Introducing Social
Research Methods

About the Website

The companion website for Introducing Social Research Methods: Essentials for Getting the Edge includes a number of resources created by the author that you will find helpful.

Please go to:
www.wiley.com\go\ruane\researchmethods

For students:
- An annotated list of TED talks on topics covered in the text
- Links to further resources available on the web

For instructors:
- A test bank with chapter-by-chapter multiple choice questions

Introducing Social Research Methods

Essentials for Getting the Edge

Janet M. Ruane

WILEY Blackwell

This edition first published 2016
© 2016 John Wiley & Sons Ltd

Registered Office
John Wiley & Sons Ltd, The Atrium, Southern Gate, Chichester, West Sussex, PO19 8SQ, UK

Editorial Offices
350 Main Street, Malden, MA 02148-5020, USA
9600 Garsington Road, Oxford, OX4 2DQ, UK
The Atrium, Southern Gate, Chichester, West Sussex, PO19 8SQ, UK

For details of our global editorial offices, for customer services, and for information about how to apply for permission to reuse the copyright material in this book please see our website at www.wiley.com/wiley-blackwell.

The right of Janet M. Ruane to be identified as the author of this work has been asserted in accordance with the UK Copyright, Designs and Patents Act 1988.

Library of Congress Cataloging-in-Publication Data
Ruane, Janet M.
 Introducing social research methods : essentials for getting the edge / Janet M. Ruane.
   pages cm
 Includes bibliographical references and index.
 ISBN 978-1-118-87425-7 (cloth) — ISBN 978-1-118-87424-0 (pbk.) 1. Social sciences--Methodology. I. Title.
 H61.R72 2016
 300.72'1—dc23
                              2015023643

A catalogue record for this book is available from the British Library.

Cover image: © Pete Turner / Getty Images

Set in 10/13pt Minion by Aptara Inc., New Delhi, India

Printed in Singapore by C.O.S. Printers Pte Ltd

1 2016

Contents

Chapter 1

How Do We Know What We Know?
Science as a Superior Way of Knowing

Introducing Social Research Methods: Essentials for Getting the Edge, First Edition. Janet M. Ruane.
© 2016 John Wiley & Sons, Ltd. Published 2016 by John Wiley & Sons, Ltd.

FIRST TAKES

Be sure to take note of the following:
Scientific vs. Non-Scientific Knowledge
- Competing *non-scientific* ways of knowing
    - Tradition
    - Authority
    - Common sense
    - Intuition
    - Rationalism
    - Strict empiricism
- Science – a superior (less error prone) way of knowing
    - A distinctive way of knowing
        - The defining traits of science

How do we know what we know? This is both a rather simple but also a rather complex philosophical question. Those who seek the path of least resistance are often willing to forgo the consideration of this question altogether. But in order to achieve a deeper appreciation of science and its distinctive edge in the production of knowledge, we need to take a moment and ponder this basic question. We need to explicitly acknowledge the common tendency of many to rely on competing non-scientific ways of knowing. These non-scientific ways of knowing are well established "go to" practices for many of us that help us cope with the dynamic nature of the social world and the flood of information we all must process every day.

To be sure, we live in an information-dominated world. Every day, like it or not, we are bombarded by facts, figures, news items, opinions, tweets, and blogs; we are connected to countless information sources about our local community, our society and our world. On any given day, *Yahoo* will present us with 100 or so "headlines" prompting us to click for more information. Many now go to bed with their electronic devices tucked under their pillows so as not to miss the latest tweets or news flashes. (Indeed sleep specialists worry that dependency on smartphones is creating vamps – i.e. youth who forgo sleep and stay connected all night long.) Those same devices travel with us throughout our days so we can stay connected 24/7. If you are old-fashioned enough to get your news from a TV screen, you nonetheless understand it is not your "father's" news broadcast. As any one story is being aired, texts of other headlines are continuously scrolling across the bottom of the screen. If you rely on the Internet for your daily news, you will experience countless links that can quickly bring you more in-depth or totally different information.

In recent years, our information age has taken an alluring, perhaps compelling, "personal" turn. To a large extent, the personal computer and the Internet allow us (even encourage us) to customize the information that comes our way. Web browsers allow us to set up personal weather forecasts, stock quote pages, or alerts for news items of special interest. We can arrange for daily emails about our favorite sports teams, current topics and celebrities. And as we all know, today's "search" on the Internet will deliver unsolicited ads and feeds courtesy of sites watching our every move or click.

Given all the ways of knowing that are available to us, and given our growing ability to get exactly the information that *we* want via cellphones and computers, students of research methods may wonder why we need to learn the methodical and labor-intensive procedures of science and research methods? Isn't all the information we need readily at our fingertips? Given the wealth of information available on the Internet, can't we be satisfied to just sit and click?

Perhaps a recent Internet banner ad for the *New York Times* offers the best answer to the question: "What's the point of an information age without the right information?" Information is only useful if it is accurate. And if there is one hallmark of science, it is its penchant for accuracy.

The incredible amount of information that confronts us (and the relative ease of accessing it) makes us all the more vulnerable to misinformation. Indeed, Internet inaccuracies are so common there are several webpages devoted to detecting and debunking falsehoods and myths: Consider four "claims" that recently circulated on the Internet:

- The state of Kansas in caving to the religious right is introducing legislation to keep the newly updated science show *Cosmos* off Kansas television.
- Google Earth detected a British woman who was lost at sea signaling for help on a deserted island.
- The use of antiperspirants causes breast cancer.
- Bananas from Costa Rica (and more recently from South Africa) carry a flesh-eating bacteria.

All of these assertions grabbed a lot of attention (and no doubt clicks) on the Internet. Yet, *not one* of these statements is true. The news about Kansas originated on a satirical webpage but nonetheless started circulating as a "fact." The Google Earth story was revealed to be a hoax but not before it traveled sea to sea. Both medical researchers and the National Cancer Institute assert that there is insufficient evidence to warrant linking antiperspirants to cancer. The flesh-eating banana bacteria story is a hoax that has been circulating on the Internet for many, many years. Internet rumors, however, are particularly hard to squelch because individuals are quite willing to believe anything they learn from the "all-knowing" computer. Though false, these rumors still exact a price. The International Banana Association has referred to the banana rumor as an incident in Internet terrorism.

The Competition: Non-Scientific Ways of Knowing

When confronted by an information glut, how are we to know which information is accurate? How are we to decide which information to trust? To answer these questions, we need to give some thought to the various sources of knowing that contribute to our "stock of knowledge" and drive our information society. We need also to consider if some sources of knowledge are more worthy of our trust than others. Hopefully, after reviewing several of the most popular ways of knowing, you will come to appreciate that not all ways of knowing are as worthy of trust as others.

Time-Based Knowing – Traditional Knowledge

Consider a popular "fact" asserted by many in today's society: marital stability is compromised when wives earn more than husbands. This twist on the long-standing norm of males being primary breadwinners has been gaining more attention in the United States since the recession of 2007, a recession that took a bigger toll on male than on female workers. And early in 2015, economic forecasters maintained that middle-class job growth will be concentrated in workplaces more open to women (Aisch and Gebeloff 2015; Searcey, Porter and Gebeloff 2015). Some marital advisors suggest that when husbands earn less than their wives, special effort should be made to restore the husband's importance in the family. Indeed, there is research to suggest that couples in these situations actually respond to the pay imbalance by embracing *more* rather than less traditional marital roles. And why not? Everyone *knows* that the male family role dictates that men should be heads of households. At least everyone "knows" this if they rely on traditional knowledge. (But it remains to be seen if this piece of traditional knowledge can survive the new economic reality of a changing job market.)

Traditional knowledge – knowledge based on the passing of time.

With **traditional knowledge** the *mere passing of time* provides the basis for claiming knowledge or making knowledgeable assertions about the world. Many of us know that all good things must end, but this knowledge is rooted in our learning this adage from parents who learned it from their parents who learned it from their parents and so on. Consequently, traditional knowledge can be particularly tenacious in its hold on us. Who are we to second guess what has been "known" for so very long? This tendency to defer to the "age" of an idea as the acid test of its veracity feeds the strength and influence of traditional knowledge. In surviving the test of time, long-standing ideas or enduring assertions about the world are automatically assumed to be true – indeed, if these assertions were not true, we ask, how could they still be around? One of the classic urban myths is the rumor about the FCC (Federal Communications Committee) banning God from TV. One of the reasons this falsehood still is given credence is because it has been circulating for the last 30 years! The same can be said about the flesh-eating banana story – it has been going strong for 15 years. Or think about the many "facts" you heard while growing up: eating carrots is good for eyesight; an apple a day keeps the doctor away; you catch cold by standing out in the cold or by getting caught in the rain; we lose the most body heat through our uncovered heads; Epsom salt baths are good for de-stressing; warm milk helps us fall asleep.

True or not (all of the before mentioned have been challenged as myths), these adages (and many, many more) are firmly planted in our everyday stock of knowledge. When we hear the same thing over and over, we frequently conclude that there simply must be some truth to it – after all everyone *knows* that where there is smoke, there is fire. But herein rests the major flaw of traditional knowledge: the mere passing of time *does NOT in itself* establish something as true. Consider the fact that for thousands of years, "everyone knew" that the earth was flat. Navigators chartered their trips to accommodate this fact. Mapmakers were content with two-dimensional maps. But claiming the earth was flat did not make it so. The mere passing of time did not verify the assertion. (If anything, the passing of time is exactly what showed this assertion to be unequivocally false.)

Similarly, until the fifteenth century, astronomers held that the earth was the center of the universe. It was unthinkable to challenge this fact. (Recall the fate of Galileo for bucking the system – he was excommunicated from the Catholic Church for promoting a sun-centered model of the universe.) Once again, however, thousands of years of asserting that all heavenly bodies revolved around the earth did not make it so. Most recently the genetic mapping evidence of the genome project challenged the traditional view of race as a biologically determined category. Despite age-old arguments to the contrary, human races are not genetically distinct. Humans share 99.9 percent of their DNA. Racial similarities, not differences, are in our genes.

Or consider one last example that has received much attention in the last few years: the danger of same-sex couples raising kids. To be sure there are still those who hold on to the long-standing belief that kids raised by two moms or two dads will suffer grave consequences. But research on this issue is consistently finding that the kids are/will be OK (e.g. see The Australian Study of Child Health in Same-Sex Families (http://www.achess.org.au/) or Gartrell and Bos's 2010 US longitudinal study of adolescents raised by same sex parents).

As these examples show, traditional knowledge with its unthinking acquiescence to the passing of time can be very risky knowledge. The "age" or enduring nature of an idea or a belief does not necessarily prove its accuracy or truth.

Box 1.1	Sharpening your research vision: father knows best … or does he?

A pretty long-standing adage is that wisdom resides in men. It is a convenient "truth" used to justify the unequal statuses and treatment of men and women world-wide. This "wise male" view is also behind one of the most outrageous and long-standing traditional practices in many countries around the world: honor killing. In the summer of 2014, a Pakistani father stoned his daughter to death. Her offense? She married a man without her father's approval. Witnesses stood by and watched but did not intervene. Some powerful evidence of the power of traditional "knowing."

Credential-Based Knowing – Authoritative Knowledge

Authoritative knowledge is another extremely popular way of coming to know what we know. After a long bullish ride, many financial experts predicted that the start of the new millennium would see a major correction in the stock market. Some smart investors took the correction warning to heart and changed their investment strategies.

Authoritative knowledge – knowledge based upon credentialed expertise (i.e. specialists or respected sources of information).

With **authoritative knowledge**, we defer to experts when looking for accurate assertions or claims about the world. In trusting experts we are deferring to their credentials and training. We accept as accurate and true that which experts tell us.

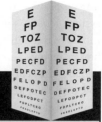

Box 1.2   Sharpening your research vision: authority addicts

The willingness of Americans to trust authorities has led some to observe that the United States is a society of "authority addicts." Many of you may already be familiar with a rather famous study by Stanley Milgram (1974) that poignantly revealed our willingness to defer to authorities. In this study, Milgram discovered that ordinary civilians would administer electrical shocks to others when directed by authority figures to do so. (Study participants were told to administer shocks to those who had failed at a learning task. While participants thought the jolts of electricity were being administered to "learners" who made mistakes, no shocks were actually delivered.) Indeed, in various replications of the study, Milgram found that a majority of study participants were willing to administer the electrical jolts even when they thought the shocks were causing others severe pain. Milgram's research indicated that humans are willing to accept uncritically an authority figure's perceptions and definitions of reality. But lest anyone think that "addiction" is unique to US culture, consider this: Milgram's research was prompted by his desire to understand the Holocaust and the failure of so many Europeans to stand up to and resist authority.

Our reliance on authoritative knowledge extends to many arenas. We take our cars in for "diagnostic" check-ups and trust our mechanic's assessment of needed repairs. In buying or selling homes, most of us rely on the expertise of realtors or credentialed home inspectors. In the area of health, many patients would not dream of second-guessing their physicians. We hesitate to question whether the pharmacist has properly filled our prescriptions. At present, countless Americans are investing for their financial futures on the basis of the economic expertise of financial planners. Many of us feel secure about the accuracy of any information if we have read it in the *New York Times*, the *Wall Street Journal* or the UK's *Financial Times*. There is no doubt about it – authoritative knowledge offers us a certain comfort zone and we like it that way.

As with traditional knowledge, however, authoritative knowledge can be wrong. Frequently our trust in experts is misplaced. Credentials do not always give experts the corner on truth. Most of us know this all too well from our first-hand experiences with such things as weather forecasts, election projections, or media hype. Meteorologists warn of a severe snowstorm and we wind up with a mere dusting. During the 2012 US presidential campaign, Republican strategists (as well as a rather authoritative polling organization) predicted a Romney victory that never happened. And let us not forget the millennium's Y2K bug which was supposed to wreak havoc on computers worldwide. Despite the big hoopla and dire forecasts, computer experts were essentially wrong about the expected calamity.

Of course, the stakes of our misplaced trust in experts can be higher than is suggested by these last examples. Many financial experts, for instance, failed to foresee the famous stock market crash of 1929 – they were confident that stocks had achieved a new but safe high plateau. As a result, countless Americans who trusted the experts were financially ruined in the aftermath of Black Thursday (October 24, 1929).[1] Prior to 9/11, we might have thought that national security experts knew best about any significant and credible threats to the safety of US citizens and territory. Yet post 9/11 reviews of "who knew what and when" suggest that experts had trouble connecting the dots that pointed to, and forewarned us about, the worst terrorist attack on US soil.[2] Our faith and trust in experts clearly failed us on this issue of homeland security. Why? Surely, one of the reasons for the failure is that credentials do not automatically give people a corner on truth. Experts work with facts, information and ideas *as they see them*. And as 9/11 painfully showed us, there is not necessarily any common agreement regarding experts' perceptions/interpretations of facts and information. In the days prior to the US military campaign in Iraq, intelligence "experts" claimed that Iraq had weapons of mass destruction. Those weapons have yet to be found. More recently, experts lined up behind the austerity programs adopted by many European nations in order to combat recessionary times. Today, there are experts saying these programs were a huge mistake.

Note too that credentialed authorities can sometimes *intentionally* mislead us. Experts can distort information when they have a vested interest in doing so. For example, during the Vietnam War, military authorities obscured American participation in combat and doctored enemy casualty reports in order to offset resistance to the war.[3] Starting in the 1950s, the tobacco industry spent several decades denying the health risks of cigarettes despite the fact that its own research were showing the opposite to be true. As early as 1963, cigarette makers knew the addictive properties of nicotine but intentionally withheld the release of this damaging information.[4] While some consider the misinformation offered by the intelligence community prior to the US Iraqi war to be an intelligence "failure" others believe that some officials intentionally misused the information to justify the war. Or consider the recent charges that the Tokyo Electric Power Company (Tepco), operator of the Fukushima nuclear power plant crippled by the 2011 tsunami in Japan, has been misleading the public with regard to the continuing dangers presented by contaminated water leaking into the ocean.

On a less sinister note, authorities can also mislead us when they move outside their areas of training and expertise. Prior to the American Revolution, most American medical practitioners were ship's surgeons, apothecaries or clergy (Cockerham 2004). It was not until the early 1900s that the American Medical Association was able to effectively limit the practice of medicine to those with a medical degree (Starr 1982). Prior to the emergence of a secular worldview, legal rulings were frequently left in the hands of religious authorities. Divinely ordained inquisitors were given the job of deciding a person's innocence or guilt on the basis of trials by ordeal (i.e. trials by torture). Many authorities may very well be credible, but trusting them when they move beyond their areas of expertise can certainly be a foolish or misguided decision.

More Risky Knowledge Sources – Common Sense and Intuition

Two additional knowledge sources are frequently employed: common sense and intuition. As with tradition and authority, each of these ways of knowing can be compelling.

> **Common sense knowledge** – knowledge based on personal experiences.
>
> **Intuitive knowledge** – knowledge derived from extraordinary or paranormal sensations or sources.

Common sense uses our personal experiences and the experiences of those we know as the source of "practical" knowledge. Common sense tells us that 6-year-olds should not be in charge of family meal plans or setting bedtimes. Common sense tells us that the mentally ill should not own guns. And common sense tells us that if someone hits us before marriage, he or she is likely to hit us after marriage as well.

Intuition can be thought of as "direct access" knowledge; it refers to a way of knowing that operates on "gut feelings" without the use of intellect. Intuition can be a powerful source of information – even a real lifesaver. (My intuition saved me from an assault and robbery when I was in graduate school.) Many of us have experienced occasions where our intuition has steered us away from making bad choices or steered us into "good bets." (My only winnings at the racetrack have come from betting hunches.)

Still, as with traditional and authoritative knowledge, common sense and intuition are not error-free ways of knowing. Common sense places a very high premium on *personal* experiences as a basis for *universal* truths. To be sure, deferring to personal experiences can be a very powerful and influential source of knowledge. Consider how often you turned to others who have already "been there, done that" in order to get some useful guidance or feel securely "in the know." Young mothers will ask their mothers what to do with fussy babies. Younger siblings will often rely on older, more experienced siblings for advice about dating. Yet personal experience, because it is tied to the individual and unique circumstances, is not the best basis for generalized knowledge. Just imagine the health risks entailed when one person (say, a husband) shares his prescription drugs for high blood pressure with another (say, his wife). There is a rather high likelihood that the drugs that benefit one person could actually be less effective or even prove detrimental to another. Indeed, medical research now understands that small differences in our genes can greatly affect how we react to medicine. In order to avoid the mistakes of overgeneralizing, the medical field is also becoming more diligent about conducting research on a greater variety of research subjects.

The National Institutes of Health has encouraged scientists to include more female lab animals in their preclinical research (Clayton and Collins 2014). In doing so they are addressing a long-standing practice and problem in medical research: too many animal and cell studies rely on male-only samples and fail to consider the significance of sex-based differences in their studies. By allowing this sex bias to exist, these studies are losing an opportunity to see how drugs, supplements and treatments might impact male and female rodents differently and in turn may ultimately negatively impact health care for humans. What's good for the goose, it seems, may not be so good for the gander. And so by extension, what worked or was true for one person may or may not be true or work for someone else.

Similarly, information that is true for one nation or culture may not hold true for another. Ethan Watters in his article "We Aren't the World" (2013) draws attention to the tendency of Western researchers who rely heavily on samples of Western nations (or more pointedly on samples of American college students) to nonetheless proclaim universal truths (see Box 1.3). To paraphrase an old saying, one size experience does not fit all.

> **Box 1.3** Newsworthy research: what can we learn from the weirdest people in the world?
>
> In a paper about "The Weirdest People in the World," social scientists Joe Henrich, Steven Heine, and Ara Norenzayan consider how frequently samples of Westerners and, more specifically, Americans are used to draw conclusions about the rest of the world. But they note the problem in doing so – Westerners are very different from the rest of the world and Americans are very different from other Westerners. In the end, we wind up with generalizations based on what they call "outliers among outliers." They liken this dilemma to trying to learn about all birds by studying penguins. The experiences of penguins are not the experiences of so many other birds. And so making generalizations about all birds based on the experiences of just penguins … really won't fly.
>
> *Source:* Henrich, Heine, and Norenzayan (2010): 61–135.

Intuition might best be thought of as "extra-sensory" knowing. Because intuition operates outside the realm of intellect and reason, it is often hard to understand – indeed we are often unable to explain how we "know" something intuitively ("I don't know, I just had a funny feeling about the situation – I just knew something was wrong.") Intuitive knowledge might be described as "direct access" knowledge that occurs without use of reasons or normal learning. In fact, there is an entire psychic industry that has evolved around the *inability* of most of us to listen to or "hear" our intuitive voice. Many of us turn to intuition "specialists" to help us make sense of our extraordinary or paranormal experiences. Our reliance on intuition is further complicated by our common sense. Common sense tells us to be suspicious of intuition or of charlatans who claim to know something beyond reason. Common sense reminds us that while many of us eagerly broadcast times when our intuition has paid off, many of us will also conveniently forget all of the times when our hunches were wrong. (Think of all the losing horse and lottery bets that were placed because of hunches.)

More Reasonable and Tangible Ways of Knowing: Rationalism and Empiricism

Before we take a good long look at the distinctiveness of scientific knowing, we might consider two additional ways of knowing that can be thought of as providing a "bridge" to science: **rational knowledge** and strict **empiricism**.

The key to rationalism as a way of knowing is found in its use of the deductive syllogism: an appealing self-contained or closed system of reasoning that leads one to a logical conclusion. At first glance, rationalism seems to be a fool-proof way of knowing. In using the deductive syllogism, the

Rational knowledge – knowledge derived from the power of reasoning to deduce logical conclusions about reality.

Empiricism – knowledge based on sensory evidence: seeing, hearing, touching, tasting, smelling.

powers of critical thinking are applied to both a major and a minor premise and a logical conclusion is derived. A major premise refers to a statement about a general principle (i.e. a universal affirmative). A minor premise is a statement about a particular or specific instance (i.e. a particular affirmative). In reasoning about the major and minor premises, a logical conclusion is reached. Consider for instance the major premise: All humans are mortal. Next consider the minor premise: Janet is human. A logical conclusion follows: Janet is mortal. The simplicity of the deductive syllogism makes it an appealing way of knowing. But there is a weakness inherent in pure rationalism. Consider another major premise: All birds fly. Next consider the minor premise: Penguins are birds. What's the logical conclusion? Penguins fly! (If you have seen one flying, please let me know a.s.a.p.!) Of course, penguins waddle and swim but they do not fly. So what happened here? If either the major or the minor premise is in error, so too is the conclusion that follows. Despite its use of reason and critical thinking skills, rationalism needs something more to protect itself from logical errors; it needs a way to assess the accuracy of both major and minor premises. Without this independent empirical assessment, rationalism can also be a rather risky way of knowing (remember, penguins do not fly).

Strict empirical knowing places a high premium on sensory evidence as the basis for making informed statements about the world around us. We take to be true that which we see, or hear, or taste, or touch, or smell. At first glance, this may appear to be a foolproof way of knowing – seeing after all is believing, right? We can trust what we "heard with our own ears" can't we? Any of you who have ever had an experience where your "eyes" and ears deceived you know first hand the weakness of strict empiricism as a way of knowing. To be sure, sometimes our senses do fail us. As any contested court battle demonstrates, eye witnesses often "see" different realities. An argument can show us that two people do not necessarily hear the same things in an oral exchange. The simple fact is that not all "vision" (or hearing, tasting, etc.) is perfect. We often get less than the full picture of something and so we can wind up with faulty knowledge. Partisan talking heads have quite the talent for taking quotes out of context and making it seem as if the speaker is saying something very different than what is reported. Consider Goode's take on pure empiricism:

> Very often, information is spotty, patchy, scattered; it comes in bits and pieces. Many of the things we might want to observe are not so homogeneous that they always appear in the same way. We may observe certain things, but our observations may be flawed by the fact that we have seen only a small part of their reality … You know it rains a lot in Seattle, but you stayed there for a week and didn't see a drop of rain. Your observations were empirical – you used the data of your senses. But they were very partial, very selective, and not a good cross-section. (Goode 2000, p. 25)

To further complicate our knowing via strict empiricism, science has documented that humans are "hard-wired" to see the familiar in vague images. (A phenomenon known as pareidolia.) This tendency explains why we can look at clouds in the sky and see bunny rabbits or elephants and why we so easily can "see" the man on the moon or a face on the surface of Mars. (Perhaps some of you know of the Mazda 3's dilemma over its "smiling" car fronts. Some design critics felt the cars looked silly. Mazda dropped the smiles in its 2014 models.) As good as sensory evidence is, it nonetheless must be tempered with something more before we can be confident about accepting it as trustworthy. This is science's mission.

Figure 1.1   The "face on Mars" and a "smiling" Mazda 3. *Source:* (1.1a) NASA/JPL; (1.1b) By S 400 HYBRID (Self-photographed) [Attribution], via Wikimedia Commons

Where does all of this leave us? Hopefully, you now have a new-found realization that much of the information that bombards us every day is based on some rather popular but questionable ways of knowing what we know. Many of our most familiar and comfortable ways of knowing may be fast and easy or logically appealing – they are in our comfort zones. But we need also appreciate that they can be risky, error-prone ways of knowing. Traditional and authoritative knowledge, common sense and intuition are all alike in that they encourage an uncritical acceptance of information. Ideas that have been around a long time, ideas that are presented by authorities, ideas that are practical or "feel right" can wind up being accepted as true *even when they are false*. Pure rationalism, while featuring the power of logical reasoning can, nonetheless, lead to erroneous conclusions if major and minor premises are factually incorrect. Strict empiricism can also mislead us if we are not careful about obtaining the "full" or non-distorted picture of what it is we are "seeing" (or "hearing," tasting," "touching," or "smelling"). Still, we need not despair; there is one way of knowing that is distinctively different from those we have just reviewed: science. Science and its research methods promote a critical assessment of information before that information is accepted as accurate.

Science – Providing an Accuracy Edge

Science as a Trustworthy Way of Knowing

If we are interested in obtaining the highest quality of information, we are well advised to embrace science. In the broadest sense, **scientific knowledge** represents a hybrid way of knowing that utilizes both critical, rational thinking skills (a rational, theoretical component) *and* concrete evidence (an empirical component). Theory and evidence, Goode says, are the "lifeblood" of science. With the distinctive "tools" or techniques of science, we can evaluate the wealth of information we receive each day in light of some very

> **Scientific knowledge** – knowledge derived from the merger of theory and research; knowledge based on the integration of rational reasoning and empirical evidence.

discerning standards for assessing accuracy or validity. An understanding of the scientific method enables us to become critical consumers of information.

Theory – a set of propositions or statements about how the world or some entity operates.

Science is a Distinctive Way of Knowing

Science is distinctive in that it places a high premium on reason and logic. Scientific research is guided by **theory** – reasonable propositions or statements about how the physical and social world operates. Propositions that are unreasonable or that are untestable are beyond the realm of scientific inquiry. I may firmly believe that good people will be rewarded in a heavenly afterlife but my belief is an issue of faith not an issue of science. Or consider that science's dismissal of the paranormal turns on the simple notion that such beliefs are not plausible or reasonable. Levitation is unreasonable given the laws of gravity. (The critical relationship between theory and scientific research is explored further in Chapter 4, on design.) The ongoing debate between creationism and evolution clearly illustrates that not all theories about the origins of the universe or mankind are scientific. Creationism is essentially a belief that an intelligent designer created the universe. But since it is impossible to assess this theory with empirical evidence, creationism is outside the realm of science. It is an untestable belief based on religious faith. The theory of evolution, on the other hand, is based on the testing and assessment of empirical fossil evidence dating back tens of thousands of years.[5]

Science is also distinctive in that it employs set methodical procedures that aim to reduce or control the amount of error that creeps into the process of knowing. Indeed, Goode notes that science is defined by its *methods*, not by its content. So in the name of methods, the scientific approach demands **empirical evidence** to support any assertions about the world. Its empirical nature means that science places a high premium on the observation of concrete phenomena. Science also insists on our following systematic, methodical "rules" for gathering our empirical evidence. Evidence that is obtained in an unsystematic way is regarded as tainted or problematic; it is seen as less trustworthy. And science insists that the evidence we find in support of our assertions be *replicated* by other studies before it is considered trustworthy. This repetition of studies in search of the repetition of findings is an essential safeguard against our jumping to false conclusions. Each of these standards and a few more distinctive traits of science are elaborated below.

Empirical evidence – tangible, sensory evidence.

Empirical Evidence

Empirical evidence – Science as a way of knowing – is not willing to accept assertions about the world at face value. In science, it is not sufficient, for instance, to maintain (as traditional knowledge does) that gays in the military are bad for soldier morale. Science demands tangible evidence to substantiate any claims of fact. Science requires that assertions be backed by concrete, objective evidence that shows or reveals the accuracy of the statements. With this demand for empirical evidence, science is highlighting its inherently skeptical nature – unless we "show it" to be so (via the empirical world around us), claims about reality are merely that – just "claims" and nothing more. Science is not willing to trust a mere assertion – it demands empirical documentation that allows us to assess the accuracy of any assertion. The insistence on empirical evidence may be one trait of science that the public readily appreciates.

In March 2014, Malaysia Airlines Flight 370 mysteriously disappeared from the sky. The plane's black box had yet to be recovered and more than a year after the incident the world is still clueless as to what happened to the plane. The Malaysian government has officially declared the disappearance an accident. But more telling is the response of the families and friends of the flight's passengers. They have said that as long as there is no evidence to show what happened to the plane, they will not accept that their loved ones are gone. The wife of one passenger put it as follows: "How can they presume they are dead? There is no evidence. There is nothing" (Tan 2015).

Systematic, Methodical Rules

In the interest of curtailing error, science utilizes standardized procedures that guide our search for accurate information about the world around us. There are rules for developing and assessing the accuracy of the ways we try to document or measure the world around us. In Chapter 6 we review several "tests" that are used to check whether or not measures are really measuring what they claim to be measuring (i.e. criteria for establishing measurement validity). There are "rules" that govern our ability to discern causal connections between events or between characteristics and behaviors (i.e. criteria for establishing internal validity). There are rules that govern which people, things, or events we should focus on when studying the world around us (i.e. criteria for selecting units of analysis). And there are rules that govern whether or not it is appropriate to generalize our research findings beyond the study at hand (i.e. criteria for establishing external validity). These rules constitute the heart of research methods. And while learning these rules is challenging work, they promise a benefit not offered by any other way of knowing. The methodical rules of scientific research minimize the likelihood of error. In abiding by the discerning methodical rules of research, we gain confidence that our findings are accurate or error free.

Box 1.4	Sharpening your research vision: the most powerful women in the world

Forbes regularly keeps tabs on the most powerful people in the world. In constructing the 2015 list of the world's top 100 powerful women, Forbes considered three factors: (1) money, (2) media presence, and (3) spheres of influence. Women's monetary standing was assessed in terms of either their company earnings (for CEOs), their personal earnings or net worth (for celebrities or billionaires), their countries' GDPs (for politicians), or the money spent by their non-profits or NGOs. Media presence was determined by the total number of media mentions in the past 12 months as well as by the women's media presence as indicated by Facebook fans, Twitter followers, and so on. Lastly, the most powerful women had to be actively powerful in multiple spheres of influence. So … who made it to the top five using these measures?

(1) Angela Merkel, Chancellor, Germany; (2) Hillary Clinton, former Secretary of State, United States; (3) Melinda Gates, philanthropist, United States; (4) Janet Yellin, Chair, Federal Reserve, United States; (5) Mary Barra, CEO, General Motors, United States. Do you agree with the results and/or the measures used?

Source: *http://www.forbes.com/sites/carolinehoward/2015/05/26/ranking-the-2015-worlds-100-most-powerful-women/.*

Commitment to Causal Analysis

Science is also distinctive in embracing a causal view of the world; an underlying assumption of science is that every outcome has a cause. With this causal commitment, science rejects any unnecessary mystification of the world. Instead, science proceeds by applying its rules and its tools in the service of discovering causal mechanisms. It remains open to the possibility that mysteries can be solved. An entire chapter of this text will be devoted to the issue of causal research.

Replication

Replication – repeating a study to see if original results/findings are obtained again with different subjects or under different settings.

To regard findings as true and reliable, science insists that those findings be observed more than once. This insistence on repetition of studies and findings reveals a fundamentally conservative side to science. **Replication** is a safeguard against our drawing premature, and therefore possibly false, conclusions about the world. Findings that cannot be replicated arouse suspicion – isolated findings are regarded as flukes and are not considered worthy of our trust. (Recall the earlier discussion of Milgram's study of obedience to authority. He was not willing to draw any conclusions on the basis of just one study. Instead, he repeated the study over and over again to see if the findings continued to hold.) Indeed, the insistence on replication is simply the skeptical "show me" attitude of science coming full circle – if the findings are true, they should show up time after time under similar research conditions. One-time findings (like one-time sales offers) are usually too good to be true. Our confidence that our findings are accurate is further bolstered each time our findings are replicated by others employing the same rigorous methods of research to examine the same research question.

Science is a Public Endeavor

Science must be committed to an open or public distribution of its workings. There should not be any secrets in science. This public commitment serves science's high regard for accuracy. The researcher must be willing to show others their work: what research design, what measures, what sampling, what analysis was done in the name of their research? This sharing enables others to review the work with a critical eye. Putting research out there for public review provides others with the opportunity to see if any errors can be detected. Science's commitment to "going public" also supports the interest in replication. The ability to "reproduce" and study and verify if findings "hold" beyond any one study only is possible if subsequent researchers have unfettered access to previous studies.

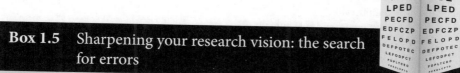

Box 1.5   Sharpening your research vision: the search for errors

In their very informative book *Evaluating Information*, Jeffrey Katzer, Kenneth Cook, and Wayne Crouch explain how they adopt the "error model" in their approach to research. Good research is about minimizing error – the researcher and those evaluating research must become aware of potential errors and the steps that can be taken to minimize them. No matter what the research, there are some "likely suspects" when thinking about sources of error. Error, for instance, might be due to a bad sampling strategy or execution. Error can arise from extending findings beyond their limits. Error might be due to poor measurement decisions or to poor research designs. Error can result from using inappropriate techniques or statistics for data analysis. The point is a simple but important one: science more than any other way of knowing engages in a relentless search for "possible errors" and ways to offset or correct them. It is this dedication that gives it the edge in the production of knowledge. Hopefully, by the time you finish this book, you will have improved your skill level for spotting errors.

Tentative

Perhaps somewhat ironically, science is also a tentative enterprise; when it reaches a conclusion it does so with an understanding that future revision may be needed or be in order. This may surprise some readers given science's efforts to minimize error in the research process. Why not have more faith in its product? The tentative or provisional nature of science has everything to do with its concern with accuracy and with an unrelenting concern with keeping an open mind to new research possibilities: new discoveries, new tools, new theories, and so on. Rather than speaking in terms of certainty, science adopts the langue of *likelihood* and *probability* and *increasing confidence* in findings that are replicated. But ultimately, science must remain open to new developments that might well challenge current ideas and propel us into new territories and findings. Members of the Cloud Appreciation Society (37,000 gazers worldwide) have found a new cloud – *undulatus asperatus* – and are asking for its official designation by the United Nations World Meteorological Organization. If the designation goes through (and it is expected) this will be the first new cloud discovered in over 50 years (Phillips 2015).[6] And thanks to the powers of DNA testing, oceanographers are swimming in the glory of a new discovery: scientists have now discovered a third species of seadragons. A CT scan of the new species, Ruby Seadragon, also revealed a distinctive skeletal structure of the deep red sea dragon. For over the last 150 years, oceanographers thought there were only two seadragon species; the Ruby seadragon demonstrates the need to amend this position (Cuthbert 2015). And recently in Myanmar, a bird thought to be extinct for nearly 75 years was found to be alive and living in the grasslands of an abandoned agriculture station (*Yahoo* News 2015).

Table 1.1   Strengthening your research vision: defining traits of science

Science is …
- theory based
- empirical
- systematic and rule guided
- committed to causal model
- invested in replication
- a public endeavor
- tentative
- an essentially skeptical enterprise

Science as an Exercise in Skepticism

To truly appreciate the distinctive nature of scientific knowing, we must recognize one last important trait, one that is clearly foreshadowed by the last few traits: skepticism. Science is a highly skeptical way of knowing. When confronted by a claim or "assertion" about the world, science's first reaction is to "doubt it." This knee-jerk or reflexive reaction is the driving force of good science. Scientific skepticism is essentially about unrelenting fact-checking. Every time science is skeptical it forces those making claims to up their game. Scientific skepticism insists that the quality of evidence being offered in support of a claim be of the highest order. Indeed, it is this theme of skepticism that helps explain science's insistence on collecting empirical evidence, on the use of standard, logical methodical rules and procedures and on the value of replication. It is no accident that meteorologists have been *considering* the recognition of a new cloud type for nearly a decade! (mentioned above). And more than ten years after the first sighting of the presumably extinct ivory-billed woodpecker, there are those who still doubt the bird's return from the great beyond (see Box 1.6).

Box 1.6   Newsworthy research: birds take flight

In 2005, the birding world was aflutter with news that the ivory-billed woodpecker thought to be extinct in the United States for over 60 years was alive and living in the swamps of Arkansas! Initial 2004 claims about the bird's return were met with great skepticism and demands for additional evidence. (Those claims were based on a snippet of a very blurry videotape.) Further evidence was offered in the form of audio recordings made over the course of several months. Ornithologists who reviewed the new audio recordings were persuaded and declared the ivory-billed woodpecker to be back in business. To be sure, some ornithologists still remain skeptical (i.e. they believe that the audio recordings were from the Pileated woodpecker) and not all birding sites have closed the book on this case. One thing we can say for sure is this: skepticism will never be extinct in the workings of science.

Using Research Methods to Become Critical Consumers of Information

While relatively few of us will be directly involved in the *production* of research, all of us will be involved in *consuming* such information. Thus, you might regard the learning of scientific research methods as a matter of personal empowerment. We stand to gain by arming ourselves with scientific know-how. Our stakes in obtaining accurate information about our world are higher than ever. The sheer volume of information and the speed with which it travels carries grave ramifications concerning the consequences of misinformation. The damage of erroneous information can be as insidious as a computer virus. Consequently, the ability to evaluate information as more or less trustworthy is a crucial skill.

> **Tip 1.1**
>
> Failure to Replicate – a Warning Sign
>
> The failure to replicate findings is often the first "clue" that something is amiss in scientific research. Dr. Andrew Wakefield's early 1998 findings suggesting a link between childhood vaccines and autism could not be replicated in subsequent studies. Concerns about the accuracy and ethics of his research arose. Eventually, co-workers withdrew their support of the research and the journal that published Wakefield's original study, the *Lancet*, retracted the paper.

Our ability to evaluate information is directly tied to our knowledge of scientific research methods. Information that is the product of carefully conducted scientific research is less likely to be in error, more deserving of our attention and trust. In the end, it may be your understanding of research methods that helps you make some critical life decisions. What is the most prudent diet or health regime for someone of your age, race, or gender? Which course of medical treatment is the best for you if you are a female heart attack victim rather than a male victim?[7] Can e-cigarettes help smokers quit? Are genetically altered foods safe for us to eat? Is there a real danger to using cell phones? Is there a good reason to pay higher prices for organic fruits and vegetables? Can nations halt global warming? Is home schooling the right choice for your family? Should parents have their children vaccinated? Or is feeding infants peanut butter a good way to offset the development of later and more dangerous peanut allergies? Is your retirement fund safer in the hands of the government or in the hands of private investors? In large measure, finding the right answers to these and other questions will depend on our ability to judge the quality of relevant information. In the end, your knowledge of research methods could very well be a life-enhancing, even a life-sustaining, resource.

TAKE AWAYS

- Non-scientific ways of knowing, while common, are nonetheless prone to error
  - Traditional knowledge – knowledge based on the passing of time; not all enduring ideas are correct
  - Authoritative knowledge – knowledge that relies on credentialed experts or respected sources of information; credentials don't assure accuracy of information
  - Common sense knowledge – knowledge that relies on personal experiences; personal knowledge is not necessarily generalizable

(Continue)

(*Continued*)

- ○ Intuitive knowledge – knowledge derived via a special, paranormal "sixth" sense; operates beyond realm of empirical evidence
- ○ Rationalism – knowledge derived via the use of deductive reasoning; faulty premises will lead to erroneous conclusions
- ○ Strict empiricism – knowledge derived from senses; faulty or distorted "vision" or incomplete evidence can lead to erroneous conclusions
- Science is a distinctive and less error prone way of knowing
  - ○ Linked to theory
  - ○ Requires empirical evidence
  - ○ Embraces a causal view of the world
  - ○ Adopts standard methodical rules to assure "quality control"
  - ○ Values replication – recognizes the importance of consistency in the verification of findings
  - ○ Must be a public endeavor – rejects secret science
  - ○ Values a healthy amount of skepticism

Sharpening The Edge: More Reading and Searching

- Listen to a short lecture by Ethan Watters on how cultures influence perceptions of trauma and mental illness and how American culture is often at odds with views in other settings at:

  http://on.aol.com/video/author-ethan-watters-discusses-crazy-like-us-502044888
- The top sites for debunking urban myths can be found at:

  http://www.techrepublic.com/blog/tech-of-all-trades/top-10-sites-to-debunk-urban-legends/
- Internet information – should we trust it or not? The query is prompted by the fact that information on the Internet is not screened for accuracy. Anyone, after all, can post anything on a webpage. For a good tutorial on how to evaluate a webpage, visit the following site maintained by the University of California, Berkeley: "Evaluating Web Pages: Techniques to Apply and Questions to Ask":

  http://lib.berkeley.edu/TeachingLib/Guides/Internet/Evaluate.html
- Those wanting to delve further into the questions of knowing and truth and objective reality should take a look at the first few chapters in:

  Earl Babbie's *Observing Ourselves: Essays in Social Research*. Prospect Heights, IL: Waveland Press, 1998
- For any number of the topics covered in this text, you will find additional reader-friendly information at Bill Trochim's Web Center for Social Research Methods:

  http://socialresearchmethods.net/

  Once on the page, click on the Knowledge Base link, and then click the Contents link. Scroll down until you find the topic of interest to you. A good place to start would be with the links to "Language of Research" and "Five Big Words."

Exercises

1. Visit one of the sites devoted to debunking urban legends (see second entry under Sharpening the Edge above). Review several of the legends and see if you can identify the "way of knowing" on which they are based. Do you see any pattern?

2. Review a week or two of letters to the editor in your local newspapers. Identify the dominant knowledge source being used to support the claims/assertions made in the letters.

3. Carefully consider current print or television commercials or some political campaign ads. For each of the knowledge sources reviewed in this chapter, locate one or two commercials/ads that invoke non-scientific sources in order to convince us of the merits of their product or candidate claims (e.g. an old Hebrew National hot dog commercial had the voice of God telling us the product is good – this is clearly asking the consumer to defer to the ultimate authority figure).

4. Do a quick search on *Yahoo!* or your favorite internet search engine and locate a few science articles that discuss some newly released study. As you read through the articles, can you see evidence of the major traits of science discussed in this chapter?

Notes

1 In the three years following the 1929 crash, national income was cut in half and there were some 15 million unemployed Americans – up from 1.5 million in 1929 (Garraty and Gay 1972; Wiltz 1973).

2 FBI superiors elected to dismiss warnings from local agents in Minnesota and Arizona who were concerned about flight training activities of individuals under surveillance (Hirsch and Isikoff 2002). INS authorities failed to stop Mohamed Atta from entering the United States despite the fact that he had an expired visa and links to known terrorists. On the very day of the attacks, airport security agents singled out nine of the terrorists for special scrutiny but did not prevent them from boarding the planes (*The New York Times* 2002).

3 The efforts by President Johnson and military advisors to paint a positive picture of US involvement in the war eventually contributed to a serious "credibility gap" with the American public (Braestrup 1982).

4 These cover-up efforts by the tobacco industry lasted decades coming to light only in 1994 with the leak of a "smoking gun" (no pun intended). An anonymous "Mr. Butts" released over 40 years of internal company documents detailing how much tobacco industry experts knew but wouldn't tell about the dangers of its product (Zegart 2000).

5 To look further into the creationism/evolution debate, see the ongoing discussions by Bill Nye (aka the science guy) and Ken Ham the founder of the Creationism Museum: http://www.christiantoday.com/article/bill.nye.vs.ken.ham.debate.live.stream.free.watch.online.creation.vs.evolution.debate.here.start.time/35688.htm.

6 For a stunning video of the new clouds see: http://www.weather.com/news/news/undulatus-asperatus-clouds-20140925#.

7 The need for gender-based clinical studies is finally receiving more focused attention of medical researchers.

References

Aisch, Gregor, and Robert Gebeloff. 2015. "The Changing Nature of Middle Class Jobs." *The New York Times*. Economy. February 22. http://www.nytimes.com/interactive/2015/02/23/business/economy/the-changing-nature-of-middle-class-jobs.html?hpw&rref=business&action=click&pgtype=Homepage&module=well-region&region=bottom-well&WT.nav=bottom-well&_r=0.

Braestrup, Peter. 1982. Transcript of Interview with Peter Braestrup. Lyndon Baines Johnson Library. http://www.lbjlib.utexas.edu/johnson/archives.hom/oralhistory.hom/Braestrup/Braestrup.PDF.

Clayton, Janine A. and Francis S. Collins. 2014. "Policy: NIH to Balance Sex in Cell and Animal Studies." *Nature*. http://www.nature.com/news/policy-nih-to-balance-sex-in-cell-and-animal-studies-1.15195.

Cockerham, William. 2004. *Medical Sociology*, 9th ed. Upper Saddle River, NJ: Pearson/Prentice Hall.

Cuthbert, Lori. 2015. "New Seadragon Species a Deep Ruby Red." Discovery.com. February 19. http://news.discovery.com/animals/new-seadragon-species-a-deep-ruby-red-150219.htm.

Garraty, John and Peter Gay. 1972. *The Columbia History of the World*. New York: Harper & Row.

Gartrell N., and H.M.W Bos. 2010. "The US National Longitudinal Lesbian Family Study: Psychological Adjustment of 17-year-old Adolescents." *Pediatrics* 126: 1–9.

Goode, Erich. 2000. *Paranormal Beliefs: A Sociological Introduction*. Prospect Heights: Waveland Press.

Helmstadter, G.H. 1970. *Research Concepts in Human Behavior*. New York: Appleton-Century-Crofts.

Henrich, J., Heine, S., and A. Norenzayan. 2010. "The Weirdest People in the World." *Behavioral and Brain Sciences* 33: 61–135.

Hirsch, Michael and Michael Isikoff. 2002. "What Went Wrong?" *Newsweek* (May 27): 28–34.

Katzer, Jeffrey, Cook, Kenneth, and Wayne Crouch. 1998. *Evaluating Information: A Guide for Users of Social Science Research*. Boston: McGraw-Hill.

Phillips, Mark. 2015. "Sky Gazers Discover New Cloud." *CBS News*., February 17. www.cbsnews.com/news/cloud-gazers-discover-new-cloud/.

Searcey Dionne, Porter, Eduardo, and Robert Gebeloff. 2015. "Health Care Opens Stable Career Path, Taken Mainly by Women." *New York Times*. Economy. February 22. www.nytimes.com/2015/02/23/business/economy/health-care-opens-middle-class-path-taken-mainly-by-women.html.

Starr, Paul. 1982. *The Social Transformation of American Medicine*. New York: Basic Books.

Tan, Lincoln. 2015. "MH370 Relatives Still Seeking Closure." *The New Zealand Herald*. March 7. www.nzherald.co.nz/world/news/article.cfm?c_id=2&objectid=11413215&ref=rss.

Watters, Ethan. 2013. "We Aren't the World." *Pacific Standard*. February 25: 46–53.

Wiltz, John. 1973. *The Search for Identity: Modern American History*. Philadelphia: J.B. Lippincott Company.

Yahoo! News. 2015. "'Extinct' Myanmar Bird Rediscovered after 73 Years" March 7. http://news.*yahoo*.com/extinct-myanmar-bird-rediscovered-73-years-071530160.html.

Zegart, D. 2000. "The Cigarette Papers: A Docu-Drama in Three Acts." http://www.pbs.org/wgbh/pages/frontline/smoke/webumentary/.

Chapter 2

The Language of Science and Research: Learning to Talk the Talk and Walk the Walk

Introducing Social Research Methods: Essentials for Getting the Edge, First Edition. Janet M. Ruane.
© 2016 John Wiley & Sons, Ltd. Published 2016 by John Wiley & Sons, Ltd.

FIRST TAKES

Be sure to take note of the following:

The "trouble" with science: "What we got here is failure to communicate" (*Cool Hand Luke*)

- Terms of endearment: variables, relationships, causal analysis, and more ...
- Styles of research
  - Quantitative vs. qualitative
  - Inductive vs. deductive
- Goals of research
  - Descriptive
  - Exploratory
  - Explanatory
  - Evaluation
- Validity issues
  - Measurement
  - Internal
  - External

Science, who doesn't love it? Well, today it seems that more and more people are leaving the fan club. Back in the 1950s and 1960s, scientific advancement was a source of national pride as various countries around the world competed in the race to space or in the arena of medical research. But today, the love affair appears to be waning if it is not over. Between 1966 and 2012, the percentage of Americans reporting great confidence in men and women of science fell from 76% to 34% (Harding 2014). A 2013 *Huffington Post* poll found that only about one-third of Americans report having "a lot" of trust in the information they get from scientists (Swanson 2013). On the European stage, the BSE (mad cow disease) crisis of the late 1980s as well as the growing concern over the genetic modification of foods prompted the BBC to ask, in 2000, if science was to be trusted anymore. Since 2005, the EU has witnessed a double digit decline in Europeans general trust in science from 78% to 66% (Innovation Union Competitiveness Report 2011). The United States has seen similar divides between science and the public over genetically modified (GM) food. In 2015 the Pew Research Center reported that 87% of the American Association for the Advancement of Science (AAAS) scientists think GM food is safe as opposed to just 37% of the general public. In that same survey, Pew also found a possible explanation for this striking gap: 67% of the public thinks that scientists do not understand the health risks of GM food! And for their part, scientists today may be feeling the loss of love as well. Only 52% of AAAS scientists feel that it is generally a good time for science, down from 76% in the late 1970s (Funk 2015).

To be sure, it is not just the lack of good feelings we are currently witnessing. Instead, we see an alarming reversal where some people readily express their rejection of, or even contempt for, science. Witness, for instance, how during the 2012 US presidential election, almost all the Republican candidates tried their best to distance themselves from science. Or consider the persistent dismissal by so many people from around the world of the scientific community's warnings about global warming. To be sure, the infamous "Climategate"[1] of 2009 did much to add wind to the sails of climate change deniers and others who allege that climate change is some sort of scientific conspiracy. And while the overwhelming majority in the scientific community believes that climate change is occurring and that humans have a hand in it, a sizeable chunk of the public, nonetheless, remains skeptical about climate change and/or humans' contribution to it. In fact, the percentage of non-believers is growing: as of 2014, nearly one-quarter of Americans indicated that they did not believe global warming is occurring (Pappas 2014). In the spring of 2015, it came to light that the governor of Florida, Rick Scott, directed employees of the state's environmental agency to refrain from using such terms as global warming and climate change or rising sea levels. The governor denied the ban but state workers and scientists verified that they were warned to select their words wisely when constructing formal communications and writing emails. And there is evidence that other states have tried to invoke similar policies to cool the discussion of global warming (Liston 2015; Plumer 2015). Or consider the ongoing concern and debate about GM food. Scientific reports of the safety of such efforts seem irrelevant to the public's stand on the issue and its rejection of Big Agriculture. The "Eurobarometer" survey of attitudes finds that European support for genetically modified food is falling. Indeed, in some nations of the world, support for GM food is in the single digits, this despite the scientific community's positive views.

Consider one final and rather persistent example: the rejection by so many parents the world over of the medical community's advice with regard to the safety and the benefit of the measles vaccine. In 2015, the US measles vaccination rate was is over 90%. Still the disease has made an alarming comeback in recent years (even though the disease was declared eradicated in the United States in 2000). Despite the medical evidence supporting the safety of the measles vaccine, many parents fear it is linked to autism and refuse to have their children vaccinated. This is particularly worrisome since measles is such a highly contagious disease – it is estimated that 90% of those exposed to the virus and lacking immunization will become infected.[2] Between 2007 and 2014, the number of personal belief vaccination exemptions in California rose from 7800 to 13,000. A 2014 outbreak in Disneyland is attributed to people coming into contact with unvaccinated travelers. Just about two months into 2015, the measles outbreak had spread to 17 states. In 2014, the United States saw 644 cases of measles and more than half of them were found in a single unvaccinated Ohio community (CBS News 2015). While the US outbreak received headlines in 2015, outbreaks have been reappearing in many industrialized nations of the world as well. At the end of February 2015, the World Health Organization (WHO) called for an increase in vaccination campaigns in response to the alarming number of cases reported in the last year: more than 22,000 cases in seven European nations. Since 2014 Italy has seen over 1600 cases and Germany has recorded nearly 600 cases of measles. Berlin also recorded the first infant death from this measles outbreak in February 2015 (Kelland 2015; Moulson 2015). Public health officials attribute these outbreaks to lack of immunizations (Koleva 2012).

Clearly there are many forces at work in the effort to undermine science's stand on the safety of the measles vaccine and of GM food or on the reality of climate change. Science offerings have met with resistance from special interests, corporations, or in the case of the measles vaccine controversy, intentional deception (see Box 2.1). But part of the public's willingness to reject science must be traced back to science itself. Some critics argue that the failure of the public to be open to, and embrace, science is due to science's own failure at effective communication. Science does not make a sufficient effort to connect with the public. Rather, in adopting the modus operandi of many elite disciplines, the scientific community all too often surrounds itself with like-minded individuals and engages in a level and style of discourse requiring PhD level training. While this "works" for the efficient exchange of information for the "in-group," it is a non-starter in communicating with the general public. According to a 2015 Pew Survey of scientists in the AAAS, 52% of members express concern that the media fails the cause of science by oversimplifying research findings. And 79% of the surveyed scientists believe that the media does not do a good job in distinguishing "good" science (well-founded research findings) from "bad" science (not well-founded findings.) (All the more reason for us to take up this mission in this book!) It really should not surprise us, then, to learn that these scientists also think that the public does not know much about science. 84% of AAAS scientists believe that the lack of scientific knowledge among the public is a major problem for science (Rainie, Funk and Anderson 2015). Given all of this, it is quite understandable if the public is all too willing to forgo even attempting to understand the scientific community and its methods. Even more disturbing, when encouraged by groups with their own nefarious agendas, the public is often willing to demonize the unfamiliar, and too often that includes science.

Box 2.1   Newsworthy research: The Wakefield Affair

The continuing controversy over the alleged link between childhood vaccines and autism has been kept alive in large measure by the "research" carried out by Britain's Dr. Andrew Wakefield. As suspicions started surfacing about the validity of Wakefield's 1998 study, co-researchers withdrew their names from the study. In May 2010, the British government stripped Wakefield of his medical license. In early 2011, the *British Medical Journal* (*BMJ*) published an investigation which concluded that Wakefield had fabricated data in order to support the claim of a link between vaccines and autism. Financial incentives provided by lawyers planning to sue pharmaceutical companies are thought to be a primary reason for Wakefield's fraudulent "research."

Some within the scientific community have come to appreciate how they must improve their outreach and their ability to connect with the general public. Attempts are being made to do a better job at engaging the public. Currently, there are several online efforts devoted to bringing science to the general public (e.g. *Publiscize*, *Futurity*, and *The Conversation*).[3] Visit the homepages of any number of science museums from around the world and you will see how they are making concerted efforts to offer more dynamic exhibits as a way of bringing more people into the fold. Many museums also feature special programs for children – a clear effort to recruit new members for the science fan club. Indeed, it is worth noting that "watching" science at work still has tremendous "draw" for the public – witness the buzz that surrounded the new 2014 documentary series, *Cosmos: A Spacetime Odyssey*. (The show is an updated version of the 1980 Public Broadcasting System's series by Carl Sagan, *Cosmos: A Personal Voyage*). Consider also that one long-running commercial television show, CSI, has a very clear allegiance to science (see Box 2.2). Science, it would seem, still has an ability to win us over. When the beforementioned AAAS scientists offered suggestions on how to better engage the public, 24% mentioned the importance of communication but only 5% suggested communicating more clearly – that is, communicating without relying on technical terms (Rainie, Funk, and Anderson 2015). It seems then that our work is cut out for us! (If the mountain will not come to Muhammad …) With this in mind, we will do our part in this chapter to help the reader prepare for a more meaningful and satisfactory conversation with science in general and, more specifically, with the terms and language of the social sciences. An understanding of the scientific enterprise does not require a PhD but it does necessitate learning how to talk the talk. And so "parlez-vous" … science?

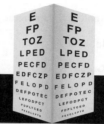

Box 2.2   Sharpening your research vision: science and the CSI

Crime Scene Investigation is a popular television show that has been on the air for 14 years and has spawned two spin-offs (*CSI: Miami*; *CSI: NY*). The CSI series shows us that the public can find the scientific mindset engaging. For any given episode, solving the case is really an exercise in science. First, a theory of the case is presented – detectives come up with their best ideas about who did what to whom. Then the hardworking crime fighters gather the empirical evidence and run the analysis that allows them to "test" their theory. Each week, the CSI crew gets a scientific lock on their case.

Units of Analysis

There is no quicker way to establish that science has its own challenging lingo than to introduce the term **unit of analysis**. The unit refers to the elements being studied in a research project. Units are the "what" or "who" of your analysis. In the social sciences, it is perhaps helpful to think of units as the *level* of social life being analyzed. With this distinction, we can note several different levels of social life that we study: the individual, the group or formal organization, the geographical area, the social program, and the social artifact (products that solve a problem of living) are some of the most common distinctions. For most sociological research, the unit of analysis is the individual – we frequently administer surveys where we ask questions about the behaviors and traits of the individual respondent. But social research might also focus on a "higher" aggregate level of life: groups (families, bowling teams, military units), or formal organizations (*Fortune* 500 companies or NGOs), or geographical areas (cities, nations), or social programs/policies (Affordable health care policies, Cap and Trade

> **Unit of analysis** – the what or who being analyzed; the level of life about which data is collected.

Ecological fallacy – an error that occurs when data is collected about groups or aggregates but conclusions are drawn about individuals; an analysis mistake that occurs when findings that occur at the group level of analysis are assumed to apply as well at the individual level of analysis.

programs), or social artifacts (national anthems, public apologies or subway graffiti). Being very clear about one's unit of analysis is essential for precluding mistakes in analysis and generalizations of research findings. One such mistake is the **ecological fallacy** which occurs when researchers use "extra-individual" units of analysis (i.e. groups or geographical areas) but mistakenly end up generalizing about individuals. A renowned sociologist, Emile Durkheim, made this mistake in his famous analysis of suicide rates for various nations. Durkheim collected data about the suicide rates of various geographical areas/nations. His conclusions about suicide, however, were stated about individuals living in the selected areas – a unit of analysis different from what he actually analyzed.

Table 2.1   Strengthening Your Research Vision: Common Units of Analysis

Individual	worker, student in college, member of the military
Group	military families, fraternities, bowling teams
Formal organization	Fortune 500 companies, universities, NGOs
Social programs/policy	social security, austerity programs, drug treatment programs
Social artifacts	gravestones, magazine ads, tattoos

Tip 2.1
Finding the Unit

Many find it challenging to correctly identify the unit of analysis in a study. Here's a tip that might help: Check to see what the researcher "sampled" to get the data. For example, did he or she sample students, or voters (individuals), or cities (geographical areas), or newspapers (social artifacts)? This approach should help "reveal" the unit of analysis.

Variable – any trait or characteristic that can vary or have more than one value/category.

Value – a specific category or attribute of a variable (for the variable car transmission, the values are stick shift or automatic).

Variables

Once a unit of analysis is clearly specified, science then sets about describing or analyzing that unit via the language of **variables**. Arguably, a hallmark of the scientific method is its "variable" vision – that is, science sees the world as a collection of variables, variables just waiting to be analyzed. In the simplest terms, a variable is any trait or characteristic that can vary (the opposite of a variable is a constant). Find something that can vary, and you have found yourself a variable: age, height, gender, race, self-esteem, generosity, foreclosure rates, divorce rates, and so on. To make the definition of a variable a bit more concrete, we might also say that a variable consists of a logical grouping of attributes or **values** of the unit we are studying. So, where the average person "sees" a man or a woman, the scientist who is working with individuals as the unit of analysis will "see" the attributes "male" and "female" as values on the variable "gender." Where the average person "feels" a cold winter morning, the scientist recognizes the variable "temperature" and values such as −20° or 0° or 32° (and thus consistent with staying inside!). When the average person "feels" a bit tipsy and hands his car keys over to a friend, the scientist considers the variable "blood alcohol level" and a value consistent with impairment (i.e. in all 50 of the United States a person with a blood alcohol level of .08 and above is considered legally drunk. Many European nations set the legal limit at .05).

Virtually everything of interest to the scientist is cast in the language of variables. And this is for a very good reason: variables enable/allow the essential work of science – that is variables facilitate the empirical documentation of the world around us. Indeed, variables are the heart of the research enterprise. Said another way, variables are what we *measure* by way of pursuing an essential trait of science: gathering empirical evidence of the world around us (see traits of science in Chapter 1).

Imagine for a minute that you are a parent worried that your baby has a fever. The concept or idea of "fever" is something beyond the comprehension of an infant so you as the parent need to figure out a way to gain some empirical evidence to help you address your concern. Empirical evidence is tangible evidence (i.e. evidence, or data that we can "observe" via our senses). We can see, taste, touch, hear, or smell tangible evidence. So, in the interest of doing the right thing, you as a concerned parent will take some steps to empirically document (i.e. measure) your child's temperature. You might touch their forehead to see if they "feel" warm (sensory evidence) or you might use a digital thermometer to get a more exact reading of your child's body temperature (more sensory evidence). In trying to assess whether or not your child is sick, you had a scientific moment. You saw the world in terms of a variable (body temperature) and you sought a way to measure the value of that variable in order to determine whether your child has a fever or not.

So step one in the process of developing an appreciation of science and learning how to talk the talk is our understanding the significance of variables. Start noticing all of the traits or characteristics of people, places, things, ideas and you will start noticing variables. Start thinking about the ways in which we might measure any/all of these variables and you will have some immediate insight into the empirical work of scientific research. Scientific research is all about gathering and analyzing empirical evidence. Indeed, science *demands* the examination of empirical evidence (aka the collection of data). As indicated in the previous paragraph, the examination of empirical evidence is carried out via the process of measurement – or, more specifically, the process of measuring variables. *If we can't figure out a way to measure something, it will remain outside the domain of science.* The good news is that science has been remarkably adept at figuring out how to measure a vast array of variables: the age of the universe, the temperature on mars, the blood pressure of humans, the magnitude of earthquakes, the force of gravity, the speed of light, the size of stars, the depth of oceans, the rate at which polar caps are melting, the force with which the average soccer ball hits the head of a goalie, and so on. The social sciences also have an impressive track record in the area of measurement. Think of just about any human trait and chances are someone has developed a way to measure it. Shyness, altruism, happiness (see Box 2.5), depression, loneliness, gregariousness, grit (yes, there is a grit measure).

> **Tip 2.2**
> How to speak variable
>
> Learning to "talk" variables may be awkward at first. You might find it useful to try the following exercise. Focus on one specific object (e.g. a car). Now think about all the ways in which cars can differ from each other. (Sales people often highlight these differences in their sales pitches.) Cars can differ in style (sedans, coupes, hatchbacks, etc.) They can differ in trims (basic, sport, luxury). They can differ in transmissions (automatics or stick shifts). All of these differences represent variables that a market analyst might look at when trying to figure out if there are gender differences (another variable) in car purchases!

The Nuanced Language of Variables

Given the centrality of variables to scientific vision, it should not surprise you to learn that science denotes many different type of variable – for example, independent and dependent, antecedent and intervening, qualitative vs. quantitative, dichotomous, continuous vs. discrete, to name but a few distinctions. Several of these terms are addressed in the sections on causal research and the various styles of research. Others can be found in Box 2.5 towards the end of this chapter and still others are discussed in later chapters (e.g. see Chapters 4 and 7). But for now you should note how this specialized terminology only serves to reinforce the fundamental importance of variables in the world of scientific research.

Table 2.2   Strengthening your research vision: some examples of variables, values, and possible measures

Variable	Values	Possible measure
Gender	male/female	Question: What is your gender?
Political affiliation	Republican/Democrat/Independent/Other	Question: What is your political affiliation?
Height	short/average/tall	Direct Observation
Car style	sedan/coupe/hatchback	Direct Observation

Data – the information collected via research efforts; the result or outcome of the measurement process.

Quantitative data – research information that is expressed via numbers; the result of a measurement process that expresses values of variables via real numbers.

Data

It is often noted that money makes the world go around. In science, however, it is data that has this power. Where you and I might talk about *information*, scientists talk of *data*. Data results from the measurement process – the process whereby we gather empirical documentation of a variable (see definition). We might measure something by direct observation, such as visually inspecting and recording the amount of damage caused by a tornado, or observing the growth of your child over time by marking lines on a doorframe. In the social sciences, measurement is often done indirectly – in other words, it is the result of our asking questions about our units of analysis: such as asking individuals about the time they spend on the Internet and their feelings of loneliness. **Quantitative data** is the result of a measurement process that uses numbers as the values of variables (e.g. measuring body temperature by the numbers flashing on a digital thermometer or measuring body weight by the numbers appearing on a scale). **Qualitative data** is the result of a measurement process that focuses on words or images (narratives) to document the social world (e.g. measuring spousal love via the words of personalized marriage vows or measuring anti-government sentiment by the words or images used in public graffiti).

> **Qualitative data** – research information that is expressed via words/images.

Correlations

To be sure, nothing is ever as simple as it seems. And this is certainly true of the social world in which we live. Consequently, while there is much to be learned by studying and measuring variables in isolation, science moves well beyond such univariate (science-speak for one variable) analysis. Much research is devoted to assessing the relationships *between* variables – that is, documenting correlations or associations between variables. So while parents might want to know if their child is happy, the social scientist will not only figure out how to measure the variable happiness but may very well up the ante and see if there is an association between happiness and a second variable. In the name of correlational analysis, the social researcher might ask if higher levels of happiness are associated with higher levels of education or higher levels of financial security (perhaps a bigger allowance!). Or a social researcher might want to investigate whether the ability to empathize is associated with self-esteem or if one's grit level is associated with success.

> **Correlation** – a patterned connection or relationship between two variables.

In pursuing correlational analysis, researchers consider both the strength and the direction of associations. The extent to which two variables co-vary (or move in tandem) addresses the *strength* issue and is expressed via the *size of a correlation coefficient*. A correlation coefficient is a number that can range from 0 (indicating no connection between the variables at all) to 1 (indicating a perfect connection between two variables – i.e. the value of one variable can be used to accurately [perfectly] predict the value of the other). Correlation coefficients are also expressed as positive or negative numbers – use of these signs addresses the direction of the correlation. More on this point a little later.

Take a look down at your feet – direct observation should convince you that there is a strong (if not perfect) association between the size of your left foot and the size of your right foot. (Ergo, most of us are able to buy one size shoe to fit both of our feet!) There is a strong (albeit not totally perfect) correlation between level of education and total lifetime earnings. There is a strong (but again not perfect) relationship between smoking and lung cancer. Or finally, consider the likelihood of there being a correlation between a student's high school grades and college grade point average (GPA). It seems reasonable to expect a relatively strong association between these two variables.[4]

Box 2.3   Newsworthy research: happiest countries

In the summer of 2014, Gallup reported that Paraguay was the happiest country in the world with Panama, Guatemala, Nicaragua and Ecuador rounding out the top five. The inquiring scientific mind would want to know exactly how happiness was *measured* in order for Gallup to reach this conclusion. Gallup collected data from 1000 individuals in 138 countries about five factors: (1) whether they felt rested, (2) whether they were treated with respect,(3) whether they laughed or smiled a lot, (4) whether they enjoyed themselves, and (5) whether they did or learned something interesting on the previous day. (By the way, using these indicators, how does your own happiness measure up?)

Source: *www.nbcnews.com/health/health-news/worlds-happiest-country-would-you-believe-paraguay-n110981*.

Positive correlation – a connection between two variables which sees the values of each variable moving together in the same direction.

Negative correlation – a connection between two variables which sees the values of each variable moving together but in the opposite direction of each other.

As indicated earlier, the connection between variables can also have a direction. The direction of relationships can be linear (a plot of the values of the two variables will resemble a straight line) or non-linear (a plot of the values resembles a curved rather than a straight line). In talking about linear relationships we note **positive** or **negative correlations**. Non-linear relationships are identified as curvilinear.

A positive relationship exists when the values of two variables move together in the same direction – that is, either both values increase together or both decrease together. High values on one variable are associated with high values on the other variable or low values on one variable are associated with low values on the other variable. So we can speak of a positive relationship between level of education and income: more years of education are associated with higher levels of income. Medical research has documented a positive relationship between exercise levels and mental wellbeing. A recent study found a positive correlation between high school GPA and later adult salary of Americans (French, Homer, Robins, and Popovici 2015). Research has also documented a positive relationship between loneliness and Internet addiction among Swedish students (Engelberg and Sjoberg 2004) as well as a positive relationship between loneliness and shyness among West German students (Lamm and Stephan 1987). A positive relationship is indicated by including a positive sign (or no sign at all) before the correlation coefficient – e.g. +.35 would indicate a moderate positive correlation between two variables.

A negative relationship between two variables exists when the values of the two variables move in *opposite* direction: as the values of one variable *increase*, the values of the second *decrease* (or as the values of one decrease, the values of the second increase). So we can speak of a negative relationship between exercise and stress; higher levels of exercise are associated with lower levels of stress. We can also note a negative relationship between social class and rates of mental illness. Research documents a negative relationship between emotional intelligence and loneliness levels among Israeli students (Zysberg 2012) as well as a negative relationship between loneliness and self-rated physical attractiveness among West German students (Lamm and Stephan 1987). A negative correlation is indicated by including a negative sign before the actual correlation coefficient – for example, –.35 would indicate a fairly weak relationship where two variables are moving in opposite direction. Neil Salkind (2012) suggests possible cut-offs for an "eye-ball" assessment of correlation coefficients (see Table 2.3).

Table 2.3   Sharpening your research vision: how strong is the relationship?

.8–1.0	very strong
.6–.8	strong
.4–.6	moderate
.2–.4	weak
0–.2	not really strong enough to mention

Source: Based on Salkind (2012)

Once again to show that things are not always so simple, science also recognizes that variables are not always connected in a simple, clear-cut linear fashion (i.e. where plotted values resemble a straight line). The relationship between some variables can best be described by a curved, not a straight, line. Such associations are referred to as curvilinear (see Figure 2.1 and Box 2.4). So consider how the two variables, number of friends and happiness, might be associated. As we might expect, there is most likely initially a positive relationship between number of friends and happiness. But consider what might also be likely as the number of friends grows and grows to Facebook quantities! It may well be that with more friends than one can count, happiness might actually take a hit and the original "positive" association may reverse itself and take a downward (negative) turn with the increase in number of friends actually hurting one's happiness. Finally consider how efforts to fight boredom by engaging in a new novel activity might reach a point of reversal as a "been there, done that" attitude sets in (see Figure 2.1). (Reporting a correlation coefficient is only appropriate for either a positive or a negative relationship. No correlation coefficient can be calculated for a curvilinear relationship.)

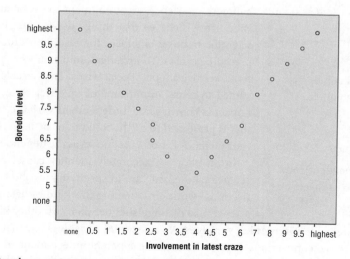

Figure 2.1   Involvement in new craze and boredom level

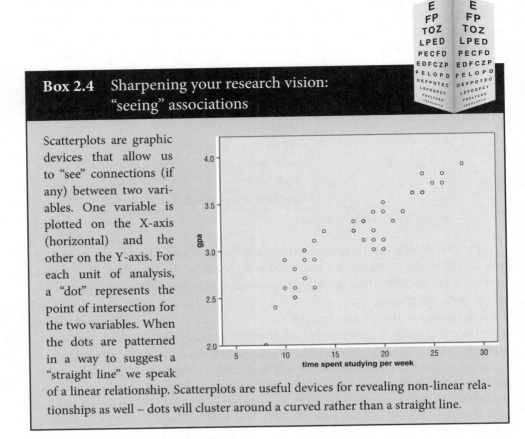

Box 2.4   Sharpening your research vision: "seeing" associations

Scatterplots are graphic devices that allow us to "see" connections (if any) between two variables. One variable is plotted on the X-axis (horizontal) and the other on the Y-axis. For each unit of analysis, a "dot" represents the point of intersection for the two variables. When the dots are patterned in a way to suggest a "straight line" we speak of a linear relationship. Scatterplots are useful devices for revealing non-linear relationships as well – dots will cluster around a curved rather than a straight line.

Independent variable – the variable presumed to cause or impact another variable; aka the predictor variable.

Dependent variable – the variable presumed to be the result or consequence of another variable; aka as the outcome.

Antecedent variable – one that comes earlier in a causal sequence or chain, preceding both the independent and dependent variables.

Intervening variable – one whose placement is between the independent and dependent variables; it serves to explicate or mediate the causal connection.

The Causal Relationship

Correlational analysis starts us down the path of yet another hallmark of science: a commitment to causal analysis. Science firmly believes that things do not just happen. The scientific mindset embraces the idea that "outcomes" have preceding causes. To investigate and express causal connections, science adopts special terms. The variable that is presumed to cause an outcome or an effect or to produce an impact is known as the **independent variable**. The variable that is presumed to be the result of or be impacted by or be the outcome of another is known as the **dependent variable**.

In an effort to accurately identify causal connections, science takes great care in specifying just how causal connections "work." In pursuing this kind of detailed analysis, science also distinguishes between two other kinds of variables: **antecedent** and **intervening variables**. An antecedent variable is one that comes early in a chain of causal connections. It precedes both the apparent independent and dependent variables in time. So, in exploring the causal link between education level and income, one might also want to consider a variable that precedes both (i.e. social class). The apparent causal connection between education level and income might really be driven by social class.

An intervening variable is one that is situated "between" the alleged independent and dependent variable. In identifying intervening variables, the researcher helps to specify or elaborate the causal process. So while one may believe there is a causal link between income and happiness, one might discover that a life stress variable intervenes and is really the key to understanding or explaining the link between income and happiness. It may be that a higher income can help eliminate major sources of stress and that this in turn helps to increase happiness levels.

Styles of Research

In addition to learning the language of variables, data, measurement, and relationships, science also offers a specialized vocabulary for characterizing essentially different styles or approaches to the overall research process. One such distinction is made with regard to quantitative vs. qualitative research. Another useful distinction is noted by the terms inductive vs. deductive research.

The Quantitative/Qualitative Difference

The term **quantitative research** reflects an approach that documents variables through a measurement process that emphasizes numbers. Indeed, a numerical orientation is key to one very common definition of measurement: measurement is the process by which *numbers are attached to the values of variables.* Following this definition, the variable family size can be measured by using numbers to count the total number of people in a family. Personal income might be measured by indicating the total amount of money earned in a year. The variable temperature might be measured by noting the numerical value displayed on a digital thermometer. The speed of a pitch or of a car might be measured by noting a numerical reading (i.e. miles per hour) on a radar gun. In its reliance on numbers in the research process, quantitative research recognizes the value of numbers with regard to yielding precise measurement as well as yielding measures and data compatible with statistical analysis. In Chapter 5, on measurement, we see that when real numbers are used in the measurement process, it is possible (and appropriate) to perform analysis that incorporates or relies on mathematical procedures (addition, subtraction, division, multiplication, etc.). Quantitative research is often interested in offering as detailed a picture as possible of its topic of inquiry and numbers can serve this task very well. For instance, in order to provide details, quantitative researchers typically work with large samples sizes (a numbers issue) and then resort to statistics (again a numbers issues) to offer summaries of the numbers across a wide array of variables. So, research on global alcohol consumption might offer statistics on a number of variables: the overall consumption rate as well as consumption rates by gender, or by age, race and ethnic groups or by religious groups, the number of alcohol-related deaths, the number of alcohol-related illnesses, the variation in rates between groups, and so on (see WHO 2014).

> **Quantitative research** – an approach to documenting reality that relies heavily on numbers both for the measurement of variables and for data analysis.

There are some researchers, however, who reject this reliance on numbers and are wary of putting them at the front and center of their research endeavor. While measurement can have a "quantitative" definition, **qualitative research** also

> **Qualitative research** – an approach to documenting reality that relies on words and images as the primary data source.

recognizes that numbers do not necessarily tell the whole story or provide the best road to empirical documentation and understanding. Consider, for instance, using numbers to "measure" a variable such as gender. To be sure, social scientists do this all the time: we might attach the number 1 as a label for the value "male" and a number 2 as a label for the value "female." When we use numbers to merely label the values of a variable, we acknowledge the non-quantitative use of numbers and refer to such measures as qualitative rather than quantitative measures. There are also times when the use of numbers for documentation seems totally inappropriate or ill advised. Imagine, for instance, efforts to measure how much two people love each other. How do numbers help us capture (document) this variable? While it is true that quantitative researchers do try to quantify love (e.g. on a scale of 1–10, how much do you love your spouse?), qualitative researchers would rather pursue a different (and, they might argue, qualitatively superior) route to empirical documentation. Rather than relying so heavily on numbers, qualitative researchers will rely on talk or direct observation as important tools for documenting reality. So, in an effort to measure the love between spouses, I might talk to both partners and ask them about what love means to them and how they express or experience it in their relationship. I might spend time observing them in their day-to-day exchanges and note if or how they engage in loving gestures towards each other. Because qualitative research relies on talking, listening, and watching, it frequently requires researchers to work with smaller samples than typically used in quantitative research. With smaller samples, more time can be given to analyzing the "richer" more nuanced and demanding qualitative data.

While the quantitative/qualitative distinction is an important one for understanding these fundamentally different approaches to research, it would be wrong to think these differences are absolute. Mario Small argues that the social sciences are "beyond" the quantitative/qualitative divide and that a merger of the two styles of research best serves the task of causal analysis (Small 2015). Indeed, many researchers end up using some combination of quantitative and qualitative research techniques, recognizing the benefits of employing multiple strategies for achieving more insight and increasing validity. The term **triangulation** was coined many years ago to capture this mixed methods approach (Denzin 1978). Rank in his research on families receiving public assistance combined quantitative analysis of case records, in-depth qualitative interviews with recipients and observational field research at welfare offices (Rank 2004).

Triangulation – refers to using multiple or mixed data collection strategies in the study of the same topic.

Table 2.4   Strengthening Your Research Vision: The Quantitative/ Qualitative Differences

Quantitative	*Qualitative*
Numbers as data	Words/images as data
Larger samples	Smaller samples
Descriptive	Exploratory
Statistical analysis	Narrative analysis

The Inductive/Deductive Distinction

Research can also be characterized as inductive or deductive in its approach. The distinction is made with regard to the place of theory in the research process. The key question is this: Is theory generated or formulated as the *result* of our research efforts or is theory used to *initiate* the research process?

Inductive research pursues a path of study that culminates in formulating or refining theory. It starts in the empirical realm – collecting data – and uses the empirical data to stipulate **empirical generalizations** – that is, generalizations based on observed patterns in the data. In turn, these empirical generalizations become the fodder or grist for new theory. The theory generated in this approach is often called "grounded" theory – built from the ground (empirical) up. (The origin of grounded theory is credited to Glaser and Strauss (1967).[5]

Inductive research – research that starts with data collection and looks for patterns in the data to generate empirical generalizations.

Empirical generalizations – generalizations based on observed patterns in the data.

Deductive research – research that deduces questions or hypotheses from theory and then collects data to assess/test those questions or hypotheses.

With **deductive research**, theory is used to formulate specific research questions or hypotheses (predictions of expected relationships between variables based on theory). Once the questions or hypotheses are stated, empirical data collection ensues. The evidence provides answers to the research questions or tests of the hypotheses. More discussion of the role of theory in the research process can be found in Chapter 4. For now, Figure 2.2 offers a concise visual that illustrates the distinctive "flow" of inductive and deductive approaches.

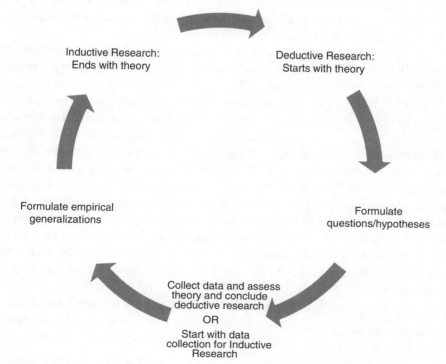

Figure 2.2　Inductive and Deductive Styles: It all Turns on the Placement of Theory

Goals of Research

Just as one's style of research can differ, so too can the reason for pursuing research in the first place. Research is typically undertaken in the name of four basic tasks: exploring, describing, explaining, or evaluating some social phenomenon, practice, event, or program.

Exploratory research – the purpose of shedding light on a little understood or researched setting, group or phenomenon.

Exploratory research is typically concerned with "getting to know" or increasing our understanding of a new or little researched setting, group or phenomenon. Such research tends to utilize relatively small samples of subjects so as to afford the researcher the opportunity to get "up-close" first-hand information about their research issue. By way of exploring, the researcher might engage in intensive one-on-one interviewing or pursue a participatory study that allows the researcher to get some direct experience of their subject/topic – that is, to "walk a mile" in the research subject's shoes or worlds. Exploratory research often (though not exclusively) produces qualitative data where empirical evidence is presented in words, pictures or some other form that best captures the research subject's genuine experiences and understanding (see for instance Early and Akers's (2015) study of suicide in the black community). To be sure, there are times when exploratory research can involve large samples and need to turn to quantitative data collection and analysis. Early studies exploring the extent of internet usage offer an example. Lastly, some researchers will conduct exploratory research as the first step in planning a larger project. When this is the case, the research is typically referred to as a pilot study. The researcher, in effect, is getting the lay of the land and seeing which elements of a larger study are feasible, which need modification and which might have to be foregone altogether. Various measures or analysis techniques might also be pre-tested in the pilot phase.[6]

Descriptive research – research that offers a detailed picture or account of some social phenomenon, setting, experience, group, and so on.

Descriptive research seeks to provide a detailed picture or account of some social phenomenon, setting, experience, group, and so on. In providing such description, this kind of research strives to be as accurate and thorough as possible. Consequently, descriptive research tends to be invested in large and representative samples and with devising accurate (and often quantitative) measures of variables. In effect, descriptive studies often provide a numbers-driven "plenty of facts" line of investigation. It seeks to find out the "what's happening" and "who is involved" details of a situation. (Good examples of large-scale descriptive research are provided by any nation's effort to present data rich overviews of its people – i.e. the US Current Population Survey or the European Union's Eurobarometer or the World Values Survey.) In the interest of description, researchers might also want to document correlations or associations between variables. In generating these basic facts, descriptive research aligns quite naturally with a quantitative approach to research (see previous discussion).

Explanatory research – research that undertakes or pursues causal relationships between variables.

Explanatory research takes us a step further than description, tackling the why and how questions of a phenomenon. So while descriptive research on domestic violence might tell us about its prevalence and identify the typical offenders and victims, explanatory research will try to identify the causes of domestic violence. Why do some and not others resort to using physical violence on their loved ones? How do family conflicts escalate into violent episodes or exchanges? Given its interest in finding explanations, this research endeavor makes a firm commitment to causal analysis and the conditions for establishing causal connections between variables (an issue that is so important in scientific research it has its own chapter in this text). The single best data collection strategy for finding explanations or answering causal questions is the experiment – a design that intentionally manipulates an independent variable in order to see its impact (if any) on a dependent variable. Yet, as Chapter 7 shows, the experiment is often a design that cannot be used when investigating causal relationships in the social realm.

Evaluation research can be thought of as a "judgmental" form of research in that it seeks to assess (judge) the merits or efficacy of some social program or policy. If we were interested in finding out if a new anti-bullying program has the desired impact of reducing bullying, we would conduct a piece of evaluation research. In order to determine if the "put the cell phones down" policy was effective in reducing auto accidents from talking/texting while driving, we would conduct evaluation research. Evaluation research has a very practical, bottom-line orientation – it wants to know if policies and programs work as planned. In the present climate of accountability and tough financial times, it is a "must do" area of research for many social institutions (e.g. education, health care, government). It is frequently a necessary condition for programs seeking both initial and continuing funding. Funding agencies or organizations often insist that programs prove their worth to get their monies.

> **Evaluation research** – research that assesses the impact of some program or policy or intervention.

Some Perfectly Valid Points

One set of terms that you will encounter repeatedly in any science talk have to do with validity. As indicated in Chapter 1, the research enterprise is very concerned with the accuracy of claims or assertions about the world around us. To state this another way, science is concerned with minimizing error. Given this concern, science devotes a lot of attention to the issues of **measurement validity, internal validity, and external validity.**

As we saw in Chapter 1, science is an empirical endeavor: it is dedicated to using concrete, sentient evidence to support its claims about the world around us. In the language of science, this evidence takes the form of variables that are subjected to the measurement process. In focusing on the issue of measurement validity, the researcher is most concerned with critically evaluating the accuracy of the empirical indicators used in a study. When we claim measurement validity, we claim that we have been successful at measuring what we claim we have measured. Much more is said about this topic in Chapters 5 and 6.

> **Measurement validity** – accuracy with regard to measures empirically documenting what they claim to document.
>
> **Internal validity** – accuracy with regard to claims of causal connections between variables.
>
> **External validity** – accuracy with regard to findings being correct when applied beyond any one study/sample.

Perhaps it is our nature, but humans have a very keen interest in causal analysis. Many are willing to share their views as to the causes of divorce, misbehaved children, terrorism, or the shrinking middle class. Yet, research that attempts to provide causal answers is treading on very treacherous ground – causes of outcomes are seldom simple. In trying to evaluate causal assertions, the issue of internal validity directs our attention to research design, the plan or strategy for data collection. The key to achieving strong internal validity in a study is a plan of action that allows the researcher to effectively satisfy the three requirements of causality: showing the causal agent (the independent variable) precedes the outcome (the dependent variable) in time, showing that the independent and dependent variable are associated, and showing that the association is not due to some rival explanation. As it turns out, one design, the experiment, is best for achieving all of these conditions. Much more discussion of experiments and internal validity follows in Chapter 7.

Even if we are satisfied with a study's measures and a study's overall design, we still must ask if the findings obtained in any one study can be safely generalized to other settings or groups. This brings us to the last validity concern: external validity. Taking one's new found knowledge and "spreading it around" can be problematic so the researcher must exercise caution. Consider for instance the findings obtained via experiments. As we will see in Chapter 7, an experiment is an extremely special data collection tool, one that exercises much control over the conditions of the research process. And while all of this control helps with establishing internal validity, it can undercut external validity. Can a contrived or manipulated research endeavor really yield information that is accurate about everyday, non-experimental conditions or settings? Even survey research, the mainstay of social research, will face external validity challenges if survey samples are not representative. Any time we are asked to trust that data from a sample accurately describes the larger population, we should have an external validity concern; we should ask if the generalization is on solid footing. Again, much more discussion of the conditions needed for maximizing external validity is found in Chapter 11.

Talking the Talk

Hopefully this introduction to the language of scientific research will help get you started and serve you well as you move through the rest of this book. It is also hoped that learning "science speak" might make it easier to connect with the scientific mindset. There is no doubt that we have much to gain by increasing our fluency in the language of science and research. To be sure, this brief introduction is just the beginning – fluency will require more language classes! Still such training will have a great pay-off: If we can "talk the talk" we will be in a better position to assess if someone is doing a good job "walking the walk" of science.

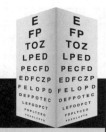

Box 2.5   Sharpening your research vision: more key terms of science

Aggregate data –information about social collectivities – groups, nations, women, men, etc.

Applied research – research undertaken to address a specific or real world problem –contrast with basic research

Attribute variable – a variable that cannot be manipulated by the researcher as it is a trait or characteristic of the individual; aka "fixed" variable

Basic research – researcher undertaken to advance theoretical understanding – contrast with applied research

Bias – a systematic or patterned error in research findings

Cases – the units about which data is collected; aka units of analysis

Concept – an abstract idea that summarizes commonalities shared across particular items

Construct – an abstract idea that cannot be directly observed

Continuous variable – one that can be measured by an infinite set of values; a variable that can be expressed as either whole numbers or as fractions – contrast with discrete variable

Control group – the group in an experiment that is not exposed to the independent variable – contrast with experimental group

Cross-sectional study – a study conducted at one moment in time; aka survey design

Design – a research plan or strategy

Descriptive statistics – statistics used to summarize or organize data

Dichotomous variable – a two-value variable – e.g. gender (male/female) grade outcome (pass/fail)

Discrete variable – a variable whose values can only be expressed as whole numbers; aka categorical variable

Experiment – a highly controlled research design where the independent variable is intentionally manipulated to see its effect on the dependent variable

Frequency distribution – a count of the number of times a value occurs for a given variable

Generalizability – the ability to accurately generalize findings from one group/sample to another group/population; aka external validity

Hawthorne effect – the tendency for study subjects to change their behaviors because they are aware of being part of a study. (The name is derived from an early industrial productivity study of plant workers in Hawthorne, Illinois. Plant workers increased their productivity in reaction to receiving the attention of researchers.)

Hypothesis – a statement or prediction of the expected relationship between two variables

Index – a composite (multiple item) measure; Rosenberg, for example, uses ten statements to measure self-esteem

Inferential statistics – statistics that estimate population values based on sample data

Inverse relationship – a negative relationship between two variables

Lurking variable – a "background" variable that is responsible for a spurious relationship – i.e. an apparent but not a genuine causal connection between two variables

Mean – the arithmetic average of the values for a variable

N – number of element in a research population

n – number of elements in a sample

Null hypothesis – the prediction that there is no relationship between two variables

Operational definition – a set of instructions for measurement

Representative sample – a subset of a research population that accurately reflects or captures the full range of variation found in the population

Research design – the plan or strategy for a research project

Research population – the total collection of elements (people, places, things) being studied/analyzed

Sample – a subset of the research population; data is typically collected from samples of research populations

Variance – the spread of individual scores around/from the mean

Variation – differences or diversity in the values of a variable; it is the heart of analysis efforts: research essentially interested in trying to explain the variance found in variables.

TAKE AWAYS

- Science has its own specialized language/terms
- Science sees and analyzes the world as a series of variables – variables that must be measured
- Much research is devoted to examining connections between variables – aka correlations or associations
  - Positive correlation is an association between two variables where the values of two variables move together in the same direction
  - Negative correlation is an association between two variables where the values of two variables move in opposite directions
  - Curvilinear relationship is an association between two variables where the values start in one direction but then reverse their direction
- Science is committed to causal analysis:
  - Independent variables are those thought to cause/influence dependent variables
  - Dependent variables are the "outcomes" of another variable
  - The casual connection can be further clarified via variables that are either antecedent to or intervening between the independent and dependent variables

- There are two basic approaches to or styles of research:
  - Quantitative with its reliance on numerical data
  - Qualitative with its reliance on narrative data
- Research is pursued for the purpose (goal) of:
  - Exploration
  - Description
  - Explanation
  - Evaluation
- Validity issues
  - Measurement validity addresses if measures are trustworthy
  - Internal validity addresses if causal claims are trustworthy
  - External validity addresses if generalization are trustworthy

Sharpening the Edge: More Reading and Searching

- A good discussion of the ecological fallacy that includes a review of Durkheim's work on suicide as well as Robinson's work on the relationship between foreign born status and literacy rates is available in "The B Files: Case studies of bias in real life epidemiologic studies.", found at:

  http://www.teachepi.org/documents/courses/bfiles/The%20B%20Files_File3_Durkheim_Final_Complete.pdf
- An oldie but goodie for anyone wanting to get some more advice on how to be a better consumer of research is:

  Jeffrey Katzer, Kenneth Cook, and Wayne Crouch's *Evaluating Information: A Guide for Users of Social Science Research*. 4th edn. Boston: McGraw-Hill, 1998
- Those interested in finding articles and studies to illustrate many of the topics and issues raised in this book should take a look at:

  Diane Wysocki's *Readings in Social Research Methods*. 3rd edn. Belmont, CA: Thomson Wadsworth, 2008
- No matter what the specific area of inquiry, the reader will always find something of worth at Bill Trochim's *Web Center for Social Research*:

  http://socialresearchmethods.net/
- Those interested in making a stronger everyday connection with science should visit the Publiscize website which is devoted to presenting science in the most accessible, jargon-free way.

  http://www.publiscize.com/
- Anyone interested in learning more about grounded theory will find a great resource in Glaser's The Grounded Theory Institute:

  http://www.groundedtheory.com/
- Those interested in learning more about "mixed methods" (integrating qualitative and quantitative techniques) should visit:

  http://personal.bgsu.edu/~earleym/MIXEDMETHODS/resources.htm

Exercises

1   Consider some common objects around your house – for example, a television, a book, an outdoor grill, a sweater. Think about the objects "like a scientist" and make a list of variables that you could use to "study" the object. For instance, televisions can vary in size (e.g. 32, 38, or 65 inch screens) and vary with regard to the quality of picture (e.g. high definition or not). See how many different variables you can suggest as potentially important for your study of a given object.

2   Access an electronic search engine via a library webpage. Do a quick search and locate about five articles on a common topic (e.g. obesity). Read the abstracts for each article. Can you determine the unit of analysis for the research? Dig a little deeper and scroll down to the "methods" section of each article to see if your initial assessment was correct. Who or what was sampled? Was the data collected about individuals, or groups, or a program/policy, or a social artifact?

3   Go back to the same articles you used for exercise two above. From the information given in the abstract, can you identify which "goal" was being pursued in each of the research articles? Can you identify which articles took a quantitative and which a qualitative approach to their research? (Here you might find it helpful to scroll down to the "findings" section of the articles and see if the researchers' analysis is focused on statistics or on narratives.)

4   Return once again to the articles you used for exercise 2. This time take a look at the sampling information presented in each article. Do you see any reason to be concerned about the issue of external validity in each of the studies?

Notes

1   In the fall of 2009, thousands of personal emails between a few scientists who wrote dismissively about critics of climate change were hacked, stolen and released to blogs denying global warming. Global warming skeptics used the emails to attack and discount climate science. The incident became known as Climategate.

2   https://gma.yahoo.com/ny-measles-patient-boarded-amtrak-train-penn-station-123050981-abc-news-wellness.html.

3   Publiscize: http://www.publiscize.com/; Futurity: http://www.futurity.org/; and The Conversation: https://the-conversation.com/us.

4   You can visit the following link to see an illustration of a hypothetical illustration: http://pirate.shu.edu/~wachsmut/Teaching/MATH1101/Relations/correlation.html.

5   See Bill Trochim's webpage for a brief but informative review of the term http://www.socialresearchmethods.net/kb/qualapp.php.

6   See http://otrec.us/news/entry/study_examines_racial_bias_at_crosswalks for a pilot study investigating the influence of pedestrian race on drivers yielding at crosswalks.

References

BBC News. 2000. "Should We Trust Scientists?" http://news.bbc.co.uk/2/hi/talking_point/713337.stm.

CBS News. 2015. "Disneyland Measles Outbreak Spreads." http://www.cbsnews.com/videos/disneyland-measles-outbreak-spreads/.

Denzin, Norman. 1978. *The Research Act*. New York: Aldine.

Early, Kevin, and Ronald Akers. 1993. "'It's a White Thing': An Exploration of Beliefs about Suicide in the African-American Community." *Deviant Behavior* 14: 277–296.

Engelberg, E., and L. Sjoberg. 2004. "Internet Skills, Social use and Adjustment." *CyberPsychology & Behavior* 7: 41–47.

French, Michael, Homer, Jenny, Popovici, Iona, and Philip Robins. 2015. "What You Do in High School Matters. High School GPA, Educational Attainment, and Labor Market Earnings as a Young Adult." *Eastern Economic Journal* 41: 370–386. http://www.palgrave-journals.com/eej/journal/vaop/ncurrent/full/eej201422a.html.

Funk, Gary. 2015. "5 Key Findings on what Americans and Scientists Think about Science." Pew Research Center. FactTank. http://www.pewresearch.org/fact-tank/2015/01/29/5-key-findings-science/.

Glaser, Barney G., and Anselm L. Strauss. 1967. *The Discovery of Grounded Theory: Strategies for Qualitative Research*. Chicago: Aldine.

Harding, Anne. 2014."Americans Trust in Doctors is Falling." *Livescience*. http://www.livescience.com/48407-americans-trust-doctors-falling.html.

Innovation Union Competitiveness Report. 2011. *New Perspectives Smarter Policy Design – Building on Diversity*. http://ec.europa.eu/research/innovation-union/pdf/competitiveness-report/2011/chapters/new_perspectives_smarter_policy_design_chapter_1.pdf.

Kelland, Kate. 2015. "WHO Calls for More Measles Vaccination in Europe as Large Outbreaks Persist." *Yahoo! News*. http://news.yahoo.com/calls-more-measles-vaccination-europe-large-outbreaks-persist-114653744.html.

Koleva, Gergana. 2012. "What Recent Measles and Rubella Outbreaks in Europe Can Teach the U.S." http://www.forbes.com/sites/gerganakoleva/2012/07/02/what-recent-measles-and-rubella-outbreaks-in-europe-can-teach-the-u-s/.

Lamm, Helmut, and Stephan Ekkehard. 1987. "Loneliness Among German University Students: Some Correlates." *Social Behavior and Personality* 15(2): 161–164.

Liston, Barbara. 2015. "Florida Bans Use of 'Climate Change' by State Agency: Report." *Yahoo! News*. http://news.yahoo.com/florida-bans-climate-change-state-agency-report-163805011.html.

Moulson, Geir. 2015. "Toddler Dies of Measles in Berlin, 1st Death in Outbreak." *Yahoo! News*. http://news.yahoo.com/young-child-dies-measles-berlin-1st-death-outbreak-114712339.html,

Pappas, Stephanie. 2014. "More Americans Don't Believe Global Warming is Happening." *Livescience*. http://www.weather.com/science/environment/news/more-americans-dont-believe-global-warming-happening-survey-20140117.

Plumer, Brad. 2015. "Florida Isn't the Only State Trying to Shut Down Discussion of Climate Change." *Vox Media*. http://www.vox.com/2015/3/10/8182513/florida-ban-climate-change.

Rainie, Lee, Funk, Carrie, and Monica Anderson. 2015. "Scientists' Views: Most Approve of Active Role in Public Debates About Science and Technology." Pew Research Center. Internet, Science & Tech. http://www.pewinternet.org/2015/02/15/scientists-views-most-approve-of-active-role-in-public-debates-about-science-and-technology/.

Rank, Mark. 2004. "The Blending of Qualitative and Quantitative Methods in Understanding Childbearing Among Welfare Recipients." In SharleneNaby Hesse-Biber and PatriciaLeavy (eds.), *Approaches to Qualitative Research*. New York: Oxford.

Salkind, Neil. 2012. *100 Questions (and Answers) about Research Methods*. Los Angeles: SAGE.

Swanson, Emily. 2013. "Americans Have Little Faith In Scientists, Science Journalists: Poll." *Huff Post*. Science. December 21. http://www.huffingtonpost.com/2013/12/21/faith-in-scientists_n_4481487.html.

WHO 2014. "Global Status Report on Alcohol and Health 2014." http://www.who.int/substance_abuse/publications/global_alcohol_report/en/.

Zysberg, Leehu. 2012. "Loneliness and Emotional Intelligence." *The Journal of Psychology* 146(1–2): 37–46.

Chapter 3

Ethics: It's the Right Thing To Do

Introducing Social Research Methods: Essentials for Getting the Edge, First Edition. Janet M. Ruane.
© 2016 John Wiley & Sons, Ltd. Published 2016 by John Wiley & Sons, Ltd.

FIRST TAKES

Be sure to take note of the following:
- Importance of ethics in research
- Major ethical issues
  - Do no harm
  - Obtain informed consent
  - Protect privacy
  - Avoid conflict of interests
- Ethics review boards
  - Institutional review boards (IRBs)

While most of this book is concerned with introducing you to the logic and specific strategies of research methods, there is one issue that must be acknowledged as infusing all others: research ethics. Ultimately, our research endeavors must abide by standards of professionalism and honesty; our efforts must strive to earn the respect and trust of both research participants and the public at large. In fact, without that well-earned trust factor, science loses its competitive edge over alternative ways of knowing. Furthermore, science without the public trust can seriously undermine other social institutions as well. Consider the following research scandal in Japan. Japan has been trying to grow its research reputation and worldwide market. It appeared that the nation was moving in this direction when a government-funded study produced promising results in the area of stem cell research. But some data discrepancies prompted a review of the study. The Japanese government announced in the spring of 2014 that data in the stem cell research was falsified.[1] The lead researcher in the lab was accused of research malpractice. The incident is seen as both a set-back for the Japanese research community and the government at large (Kurtenbach 2014). If we can't trust science, what or who can we trust?

The ethical concerns of good research extend well beyond the issue of falsifying data. Indeed, the methodical steps for conducting research provide a basic safeguard against this form of deception. Science's commitment to a public forum for its work allows others to check and see if valid but also proper procedures were followed in various stages of the research process. In addition to research fraud, we must also be diligent about such issues as safeguarding the wellbeing of research subjects, obtaining informed consent from those subjects, protecting participants' privacy, and with the ever-growing need to secure research funding, we need to be diligent about avoiding a conflict of interest. These issues are reviewed in detail in the pages that follow.

Putting Ethics in Historical Context

The explicit attention we now give to research ethics is a rather recent development. World War II provided one of our loudest wake-up calls regarding the ethics of research. Through the Nuremberg trials, the world learned about concentration camp atrocities committed in the name of science. In 1946, 23 German physicians went on trial for crimes against prisoners of war. The crimes included experiments that exposed humans to extreme temperatures, the performances of mutilating surgery and the deliberate infection of prisoners with lethal pathogens (National Institutes of Health 2008). As a result of these revelations, the Nuremberg Code of 1949 established the basic principles for research involving humans. Still decades elapsed before a formalized mechanism for enforcing the code was established and, consequently, ethical abuses continued in the interim.

Box 3.1   Sharpening your research vision: the Nuremberg code

The code consists of 10 principles designed to protect human subjects of research. Here are some of those standards:

- Voluntary consent of human research subjects is essential.
- The purpose of the research must be to yield results for the good of society.
- Risk should never exceed humanitarian importance of the study.
- Subjects must be free to discontinue participation.
- Researchers must be prepared to terminate the research if it is assessed that continuation will result in harm.

Source: US Department of Health and Human Services (2005).

Despite the fact that the Nuremberg Code was prompted by egregious research practices in Nazi Germany, it would be a mistake to think that unethical practices were confined to Germany or even to the context of war. At about the same time the Nuremberg trials were being conducted, the Canadian government was engaged in a major study of 1300 aboriginal adults and children. At the time, researchers took advantage of the natives' "natural" state in order to run nutritional experiments that continued for an extended time period. Subsequent revelations about this decade-long study brought rousing criticism of the government's disregard for the wellbeing of the research subjects and the decision to put a research agenda ahead of humanitarian efforts (Weber 2013). Without the means to enforce ethical codes, it should not surprise the reader to learn that there have been many more ethical lapses by those engaged in research. In 1959, a Senate subcommittee investigated routine drug-testing practices by pharmaceutical companies. The companies would provide physicians with samples of experimental drugs not yet established as safe and pay the physicians to collect data on their unwitting patients. In 1963, the director of the National Institutes of Health (NIH) exposed some troubling federally funded research being conducted by physicians at the Sloan-Kettering Cancer Research Institute. The physicians had injected live cancer cells into indigent elderly patients without their consent (ACHRE 1995).

In the 1970s the Senate held hearings on the Tuskegee Syphilis Study. In this research that began in the 1930s under the auspices of the US Public Health Service approximately 400 black men in Tuskegee, Alabama were involved without their knowledge in a longitudinal study of syphilis. In order to better understand the nature and course of the disease, the men in the study were denied penicillin even after it became the standard course of treatment for the disease. At least 28 research subjects died and 100 more suffered blindness and insanity from the effects of their untreated disease (or perhaps more to the point, from the effects of the study) (ACHRE 1995).

Most recently in the 1990s a Presidential Advisory Committee was formed to investigate ethically questionable government radiation experiments conducted in the United States between the late 1940s and early 1970s (ACHRE 1995). Toward the end of World War II, some Americans were injected with plutonium in order to study the element's effects on the human body. (The goal of the research was to gain information that would limit hazards to workers involved with the atom bomb project.) During the same time period radioactive oatmeal was reportedly fed to patients at a school for the retarded in Massachusetts. In the postwar period, the government sponsored research that entailed releasing radiation into the environment in Utah, New Mexico, Tennessee, and Washington without notifying the affected populations.

To be sure, the social sciences do not often entail the highly dramatic ethical issues encountered in medical, or drug, or nuclear research. Answering survey questions or being the focus of field studies may not pose serious threats to one's physical safety or wellbeing. Still, the social science researcher would be ill advised to treat ethics as an irrelevant or secondary topic. Every research decision we make, from planning to the disclosure of results, should be made with an eye to ethics.

For our work to be ethically grounded we must be prepared to evaluate our research plans and activities in light of generally accepted rules of conduct (e.g. see Nuremberg Code). For the sake of structuring this chapter, the discussion that follows focuses on several key ethical standards contained in the *American Sociological Association*'s Code of Ethics. As you read through these principles, however, you will no doubt appreciate that they are not unique to the field of sociology. Rather the ethical principles that follow transcend any one specific discipline or field of study. Anyone embarking on the research path should be prepared to abide by these standards.

Research Should Not Cause Harm to Subjects

On first inspection, the "cause no harm" dictum may be the "no brainer" of all ethical guidelines for research. Any research activity that harms or poses unreasonable risks to subjects is incompatible with a fundamental ethical obligation to safeguard the physical, psychological and emotional wellbeing of participants. Research that carries the risk of harm to participants without offering any clear benefits is ethically untenable. But even an obvious guideline such as "cause no harm" can be a difficult rule to fully honor. The simple fact is that it can be hard to predict or know in advance the negative consequences of research. Research that appears safe and innocuous may have very different effects than those anticipated. Consider, for instance, the Cambridge-Somerville Youth Study of the 1930s.

In 1939, Richard Cabot initiated an experimental treatment program for the prevention of delinquency among Boston youth. The research involved over 500 boys, half of whom were assigned to an experimental treatment group while the other half were assigned to a no-treatment control group (Powers and Witmer 1951). In the mid-1970s, a research team led by Joan McCord conducted a follow-up assessment of the effectiveness of the program. Despite the honorable intentions of the original research program, McCord and her team found evidence that the boys in the treatment condition may well have been harmed by their participation in the original study:

> Treated subjects were more likely than controls to evidence signs of alcoholism and serious mental illness, died at a younger age, suffered from more stress-related diseases, tended to be employed in lower-prestige occupations and were more likely to commit second crimes. (Kimmel 1988, p. 19)

As another example of just how hard it is for researchers to know in advance the consequences of their research, consider Haney, Banks, and Zimbardo's (1973) now famous simulated prison experiment. These researchers carefully screened and selected 24 male college students for participation in a study of the behavior of "prisoners" and "guards" in a mock prison. The students knew they would be role-playing and they were paid for their participation. What *nobody* knew, however, was the impact the mock prison experience would have on the research subjects. Soon after the start of the study, some of the prisoners experienced depression, anxiety, and psychosomatic symptoms. Some of the guards displayed abusive and aggressive behaviors. Zimbardo and his colleagues became so alarmed by what they witnessed that they cancelled the experiment after only six days of its planned two-week run.

Social media sites offer new possibilities for research projects. Many regard Internet forums or locations to be rich and vital data sites. But these sites bring with them their own possibilities for harm. Not too long ago, the Centers for Disease Control embarked on a research agenda that took advantage of the popularity of *Second Life. Second Life* is a virtual reality site where individuals via their avatars can behave in ways far different from their ordinary lives. Virtual reality sites force us to wonder if these sites actually "allow" participants to engage in activities that would be deeply discrediting in another "here and now" world. If so, there is a possibility that virtual reality research could set up participants for some disturbing or even harmful "self-knowledge." Or consider the revelation by Facebook concerning its weeklong 2012 "experiment" wherein news feeds of nearly 700,000 users were intentionally manipulated in order to see the impact of positive versus negative feeds on the moods of users. Facebook, of course, defended its research saying that all users have agreed to such studies by virtue of "signing" the terms of service (TOS) agreement upon joining Facebook.[2] Still, news about the experiments disturbed many who reject the idea of Facebook (or any group) intentionally manipulating our emotions. (One observer tweeted that given the small effect size of the alterations, "probably" no negative news feeds resulted in any suicides!) (Forbes 2014).

Another human experiment that received much attention was conducted by Okcupid. This online dating service intentionally fed users false information about potential matches, telling users that selected individuals were good matches when in fact they were not. The CEO of Okcupid defended the intentional lying claiming that the company did not *intend* any harm to its users. But as we saw in the earlier Cambridge Study account, good intentions can nonetheless have negative results.

Clearly, without the ability to see into the future or when entering into largely uncharted territories as in the Facebook experiments, it is impossible for researchers to know in advance all the possible or the final consequences of their research. Uncertainty about outcomes, however, should not void or weaken the "do no harm" directive. The ethical obligation remains for researchers to anticipate likely outcomes and to take those steps that would mitigate the harm and maximize the benefits that might come to participants.

Researchers Should Obtain the Informed Consent of Subjects

Informed consent – an ethical mandate that stipulates that potential research participants must be fully informed about all aspects of a research project that might influence their decision to participate.

The principle of **informed consent** is about the right of individuals to determine for themselves whether or not they want to be part of a research project. More specifically, informed consent refers to the right of research participants to be fully informed about all aspects of a research project that might influence their decision to participate. Consequently, freedom of choice and self-determination are at the heart of the informed consent principle. No one should be forced or duped into participating in a research endeavor. Informed consent is such an important principle of ethical research that it is a required condition of any federally funded research project in the United States. That said, we must also acknowledge that informed consent is a principle that is all too frequently violated.

If we dissect the principle of informed consent, we will see that it really consists of four separate elements: the assumptions of competence, voluntarism, full information, and comprehension (Reynolds 1979). Understanding these elements provides some immediate insight into why informed consent is so often violated.

Competence

This element of informed consent presumes that informed consent can only be given by competent individuals – that is, individuals capable of deciding for themselves if participation in a study is in their best interest. Given the incredible diversity of social research topics and populations, research often involves subjects who lack the maturity or responsibility or even the language skills required for competent decision-making. For instance, obtaining informed consent from individuals in developing countries can be problematic given the cultural and language differences that often exist between the researcher and subjects. The most obvious categories of those incapable of providing consent are children and mentally challenged or seriously ill individuals. To pursue research on these populations, informed consent must be obtained from parents or guardians.

Box 3.2   Newsworthy research: informed consent and the search for the Polio vaccine

By the early 1950s, medical researchers had been engaged in a long 10-year search for a vaccine to stop the highly contagious and highly feared polio virus. (Survey research at the time indicated that polio was second only to the atomic bomb as Americans' greatest fear.) The head of the March of Dimes campaign to combat polio had years before assured the public that a vaccine was near. In 1952, several years after the "cure is near" promise was made, the United States was experiencing its worst polio epidemic. Enter Jonas Salk. Salk had achieved some promising results with his vaccine in his research using monkeys. Now he wanted to test the vaccine on humans. And test it he did. In 1952 he injected 43 children at the D.T. Watson Home for Crippled Children with his vaccine. A few weeks later he injected more children at the Polk State School for the retarded and feeble minded. To be sure, the principle of informed consent was yet to be an ethical mandate but there were those who thought Salk's testing on humans was premature and posed too great a risk to innocent children.

Source: "The American Experience. 2009. The Polio Crusade." *http://www.pbs.org/ wgbh/americanexperience/features/transcript/polio-transcript/.*

When honest sincere efforts are not made to attend to all the elements of this principle, informed consent can be easily violated. For instance, there had been a long-standing complaint in education research that informed consent was all too frequently given little more than lip-service. Informed consent would often be obtained via "passive" or "opt out" consent forms – that is, forms that made consent the "no action" default position while non-consent would require subjects to take an extra step to "opt out" of the study. For example, to obtain "passive" consent, forms might be sent home with elementary school students with the instructions that slips need only be returned if parents *objected* to their child's involvement. This tactic guaranteed higher consent rates since many children would either forget to present the slips to their parents or forget to return them to school officials. Of course some researchers are guilty of more blatant violation of the competence element. In 2009, the UK's General Medical Council ruled that Dr. Andrew Wakefield showed callous disregard for children when he solicited blood samples from children attending his son's birthday party (Harrell 2010).

Voluntarism

This element presumes that informed consent can only be given by individuals who are truly free to say yes or no to a research project. If any hint of coercion exists, the principle of informed consent is violated. Again, this presumption is not always so easy to satisfy. It is not hard to imagine conditions where research subjects might agree to a study for fear of negative consequences following their refusals. Charges of coercion, for instance, were levied against a long-term (1956–1972) hepatitis study conducted at the Willowbrook State School for the Retarded on Staten Island. Critics alleged that parents seeking to enroll their children in the school were offered "fast" admission to the school if they would consent to their children's involvement in the hepatitis study (wherein some of the children would be intentionally injected with the hepatitis serum).

An argument can easily be made that *any* research in institutional settings – hospitals, schools, prisons – has the potential to violate voluntarism. Institutional settings entail authority relationships that are inconsistent with true voluntarism. Following this reasoning, research participation that is a condition of fulfilling course requirements would be vulnerable to charges of coercion. Similarly, we must consider the possibility that any research that offers financial compensation to participants might have a coercive dimension. Indigent subjects may find it hard to say no to the offer of money as a participation inducement. Similarly, studies conducted in developing nations need to give serious thought to the voluntary participation of research subjects since these individuals may fear that services or assistance might be denied them if they refuse to give consent. The condition of being free to say yes or no to research is often problematic in field research. Some researchers feel that obtaining informed consent is not necessary when the observation is being conducted in a public setting. And other researchers turn to significant gatekeepers for a general informed consent for their studies and thus sidestep the issue of giving individuals in the field the chance to exercise their own free choice. Indeed, this is often the situation for research in developing nations. Community leaders rather than individuals will provide a general informed consent for the study. Lastly, some have argued that for the element of voluntarism to be met, egalitarian relationships must exist between the researcher and participants. The fact that participants are so often regarded as research *subjects*, however, indicates that any assumption of equality in a research endeavor is clearly problematic.

Box 3.3   Newsworthy research: The Guatemalan/Pan American STD studies

In the late 1940s, several Guatemalan government agencies in conjunction with the US Public Health Server and the Pan American Sanitary Bureau conducted medical research that deliberately exposed soldiers, prostitutes, prisoners and mental patients to sexually transmitted diseases. Aside from violating the basic mandate that research should do no harm, this study also violated the principle of informed consent. And note, even if informed consent were obtained, the populations used in the study (soldiers, prisoners, mental patients) suggest that the element of "voluntarism" could not be reasonably assumed.

Source: Stobbe 2011 Panel Reveals New Details of 1940's Experiment, *http://news. yahoo.com/panel-reveals-details-1940s-experiment-012040543.html.*

Full information

This element presumes that research subjects will be given all the relevant information they need to make an informed choice. But this standard is far from self-evident. How much information is enough? How relevant is relevant? Must every detail of a study be shared with participants? Will some details actually increase the chance of confusing respondents or biasing results? Some researchers contend that withholding select information is necessary in order to maintain the integrity of the study. This was certainly Milgram's position in his study of obedience to authority (1974). Milgram's research was intended to see if there were moral limits to what ordinary citizens could be ordered to do by authority figures. He did not, however, share this information with his research subjects. Instead, he simply told his participants that the study was about the effects of punishment on learning. In the course of the study, unwitting participants were "ordered" to administer electric shocks to individuals whenever they made mistakes in a learning exercise. In fact, the "learners" never received any electrical shocks but the research participants did not know this. In retrospect we must now ask if Milgram's misleading explanation of his obedience study was ethical. Over the years, the adopted standard has been to provide as much information as the "reasonable" person requires for decision-making. While this standard offers some guidance, it really does not adequately clarify the issue. Indeed, the US legal system has devoted much time and attention over the years to debating the reasonable person doctrine and such cases have shown that what is "reasonable" to one group may be "unreasonable" to another. Or consider again the Facebook experimentations involving the intentional manipulation of users' emotions. Facebook's defense was that all its users have "signed" an informed consent form by virtue of becoming users. But the Facebook consent form is very lengthy and in all probability it is not read by many (perhaps most) users.

Comprehension

This element presumes that in order for individuals to provide informed consent, they must be able to *understand* the information received. By way of offering guidance, the Department of Health and Human Services advises that the consent document should be regarded as a *teaching* tool rather than as a legal instrument. At minimum, the comprehension aspect requires that research recruits be provided information in non-technical "lay language" (i.e. forms should not read like a contract!). Furthermore, to facilitate comprehension, participants should also be allowed to consult with others and to take some time between receiving information and making a decision about participation. Consequently, oral consent or consent procedures that do not give subjects any time to think over or reconsider their decision are not really fully abiding by the informed consent principle. The comprehension element can also prove problematic for online surveys asking participants to indicate that they have "read" the terms of consent by "checking" a box. Think about how many times you have checked the box indicating your acceptance of the terms of a computer download when in fact you have not read the terms at all. If you are a Facebook user, did you read the 9000-word consent form before agreeing to "sign" it? Surely we must be aware that similar "artificial" acceptance will occur with informed consent agreements.

Organizations that are involved in research typically have in-house Institutional Review Boards (IRBs) to evaluate planned research projects. These boards will provide specific details about their informed consent requirements. But in the meantime, to get a better idea of what these forms entail, you can access informed consent templates offered by the World Health Organization (http://www.who.int/rpc/research_ethics/informed_consent/en/).

Box 3.4   Newsworthy research: informed consent: for how long?

A new dilemma regarding informed consent is causing some to rethink its time limits. In the area of medical research, informed consent is typically sought for studies that collect blood samples or genetic materials from participants. For instance, blood samples of newborns are routinely collected in order to do early screening for serious medical disorders. However, some research participants have gone to court to stop researchers from re-analyzing blood samples for research purposes beyond the original study. Members of the Havasupai tribe of the Grand Canyon in the United States originally gave their informed consent (and samples of their blood) to University of Arizona researchers interested in learning why the tribe had exceptionally high rates of diabetes. All was well and good until the tribe learned that their "informed consent" was being extended to other studies utilizing their blood samples – studies about which they were not "informed" and to which they did not consent. The tribe members rejected the idea that their consent was a "general" one that covered subsequent studies of any behavioral or medical disorders. For their part, researchers pointed out that the informed consent document indicated that additional research beyond the original study was a possibility. It took six years of legal litigation before the issue was resolved with the blood samples being returned to the tribe along with a sizeable cash settlement.

Source: Harmon. 2010. "Indian Tribe Wins Fight to Limit Research of Its DNA." *New York Times.* April 21. *http://www.nytimes.com/2010/04/22/us/22dna.html?pagewanted=all&_r=0.*

Researchers Should Respect Subjects' Privacy

Right to privacy – the right to control when and under what conditions others will have access to information about us.

The **right to privacy** refers to our ability to control when and under what conditions others will have access to information about us. Anyone familiar with the US culture and legal system should appreciate just how passionate people can be about this cherished principle.[3] But with the remarkable reach of technology, the privacy issue is really a problem for the world community at large. Indeed, in 2013 the UN General Assembly passed a resolution that recognized our current digital age has brought with it "an international right to privacy." Technology enables governments, corporations, and special interest groups to follow our clicks, our calls and tweets, our purchases. Far too many of us, however, remain unaware of the degree to which our activities are tracked and how our lives are becoming an open book for others. Edward Snowden's revelations about the NSA surveillance activities came as a rude surprise to both ordinary citizens and world leaders. (German chancellor Angela Merkel and Pope Francis may never look at their cell phones in the same way again!)

Since research is essentially an endeavor for "finding out," virtually any attempt to collect data from or about people can raise a red flag for the privacy issue. An invasion of privacy does not just occur when researchers sort through a town's garbage site or review private school records, or utilize social media sites that participants think of as private. An invasion of privacy can also occur when a researcher poses questions that the respondent considers "out of bonds." A subject's right to privacy requires the researcher to pay attention to three different privacy issues: (1) the sensitivity of the information being solicited, (2) the location or setting of the research, and (3) the disclosure of a study's findings (Diener and Crandall 1978).

Sensitivity of Information

The privacy issue is undoubtedly complicated by the fact that any kind of personal information may be potentially threatening for some respondents. The greater the sensitivity of the research topic, the more safeguards are called for in order to protect the respondent's privacy. For instance, when surveys contain threatening questions (e.g. about discrediting behaviors or illegal activities), respondents should be forewarned and reassured about the steps that will be taken to protect their privacy. If sensitive topics are being covered in a person-to-person interview, researchers should consider resorting to an alternative "anonymous" format as a way to safeguard privacy (for a discussion of such a technique, see section "Covering Sensitive Topics" in Chapter 9). The sensitivity issue is particularly relevant to online research that utilizes sites such as blogs and virtual reality venues where participants may engage in potentially embarrassing behaviors. Informed consent forms should remind respondents that they have the right to withdraw consent at any point in the study.

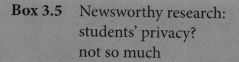 

Box 3.5 Newsworthy research: students' privacy? not so much

Reading, writing and … data collection. This is the life of the typical US student today. Parents are concerned and are speaking out about it. Students often complete surveys with very personal questions about their health, sleeping habits, sexual activities, and alcohol and drug use. The Electronic Privacy Information Center claims that the information collected is sometimes sold for commercial use and winds up providing companies with opportunities for target advertising. Scholarships.com, for instance, transferred the data it collected to a business affiliate who sold it for general marketing. The privacy violation extends to entire families. Some cafeteria software tracks financial aid data about family income and palimony payments. The current federal laws protecting children's privacy have many loopholes creating what some critics call an Orwellian "Big Brother" situation in our schools. As one concerned mother said: "I think people have forgotten these are my kids, not the school's. When you start linking all this data – my kid's biometrics, with an address, a juvenile record, voter registration, you get a profile, and there's so much wrong with that."

Source: Beth Greenfield (2015).

Research Setting

Just as the topics and populations of social research are extremely diverse, so too are the settings of social research. Research might be located in private homes, schools, work sites, neighborhood bars, street corners and shopping malls, or on the Internet to name but a few likely locations. In considering the privacy issue, the researcher should be prepared to evaluate the research site on a continuum of locations ranging from private to public. On first inspection, one might assume that locating sites on such a continuum would be a relatively easy task. But the extent to which a setting is private or public is not really all that obvious. Even the most public of settings may be perceived as an "off limits" private territory to the occupants. Indeed, the argument can be made that public settings actually intensify our need for privacy (see Aalbers 2008; Goffman 1971; Lofland 1973).

Consider, for instance, a public beach. Surely beachgoers understand that no one has a right to privacy on a public beach. Or do they? Think about the typical beach territory marking rituals we have all utilized. We mark off our territory with blankets and ice chests and with strategic placements of chairs and umbrellas. In effect, we are serving notice to other beachgoers that we have created a domain of privacy and woe to the person who ignores our privacy shields. Or think about your behaviors while driving your car on public streets. Despite the fact that we realize we are driving "in public" many of us will treat our cars as a "private" zone. We expect other drivers to engage in what Goffman (1963) called "civil inattention" (i.e. to pretend they don't see or hear us belting out a tune or yelling at our kids when we are stopped at traffic lights or tollbooths). Or for a still more vexing location, think about the private/public divide on social media sites. Despite Mark Zuckerberg's original intention for Facebook (a place for open information flow between friends) many early users were oblivious to the reality that non-friends were recognizing the "background check" potential of Facebook pages. And so businesses and schools and agencies started using Facebook pages to learn more about prospective employees or applicants or clients. Is a Facebook posting or picture of one's spring vacation in Mexico a "private" or "public" posting? In short, the privacy of a location is often problematic. Determining whether a research site is private or not requires more than merely noting its spatial setting.

One of the most notorious examples of the privacy dilemma in a public research setting is offered by Laud Humphreys' study (1969) of tearooms (i.e. public restrooms used for impersonal homosexual encounters). Humphreys defended his selection of the research setting on the basis of the "democratic" nature of public restrooms. He felt that public restrooms would give him access to the most representative sample of tearoom patrons. What he failed to explicitly consider was that these very public locations were chosen by the patrons as a way to *safeguard* their own privacy. More private settings would be more restrictive in terms of access and would increase the chances of individuals' identities being or becoming known. Public restrooms allowed participants to enter under conditions of anonymity.[4]

Anyone who is considering Internet-based research must give some serious thought to the private/public divide. At the time of writing there are several organizations currently at work trying to establish guidelines for social media sites research. One of the key issues in making this determination is the degree to which sites (blogs, discussion forums, etc.) have restricted membership. With restricted access, it is hard to regard the location as a public site free of privacy concerns. But even wide-open public forums should also be evaluated for the participants' expectations of privacy. Joining a public site for the purpose of eavesdropping (listening in on the exchanges of other members for the sake of research) flies in the face not only of privacy expectations but also of the principle of informed consent. While many researchers believe that public blogs should be free of the need to obtain informed consent, others say it all depends on the context and sensitivity of the information and the expectations of the bloggers (Sveningsson 2004).

Disseminating Research Findings

One clear way to violate a person's privacy is to go public with their personal identifying information. While courts of law have ruled that certain groups that are "in the public eye" (e.g. politicians and celebrities) may forfeit some of their rights to privacy, the ordinary citizen should be able to enjoy this protection without qualification. Research poses a risk to privacy when findings are disclosed in a way that allows private information provided by individuals to be publicly linked to those individuals. Typically, researchers will offer protections of privacy by extending the guarantee of either **anonymity** or **confidentiality** to research subjects.

> **Anonymity** – collecting data in such a way as to preclude being able to identify or link specific persons with the information they have given the researcher.
>
> **Confidentiality** – protecting the privacy of research subjects by promising not to disclose the person's identity or link their information to them personally.

To meet the promise of anonymity, the collection of data is structured so that the researcher cannot link specific information with the individuals who provide it. One way to accomplish anonymity in the research process is to purposely omit any self-identifiers during data collection. This strategy is frequently employed on questionnaires where items that could identify the respondents (e.g. names, social security numbers, addresses) are not requested. As a variation on this procedure respondents might be instructed to keep identifying information separate from the rest of their responses (i.e. they might be instructed to mail identifying information in one envelop and the actual survey in another). This would allow the researcher to know that a respondent has returned a questionnaire but would not be able to know which surveys belong to which respondents. Under conditions of anonymity, the names attached to specific data points cannot be revealed because they simply are not known.

The promise of confidentiality is an assurance by the researcher that the information provided by participants will never be linked to them publicly. Unlike anonymity, in confidential exchanges the researcher actually knows which names are linked to specific information but makes a promise not to go public with this information. In essence, the researcher agrees to a type of "secret-keeping" where she or he promises to refrain from making any "he said/she said" revelations.

Once having made the offer to protect research participants' privacy, researchers clearly have an obligation to take the steps necessary to support their promises of anonymity and/or confidentiality. For instance, researchers should plan on assigning case numbers to replace any personal identification and to protect personal data. If lists that link case numbers with personal IDs exist, they should be kept in secure settings. Once data has been entered into computers for analysis, original surveys containing self-identifiers might be shredded.

On the face of it, the promises of anonymity and confidentiality would appear to be sufficient for safeguarding privacy. Revelations will not be made because we do not have names to reveal or because we promise not to do so. But the truth is that our guarantees of anonymity or confidentiality can be hard to keep. In the 1950s a rather telling privacy debacle occurred in Vidich and Bensman's (1958) field study of the political and social life of a small upstate New York town. The researchers thought they had adequately addressed the participants' privacy concerns with promises of anonymity and confidentiality. The researchers agreed to use fictitious names for both the town and the inhabitants when it became time to write up their findings. Unfortunately, their disguise for the town and its townspeople was not effective. The locals could easily recognize themselves and their neighbors in the often critical and unflattering research narrative. Some concrete proof of the townspeople's dissatisfaction with the researchers' privacy guarantees can be gleaned from the fact that the town publicly lampooned the researchers at their annual 4th of July parade (Kimmel 1988).

Internet-based research also presents its own set of challenges with regard to promising conditions of anonymity and confidentiality. Far too few users of the Internet realize just how easy it is to trace user identity. So while bloggers or online survey respondents might think they are totally anonymous presences on a website, this is actually more wishful thinking than anything else. (In March 2015, former major league pitcher Curt Schilling quickly discovered and then revealed the names of Twitter trolls who had posted threatening posts about his daughter.) IP (internet protocol) addresses as well as seemingly benign information such as zip codes or movie ratings can be tools used for the "re-identification" of an "anonymous" individual (Schwartz and Solove 2011). And even if a researcher does obtain informed consent from online groups, care must also be given to how the data from the research will be safeguarded and shared. Some guidelines for Internet research recommend that any data collected over computer networks should be encrypted to preclude it falling into non-research hands. There are many anecdotal stories about study participants being surprised and dismayed to find their postings quoted verbatim in a study report. The reaction of dismay or concern is not unreasonable, given how easy it is for nefarious parties to work back from a "posting" to the identity of the author.

In making promises of confidentiality, researchers should also realize they may actually be promising more than they are prepared or willing to deliver. For instance, while we may offer the promise of confidentiality to research subjects, the courts have not always agreed that the exchanges between researchers and subjects are privileged communication and thus worthy of this protection. Consequently, social research data does not automatically enjoy the assurance of confidentiality offered in other exchanges, for instance, lawyer–client, doctor–patient, or clergy–penitent relationships. When push comes to shove, courts may subpoena research data and thus threaten the privacy promises made by researchers. For their part, researchers must make a tough decision – whether to comply with the court order (and in so doing break their privacy promise to participants) or risk spending time in jail if they ignore the court order. In failing to comply with court orders, the researcher is vulnerable to legal sanctions (see Case 99 of the ASA's Teaching Ethics Throughout the Curriculum for an account of a sociologist refusing to turn over data gathered about animal rights activists and his extended jailing for contempt of court. http://www.asanet.org/ethics/detail.cfm?id=Case99). Consequently, researchers who are embarking on projects that will gather sensitive information from respondents (e.g. information on sexual preferences or practices, on illegal activities, on psychological wellbeing) should consider obtaining a **certificate of confidentiality** for their projects. These certificates can be obtained through the NIH and are intended to prevent forced disclosure of confidential research information. However, they should not be considered absolute protections. While certificates offer protection, they can be voided if participants themselves consent to disclosure and certificates lack enforcement for research that transcends US boundaries. In addition, the issuance of certificates is totally discretionary – they are not an "entitlement" for research projects on sensitive topics (NIH 2014).

> **Certificate of confidentiality** – a form obtained through the National Institutes of Health (NIH) to safeguard against forced disclosure of confidential research information.

In the final analysis, researchers are well advised to explicitly state conditions of confidentiality (including any limits to confidentiality agreements) and to know how they will honor such agreements. And given the unique challenges faced with internet research, some internet ethics guidelines advise that researchers should refrain from making *any* guarantees of confidentiality or anonymity (e.g. see Penn State Internet Research 2007).

Researchers Should Avoid Conflicts of Interest

At first glance, an explicit dictum about conflict of interest may seem unnecessary in a research code of ethics. After all, researchers are dedicated to an objective and seemingly impartial collection of information. In truth, of course, researchers, like all social actors, are influenced by their social contexts. A context that can be extremely influential is that involving the corporate funding of research. Corporate-campus liaisons are becoming more and more common as universities search for new sources of funding. These liaisons carry major implications for research. Corporate funders can dictate the direction and scope or the specific questions of research projects. This in itself may not strike the reader as a cause for alarm – after all, it is hardly unreasonable for funders to want a say in how their money will be spent. But corporate funders can also set the terms and conditions for the publication of findings. Here the funders' reasoning is simple but extremely troubling: corporations that fund research projects may claim that they "own" and therefore can control the data. This notion, however, flies in the face of one extremely important scientific principle: research should be a public endeavor committed to sharing its findings (bad or good) in a public forum. There should be no "secret data" in science (see Chapter 1). Yet in medical research it is not uncommon for pharmaceuticals to place no-publishing clauses in contracts with university-based researchers. (This was the very condition that led to the Olivieri scandal in Canada – see Box 3.6). Or consider the restrictions that BP wanted to impose on researchers hired to study the aftermath of the Deepwater Horizon oil spill in the Gulf of Mexico. BP contacted numerous research universities in the area of the oil spill and offered lucrative contracts for research *provided* that the researchers agreed to terms that precluded going public with results for three years or longer and/or terms that restricted researchers from pursuing other research if it conflicted with the work for BP (Lea 2010).

Box 3.6   Newsworthy research: conflict of interest and Dr. "No"

At times, the wishes of corporate sponsors can be directly at odds with the ethical and the scientific principles of researchers. Consider, for instance, the case of Dr. Nancy Olivieri, a professor of pediatrics and medicine at the University of Toronto. Dr. Olivieri was involved in research on a genetic blood disease that was funded by Apotex, a Canadian drug company. During the course of her data collection, Dr. Olivieri discovered that a drug manufactured by Apotex was having adverse life-threatening effects in some of her patients. Her first move was to inform Apotex that she felt duty bound to notify her patients. The drug company reminded her that there was a no publishing clause in her funding contract and threatened to sue her if she went public. Dr. Olivieri decided to tell her patients about the drug and then published her findings in the *New England Journal of Medicine*. The drug company immediately terminated their funding and continued to threaten litigation. Additionally (and perhaps even more disturbing), the University of Toronto, fearing loss of corporate funding, dismissed Olivieri from her job as director of the blood disorder clinic at the university's Hospital for Sick Children! The case prompted a formal independent committee of inquiry. After two years, the committee found that Dr. Olivieri acted ethically and that the University of Toronto was faulted for not defending the right of clinical researchers to disclose risks to research subjects.

Source: Thompson, Baird, and Downie (2002)

Corporate sponsorship raises yet another concern: it seems that corporate funders can also influence the actual findings obtained via research. A recent study by Danish researchers in 2002 found that sources of funding affected researcher's findings in randomized clinical experiments. In a review of 159 articles published in the *British Medical Journal* between 1997 and 2001, researchers found that studies were more likely to show a positive result from an experimental intervention if the study *was funded by a for-profit organization*. Such positive results were missing from studies funded by non-profit organizations (Kjaergard and Als-Nielsen 2002). A case involving a renowned Canadian researcher reveals one possible way in which funding influences results. Dr. Chandra was involved in over 20 years of research on child nutrition and was considered to be a world expert on the topic. In 2000, Dr. Chandra submitted one of his studies to the *British Medical Journal*. The article, however, was rejected – the editors suspected that the data was fake. Additional scrutiny confirmed that Dr. Chandra was engaged in fraud and *manufacturing* results that benefited his funding sources. Indeed Dr. Chandra produced a study purportedly showing the benefits of Nestlé's "Good Start" formula yet no such research was ever actually conducted by Dr. Chandra (Infact Canada 2006).

Box 3.7 Newsworthy research: knocking heads over conflict of interest

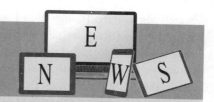

In the past few years, there has been a growing interest in the negative health effects of playing contact sports, especially the prevalence of concussions in both amateur and professional football players. More and more communities across the United States are running clinics to help young players learn how to tackle safely and avoid serious injuries. In recent years, two class actions suits were filed by over 5000 former professional players against the National Football League (NFL). The suits contend that the league deliberately hid information about head injuries from the players. The allegation stems in part from the NFL's long-standing dismissal of any independent research that documented cognitive decline in former professional players. Indeed, whenever confronted by research that challenged the NFL's position that football is a safe sport, the NFL would insist that they were waiting for the results of the only study they considered trustworthy. And which study was that? Believe it or not, the study was one conducted by the NFL's own committee on concussions! (If a warning bell is going off in your head, don't be alarmed.) Critics of this arrangement argue that the league's "in-house" study suffers from a poor design, a paucity of subjects and a clear conflict of interest in that the lead investigator is someone with long-standing ties to the NFL and thus in a untenable position to maintain objectivity.

Schwarz, A. 2009. "N.F.L.'s Dementia Study Has Flaws, Experts Say." *New York Times*, October 26.

Kelsey, E. 2014. "Dan Marino will Withdraw from NFL Concussion Suit." *http://sports.yahoo.com/news/marino-joins-latest-lawsuit-against-nfl-over-concussions-150835661—nfl.html;_ylt=AwrBJR8urLFTcBcA6.zQtDMD*

Clearly researchers are within their rights to purposely elect to align themselves with a cause or a research sponsor. In order to maintain the ethical high ground, however, they should make their allegiances known to their audience. Such acknowledgments put all on notice to possible biases in research efforts and findings. Indeed the authors of the previously cited study of randomized clinical trials maintain that their study clearly indicates the need for researchers to explicitly state their competing interests.

Reinforcing the Ethical Route: Institutional Review Boards

History has taught us about the danger of allowing ethical considerations to be the sole responsibility of individual researchers. Consequently, in order to reinforce the ethical behavior of researchers, ethical review boards are now routinely found in the international research community. Though these boards go by various names – for example, Institutional Review Boards (IRBs) in the United States; Human Research Ethics committees (RECs) in Australia, or Research Ethics Boards (REBs) in England – all have the common goal of protecting research participants. In the United States any institution that is involved in human research and all that receive federal funding are required to establish IRBs.[5] IRBs are charged with the ethical assessment of proposals for all research projects under the institution's auspices. Today's IRBs are byproducts of efforts to pass the National Research Act of 1974. In large measure, this Act resulted from Congressional hearings on the Tuskegee study (see earlier discussion in this chapter) and other research abuses receiving public attention in the 1960s and 1970s. Both the National Research Act and IRBs are regarded as critical milestones in the development of federal standards for the protection of human research subjects. IRBs are generally composed of members with expertise in science and ethics as well as other non-scientific areas. The diversity of board members is seen as a strategic step for safeguarding the rights and welfare of research subjects. In assessing research proposals, IRBs invoke federal standards and regulations concerning the protection of human subjects. Still, the use of IRBs is not in itself a guarantee of researchers "doing the right thing." Consider for instance that the Facebook experimentation detailed earlier in this chapter was subjected to IRB approval![6]

Box 3.8   Sharpening your research vision: reviewing review boards

Despite their good intentions, ethics review boards often draw critical reviews from researchers. Some researchers charge that rather than focusing on research participants, they have become overly concerned with "protecting" institutions and thus wind up mandating needless hurdles for researchers. There is also the criticism that review boards have become overprotective of research participants. Consider some of the points raised by Sharon Begley in her piece "Coddling Human Guinea Pigs." In the late 2000s, an anthropologist from the University of Michigan sought IRB approval to interview jailed terrorists who were responsible for the 2005 Bali bombing. The board rejected the initial request citing concerns about obtaining informed consent from prisoners and invading inmates' privacy. Indeed, concerns over review board negative reactions to medical research involving humans is cited as a reason why clinical studies have lower funding success than basic research proposals involving the use of cell cultures or animals. In 2008, Begley reported that clinical trials for cancer research could expect to face about six months of red tape delays. Begley argues that this kind of paternalistic over-protectionism is ultimately detrimental to research for the common good.

Begley, S. 2008. "Coddling Human Guinea Pigs." *On Science. Newsweek.* August 18–25.

Ethical Fusion

While we have anchored our review of research ethics in the American Sociological Association's code of ethics, the ethical standards of many professional associations are remarkably similar (you should be able to find the code of ethics for various professions on their official webpages.) Regardless of their specific discipline, researchers are generally charged with the responsibility of following rules of conduct that will safeguard the wellbeing of research subjects and treat them with dignity and respect. At minimum, researchers should judge their planned research activity in terms of its potential benefits, the amount of risk it poses to participants, whether potential benefits outweigh the risks and whether or not adequate safeguards have been adopted to minimize any risks. In starting with these basic standards, the researcher should be able to maintain the ethical high ground in their work.

Hopefully, by the time you have worked your way to the end of this book, you will have learned much about the logic and techniques of social research. As you reach the end of this chapter, however, I hope that you have already realized that research needs to be conducted in an ethically responsible way. Troubling lessons of the past remind us that good research cannot afford to cast a blind eye to ethical standards. Good research demands that ethical concerns occupy a central place in the entire research process: from planning to data collection to reporting. And with the growing reliance on the internet as both a location, as well as a tool, for research, ethical issues and concerns become increasingly vexing and important. Treating ethics as a secondary or marginal issue is an unjustifiably perilous path that will only serve to undercut the cause and value of research.

TAKE AWAYS

- Ethical lapses are fairly common
- Internet research presents new ethical concerns/issues
- The key issues are:
  - Doing no harm
  - Obtaining informed consent
    - Competence – participants need to have the ability to know what is in their best interest
    - Voluntarism – participants must have freedom of choice about study involvement
    - Full information – participants should receive all relevant information about study
    - Comprehension – participants must understand information presented
  - Protecting privacy
    - More complicated in our technology saturated world
    - Many public settings still have privacy expectations
  - Avoiding conflict of interest
    - A challenge given prevalence of corporate funding of research
- Ethics review boards
  - Essential for safeguarding ethical practice

Sharpening the Edge: More Reading and Searching

- The full code of ethics for the American Sociological Association can be found at the following:

    http://www.asanet.org/about/ethics.cfm

- The Office for Human Research Protection in the US Department of Health and Human Services provides a tip sheet on informed consent:

    http://ohrp.osophs.dhhs.gov/humansubjects/guidance/ictips.htm

- Additional information about Certificates of Confidentiality can be obtained from the Confidentiality Kiosk at the National Institutes of Health webpage:

    http://grants.nih.gov/grants/policy/coc/index.htm

- A short but informative discussion of explicit vs. implicit confidentiality agreements as well as of the overall importance of confidential exchanges in social research can be found in Wes Jamison's article "Confidentiality in Social Science Research" at:

    http://www.wpi.edu/Academics/Projects/confidentiality.html

- For an informative review of the array of ethical challenges encountered via online research see E. Buchanan and M. Zimmer's 2012 article "Internet Research Ethics" in Stanford Encyclopedia of Philosophy:

    http://plato.stanford.edu/entries/ethics-internet-research/

Exercises

1. What ethical "red flags" might arise with the following research endeavors?

    - observing people's routines at ATM machines
    - interviewing residents at an assisted living facility
    - using an online bulimia discussion forum to gain insight into this eating disorder
    - conducting university sponsored research to assess student satisfaction
    - using Second Life as a vehicle for studying people's willingness to use violence against others.

2. Find out if your local university (or work) institution has an IRB. If so, see what you can learn about the board's procedures: who sits on the board; what is the time frame for the review process; does the board exempt any categories of research, and so on.

Notes

1 The lead researcher denies any wrongdoing and is appealing the review decision.

2 It should be noted that one reviewer of the Facebook incident has noted that Facebook's user consent form is over 9000 words long and takes about 40 minutes to read!

3 In the summer of 2014, the US Supreme Court issued a ruling denying police the right to immediately search cell phones of arrested individuals saying that such warrantless cell phone searches trampled privacy rights.

4 Ethical concerns are raised by the Humphreys' study on still other fronts. Humphreys conducted follow-up

in-home interviews with tearoom patrons. How was he able to do this? As individuals drove up to the public restrooms, Humphreys recorded the license plate numbers of their cars. He used this information to obtain home addresses. A year after his restroom observations, he changed his appearance and showed up at the patrons' homes posing as a health services interviewer.

5 The Department of Health and Human Services requires all institutions that receive federal research monies to establish IRBs in order to scrutinize all proposed studies sanctioned by the institutions. Furthermore, any researcher seeking federal support for their research must receive IRB approval before applying for federal monies.

6 Facebook had the experiment reviewed by an IRB at Cornell University. For its part, Cornell indicated its IRB did not have sufficient lead time to stop the research.

References

Aalbers, Manuel. 2008. "Big Sister is Watching You! Gender Interaction and the Unwritten Rules of the Amsterdam Red-Light District." In Robert Heiner (ed.), *Deviance Across Cultures*. New York: Oxford.

Advisory Committee on Human Radiation Protection Experiments (ACHRE). 1995. *Advisory Committee on Human Radiation Protection Experiments, Final Report.* Washington, DC: US Government Printing Office, October 1995. http://www.scribd.com/doc/182971267/Advisory-Committee-on-Human-Radiation-Experiments-Final-Report-Original#scribd.

The American Experience. 2009. "The Polio Crusade." http://www.pbs.org/wgbh/americanexperience/features/transcript/polio-transcript/.

Begley, Sharon. 2008. "Coddling Human Guinea Pigs." *On Science. Newsweek.* August 18–25.

Buchanan, E. and M. Zimmer. 2012. "Internet Research Ethics" Stanford Encyclopedia of Philosophy. http://plato.stanford.edu/entries/ethics-internet-research/.

Diener, Eduard and Rick Crandall. 1978. *Ethics in Social and Behavioral Research.* Chicago: University of Chicago Press.

Forbes. 2014. "Facebook Manipulated 689,003 Users' Emotions For Science." http://www.forbes.com/sites/kashmirhill/2014/06/28/facebook-manipulated-689003-users-emotions-for-science/.

Goffman, Erving. 1963. *Behavior in Public Places.* New York: Free Press.

Goffman, Erving. 1971. *Relations in Public: Microstudies of the Public Order.* New York: Basic Books.

Greenfield, Beth. 2015. "Data Collection at Schools: Is Big Brother Watching Your Kids?" *Yahoo! Parenting.* February 23. https://www.yahoo.com/parenting/data-collection-at-schools-is-big-brother-111889795072.html.

Haney, C., C. Banks and Philip Zimbardo. 1973. "Interpersonal Dynamics in a Simulated Prison." *International Journal of Criminology and Penology* 1: 69–97.

Harmon, A. 2010. "Indian Tribe Wins Fight to Limit Research of Its DNA." *New York Times.* April 21. http://www.nytimes.com/2010/04/22/us/22dna.html?pagewanted=all&_r=0.

Harrell, E. 2010. "Doctor in MMR-Autism Scare Ruled Unethical" *Time.* January 29. http://content.time.com/time/health/article/0,8599,1957656,00.html.

Humphreys, Laud. 1969. *Tearoom Trade: Impersonal Sex in Public Places.* Chicago: Aldine.

Infact Canada. 2006. "How Nestlé-funded Research Supported Deceptive 'Hypoallergenic' Claims." Scientific Fraud and Child Health https://www.infactcanada.ca/Winter_2006_Pg_1_2.htm.

Kelsey, E. 2014. "Dan Marino will Withdraw from NFL Concussion Suit." *Yahoo! Sports,* June 23. http://sports.yahoo.com/news/marino-joins-latest-lawsuit-against-nfl-over-concussions-150835661-nfl.html;_ylt=AwrBJR8urLFTcBcA6.zQtDMD.

Kimmel, Allan. 1988. *Ethics and Values in Applied Social Research.* Newbury Park, CA: SAGE.

Kurtenbach, E. 2014. "Japan Says Stem Cell Research Falsified (Update 3)," April 1. http://phys.org/news/2014-04-japan-lab-stem-cell-falsified.html.

Kjergard, Lise and Bodil Als-Nielsen. 2002. "Association Between Competing Interests and Authors' Conclusions: Epidemiological Study of Randomized Clinical Trials Published in the *BMJ*." *British Medical Journal* 325: 249–252.

Lea, R. 2010. "BP, Corporate R&D, and the University." *Academe.* November–December 2010.

Lofland, Lyn. 1973. *A World of Strangers: Order and Action in Urban Public Space.* New York: Basic Books.

Milgram, Stanley. 1974. *Obedience to Authority: An Experimental View*. New York: Harper & Row.

National Institutes of Health. 2008. "Protecting Human Research Participants." http://www.soc.iastate.edu/sapp/IRBCourse.pdf.

National Institutes of Health. 2014. "Certificates of Confidentiality Kiosk." http://grants.nih.gov/grants/policy/coc/index.htm.

Penn State Research. 2007. "IRB Guideline X–Guidelines for Computer- and Internet-Based Research Involving Human Participants." http://www.research.psu.edu/policies/research-protections/irb/irb-guideline-10

Powers, E. and H, Witmer. 1951. *An Experiment in the Prevention of Delinquency: The Cambridge-Somerville Youth Study*. New York: Columbia University Press.

Reynolds, Paul. 1979. *Ethical Dilemmas and Social Science Research*. San Francisco: Jossey-Bass.

Schwartz, P. and D. Solove, 2011. "The PII Problem: Privacy and a New Concept of Personally Identifiable Information." *New York University Law Review* 86: 1814.

Stanford Encyclopedia of Philosophy. 2012. "Internet Research Ethics." http://plato.stanford.edu/entries/ethics-internet-research/.

Stobbe, M. 2011. "Panel Reveals New Details of 1940's Experiment." http://news.yahoo.com/panel-reveals-details-1940s-experiment-012040543.html

Sveningsson, M. 2004, "Ethics in Internet Ethnography," in E. Buchanan (ed.), *Readings in Virtual Research Ethics: Issues and Controversies*, Hershey: Idea Group, pp. 45–61.

Thompson, J., Baird, P. and J. Downie. 2002. "Supplement to the Report of the Committee of Inquiry on the Case Involving Dr. Nancy Olivieri, the Hospital for Sick Children, the University of Toronto, and Apotex Inc." January 30. http://www.caut.ca/docs/academic-freedom/supplement-to-the-report-of-the-committee-of-inquiry.pdf?sfvrsn=0.

US Department of Health and Human Services. 2005. "The Nuremberg Code" http://www.hhs.gov/ohrp/archive/nurcode.html.

Vidich, Arthur and Joseph Bensman. 1958. *Small Town in Mass Society: Class Power and Religion in a Rural Community*. Princeton: Princeton University Press.

Walton, N. 2013. "Research Ethics Scandals in Canada, You Ask? Sadly, Yes." *Research Ethics Blog*. http://researchethicsblog.com/2013/07/23/research-ethics-scandals-in-canada-you-ask-sadly-yes/.

Weber, Bob. 2013. "Canadian Government Withheld Food from Hungry Aboriginal Kids in 1940s Nutritional Experiments, Researcher Finds" *The Canadian Press*. July 16. http://www.theglobeandmail.com/news/national/hungry-aboriginal-kids-adults-were-subject-of-nutritional-experiments-paper/article13246564/.

Chapter 4

Designing Ideas: What Do We Want to Know and How Can We Get There?

Introducing Social Research Methods: Essentials for Getting the Edge, First Edition. Janet M. Ruane.
© 2016 John Wiley & Sons, Ltd. Published 2016 by John Wiley & Sons, Ltd.

FIRST TAKES

Be sure to take note of the following:
PLANNING A RESEARCH PROJECT
- Finding a good research question
  - One that is researchable and interesting
- Conducting a literature review
- The role of theory
  - Deductive vs. inductive research
  - Levels and paradigms
- The kinds of questions
  - Causal questions
  - Non-causal questions
  - Process questions
- The timing element
  - Here and now: cross-sectional
  - Overtime to see change: longitudinal
- Validity concerns
  - Measurement
  - Internal
  - External

The Research Plan

To say the least, scientific research *is very methodical*. The methodical nature of scientific research is most clearly revealed in its high regard for careful planning and strategizing. Indeed, scientific research is so methodical that virtually every research methods text contains essentially the same content matter – the steps or "ingredients" required for good research or roughly the information shown in Box 4.1. The typical text will offer a chapter on measurement, sampling, data collection techniques and so on. There is also a chapter devoted to design (i.e. the research plan). As we will see in this chapter, good research requires careful planning and careful planning requires us to consider several issues.

Box 4.1   The "steps" of the research process

Idea phase – formulate a good research question
  Review the literature
  State/share your theory
  Ask your questions or state your problem or hypotheses.

Design phase

Given your research question/issue, develop an overall design or blueprint for:
Collecting the data
Selecting units of analysis
Sampling
Measurement
Planned analysis

Data collection phase

Pretesting
Pilot studies
Final data collection

Analysis phase

Select the right statistics/techniques for answering the research question

Writing/communication phase

Share the details as well as the results of your executed study in a well-crafted written report/article

Coming up with the Right Question

Coming up with a good question for research is not as simple as merely asking a question. The truth is that not all questions are "worthy" of research. Some work must go into finding a question that will carry the day. Firebaugh (2008) maintains that research questions must meet two bars: the question must be *researchable* and it must be *interesting* to both the researcher and to others. If a research question does not satisfy both criteria, another should be selected. By researchable, Firebaugh means that the question must be "answerable" by using current scientific methods and empirical data. You might want to pose a question about the gender distribution of heaven, but it would not survive Firebaugh's first standard since no data collection is possible. A good research question must also be interesting. As it turns out, this standard is the more demanding one – real work (often of the detective variety) must be done to show that a question is interesting enough to be given the "green light" for research. In the interest of posing an interesting question, attention must be paid to a number of issues.

Interesting questions might *resolve a conflict* in findings found across a variety of other studies. Or an interesting question might be one *that extends an established question* to a new population or subpopulation or to a new time period. An interesting question might be one that *employs a new strategy or new measures* for addressing an old question. An interesting question might be one that *addresses a gap* in the research literature or, perhaps, replicates new findings (Firebaugh 2008). As you can see, there is work to be done to convince skeptics that any new research is needed and it is the researcher's job to make the case. Or as Firebaugh puts it, the researcher should try to keep a "surprise" element in the research process – that is, by putting a new twist on an old problem or finding a new answer to an old question. Still, the search and justification of a good research question should not discourage the pursuit of research. With some work and a good literature review, many questions can be "worked" into shape and provide a good launch pad for a research project. (In fact a useful touchstone for a researcher to use over the course of a study is to remember that the burden is always on the researcher to convince others that she or he has made the right decision or choice at every single step of the research process.)

Reviewing the Literature

Of all the steps entailed in the research process, arguably none is more important than the review of the relevant research literature on the topic or question being investigated. Yet, truth be told, those new to the research process often recoil at the idea of immersing themselves in the research literature. This reaction is very consistent with the general reluctance of so many of us to engage science on its own terms (see Chapter 2). Research articles and books, after all, are full of jargon and tables and statistical analysis that can leave many feeling lost or, at the very least, stressed. By introducing readers to the logic and language of research, this book hopes to make significant inroads into turning this resistance around. The sooner students of research turn to and embrace a review of the relevant literature, the easier they will find the task of planning and executing their own research project. In particular, literature reviews give students a chance to see how others have approached or tackled similar questions/issues. Reviews will help with the theoretical framing of an issue or the formulation of research questions. Reviewing the literature also allows one to see just how successful others have been in finding answers to their questions. In short, a review of the literature provides an extremely useful "heads-up" for many of the factors that go into formulating a good research question (see previous section) as well as the factors that go into planning and executing a successful piece of research. Because it is a dreaded process, though, many students will delay starting a literature review. This really is a terribly misguided, even self-defeating idea. You can start small if you are trepidacious but you will definitely be well served by starting as soon as possible. Knowing how to proceed in a research project presumes some previous knowledge. Or as Firebaugh puts it, in order to learn something you first need to know something. A literature review is the fastest and most efficient way to "know" your research topic.

At the beginning, the literature review can help with the clarification and or refinement of research questions and issues. Those new to the research process frequently lack the degree of focus required for a quality project and consequently they too often start with overly broad research topics. For instance, someone might have a very general interest in eating disorders or in technology. If they start a literature search using either one of these terms, however, they will be overwhelmed by information and quickly realize the need to further specify their interests. Consider for instance a search I conducted on the term "eating disorders" in the online database, *Academic Search Complete*. The search indicated that there were nearly 20,000 entries (articles and books) on the topic. (If you repeat the search today, chances are you will find the number of "hits" will have grown even larger!) One of the goals of a good review of the literature is for the researcher to use the review to gain expertise in their area of interest and thus establish some credibility. Gaining this expertise means reading as much as one can about the topic. Yet, it is unreasonable to expect anyone to digest 20,000 articles/books by way of preparing for a research project. So in the interest of carving out an area to "master", some refinement of topics is typically in order.

There is then a very practical side to starting the literature review as early as possible. Let us stay for a moment longer with the previous search conducted on eating disorders. Recall this search yielded close to 20,000 results. Though the number of hits is large, we need not despair. Even such an overly broad start to a review can yield some useful information. Faced with 20,000 search results, one might want to scroll down through some of the listed articles. Reading titles and abstracts will offer a good idea of all the different paths pursued by other researchers interested in the stated topic. This quick scroll might also help new researchers become more focused as they starts a process of "screening out" certain articles that are too far removed from their own interests. This overly broad start, then, can nonetheless yield some useful results. The new researcher might decide to re-launch their search and this time insert some refining or qualifying terms. So, by way of example, the earlier eating disorders search might prompt a second search which now pairs eating disorders with a second "qualifying" term: adolescents. Running this second search yielded a list of just over 3000 entries. While this is still a rather large number of results, the lesson is clear.

Launching a review earlier rather than later is a smart way to proceed. It will give those new to research the time to think and re-think (and perhaps re-think yet again) their research focus. As the previous example illustrates, there will be many "false starts" in the review process, but even false starts can be useful. As topics or questions are specified, refined or transformed into totally new questions, the direction of the literature search will change. The researcher needs to allow for these twists and turns in their planning timelines. Since reviewing the literature really is the only way for someone to become grounded in an area of study, one should not truncate or short-change the process simply because not enough time has been allotted for a good review.

A second compelling reason for starting the review of the literature as early as possible is also about time – good literature reviews can be time savers. Remember, the idea behind conducting a literature review is to learn something. Knowing how others have grappled with the theoretical framing of an issue as well as the many design decisions, sampling decisions, measurement options, analysis strategies affords the reviewer a wealth of potentially useful information. Researchers are not obligated to "re-invent" the wheel. Recall from Chapter 1 that science is an enterprise that values replication – if someone else has made a persuasive theoretical argument or developed quality measures or has figured out a great sampling procedure or an effective plan of analysis, it is totally reasonable and appropriate for later researchers to recognize and incorporate (with proper acknowledgment and citations) these efforts in their own projects. In short, any researcher who short changes the literature review is really short-changing their own research efforts.

Tip 4.1

A good start to a literature review: summary articles

A good short-cut to getting into a research literature is to find "summary" review articles on your topic. These articles provide an overview of the major theoretical arguments or positions as well as the research activity that surrounds a topic. Review articles tend to focus on the best and/or most interesting research being conducted. These review articles, then, are great ways to get up to date as fast as possible with the literature you need to master. In the social sciences, there are "Annual Review" publications that provide these summary articles. Look for them in your discipline and search them for a recent review of your area of interest. Below is a partial list of some of the Annual Review Series:

Anthropology	Psychology
Economics	Public health
Law and social science	Sociology
Political science	

The Case and Place for Theory

As indicated in Chapter 1, science is very much committed to logic and reasoning. Indeed, this commitment is precisely why scientific research should *always* be connected to theory. And when searching for a "good" research question, Firebaugh (2008) advises that the question must have a theoretical connection for it to be interesting. **Theory** can be thought of as a series of reasonable propositions about some social or natural phenomenon, propositions that can be tested or assessed against empirical evidence. A-theoretical research is an exercise in futility – in fact, it is usually dismissed by critics as mindless empiricism. Counting the grains of sand on a beach might be "tangible" empirically grounded work but it is a meaningless exercise without a theoretical purpose for the counting. And conversely, theory that is too abstract for empirical testing is deemed to be equally useless. As indicated in Chapters 1 and 2 as well as Chapter 5 on measurement, concepts or ideas that cannot be "translated" into their observable counterparts necessarily must remain outside the realm of scientific investigation. Indeed, by way of assuring that the theory/research connection be productive, one sociologist of note, Robert Merton, made the case that "middle-range theory" is the appropriate goal for science – that is, science should be oriented to both the theoretical and empirical realms. If the empirical evidence repeatedly confirms our theoretical ideas, we are in a good position to start trusting and believing our theory to be correct.

Theory – a set of propositions or statements about how the world or some entity works or operates.

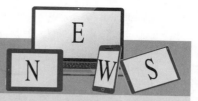

Box 4.2 Newsworthy research: creationism: is it science?

Off and on since the Scopes Trial of 1925, local communities and school districts across the United States have had debates on whether or not creationism (which adheres to a biblical account of the origins of the universe) or, more recently, intelligent design (the claim that the complexity and diversity of life can only be explained by some supernatural being/force) should be part of a science curriculum. In 2005, the intelligent design debate reached the US federal courts. In 2004, the Board Curriculum Committee for the Dover, Pennsylvania, public schools instructed science teachers to inform high school biology students that intelligent design was an alternative to Darwin's theory of evolution. Eleven parents who were opposed to this new mandate filed suit against the Dover school board contending that its new policy violated the separation of church and state. In effect the case (*Kitzmiller* vs. *Dover School Board*) amounted to a legal test of intelligent design as a *scientific* theory. The judge in the case ruled in favor of the plaintiffs arguing that intelligent design was at its core a religious, *faith-based* theory and thus it was *not* science. In spelling out his reasoning for denying intelligent design any scientific status, the judge noted that intelligent design allows for *supernatural* causation and thus fails to abide by the scientific standard of seeking natural causes for natural phenomenon.

The Placement of Theory in the Research Process

In general, theory and research feed off of each other in one of two ways. Theory is used either as a starting point for data collection, or it is the result, "outgrowth," or end point of data collection. In the first scenario, we speak of **deductive research**, in the latter we speak of **inductive research**. With deductive research, specific propositions or hypotheses are reasonably derived (deducted) from theory and then "tested" against the empirical evidence. This evidence then is used to support or reject the original hypotheses and in turn to strengthen or challenge the original theory. With inductive research, data collection precedes theory. The data are allowed to take the lead as it were. The patterns found in the empirical evidence are then used as the basis for generating (inducing) new theoretical ideas or advancing what are known as empirical generalizations. In either case, however, theory has a key place in the research process.

Deductive research – research that starts in the realm of theory and deduces questions or hypotheses to be tested with empirical data.

Hypothesis – a statement or prediction of an expected relationship between variables.

Inductive research – research that starts in the realm of empirical data and uses the patterns found in the data to induce/generate broader empirical generalizations.

Empirical generalizations – generalizations based on or drawn from observed patterns in the data.

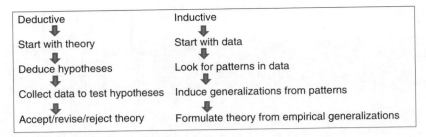

Figure 4.1   Theory's Place in Research

The Levels of Theory Guiding or Resulting from Research

> **Macro theory** – very broad explanations of large scale social processes or institutions.
>
> **Micro theory** – explanations of social processes that focus on behaviors of small group or person-to-person interactions.

Students of social sciences (anthropology, economics, education, social work, criminology, sociology, etc.) frequently encounter macro, or micro, or meso-level theories of social life. **Macro theories** offer grand or broad explanations of large-scale social processes or institutions. Macro-economic theories, for instance, are interested in explaining broad trends such as the unemployment or the productivity rates of an entire society's economy. Its broad focus makes macro-economics a perennial interest of governments. Macro-sociology theories consider how overarching social structures or patterns regulate or impact social life – such as how the age structure of a society impacts retirement programs, or how changes in food production impact the health of a nation. Durkheim's work on the functions of deviance and his theory of suicide offer a macro-level analysis (1951). **Micro theories** switch the focus to the "up close" and personal levels of interaction – they bring individuals back into the picture and concentrate on smaller slices of social reality. So a micro-economic theory is concerned with the behavior of specific individual consumers or businesses. Micro-sociology theories are interested in understanding behaviors of small group, or person-to-person, interactions. Many, for instance, are interested in documenting how aging Baby Boomers will experience (and perhaps totally redefine) "old age" or in identifying the new expectations millennials bring to the workplace. Sutherland and Cressey's differential association theory (1934) offers a micro-level theory of deviance with its focus on interpersonal "pro" and "anti" social learning.

> **Meso theory** – explanatory framework that focuses on mid-size groups or levels of interaction that occur between the macro and micro levels.

Meso-level theories shoot for the best of both worlds and try to merge macro- and micro-level analysis and offer an intermediate level of theoretical explanations. A meso-level analysis displaying both economic and sociological interests might focus on the effect of labor unions on corporate decision-making in a specific industry. White and Terry (2008) offer a meso-level analysis of the Catholic Church's sexual abuse crisis and argue that an opportunity structure and an organizational structure facilitate deviance among Catholic clergy. Kai Erikson takes the insights offered by Durkheim regarding the functions of deviance and applies them in his theory of establishing moral boundaries in local communities. Appreciating the "level" of theory that is informing a research project will help researchers clarify their specific research questions as well as help guide them in selecting an appropriate unit of analysis for research (see Chapter 2 for a full discussion of units of analysis). Macro-level theories will utilize aggregate level units (society, nations, etc.) while micro-level theories tend to align with individuals or small groups as units of analysis and meso-level theories align with groups or formal organizations.

Students of social sciences are often introduced to very general theoretical paradigms of the various fields of study. **Paradigms** are theoretical tools or frameworks (schemata) that offer very broad views of how the social world operates. Paradigms make certain assumptions and offer distinctive concepts or ideas and even distinctive methods for understanding the world. Students of sociology are routinely introduced to three such frameworks: the order, conflict, and the symbolic interactionist paradigms. The **order paradigm** holds the social world to be a rather consensus-based orderly arrangement of interdependent parts: social institutions (family, education, governments, etc.) complement each other and make for a smooth overall operation of the social system. The **conflict paradigm** envisions the social world as a far less consensual place and instead maintains that social dissensus abounds and any sense of order is the result of power and coercion. Both of these paradigms are considered macro-level theories. The **symbolic interactionist paradigm** takes a

Paradigm – a grand theoretical framework, schemata or orientation for viewing social phenomenon.

Order paradigm – a theoretical framework that presents the world as a well-integrated whole with interdependent and functional parts.

Conflict paradigm – a theoretical framework that presents the social world as conflict-laden where special interest factions compete for dominance or control.

Symbolic-interactionist paradigm – a theoretical framework that views social reality as socially constructed via the social interactions of individuals and groups.

"micro" orientation to understanding social life and envisions the order around us as the result of ongoing interpersonal negotiations. Committing to any one of these paradigmatic visions influences research by way of the abstract concepts and specific variables that will be brought into play or highlighted in research efforts. The order view will highlight concepts that feed consensus: social solidarity, social stability, social integration, collective conscience, and so on. The conflict view will highlight concepts that further the understanding of dissensus: coercion, power, force, special interests, and so on. The symbolic interactionist paradigm will focus on concepts that help explicate the micro level give and take of negotiating and constructing reality: impression management, social context, verbal and non-verbal communication, and so on.

In addition to presenting researchers with a variety of concepts and variables to inform or direct the research process, theoretical visions or paradigms can also influence the selection of specific data collection techniques. For instance, the symbolic interactionist's micro focus on interpersonal exchanges and the construction of meanings aligns quite naturally with qualitative data collection techniques that facilitate tapping into meaning (i.e. direct observation or intensive interviewing). Allegiance with a conflict paradigm calls for more innovative strategies that are better suited to reveal conditions of power imbalances (think a Michael Moore film, e.g. *Capitalism, A Love Story*, for a flash of insight). Certain ethnomethodology techniques or disruptive experiments might prove useful strategies for investigating conditions of "hostile contrast" – that is, where dominants have a vested interest in obscuring information from researchers (Lehmann and Young 1974).

The main take-away from this brief review of theory is to highlight the centrality of the relationship between theory and research. The theory/research link is a necessity in the realm of scientific knowing. Theory that cannot be empirically tested and assessed is simply not part of the scientific model. (It is for this reason that so many reject the proposal that intelligent design be included in science curriculums. Since the tenets of intelligent design are beyond empirical testing – they are "faith-based" – it is not properly a scientific theory. See Box 4.2.) Theory should feed research and in turn research should feed theory. This is what keeps knowledge moving forward and growing. As one writer puts it: science is best thought of as a continuous reworking or refining of theory (Hanson 1999). And as indicated in the previous section, a good review of the research literature is one sure way to get up to speed on the theoretical context of a given topic. In most research articles, the theoretical foundations for a given project are offered in the opening paragraphs or pages of articles.

More Planning and Strategizing: Considering Questions and Timing

Its importance notwithstanding, good research needs to plan beyond theory. Theory can set the direction for a research project but more specific strategizing is still needed. Consider this simple analogy: you might have a good theory for setting up an efficient hospital intensive care unit or a "smart classroom" but it will take much more strategic or "nuts and bolts" planning to execute these specific projects. Indeed, the scientific method might be thought of as a blueprint for action. It is akin to an architect drawing up the "plans" for building something. To achieve the desired end, the builder must pay attention to the needed parts/components and be able to execute the design plans. There are many ways to go about the collection of data needed to address or evaluate theoretical ideas about how the world operates. What we will take up in this section is a review of some of the "nuts and bolts" considerations when planning any research project.

Good planning must also attend to the exact research task or question at hand. Are we interested in how something works or in getting an accurate description of some population or phenomenon? Are we interested in finding the causes of something or are we interested in seeing if certain variables are merely associated? Are we interested in documenting change or are we concerned with understanding a process? All of these questions are fairly common ones for social research. And all of them would best be pursued via decidedly different research designs.

What's the Question? Causal vs. Non-Causal Questions

Causal Questions

One of the most basic distinctions we can make regarding research questions is whether or not they are concerned with causality. Is the researcher interested in finding answers to causal questions or non-causal questions? Many times, our research focus has a very clear causal focus. Does buckling up saves lives? Does texting while driving lead to accidents? Do electronic cigarettes help smokers quit? Does drinking red wine lead to health benefits or health problems? All of these questions focus on a causal connection (e.g. the causal link between use of e-cigarettes and smoking habits). While there are several research strategies that might be employed to address causal questions, one design is superior to all others: the experimental design. Here's the golden rule: if you want to find out if there is a cause and effect connection, use the experimental design (if possible). An **experiment** is a contrived method of observation where the researcher intentionally manipulates the independent variable in order to assess its impact on an outcome (i.e. the dependent variable).

> **Experiment** – a contrived data collection strategy where the researcher intentionally manipulates the independent variable in order to assess its impact on the dependent variable.

The experiment is superior to all other designs for finding causal relationships because of the *control* it introduces and maintains over the research process. The classic experimental design entails randomly assigning research participants to two groups: the **experimental** and the **control** groups. Ideally, these two groups should start off as virtually "identical" to each other – that is the idea behind random (or chance) assignment. The experimental group will be intentionally exposed to the alleged causal agent (aka the independent variable). And in the interest of control, the independent variable is intentionally withheld from the control group. This "design" allows a clear focus on the connection, if any, between the independent variable and the outcome being investigated (aka dependent variable). (The criteria for establishing causal connections and the logic of experimental design are both thoroughly reviewed in Chapter 5.) To be sure, not all researchers who study casual questions employ the experimental design. (Chapter 5 offers a thorough review of the limits or obstacles to utilizing experimental design.) Still, the "logic" of the experimental design should inform all design decisions for causal analysis and help the researcher find reasonable alternatives to pure experiments.

> **Experimental group** – the group in an experiment that is intentionally exposed to the independent variable.
>
> **Control group** – the group in an experiment that does not receive the independent variable.

Non-Causal Questions

Despite humans' perennial interest in explanations, not all research questions are causal ones. Indeed, most often social researchers pose questions that are non-causal in nature. Researchers might want to describe the current population of Facebook users or climate change deniers or victims of sexual violence on college campuses. Researchers might want to pursue correlational analysis and thus be interested in documenting relationships between variables. For instance, are climate change deniers more likely to be found in certain social classes, or religious groups, or political parties? Researchers might be interested in knowing more about social processes, for example: how do terrorist organizations recruit new members; how do people who have undergone transformative weight loss manage their new identities; how do people transition from one gender to another? Or researchers might want to know if social programs or policies have had the desired impact, for example: have austerity programs in European nations produced the desired results; do "put the cell phone down" campaigns work? Or researchers might ask questions about social change, for example: are today's senior citizens better off than those of previous decades; do millennials view careers differently than previous generations? Research agendas that pursue description, correlational analysis, exploration or evaluation, or pose questions about process or change can utilize an array of non-experimental research designs. When discussing non-experimental designs we distinguish between two major approaches: cross-sectional and longitudinal designs. The key to understanding these fundamentally different strategies is *timing*.

Timing is Everything

Ever since life as we know it began, humans have been fascinated and preoccupied with time. Einstein observed that "space and time are modes by which we think …" The 60-second minute and the 60-minute hour have been with us since Babylonian days. We structure our days, weeks, even our lives with an eye to time. Ignore time and we run the risk of losing jobs, money, our health, and even our friends and loved ones. Many would argue that success in life is all about time management – learning how in some instances to seize the moment and in other instances to take things in one's stride. (There is even a science of timekeeping – horology.)

As you might now suspect, time is also a significant factor in planning research. Researchers often find themselves occupied with projects interested in documenting *select moments in time*: What percentage of Americans support immigration reform today? What is the current average age of retirement in France or Germany or Great Britain? What percentage of families today are "blended"? How do Americans or citizens of the world feel about Edward Snowden? Who are the most powerful people in the world today? To answer any of these questions we need a research plan that is a one-shot or one moment in time data collection endeavor – that is, we need a cross-sectional research design. On the other hand, many research questions necessitate our assessing some kind of change over time: Has support for immigration reform changed in light of the child exodus from Central American countries in the summer of 2014? Have the austerity measures of European nations affected the average retirement age? Are there more blended families today than there were a decade ago? Are today's youth more or less enamored with the concept of marriage than their parents? How has the terrorist attack on Charlie Hebdo changed the way European nations are addressing national security? To answer these various questions, the researcher must employ research strategies that accommodate the passing of time and/or change (i.e. a longitudinal research design).

Cross-Sectional Research Designs

Cross-sectional research – research where data is collected at one single moment in time.

The **cross-sectional** research design addresses our need to document facts or collect data at a *single moment in time* – it is the research equivalent of the "Polaroid moment" – that is, an attempt to produce a "snap-shot" (frozen in time) picture of something. Just as a snapshot freezes a moment in time, cross-sectional research "captures" information at one moment in time. In using a cross-sectional design, the researcher gathers data on all pertinent variables via a singular data collection effort; there is no attempt to follow up or extend the data collection over time. In executing a cross-sectional study, the researcher might ask a series of questions of a broad *cross-section* of people in order to address the topic of interest (ergo the phrase cross-sectional design). The most frequently utilized cross-sectional tool for collecting information is the survey (so cross-sectional design is also known as survey design). Typically, the survey is delivered to individuals in person, or via the computer screen, or via the phone and once all of the survey questions have been asked and answered, the data collection phase is finished. (Although the data collection process may go on for days or weeks, especially if one is working with a large sample, respondents' participation is limited to a one-time affair.) As you may well know from your own experiences, many surveys are done under conditions of anonymity which precludes any later follow-up or re-contact.

The cross-sectional or survey design is a remarkably robust or versatile design – one that can take on many research tasks. Consequently, cross-sectional research is quite common in social research. Obtaining information from a cross-section of a population at a single point in time is a reasonable strategy for pursuing many descriptive and exploratory research projects (see Chapter 2). Where do Americans currently stand on immigration reform? How do today's youth feel about marriage? What are Baby Boomers' thoughts on retirement? How do the people of the world regard Edward Snowden? Since the answers to these questions are about "now", they all can be addressed via a cross-sectional design employing a survey: Indeed, until 2010, the cross-sectional design was the heart of the General Social Survey (GSS) conducted by the National Opinion Research Center (NORC) at the University of Chicago – a major research effort that documents a large array of Americans' attitudes and behaviors. Through 2010, the GSS interviewed a cross-section of Americans every year or two in order to learn their views on a variety of topics. While it takes the GSS approximately two months to complete a surveys, it was still considered a single point in time study design (i.e. each respondent is only contacted once). This slice into time and across the population provided an extremely valuable and timely look at what Americans are currently thinking and doing. (In 2008, the GSS started transitioning to a panel design which was fully implemented in 2010 – see an explanation of this in section "Fixed-Sample Panel Designs".) The United States is not alone in relying on massive cross-sectional studies to generate the most up-to-date "picture" of society. Australia, Britain, Canada, Germany, and many more nations around the world all have a vested interest in conducting some form of a general survey of its people.[1]

Cross-sectional design is also useful for pursuing correlational analysis – that is, answering questions about associations between variables – a mainstay of much sociological research. Who has the higher voter turn-out rates, men or women? Are the elderly more likely than other age groups to be pro-government? Does support for measures to fight global warming vary by education? Does support for immigration reform vary by ethnicity? All of these questions are essentially about seeing if two variables are correlated at any given moment in time. Cross-sectional designs are once again up to the task of answering this type of question – of documenting or investigating associations between variables. At one select moment in time, researchers can administer surveys asking questions about key variables (e.g. gender and voting or views on global warming and education levels) and then resort to some analysis package like SPSS or STATA to check for key associations. To be sure, the cross-sectional design is a real work horse for all the social sciences.

As we will see in Chapter 7, the cross-sectional design is also frequently used to address causal relationships. To be sure, cross-sectional design with its "one moment in time" data collection presents some challenges for satisfying the conditions for establishing causality. But where there is a will, there is a way and cross-sectional research can be amended to better equip it for pursuing explanatory analysis.

Longitudinal Research Designs

As useful and popular as cross-sectional research is, it nonetheless has its limitations. Anytime we are pursuing an analysis of change over time, we must be prepared to go beyond the simple cross-sectional design. While one-moment in time data collection is perfectly adequate for assessing or describing current situations or for documenting relationships between variables, if we want to know whether or not situations or conditions have changed over time, we must select a research design that can "capture" change – that is, we must commit to a plan that collects data at multiple points in time. This "time-extension" is the defining feature of longitudinal designs. **Longitudinal research** collects data at two or more points in time. It is the presence of multiple data points that allows the researcher to confidently address the issue of change. In selecting a longitudinal design the researcher has several options to consider: the fixed-sample panel design, repeated-cross sectional design (aka trend analysis), and an event-based design.

Longitudinal research – research that collects data at two or more points in time.

Many researchers are interested in the process or question of change. Do individuals change their views about marital fidelity over time or their views about life after death as they age? How are individuals impacted by having near-death experiences? Do communities or nations change their views about the government after disasters or political scandals? Have Europeans' attitudes about the war on terrorism changed in light of the Charlie Hebdo attack in Paris? Were American attitudes about gun control changed by the Sandy Hook elementary school shootings or the AME church shootings in Charleston, South Carolina? To answer any of these questions, we need data from at least two time periods: pre and post the Charlie Hebdo attack and pre and post the Sandy Hook or Charleston shootings. Similarly, if we want to know how Russia's annexation of Crimea in the spring of 2014 has affected European's view of Russia, we would need to compare data from pre and post annexation. If we want to know how the profile of families from across the world has changed in the past decade, we would want data from at least two time periods: current family information and information from ten years ago.

If you look carefully at the various questions about change posed in the previous paragraph, you will see that change can occur at two basic levels. We might be interested in documenting change in individuals over time as they grow, mature, and accumulate more and more life experiences. On the other hand, our interest in change might be at a "higher" aggregate or social level. We might want to study how groups or communities or entire populations change over time. Questions about individual vs. social change require different research strategies. Questions about individual change require a fixed sample panel design while questions about social change require a repeated cross-sectional design.

Fixed-Sample Panel Design

Sometimes the question of change we need to address occurs at the individual level of analysis. (Do individuals change their views of marital fidelity as they age?) To study this kind of change in individuals, we need to utilize the **fixed-sample panel design** (aka panel study). As the name fixed-sample suggests, data is collected from the *same* sample of respond-

> **Fixed sample panel design** – a plan that sees data collected at two or more points in time from the exact same sample – i.e. exact same group of people.

ents at multiple points in time. In longitudinal designs, each data collection point is referred to as a wave of the study. By repeatedly gathering data from the same individuals at multiple points in time, the panel design allows the researcher to track/examine change in those individuals over time. So to see if or how a person's views about religion or about the aging process change across a lifetime, I would need to collect data on their views across multiple time periods. Since the panel study follows the *exact same people through time*, it is a superior way to analyze the process of change as it occurs in specific individuals. The panel design, for instance, would allow us to document changes (if any) in an individual's attitude toward physician assisted suicide as they age or to document changes in how individuals cope with personal tragedy over time or to see if near-death experiences change a person's attitudes toward life. After years of using a cross-sectional design, in 2008 the GSS starting transitioning to a fixed sample panel design. In 2010, the GSS implemented a four-year rotating panel design where they follow respondents across three waves of data collection. Each new GSS study will entail (1) a new representative sample of participants (who will be followed for four years), (2) a first re-interview of an earlier panel, and (3) a final re-interview of yet another panel.[2]

Despite its recognized strength for studying individual change, the panel design can be a difficult one to execute. For instance, there is the task of tracking people and data over time. Keeping such records is challenging, expensive,

> **Panel mortality** – the loss of research participants over time from a fixed sample.

and frequently frustrated by the mobility of respondents. While they may let friends and the motor vehicle agency know when they move, notifying the local researcher is probably not such a high priority. Consequently, panel studies always face a very real problem of **panel mortality** (i.e. the loss of research subjects over time). Subjects may drop out of panel studies because they die, move away or simply lose interest. Whatever the reason, attrition is a serious issue. If our respondents are not available for subsequent waves of our study, we have lost the defining feature – the *raison d'être* – of the panel design.

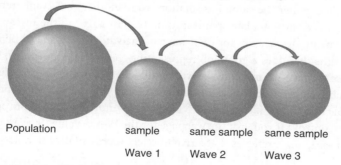

Figure 4.2 The Fixed-Sample Panel Design

Repeated cross-sectional design – a longitudinal research plan that sees data collected at two or more points in time from different samples of the same research population (aka trend design).

Repeated Cross-Sectional Design

If the change question being posed is about an entire collective or a population at large, the researcher need not go the route of a panel design. Instead, social change can be assessed via an alternate longitudinal design: the **repeated cross-sectional design** (aka trend design). As the name implies, this design essentially "repeats" two or more cross-sectional studies in an effort to address time and change. Note that it is still a longitudinal design since it still entails multiple points (waves) of data collection. It differs from the fixed-sample panel design in that it utilizes different samples at each wave of data collection. More specifically, the trend design calls for data collection at two or more times from *different* samples of respondents who are nonetheless part of *the same population*. Unlike the panel design where the exact same people are used in each wave of data collection, the repeated cross-sectional design selects a new sample at each wave of data collection (and thus prevents many of the practical problems associated with the panel design). The one essential requirement for the trend design is that each new sample must be drawn from the same population of interest. When this strategy is used, the researcher can detect or document any *social change* in the population as a whole.

One of the most ambitious trend analysis projects is the World Values Survey. This repeated cross-sectional project was initiated in 1981 and since then has investigated the impact of changing social values on the social and political life in nearly 100 countries of the world. Since 1981 there have been six waves of data collection and preparation is now underway for the seventh wave that will be conducted worldwide in 2016–2018. One of the most intriguing findings of this study is its challenge to the popular belief that globalization (or what is often called the "McDonaldization" of the world) brings a "convergence of values" with it. Findings from the World Values Survey over the last three decades indicate that no such convergence is taking place.[3]

The defining design feature of trend analysis (repeated cross-sectional surveys using different samples at each wave of data collection) carries a major implication for the analysis of change. Trend analysis permits or supports the investigation of aggregate level change (social or population) but it no longer allows the researcher to address change in particular individuals over time. So if we want to know if urban Americans' views on gun control are changing, we would need to gather such information from a sample of urban Americans in 2014 and then gather the same information from another (but comparable) sample of urban Americans drawn at a later point in time (e.g. in 2016). If the researcher has done a good job drawing the samples for each wave of the study (i.e. if she or he has selected a sample each time that does a good job representing the entire population), then a simple comparison of the data from each wave will reveal whether or not the population of urban Americans has changed its attitudes toward gun control. (But again note, the trend design will not enable us to know if specific individuals have undergone any "conversion" in their views on gun control.) If you visit the webpage for the World Values Survey, you will find a discussion of sampling strategies that strive to select representative samples of the various

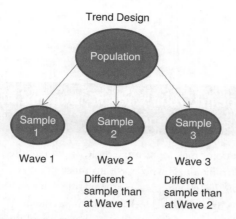

Figure 4.3 Strengthening Your Research Vision: Trend Design

participating countries at each wave of data collection. The ability to document population change depends on such careful sampling.

If you have followed the discussion of the essential features of panel and trend designs, you should appreciate that sample selection is the critical difference between these two kinds of longitudinal designs. While the panel study must repeatedly contact the exact same respondents in each wave of the study, the trend study selects a different sample of respondents from the same population at each wave of data collection. This feature of the trend study frees trend analysis of the major drawbacks of the panel design. Since the trend design allows us to work with a new sample at each wave of our study, the researcher is not encumbered by excessive record keeping or by the threat of panel mortality.

This change in sampling strategy also carries an important implication for the conclusions about change that we can draw from trend analysis. Given the fact that the targeted population remains the same in each wave of trend analysis (i.e. it is the *samples* that change from wave to wave, not the targeted population), the trend researcher can only document change at the population level. That is, by comparing data from a 2014 survey about gun control with data drawn from a 2016 survey, we can say if the *population* has changed its views on gun control. We are not in a position to say if the individuals we interviewed in 2014 have changed their views since we did not re-interview those same people again in 2016. Again, to answer a question about individual change we would need to adopt a fixed-sample panel design.

While initially started as a repeated cross-sectional design, the GSS is now trying to have the best of both worlds. For most of its history, the GSS employed a repeated cross-sectional design. However in the late 1990s, the sampling strategy was modified and fixed panels were worked into the data collection strategy. In 2010, the new three-wave panel design was fully implemented. After three waves of data collection, the panel is retired and a new panel is selected.

Box 4.3   Sharpening your research vision: not all change is the same

At first glance, this point may seem impossible. If populations change with regard to some variable don't individuals who make up those populations change as well? Not necessarily. Consider the following scenario. Imagine that we want to know how current college students at Whatsamatter U feel about climate change. We draw a representative sample in 2014 and learn there is a moderate concern about the issue. Now imagine we repeat our study in 2018. This time around we learn that the students at Whatsamatter U are quite passionate about the heating of the planet. Have those individuals from the 2014 sample changed their views? We really cannot say. All we know is that the *population at large* is more concerned. How might this happen if we can't assume that the 2014 students have changed? Well, in the four years between the two waves of the study, new environmentally astute students may have entered Whatsamatter U (and consequently show up in the 2018 sample) while the former "moderate" students of 2014 may have graduated (and are missing from the 2018 sample). The end result is that the overall population may change over time without any change in the those individuals who participated in earlier waves of a study. To be able to answer this kind of question – the question of individual change – we would, of course, need to conduct a panel design.

One final point should be made about trend designs. Our ability to use such designs to document population change is dependent on two conditions. First, for successful trend analysis, we must make sure that *each wave of the study employs a representative sample of the same population*. A trend study of recent college graduates should not use a sample from Ivy League colleges at wave one and a sample of state colleges at wave two. A trend study of American voters should not use registered Republicans at wave one and registered Democrats at wave two. A trend study of views about the Crimea annexation should not sample Crimean Tartars at time one and the general population at time two. And as noted earlier, obtaining representative samples of the national populations of participating countries is a major concern of the World Values Survey. Successful trend analysis is also dependent on *consistency in the measurement process*. In other words, to accurately document change, we must be certain that the exact same measures of variables being investigated are used in each and every wave of data collection. (A set of core questions have been repeated in the GSS since its inception.) If these conditions are not met, then any "change" we observe from one wave to the next *may* be due to population differences but they may also be due to measurement differences and not be reflective of true population change. Box 4.4 illustrates the complications that can ensue from even rather subtle changes in the measures used over the course of a trend analysis.

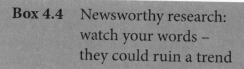

Box 4.4 Newsworthy research: watch your words – they could ruin a trend

If you are political junkie you might remember the scandal that almost brought down Bill Clinton: Clinton's affair with White House intern Monica Lewinsky. Initially, President Clinton denied any wrongdoing but on the night of August 17, 1998 he delivered a speech to the American public where he admitted he had an inappropriate relationship with Miss Lewinsky. Gallup immediately went to work to see what American's now thought of Clinton. The poll results indicated that only 40% reported having a favorable impression of Clinton, down from a 60% favorability rating reported just a week earlier! Such a ratings drop should have been the kiss of death for Clinton's presidency, but it was not. Why not? Richard Morin, who was then director of polling at *The Washington Post*, argued that the drop in favorability ratings was the result of a discrepancy in how Gallup asked its "favorability" question at time one (pre August 17) and time two (post August 17). The time one question asked respondents to indicate if they had a favorable or unfavorable opinion of various people in the news. Clinton's name was part of the list presented to respondents. This question produced the 60% favorability rating. After his mea culpa speech on the night of August 17th, Gallup asked respondents: "Now thinking about Bill Clinton as a person, do you have a favorable or unfavorable opinion of him?" This question produced the 40% favorability rating.

Morin put his finger on the very issue that can undo trend analysis: changing the measurement process between waves. Rephrasing the question at time two put the focus on Clinton's *personal* character and really was not comparable to the earlier question. Morin suggested that the time one question kept the focus at a more general "job approval" level. Indeed when Gallup saw the 20% point drop, they suspected something was amiss. So Gallup conducted yet another poll the day after the speech where they used the time one "general" question again. Respondents in this third wave of data collection reported a 55% favorability rating of President Clinton – only a 5% drop from his pre August 17 rating. Clearly words matter. We need always be mindful of how they are used in surveys, especially if we are trying to accurately document change.

We have devoted quite a bit of space to trend analysis for the simple reason that it is a popular design, especially in realm of political and social analysis. If you have paid attention to any of the major social issues of the day (climate change, national security, marriage equality movement), chances are great that you have encountered a sizable share of trend analysis. Every four years, for instance, Americans are fed a rather constant diet of preference polls that track how presidential candidates are faring with the public. Throughout the course of any presidential term, the Gallup Poll will document the trend of a president's favorability ratings. And while earlier, we identified the GSS as offering (through 2010) an example of cross-sectional research, it is also the case that the GSS is set up for trend analysis. Starting in 2010, the GSS initiated a four-year three-wave rolling panel design. Since the GSS makes concerted efforts to use the exact same questions over and over again, the GSS is capable of pursuing trend analysis. (And with its latest reliance on following the same respondents for three-year periods, the GSS is also able to address change at the individual level via its new fixed sample panel design.) You can find a discussion of the GSS design and its commitment to both trend and panel analysis by following relevant links on the GSS homepage (http://www3.norc.org/GSS+Website/). Similar trend analyses is also conducted in other nations as well – see for instance the trend studies of the European Union or the social change studies of the World Values Survey.

Event-Based Designs

> **Event-based design** – a plan that sees data collected at multiple points in time from a specific segment of a population that shares a common event; aka cohort analysis.
>
> **Cohort** – a group defined by a common event (i.e. experiencing a common life circumstance within a specified period of time).

Researchers considering longitudinal designs also have the option of employing an **event-based design** (aka a cohort design). With the event-based design, data are collected at multiple points in time from a specific segment of a population (i.e. a **cohort**). A cohort consists of people who are defined by a common event – they experience a common life circumstance within a specified period of time. Some typical events used to define cohorts are common birth periods (e.g. Baby Boomers), same year of graduation (class of 2000), same period of military service (Vietnam Veterans), and so on. Cohort analysis should be considered whenever the researcher suspects that change in specific subpopulations (cohorts) may be different than change in the general population. Cohort analysis allows the researcher to consider how certain life events (e.g. coming of age during the depression, serving in the Gulf War, being born at the start of the new millennium) may have an impact on life change and development. For instance, cohort analysis would enable a researcher to see if retirement experiences of World War II veterans are significantly different than those of Vietnam or of Gulf War veterans.

Questions About the Process

Sometimes our research interest concerns processes: how do people "fall in love" or cope with long-term unemployment or handle the transition from independent to nursing home living? How do soldiers readjust to civilian life when they return from war? For these kinds of questions, researchers often opt for qualitative research plans and data collection techniques (i.e. field research or intensive interviewing). Fieldwork entails the research entering the world of the research participant and learning about that world from the "inside" or by "walking a mile in their shoes." Fieldwork is distinctive in both its location and the depth of analysis. By meeting the research subjects in their natural settings, the researcher has a chance to gather what some consider the most authentic data – first-hand data from watching and listening to the researcher subjects as they go about their lives. Because the researcher is in the field with the research subjects, fieldwork also permits a more in-depth level of understanding gained from varying levels of immersion into the social worlds of their subjects. Chapter 10 reviews fieldwork in much greater detail and reviews the various levels of involvement that might be realized by the researcher.

Regardless of the researcher's level of field participation, the time spent in the field is typically extended – it is not uncommon for field studies to continue for months or even years. Researchers leave the field only when they have concluded that further observation/participation will fail to yield anything new. Intensive interviewing is often done in conjunction with field research. Intensive or unstructured interviewing is a technique that allows the researcher to understand how subjects experience or construct their lived realities. This interviewing strategy enables the research subjects to take the reins, as it were, in explicating their worlds. For example, Tewksbury and Lees use this technique to examine how individuals deal with the practical consequences of being publicly labeled in their communities as sex offenders (2010). Leck and Galperin used unstructured interviewing to discover how victims responded to workplace bullying (2010). (See Chapter 9 for a thorough discussion of interviewing techniques.)

And Still More Planning

So far we have considered how theory, the nature of our questions (causal vs. non-causal) and the time dimension are critical issues that must be considered in the planning stage of research. Box 4.5 offers a brief review of the connection between our research interests/questions and the appropriate design strategy. One last design consideration deserves our attention: keeping the issue of validity front and center in our research planning.

Box 4.5	Sharpening your research vision: matching research agendas/questions with designs

Agenda/question	*Design*
What are the causes of …?	Experimental design (ideally)
Are two variables correlated?	Cross-sectional design
What's the impact of …?	Cross-sectional or longitudinal (before/after)
How do individuals change over time or as a result of some event?	Longitudinal (panel)
How do populations or societies change?	Longitudinal (trend)
Providing a detail description of …	Cross-sectional design
Exploring a new social phenomenon	Cross-sectional or field research
Understanding a process	Qualitative field research or interviewing.

Measurement validity – the accuracy or extent to which measures empirically document what they claim to document.

Internal validity – the extent to which a research design is capable of detecting a true causal relationship.

External validity – the extent to which research findings can be accurately generalized from a sample to a population or from one group to another.

Planning to Maximize Research Validity

Planning a research project also must be done with an eye to the major validity issues central to scientific research: measurement validity, internal validity, and external validity. Indeed, it is science's obsession with these issues that gives science the edge over alternative ways of knowing. In our pursuit of valid knowledge, we are essentially concerned with three "trust" issues. First we want to know whether or not we can trust statements or claims of measurement. This concern raises the issue of **measurement validity** and requires us to take a long hard look at the steps we take to empirically document reality. Second, we want to know whether or not we can trust statement about causal relationships. This concern raises the issue of **internal validity** and requires us to take a long hard look at whether or not our basic research design is up to the task of detecting causal connections. Lastly, we want to know whether we can trust our findings to apply beyond the study that produced them. This raises the issue of **external validity** and forces us to take a long hard look at issues of sampling and replication. Each validity issue is reviewed in more detail below.

Measurement Validity

Part of planning a study involves the careful selection of measures for key variables. For any concept, there is a variety of ways to translate it into an "observable" or measurable variable. Good planning will see the researcher considering his or her measurement options early on in the design phase. Indeed, selecting valid measures is arguably one of the greatest challenges of research. How do we measure economic recovery? Should it be via unemployment rates, or housing starts, or consumer spending? How should we measure a successful marriage? Should it be in terms of longevity (i.e. any marriage lasting 20 years or more is a "success") or should success be grounded in self-reports of satisfaction, regardless of how long the union lasts? How should we measure drug safety? Should it be by the number of adverse effects or by the number of deaths? Our decisions with regard to measurement validity are critical. Research must be clear about how variables were actually measured and be ready to defend the measures used as "on target" – that is, really measuring what is intended. (This is such an important part of the research process that Chapter 5 of this book is devoted to the measurement process and Chapter 6 is devoted to assessing the validity of measures.) An essential part of planning, then, is considering the *possible* measures one might use in a project. The literature review process can help on this front. Finding other studies on topic and seeing how they measured relevant variables can help the researcher work through this most important planning issue.

Internal Validity

Good planning also demands that researchers pay attention to the "goodness of fit" between their research agenda and their planned strategy of action. We addressed this issue earlier in this chapter (section "What's the Question?") where we considered the connection between the specific research questions posed and the various designs or strategies for answering the questions: experimental vs. non-experiment (i.e. cross-sectional and longitudinal designs). The issue of internal validity presents a high bar for researchers undertaking causal analysis. If one is pursuing causal analysis, the internal validity issue insists that careful attention be given to some type of experimental design. Experimental designs are the best for isolating the cause and effect relationship and thus are strongest for achieving internal validity. Researchers who pursue causal analysis without utilizing the experimental design must devise an effective "work around" that will satisfy to some degree the internal validity standard. The internal validity issue is discussed more directly in the Chapter 7 on causality as well as in Chapters 8 and 9 on survey research. And once again, reviewing the relevant literature can offer important information for researchers as they consider which designs yielded the best results for the questions raised.

External Validity

Lastly, good planning must also direct an eye to the issue of external validity. If the researcher hopes to secure findings that are generalizable beyond the study at hand, careful thought must be given to sampling procedures. This issue is particularly relevant to survey researchers. As we will see in Chapters 8 and 11, surveys are extremely useful tools for gathering data quickly and from those both near and far. But if one wants to be in a good position for making accurate generalizations from the available data, one must be sure to utilize some type of probability sampling. Probability sampling gives us the best chance of obtaining a representative sample (i.e. one that accurately captures the diversity present in the total population of interest). And only probability sampling gives us an opportunity to actually estimate any error due to sampling. Both of these points in turn help to strengthen external validity. External validity must also be considered by those utilizing experimental research designs. Experiments are highly contrived research endeavors and for that reason they are said to lack "mundane realism" in that they fail to replicate everyday experiences. (People might be able to lose weight under experimental conditions but that does not guarantee they will be as successful when they return to their everyday routines.) For the experimental researcher, then, the ability to generalize beyond the conditions of the experiment is highly problematic. To strengthen the external validity of such research, researchers must rely on the process of replication: repeating the experiment under a variety of conditions and seeing if the findings continue to hold.

   Whether assessing someone else's research or planning a project of your own, you are well advised to use the validity issues as "north stars" of trustworthy data. Research that does not attend to these issues is likely to lead us down the misguided path to erroneous information.

Conclusions

A successful study requires some forethought and some careful planning. Indeed, if you think that a particular piece of research is not worth planning, it probably is not worth doing either! This chapter has addressed some of the most important issues to be considered when thinking about any research project: a good "on point" literature review, a study's theoretical "legs", the specific questions or tasks addressed in the research, a study's time orientation, and the touchstone validity concerns: measurement, internal, and external validity. Theoretical considerations will "direct" a researcher's selection of concepts and variables and statement of hypotheses or questions. Clearly specifying the research question can help with the selection of either experimental or non-experimental designs. The time dimension helps us anticipate the number of data collection points needed to address the questions raised in our research. Can we learn what we need to find out, for instance, by just talking to respondents once or do we need to re-contact respondents for follow-up information? If our interest is in change, some sort of longitudinal design is in order. Paying attention to the specific research question being raised will help clarify the specific plan for collecting data. Descriptive tasks for instance will call for a design that gets all relevant information while a causal question requires the consideration of some form of experimental design. The validity issues, measurement, internal and external, bring science's skeptical nature front and center to the planning process and insist that the researcher review the quality of measures, designs and the applicability of findings.

There is, of course, more to be said about how to successfully execute a research project. Many of the issues just reviewed are taken up in greater detail in the remaining chapters of the book.

TAKE AWAYS

- Good planning entails juggling many things
- Literature reviews – don't try research without them!
  - Offer useful "roadmaps" to your own work
  - Can provide a wealth of useful and often time-saving information
- Theory always has a place in good research.
  - Deductive research – starts in the realm of theory
  - Inductive research – starts in the realm of empirical data
  - Levels and paradigms
    - Influence questions of interest
    - Influence data collection techniques
- What's your exact question? It matters in selecting a design
  - Causal questions
    - Experimental designs
  - Non-causal questions
    - Non-experimental designs
  - Questions of change
    - Longitudinal designs
  - Questions about process
    - Qualitative designs
- Overriding validity concerns are essential touchstones for making good decisions
  - Measurement
  - Internal
  - External

Sharpening the Edge: More Reading and Searching

- Treat yourself to a TED lecture that offers some insight into the challenge of coming up with the best design. Though not directly about research design per se, the lecture by Daniele Quercia hits on some interesting ideas that are relevant for "finding" new ways to think about the world around us:

  http://www.ted.com/talks/daniele_quercia_happy_maps/transcript?language=en

- The inductive style of research uses empirical evidence to "point" the way to important patterns. A TED lecture by Johnson helps illustrate this style by considering how the "data points" in a city map from 1854 London helped solve a medical mystery of the city's last cholera epidemic:

  http://www.ted.com/talks/steven_johnson_tours_the_ghost_map

Exercises

1 Try your hand at using an online academic journal database. (Most college libraries subscribe to a few. Search the library homepage or talk with a reference librarian for help in finding out which ones are available at your institution.)

   (a) Access the database and try repeating the search on "eating disorders" discussed in this chapter. First just enter the term and see how the literature has grown since the original search for this book was conducted. Next try some different "qualifier" terms and see what impact they have on the number of hits you get via the search. Try college students or limit the search to only females and then to only males. Next try pairing the original term with middle-aged adults. Come up with a few other qualifiers that you can glean from the articles listed in your search results.

2 Use an online database (Academic Search Complete, JSTOR, BioOne Criminal Justice Periodicals) and search on an issue of interest to you. Scroll down through the results and find an entry that makes the entire article available to you. Open the article and see what planning decisions were made by the author: Is a clear question or hypothesis stated? Is it clear whether the research is deductive or inductive? Do you agree with the basic strategy being used to answer the question or test the hypothesis? Can you tell if the design is experimental or non-experimental? Cross-sectional or longitudinal?

3 Test yourself. Can you identify the best design for addressing each of the following research questions?

   (a) Do training workshops help reduce the tolerance for sexual harassment in the workplace?

   (b) Do community priorities change after some natural disaster (e.g. a flood or hurricane)?

   (c) Do "no texting while driving" laws reduce traffic accidents?

Notes

1   See the International Social Survey Programme for a list of participating nations http://www.issp.org/page.php?pageId=2.

2   See http://www.ropercenter.uconn.edu/general-social-survey/ for more details.

3   See http://www.worldvaluessurvey.org/WVSContents.jsp.

References

Durkheim, Emile. 1951. *Suicide*. New York: Free Press.

Firebaugh, Gleen. 2008. *Seven Rules for Social Research*. Princeton: Princeton University Press.

Hanson, Barbara. 1999. *The Research Process: Creating Facticity*. Prospect Heights, IL: Waveland Press, Inc.

Leck, Joanne and Bella Galperin. 2010. "Responses to Workplace Bullying." In Alex D. Thio, Thomas C. Calhoun, and Addrian Conyers (eds), *Readings in Deviant Behavior*, 6th edn. Boston: Allyn & Bacon.

Lehmann, Timothy and T.R. Young. 1974. "From Conflict Theory to Conflict Methodology: An Emerging Paradigm for Sociology." *Sociological Inquiry* 44: 15–28.

Sutherland, Edwin and Donald Cressey. 1934. *Principles of Criminology*. Chicago: J.P. Lippincott.

Tewksbury, Richard and Matthew Lees. 2010. "What It's Like to be Known as a Sex Offender." In Alex D. Thio, Thomas C. Calhoun, and Addrian Conyers (eds), *Readings in Deviant Behavior*, 6th ed. Boston: Allyn & Bacon.

White, Michael and Karen Terry. 2008. "Child Sexual Abuse in the Catholic Church: Revisiting the Rotten Apples Explanation." *Criminal Justice and Behavior* 35: 658–678.

Chapter 5

Measure by Measure: Developing Measures – Making the Abstract Concrete

Introducing Social Research Methods: Essentials for Getting the Edge, First Edition. Janet M. Ruane.
© 2016 John Wiley & Sons, Ltd. Published 2016 by John Wiley & Sons, Ltd.

FIRST TAKES

Be sure to take note of the following:

The conceptual nature of humans

- Concepts as central to theory
- Concepts as central to research
- Translating concepts into variables
  - Measurement validity
  - Conceptual vs. operational definitions
  - Natural vs. contrived measures
  - Product vs. behavioral measures
  - Item vs. composite measures
  - Levels of measurement
    - Nominal
    - Ordinal
    - Interval
    - Ratio measures

Picture adults interacting with infants and you will have an immediate insight into our conceptual nature. The parent–child interaction is largely an exercise in teaching concepts. Parents will repeatedly point to themselves or their spouses while repeating the word "Mommy" or "Daddy", hoping the child will make the connection between the real live persons and the words. Or Mom will point to a dog while saying the word "dog" over and over again, once again hoping that the child will make the connection between the family pet and the word "dog." The earliest teaching lessons involve pointing, saying a word and repeating the whole routine over and over again. In these tutorial exchanges, the child is learning about the world of **concepts**.

> **Concepts** – mental abstractions/images that serve to categorize ideas, places, things, or events.

As the above examples illustrate, concepts are mental images, abstractions or terms that symbolize ideas, persons, things, or events. In the natural sciences, concepts are often expressed in symbolic notation. If you have a physics background you may be familiar with the symbol for infinity: ∞. In physics we also learn that the symbolic notation of $s=d/t$ stands for the concepts of speed being equal to distance divided by time. In high school algebra, we learn about pi (the ratio of the circumference of a circle to its diameter) and denote it with the following symbol: π. Math classes also teach us to associate the following symbol "=" with equivalence and to recognize % as a symbol for percentage. In statistics we learn to recognize Chi Square as X^2 and Σ as a summation sign.

In the social sciences, concepts are most often expressed in words. So, if the "idea" we want to express concerns a legally recognized social and economic relationship between two individuals, we would invoke the concept (or the word) "marriage." To describe the constant bickering and fighting between brothers and/or sisters, we invoke the concept "sibling rivalry." "Blended family" is the concept used to describe the merger via a second marriage of previously existing families. The rising sea levels and world temperatures are now conveyed via the concept "climate change." The wall of water that can accompany an earthquake is conveyed in the word/concept "tsunami." Criminologists, in describing a lethal exchange between loved ones invoke the concept "friendly murder."

From the early days of childhood learning through our adult years, we strive to know and master useful, relevant concepts. There is a good reason for this – *concepts are essential tools for communicating*. Concepts enable us to give and receive information efficiently. Reconsider the examples offered in the previous paragraph and you should immediately appreciate how difficult communication would be if we could not express ourselves via the mental shorthand of concepts. (If you have ever played the game TABOO, you know this challenge first hand. Players are forbidden to use the most obvious concepts/words when trying to get their partners to guess the targeted word.) Imagine the difficulty of communicating the weather on the nightly news if we could not use such concepts as "flash floods," "blizzards," or "hurricanes." Imagine the difficulty in understanding world events without the concepts of terrorism, or infidels, or improvised explosive devices (IEDs). Or imagine how lost we would be in explaining the concept of virtual reality without the concepts of avatars and telepresence and full-body immersion. Concepts are essential to our thinking; they are essential to our communicating with others. And as you might well imagine, concepts are also central to the business of social research.

Box 5.1	Sharpening your research vision: picture this!

A quick way to understand our conceptual natures is by considering the use of picture books with babies. Well before babies begin to talk, we start instructing them about concepts and words. Picture books present the concrete indicators of abstract concepts: for example, books for babies and toddlers are filled with pictures of farm animals, toys, cars and trucks followed by the "words" that stand in for the pictures. It is the beginning of our lifetime affinity with abstract concepts and our learning the words to express them.

Concepts and The Research Process

Chapter 1 established that science is concerned with the concrete and the empirical. Yet if you look again at the definition of concepts presented above, you will see that concepts are *apart from* the empirical world. Concepts are *mental abstractions* and as such they are the antithesis of concrete empiricism. Indeed, some concepts can be so "apart" from the empirical world that they lack an empirical indicator. Such concepts without empirical counterparts are referred to as **constructs**. How then do these mental abstractions come to occupy a central role in scientific research?

> **Construct** – a concept or mental abstraction that is not directly observable.

Theory – a set of propositions or statements about how the world or some entity operates or works.

Concepts work their way into research via **theory**. In Chapter 4, we reviewed the connection between research and theory. Theories are sets of logically related or linked ideas (abstractions) about how the world or some process works. The fundamental building blocks of theory are concepts. In other words, theories consist of a series of statements (propositions) about relationships between concepts.

Chapter 4 showed that different theories invoke different concepts. In sociology, order theory (aka structural-functionalism) tries to explain the world in light of such concepts as social stability, integration, consensus, and so on. Conflict theory offers explanations of social reality that invoke such concepts as dissensus, coercion, power, and social control. Symbolic interactionism theory explains the social by invoking such concepts as social interaction, social meaning, and the social negotiation of reality. Emile Durkheim's theory of suicide (1951) relates the concept of suicide to the concept of social integration. Donald Black's theory of formal social control (1976) relates the concept of law to the concepts of social organization, culture, social morphology, and social stratification. Hirschi's social control theory (1969) relates the concept of delinquency to the concept of social bonds.

Bringing Theory Down to Earth

If theory offers ideas (concepts) about how the world works, research is about empirically documenting or assessing those ideas via empirical evidence in order to see whether or not those ideas are correct. Consequently, research can be seen as either an effort to: (a) test established theory, or (b) generate new theory. (Research conducted to test established theory is called *deductive research*; research that starts in the empirical realm and tries to generate theory is called *inductive research*. See Chapter 4.) In either scenario, research must encounter concepts. Good research either begins with or ends in the realm of concepts and theory.

To put it succinctly, if we want to conduct scientific research, we must be able to work with concepts. But here is the challenge: since concepts are abstract, mental ideas, they do not immediately lend themselves to the "show me" empirical realm of research. What is the researcher to do? We must engage in a *translation process* – one that makes concepts understandable to the empiricist. In this translation process, we transform abstract concepts into their concrete, empirical counterparts. In performing this translation process, the researcher engages in the **measurement process**. Measurement, then, can be thought of as the process of transforming the abstract into the concrete; it refers to the process of converting concepts into variables. **Variables** are empirical representations or indicators of concepts. Following this logic, the concept of education might find its empirical counterpart in counting the number of years one has spent in school or noting the highest degree someone has earned. The concept of patriotism might find its empirical counterpart in our counting

Measurement process – the process by which abstract concepts are translated into empirical variables.

Variables – empirical representations/ indicators of abstract concepts; any trait or characteristic that can vary.

the number of flags flown in a local community. Civic involvement might be empirically translated via the number of hours a month one spends doing volunteer work. The MVP of a game might be empirically translated via the total number of points or assists scored by a player.

Box 5.2   Sharpening your research vision: selling concepts

Translating the abstract into the concrete is not the exclusive work of researchers. Examples of such translations abound in popular culture. For instance, consider the work of advertisement agencies. The process of translating abstract concepts into concrete empirical representations is really at the heart of advertising. For instance, ad people work hard to get us to associate success with a variety of costly consumer items: the latest luxury sedan or a De Beers keepsake diamond. Dos Equis uses the most interesting man in the world ad campaign to get us to associate its beer with intrigue. A recent ad campaign by Honda asks us to equate family diplomacy with the Odyssey mini-van. The Chase Sapphire Card offers itself as the vehicle for exploring the world while ads for the Toyota Camry claim that they will help you go places!

Any one concept, of course, can give rise to any number of empirical counterparts or variables. Consider the concept of happiness, an abstraction that can mean many different things to many different people. Back in the 1960s, a popular cigarette commercial equated happiness with smoking Kent cigarettes. A classic *Peanuts* comic strip equated happiness with a warm puppy. A standard kids' song instructs that if we are happy ♪ and we know it, we should clap our hands and stomp our feet. Today we are encouraged to equate happiness with certain automobiles, or beverages, or gourmet ice creams. All of these examples illustrate the essential process of transforming something abstract (happiness) into something concrete. All examples suggest that happiness might best be "seen" or documented in the concrete empirical world via our actions or our possessions. Happiness is the abstract concept, a warm puppy is offered as its tangible embodiment. And all of these examples also highlight the conundrum of translating concepts into variables – there can be countless "translations" and some might not be as good as others.

Consider, for instance, how the researcher might handle the translation of happiness into its empirical counterpart. While it is in the advertiser's vested interest to have us associate happiness with the services or products of the ad agency's clients, the researcher must be sure his/her concept/variable translations live up to the standards

Valid measures – measures that actually measure what they claim to measure; measures that document what they claim to document.

or rules of science. The researcher must be concerned about developing **valid measures** or with achieving measurement validity – that is, being sure that the variables used in research really do capture the true meaning of the concepts being measured. Is a warm puppy a good measure of happiness? Perhaps not for someone who is afraid of or allergic to dogs. Stomping one's feet *might* show happiness but it might also be a sign of anger or frustration. And for more and more health conscience people, happiness is certainly not a Kent (or any other cigarette). As indicated in Chapter 1, researchers embracing scientific methods, must take extra steps to ensure an error-free translation process. When researchers equate a concept with a concrete empirical variable, they should provide some evidence of the adequacy of the translation and the resulting measure.

Conceptualization

The first step toward good measurement is good conceptualization. Since concepts can mean different things to different people, the researcher must be sure to clarify the meaning of the concepts as they see it. Two different researchers may conceive of "violence" in two different ways. One may view violence as *physical action* (hitting another) while another may see violence in *verbal* as well as physical attacks ("slamming" another with a verbal putdown). One researcher might define alienation as a loss of involvement in the activity of working. Another may equate alienation with a sense of separation from our own human nature. One researcher may define civic involvement in terms of long-standing social memberships while another sees it as short-term involvement with special interest groups. One researcher might define marital success by the *length* of marriage while another might focus instead on the *quality* of the relationship. As each of the examples show, before we can devise adequate empirical measures of abstract concepts, we must work on conceptual clarity.

> **Theoretical (aka nominal or conceptual) definitions** – definitions that clarify the exact meaning of concepts being measured by offering synonyms for the concepts; aka dictionary definitions.

The researcher strives to achieve conceptual clarity by offering **theoretical (aka nominal) definitions** of concepts. Theoretical definitions are those that clarify a concept by offering synonyms for that concept. Theoretical definitions can be found either in standard or in special discipline dictionaries. In consulting a sociology dictionary, a researcher might elect to define alienation as a "feeling of noninvolvement in and estrangement from one's society and culture." Anxiety might be defined as an "emotional state characterized by extreme apprehension (and) lacking a clear focus on a specific object." Conservatism can be defined as "an ideological orientation that opposes social change" (Theodorson and Theodorson 1969). Another good source for theoretical definitions is the research literature. Part of the purpose of reviewing the literature for a given topic is to see how the major concepts of a given topic are defined by other researchers. Recognizing the different approaches others have taken to conceptualizing can be an important guide to a researcher's refinement of a research question. Indeed, many a research project has been built out of attempts to resolve conflict over the competing meaning of concepts.

Box 5.3   Sharpening your research vision: from concepts to conceptual definitions to variables

Concept: self-esteem
- Conceptual definition: an overall evaluation of one's worth or value
- Variable: Rosenberg's Self-Esteem Scale

Concept: shyness
- Conceptual definition: the tendency to feel awkward or tense in social situations
- Variable: Cheek and Buss Shyness Scale

Operationalization

Once the researcher has achieved conceptual clarity, she or he can then get on with the task of finding the best empirical counterpart for the concept. This step is referred to as the **operationalization process**. Clearly, the researcher is interested in finding the best possible fit between theoretical definitions and empirical embodiments of concepts. Devising good measures is not easy work. (Indeed, Chapter 6 is devoted to reviewing some of the key standards used by researchers to assess the adequacy of their measures.) In working our way through the operationalization process, we may be satisfied that some measurement ideas offer a better empirical fit with the abstract concept than do others. For example, if you define conservatism as "an ideological orientation that opposes social change" you might be satisfied that conservatism is best measured by a respondent's agreement/disagreement with a series of statements about proposed social innovations (e.g. voting for a female president, supporting gays in the military, approving of women in combat units, or approving of same-sex marriage). Using the same conceptual definition of conservatism, you might be less satisfied with the idea of assessing the concept by asking respondents if they believe in God or by noting their style of dress. In working our way through the operationalization process, we might also conclude that some measurement ideas will have to be abandoned (e.g. we may conclude that happiness is best measured by asking people to self-report their levels of happiness and *not* by observing their smoking habits, their pet ownership, or their clapping, or foot stomping behaviors).

> **Operationalization process** – process of finding reasonable and accurate empirical indicators for concepts.

In struggling with the operationalization process, we might find that we need to reconsider or revisit our theoretical definitions. An iterative, fine-tuning process is often needed. For instance, our measurement difficulties might be due to the fact that we really have not achieved conceptual clarity. We might discover, for instance, that we have not sufficiently specified the various dimensions of our concepts. In reviewing the literature on alienation (an essential strategy for achieving conceptual clarity) we see that alienation is really a multidimensional or multifaceted concept. Erikson's review of Marx's writing on alienation identifies four separate forms of alienation: (1) a separation from the product of our own labor; (2) a loss of involvement in the activity of working; (3) an estrangement from fellow creatures; (4) a separation from our human nature (Erikson 1986). In measuring alienation, then, we might strive to develop a measure that addresses all four dimensions of Erikson's work. On the other hand, we might elect to take a more restrictive approach and decide to zero in on just one of the concept's various dimensions – perhaps concentrating on the dimension that focuses on one's estrangement from one's fellow workers. Such give and take is appropriate, indeed it is to be expected, as we strive to produce a good fit between the abstract and the empirical.

Some Key Guidelines for the Operationalization Process

As we embark on the operationalization process, there are a few options that need to be considered.

Will Measures be Natural or Contrived?

Natural measures document concepts via naturally occurring evidence – no "artificial" or concocted measurement procedures are devised. The researcher refrains from intruding on inserting him/herself into the research context and instead merely makes use of readily (naturally) available evidence to empirically document something. A common way to measure the popularity of a museum exhibit is to notice the naturally occurring wear patterns of floors or the dirt or smudges on the walls or glass around the exhibit. The most utilized seats in a movie theatre or on a school bus can be documented by similar "wear and tear" evidence. School cafeterias can measure the "hits and misses" on a lunch menu by observing the food selections that wind up in trash cans. The appeal of social movements or campaigns can be measured by directly observing the size of crowds that show up or attend events (unless they are paid extras as was the case with Donald Trump's 2015 event where he announced he was a candidate for President of the US)! Finding "natural" measures can be an exercise in creativity and advocates of this approach to measurement praise it for eliminating **reactivity effects**. Reactivity effects occur when research participants become aware of the measurement process and consequently change or alter their behaviors as a result. Reactivity effects clearly undermine or compromise the validity of measurement. Since natural measures do not see researchers directly eliciting information from respondents, reactivity effects are a moot issue.

Contrived measures, on the other hand, are "made up" or intentionally developed or designed by researchers. Indeed when most of us think about measures, we usually have contrived measures in mind. We think about endurance or performance tests (contrived), health check-ups (contrived), memory tests (contrived), sobriety tests (contrived), or surveys (contrived). In fact, the most utilized measurement option is some sort of **survey**. A survey refers

> **Natural measures** – measures that utilize naturally occurring evidence by way of empirically documenting a variable.
>
> **Reactivity effects** – occur when research participants become aware of the measurement process and consequently change/alter their behaviors as a result.
>
> **Contrived measures** – measures intentionally designed or developed by the researcher in order to generate empirical evidence of a variable.
>
> **Survey** – a data collection tool that gathers information via questions.

to a data collection tool that relies on contrived questions by way of gathering empirical evidence needed for measurement. Surveys rule in the social sciences.

Will the Outcome of the Measurement Process be a Product or a Behavior?

The researcher should give some thought to the desired result of measurement. In the simplest of terms we might think about the "saying" vs. "doing" option: that is, will the measurement process elicit answers to questions and thus focus on what people say or will it focus on actual behaviors or what people actually do? This distinction is important since humans are remarkably capable of saying one thing but doing something totally different. (We have a concept for that: hypocrites!). Parents may *say* they never hit their kids but watching their interactions with their kids in a mall may reveal something totally different. Another way to think about this issue is to consider if the measures will generate some kind of product outcome or generate a behavioral outcome. Using a questionnaire as part of the measurement process illustrates a "product" outcome – the researcher will have an actual, tangible product at the end of the study (the completed questionnaire). Utilizing drawings to ascertain children's feelings in a study of child abuse illustrates a "product" measure.

On the other hand, a study of abused children that directly observes their play activity with other children is utilizing a behavioral response measure. Experiments that look at the effect of alcohol on reaction time in a simulated driving course would be utilizing a behavioral response option. Measuring opposition to a campaign or policy via public graffiti would be an instance of a (natural) product measure. We take the time to make this distinction so you can appreciate the variety of possible strategies one might incorporate in a study. Table 5.1 provides an informative grid of possibilities that exist when one tries to combine natural/contrived options with the product/response options.

Table 5.1 Sharpening your research vision: a matrix of measurement options

	Indicator	
	Natural	Contrived
Product	public graffiti	questionnaire
Response		
Behavior	field observations	sobriety test

Using One or More Variables in Translating Concepts

How many variables does it take to measure a concept? While this may sound like a joke, it is a serious consideration. As we are engaging the conceptualization process, we should be taking note of whether the concepts we want to measure are simple or complex. Simple concepts convey one idea or have one dimension while complex concepts are multidimensional. The previous discussion of alienation, for instance, shows alienation to be a rather complex concept (i.e. it has multiple dimensions). Alienation indicates a feeling of separation from self, others, work, and so on. Intelligence is another example of a complex, multidimensional concept. Intelligence refers to many abilities, such as the ability to learn, to problem solve, or to comprehend. Even age is thought of as a complex concept as researchers distinguish between chronological age and mental age. Other concepts are much more straightforward or unidimensional: weight, height, eye color, religious affiliation, birth order.

> **Item measure** – a single indicator used to document a concept (i.e. one question is typically used to measure gender or age or marital status).
>
> **Composite measure** – a multiple item measure; several indicators are used together to measure a complex concept (see Rosenberg's self-esteem measure in Box 5.6 for an example).

Ascertaining whether concepts are simple or complex provides important guidance on how best to measure them. Simple concepts can be measured by **item measures** while complex concepts require **composite measures**.

An item measure is a singular indicator of a concept. One question, one observation is used to document (measure) the concept. If you take a look at just about any survey, you will see that many, many item measures are used to collect basic data on respondents' backgrounds. Typically one, and only one, question is used to measure respondents' gender, race, religious affiliation, marital status, parental status, educational level, and so on.

Clearly then there is a place for item measures in the operationalization process. "One" is often sufficient to get the job done! But we live in a complex world and as we have already seen, there are many concepts that are anything but simple or straightforward. To do a reasonable job measuring complex concepts we need to push beyond singular, item measures. Composite measures utilize multiple indicators by way of empirically documenting a complex concept. These multiple item measures are referred to as indexes or scales. Typically the items are then "woven" together to provide a more valid documentation of the concept. So if you take a look at Morris Rosenberg's classic measure of self-esteem (see Box 5.6), you will see that Rosenberg used 10 items/statements by way of measuring this complex concept. Shyness is another complex concept and so it would not be well measured via a single item. (Think of how many times you have been surprised to learn that someone who you think of as outgoing claims to be shy). Not surprisingly, then, one of the most utilized measures of shyness is Cheek and Buss's 13 or 20 item Shyness Scales.[1]

While the distinction between item and composite measures is pretty clear cut, its importance cannot be overstated. Knowing just how far we must go in developing measures, whether or not we need to push beyond singular, item measures, is critical to achieving the ultimate goal of creating valid measures. Using an item measure for a complex concept is one sure way to undermine measurement validity – that is, accurately measuring what we claim we are measuring.

Levels of Measurement

In addition to considering whether to use natural or contrived measures as well as deciding the number of indicators, there is yet another important consideration for the operationalization process. We must decide the "level" at which we will measure our variables. There are four levels to consider: nominal, ordinal, interval, and ratio. To understand the differences between these levels of measurement, we need to consider the connection between numbers and the measurement process. And to make this connection clear, we also need to introduce a new definition of measurement.

> **Measurement** – the process by which numbers are attached to the values of variables (alternate: the process by which abstract concepts are translated into empirical indicators).

In the section "Bringing Theory Down to Earth" we defined measurement as the process by which we translate abstract concepts into concrete variables. But in order to better understand the various levels of measurement, we must further specify this definition. That is, measurement entails a *numerical* translation: it is the process by which we attach numbers to the values of variables. (All variables, by definition, have more than one value. If an entity has only one value it is called a constant.) (See Chapter 2, "Variables" for a quick review of the difference between variables and values.)

Why the switch in definitions? While perhaps not apparent at first glance, there is a logic to using numbers in the measurement process. First, it resonates with how many of us think about, and go about, measurement in our day-to-day lives. Tape measures are marked with numbers to indicate inches and feet. Eye exams yield a numerical report of our vision: for example 20/20 or 20/30. Blood pressure is conveyed with numbers: 80/120. Think about the simple task of baking or cooking. Measurement is central to this endeavor and recipes utilize numbers to guide the cook: 1 cup flour; ¾ teaspoon salt, 3 eggs, and so on. Or think about the typical response when you notice your clothes feel tighter. We step on a scale and note how many pounds (in numbers) we have gained. And so we should not be surprised to see that researchers also come to rely on employing numbers in the name of measuring variables of interest. Indeed, for the researcher, there are two rather persuasive reasons. Numbers are able to add some much desired precision to the measurement process. (The cook will readily appreciate this point. A recipe calling for ½ cup of sugar is better than one calling for *some* sugar.) We could "measure" the variable height by noting that someone is short, medium height, or tall. But in the name of precision, it works much better to express height via numbers: 6' 7" Using numbers in the measurement process also advances the cause of statistical analysis. Indeed certain statistical procedures (e.g. calculating means or standard deviations or running regression analysis) *require* the use of meaningful numbers in the measurement process.

So defining measurement as the process by which we attach numbers to the values of variables is not as strange as it might first sound. Still, as we think about this definition some more, we should also come to appreciate that the "fit" between numbers and the variables we want to measure is not always a good one; it can vary from good to poor. Consider first a "good" fit, for example, the variable "yearly salary." The values of the salary variable can range from no salary at all (if one is unemployed) to millions of dollars (if one is a CEO of a major corporation). By way of measuring the salary variable, attaching numbers to the different values of the salary variable works quite well. We can report the values as the actual number of dollars earned (e.g. zero dollars for the unemployed, or $43,000.00 for an "average" worker in Texas or $5,546,000.00 for the average CEO in Texas).[2] Or consider the variable height. The values of the height variable can easily be expressed as numbers: NBA star LeBron James is 6' 8" tall while Kevin Durant is 6' 9".

Now let us switch the focus and consider a variable where numbers are a rather poor fit for the values of the variable. Consider the variable gender. In general, we recognize gender as having two values: male and female. If you think about it for a moment, attaching numbers to the values of the gender variable does not make any intuitive sense at all. It is not *obviously* meaningful to express a person's gender as "1" (whereas it is meaningful to express salary as a number – e.g. $45,500). Still attach numbers we must if we want to live up to our definition of measurement. So, in the name of *measuring* gender, researchers might use the number 1 to denote male and the number 2 to denote the value female. (Or we could reverse it and use 1 to denote female and 2 to denote male since the numbers are only "labels" for the values.) We face similar incongruities when measuring variables such as religious or political affiliations, race, ethnicity, marital status, and so on. Attaching numbers to the values of any of these variables simply does not make any immediate sense.

To indicate the fit (or lack thereof) between numbers and the values of the variables being measured, researchers distinguish various levels of measurement: nominal, ordinal, interval, and ratio. As we move from nominal to ordinal to interval and lastly to ratio levels of measurement, the "fit" between numbers and the values of variables improves (i.e. attaching numbers to the values starts to make more sense). Or to put it another way: while attaching numbers to the values of nominal variables has no inherent meaning, as we increase our level of measurement to ordinal and interval and finally to ratio, the "sense" or the logic of using numbers in the measurement process becomes more apparent or meaningful. The reason for this improvement lies with some properties we attribute to numbers themselves.

Think back to when you were just learning your numbers for the first time. We were drilled a lot – put through our paces to make sure we learned the number system. In particular, we were taught four specific features of the number system. First, we were taught the *identity property* of numbers (although chances are that your teachers did not use this formal language). The identity property merely asserts that each number has its own unique identity or name: 1 is recognized as different from 2 or 3. And even though they use the same two digits, the number 12 is different from the number 21 and so on. Teachers quizzing us on this property would write numbers on the board and ask us to call out the correct name, remember? (Organized sports take advantage of the identify property of numbers when they assign players a number for their uniforms: Now batting for the Yankees, number 7, the great Mickey Mantle! Those were the days.)

We also learned about the *magnitude property* of numbers. The magnitude property of numbers refers to the fact that we recognize that there is an "order" to the numbers in the number system: some numbers are "smaller", and some are "bigger", than others. Recall your first grade experience of learning your numbers. Not only did you have to get the "names" (identity) of the various numbers correct but you also had to recite them in the correct order: 1, 2, 3, 4, and so on. We were frequently drilled on this learning as well when we were asked to recite numbers from 1 to 10 or 1 to 100 and corrected if we got any of them out of the right order! (Popular culture makes great use of the magnitude properties of numbers: 4 star restaurants are seen as superior to 1 star restaurants. A four ticket stub rating means a movie is a "must see.")

Numbers also have an "equal intervals" property. This property refers to the fact that we recognize the *distance between any two adjacent* numbers to be equal no matter where the numbers fall in the number system. The distance between 1 and 2 is the same as the distance between 2 and 3 or between 99 and 100. Rulers were often used by way of showing us this property. Take a look at a standard ruler or yardstick and you will get a good "visual" of the equal intervals property. The space between the ruler markings for 1 and 2 inches is the same distance as the space between 7 and 8 inches.

And lastly, as we mastered learning our numbers we also learned that zero in the number system had a special meaning: 0 means the true absence of something. This lesson was often taught by showing students a classic subtraction exercise. The teacher would place three objects on the desk and then take all three away and ask how many objects were left? We would proudly yell zero (if we had learned our lessons well!) As it turns out, understanding the four levels of measurement detailed here turns on our recognizing the significance of each of these four properties of the number system we learned way back in elementary school.

Nominal Level of Measurement

When the numbers we attach to the values of a variable are merely labels used for identifying qualitative differences between values, we are measuring the variable at the **nominal level**. Here the numbers used are simply names (ergo the term nominal) or labels for the various values. Nominal level measures utilize the "identity" property of numbers. The variable gender is a classic example of a nominal level measure. The numbers attached to the values male and female are nothing more than numerical labels (codes) for qualitatively different values or categories. And so when asking: "What is your gender?" the researcher might offer the options: 1. Male; 2. Female and increasingly in these times of changing gender politics, 3. Other. Similarly, variables such as "religious affiliation," "political affiliation," or "race," are typically measured at the nominal level – that is, the numbers attached to the values of each of these variables are merely used to label (identify) the categorical differences between the values on each variable.

> **Nominal level measure** – one that uses numbers to identify or label the values of a variable; aka categorical measure.

What is your political affiliation?

1. Democrat
2. Republican
3. Independent
4. Other

Ordinal Level of Measurement

The numbers attached to the values of a variable can do more than merely label or identify values. They might also indicate a ranking or ordering of the values – the variable values labeled with the number 1 might be less than the values labeled with the number 2 which in turn might be less than the values labeled with the number 3. When this is the case (i.e. when the numbers are indicating an ordering of the values) we are measuring the variable at the **ordinal level**.

> **Ordinal level measure** – one that uses numbers to rank order the values of a variable.

With regard to the properties of number, ordinal level measures make use of two properties: identity and magnitude. In developing ordinal level measures, then, we incorporate these two properties, identity and magnitude, into our measures. For instance, in measuring the variable education, we might use the following values: (1) less than high school graduate, (2) high school graduate, (3) some college, (4) college graduate, (5) more than college degree. If you look at the numbers attached to each of these values they not only identify different levels of education but they are "ordered" so as to indicate an increasing magnitude of the values – that is, an increasing amount of education. Similarly, "interest in politics" could be measured at the ordinal level:

How would you describe your interest in politics?

1. No interest
2. Low
3. Moderate
4. High

Interval level measure – one that uses numbers to identify, order and indicate equal distance between the values of a variable.

Interval Level of Measurement

Sometimes the numbers attached to the values of variables can do more than merely label or indicate the "order" of the values. Sometimes the numbers actually indicate an exact and equal distance between the values of a variable. When this is the case, the variable is measured at the **interval level**. In devising interval measures, we are utilizing three separate properties of numbers: identity, magnitude, and the equal intervals properties. The interval level of measurement is illustrated by the variable temperature. When temperature is measured using a Fahrenheit thermometer, the numbers on the thermometer indicate various distinct values (ordered from low to high) that are *an equal distance* from each other. A temperature of 34° is *exactly* two intervals above freezing (in Fahrenheit, water freezes at 32°). A temperature of 30° is *exactly* two intervals below freezing. Similarly, IQ scores also illustrate the interval level of measurement. We recognize equal distances between scores: an IQ of 150 is five intervals more than an IQ score of 145. There is a two-interval difference between a score of 100 and 98. Interval level measures, then, are considered "higher" than ordinal because they are conveying more information via the numbers used: identity, order or magnitude of, and set distance between values.

Ratio Level of Measurement

When the numbers attached to the values of a variable indicate real quantities or amounts of the variable, we have reached the **ratio level** of measurement. Ratio level measures also take advantage of all four properties of numbers: identity, magnitude, equal intervals and a true and meaningful zero. If we measure income as the total number of dollars earned last year, we have a ratio level measure. Reporting and income of

Ratio level measure – one that uses numbers to express values of variables as real numbers or counts; aka quantitative measures.

$0 indicates no dollars earned. If person A reports an income of $40,000 and person B reports an income of $30,000, person A earned a higher income and one that was exactly $10,000 dollars above person B. If we measure education as the total number of years in school, we have a ratio level measure – the number will be a "real" number featuring all four properties of numbers. If we measure pet lover via the total number of pets owned, we have a ratio level measure. (A quick way to recognize a ratio level variable is to ask if the measurement entails an exercise in "counting" – How many books did you read over the summer? How many children do you have? If measurement entails *counting*, it is a ratio level measure.) The ratio level of measurement is regarded as the highest level of measurement because there is a perfect fit between the use of numbers and the values of the variable being measured. It is the highest level of measurement also because it features the most properties of numbers – all four. Ratio level variables are truly *quantitative* measures. Ratio level measures are also regarded as the highest level of measurement because quantitative measures permit the most sophisticated data analysis – that is, analysis that entails mathematical manipulation of *real* numbers.

Box 5.4   Sharpening your research vision: "seeing" the difference between interval and ratio level measures

At first glance, many find it difficult to see the difference between interval level measures and ratio level measures. (Indeed SPSS treats the two levels as indistinguishable and refers to them both as "scale" measures.) The two can be easily distinguished in terms of one characteristic. Ratio level measures have true and meaningful zeros; interval level measures do not. If I report zero income for last year, my zero means the absence of income. If I report zero symptoms on a health measure, the zero indicates the true absence of any symptoms. However, if I report the outside temperature to be zero, I do not mean there is an absence of outside temperature. Instead, a temperature of zero means it is very, very cold outside. A zero in an interval level measure is arbitrary, not absolute; it does not mean the absence of the entity being measured. And since interval measures have arbitrary zero points, such measures can also have negative values. So, it is totally possible when measuring temperature with the Fahrenheit thermometer to find values below zero: for example, the temperature in Minnesota or Siberia might be a −35° or −50°.

One additional point about levels of measurement needs to be considered. It is the *researcher* who must make decisions about levels of measurement (i.e. levels are not necessarily *dictated* by the variables themselves). Very often, any one variable can be measured at several different levels of measurement. Again, consider the yearly salary variable. We might measure this variable at the nominal level by asking the following:

> Did you earn a salary in 2015?
>
> 1.   yes
> 2.   no

We might also measure this variable at the ordinal level:

> What was your salary for 2015?
>
> 1.   no salary for 2015
> 2. $1–$15,000
> 3. $15.001–$30,000
> 4. $30,001–$60,000
> 5. $60,001–$90,000
> 6.   more than $90,000

And we might also measure the variable at the ratio level by asking respondents to tell us their exact salary for 2015:

> What was your personal salary for 2015? (please specify an exact dollar figure)_____.

The decision regarding which level to use is one of the most important decisions a researcher makes and should be considered very early in the planning stages of research. While there is a general agreement that higher levels of measurement are better than lower levels, there is also the possibility that higher levels of measurement require a degree of specificity or respondent knowledge that may undercut the measurement process. For instance, respondents may not be able to, or want, to reveal their exact yearly salary (the information required for the ratio level of measurement). But they may be able and willing to supply information about their *salary range* (the information required for an ordinal measure of income). Similarly, respondents may be reluctant to give their exact age (and some may fib when forced to do so) but they may be willing to indicate their age range. Such considerations are most relevant when making level of measurement decisions. In deciding levels of measurement, the researcher should also think ahead to the kind of statistical analysis planned in their study. Lower level measures preclude certain statistical analysis. The researcher who plans on using regression analysis or path analysis does not want to find their plans derailed by realizing too late that their key variables were measured at levels that are not compatible with these statistical techniques.

Table 5.2   Levels of measurement

Level	Numbers used to
Nominal	identify values
Ordinal	identify and order values
Interval	identify, order and show equal spacing of values
Ratio	express values in true quantitative terms (counts or amounts)

Operational Definitions

When we have satisfactorily transformed concepts into variables (the abstract into the concrete) and grappled with the level
of measurement we want to achieve, we are ready to complete
the measurement process by stipulating or stating full operational definitions. **Operational definitions** offer a detailed
statement regarding how variables are measured – they specify

> **Operational definition** – an empirically
> based definition of a variable that indicates
> all of the steps required to actually measure
> the variable.

the exact steps or procedures employed when carrying out the measurement process. It is perhaps most useful to think of operational definitions as "recipes" for measurement. Just as recipes
tell us the exact ingredients and steps that go into producing an entrée or a dessert, the operational definition tells us the ingredients and steps required to successfully measure a concept.

Once again, consider our alienation example. In our research we may decide to focus on
just two of the four separate dimensions of alienation: loss of involvement in the activity of
working and one's sense of estrangement from fellow workers. An operational definition of
the loss of involvement in work dimension might specify that we ask the following concrete
questions by way of measuring the abstraction:

- In the past month, how many times did you call in sick to work?
- In the past year, how many times did you skip department meetings?
- In the past year, how many times did you file a grievance at work?
- In your working career, how many times have you quit a job?

An operational definition for the dimension that focuses on our estrangement from fellow
workers might require that we ask the following questions:

- In the past month, how many times did you have lunch with co-workers?
- In the past month, how many times did you socialize with co-workers outside of the
  job?
- In the past month, how many times did you discuss personal matters with a co-worker?[3]

In listing these questions, have we completed the operationalization process? Not quite.
Typically, operational definitions are not fully specified by simply listing questions or
indicators. Complete operational definitions require more detail than this. (Think about
the analogy to recipes. It is not sufficient to merely list ingredients. We typically need some
guidance about amounts, mixing, combining, baking time, etc.) A thorough operational
definition should really "instruct" us on how we might conduct the measurement process ourselves. The researcher, for instance, should also indicate whether questions will be
followed by a list of close-ended responses or if the respondents will be invited to supply
their own answers. If multiple questions will be used to measure a concept, the research
should indicate how the specific items will be combined to yield total values on the variable. For example, if four separate ordinal level questions are used to measure the concept
of alienation, the researcher should specify the acceptable range of values that results from
combining the questions into a summary score. If the measurement process depends on the
researcher making observations rather than asking questions, the operational definition
must instruct us on how to carry out the observation process.

Consider the following example of an operational definition used to measure the concept of pedestrian cautiousness. In this example, the researcher observes (rather than questions) individuals as they are about to cross an intersection. As you read through the example, think about whether or not the researcher has provided enough detail to allow us to execute this measure on our own:

Pieces of tape were placed unobtrusively on the sidewalk leading into the intersections at intervals of 1 foot or less from the curb, 2 feet from the curb, and 3 feet or beyond. Pairs of observers noted the distance from the roadway at which pedestrians stood while waiting to cross; they also noted whether pedestrians checked for oncoming traffic by recording when the pedestrians explicitly moved their head to the left or right to look for traffic. Those who first stepped into the intersection and then moved their heads were not counted as checking, nor were those who may have used peripheral vision rather than moving their heads. Pedestrians were retained for observation only if they were fully stopped at a crosswalk before the light changed and if there were in the front row (i.e. the group closest to the curb). The measure of caution was constructed by adding together a subject's score on curb position and traffic checking. A person standing 1 foot or less from the curb was assigned a value of 1; a person 2 feet away, a value of 2; and a person 3 feet or more away, a value of 3. A person who did not check for traffic was assigned a value of 0, a person who looked in only one direction was given a value of 1, and a person looking both ways received a value of 2. (Harrell 1991)

Box 5.5   Newsworthy research: "A spoonful of sugar helps the medicine go down"

Anyone familiar with Mary Poppins knows that this was her directive on how to get kids to take their medicines. But a recent study reveals that there is a problem with the operational definition of a "spoonful." As it turns out, a "spoonful" is not an adequate measurement instruction. According to the study, parents using spoons to administer liquid medicines were 50 percent more likely to make dangerous dosing errors than parents using droppers. So, the lesson here? Operational definitions are important not only in research but for our health care as well! Take care and measure well.

Source: http://americanlivewire.com/2014–07–14–spoonful-measurement-medications-spell-trouble/.

Good Operational Definitions Aid Replication

Specifying operational definitions as detailed instructions for measurement helps support a defining characteristic of science: replication. If we report the exact steps and procedures we use in the measurement process, we then give other researchers the tools and information they need to reproduce our research efforts. Recall from Chapters 1 and 2 that replication is an important feature of science – only findings that are replicated are considered trustworthy and reliable information. If we fail to specify our operational definitions, we block the all-important work of replication.

Box 5.6   Sharpening your research vision: the Rosenberg Self-Esteem Scale

Here are the exact items and a set of instructions (the operational definition) for using the Rosenberg Self-Esteem Scale.

Present the items with these instructions. Do not print the asterisks on the sheet you provide to respondents.

BELOW IS A LIST OF STATEMENTS DEALING WITH YOUR GENERAL FEELINGS ABOUT YOURSELF. IF YOU STRONGLY AGREE, CIRCLE SA. IF YOU AGREE WITH THE STATEMENT, CIRCLE A. IF YOU DISAGREE, CIRCLE D. IF YOU STRONGLY DISAGREE, CIRCLE SD.

		1. Strongly agree	2 Agree	3. Disagree	4. Strongly disagree
1.	I feel that I'm a person of worth, at least on an equal plane with others.	SA	A	D	SD
2.	I feel that I have a number of good qualities.	SA	A	D	SD
3.	All in all, I am inclined to feel that I am a failure.**	SA	A	D	SD
4.	I am able to do things as well as most other people.	SA	A	D	SD
5.	I feel I do not have much to be proud of.**	SA	A	D	SD
6.	I take a positive attitude toward myself.	SA	A	D	SD
7.	On the whole, I am satisfied with myself.	SA	A	D	SD
8.	I wish I could have more respect for myself.**	SA	A	D	SD
9.	I certainly feel useless at times.**	SA	A	D	SD
10.	At times I think I am no good at all.**	SA	A	D	SD

1. To score the items, assign a value to each of the 10 items as follows:
• For items 1,2,4,6,7: Strongly Agree=3, Agree=2, Disagree=1, and Strongly Disagree=0.
• For items 3,5,8,9,10 (which are reversed in valence, and noted with the asterisks** below): Strongly Agree=0, Agree=1, Disagree=2, and Strongly Disagree=3.
2. The scale ranges from 0–30, with 30 indicating the highest score possible. Other scoring options are possible. For example, you can assign values 1–4 rather than 0–3; then scores will range from 10–40. Some researchers use 5– or 7–point Likert scales, and again, scale ranges would vary based on the addition of "middle" categories of agreement.

Source: Rosenberg, Morris. 1989. Society and the Adolescent Self-Image. Revised edition. Middletown, CT: Wesleyan University Press. *http://www.socy.umd.edu/quick-links/rosenberg-self-esteem-scale.*

By now some of you may be feeling a bit overwhelmed by all of the decisions that need to be made with regard to measurement. But here is the good news – news you have heard before. When it comes to making measurement decisions, there is help awaiting you in … a good literature review. One of the *best* reasons to invest in a thorough review of research on a given topic is to discover how others approached and solved the measurements issues. Every good research article that lays claim to following the rules of science will present information about how they measured key variables. Indeed, this is such a standard practice in research methods, that there is actually a section in every research article devoted to reporting on measurement issues: the methods section of an article. Scroll through any article to its methods section and you will find discussions of details about how variables were measured: that is, the names of "borrowed" indexes or scales, the levels of measurement, any available information about the measures' validity and reliability and in some cases (issues we will take up in the next chapter), an exact copy of the measured used (if presented, it is likely to be in an appendix). Look and you shall receive! Why such a "gift"? The answer is in keeping with one of the key traits of science: science values replication (see Chapter 1). But to engage in replication, researchers *must* share the details of how they conducted their studies and in particular how they measured their key variables. So yes, empirical measurement is key to good research but you can get major assistance from a good literature review.

Conclusion

From our earliest years, we learn how to see the world and communicate with each other via concepts. We are conceptual beings. Research, however, with its feet firmly planted in the empirical world, puts a slightly different spin on our conceptual nature. Our earliest training teaches us how to move from the concrete (seeing a creature with four legs and a tail) to the abstract (invoking the word "dog" as a name or label for the four-legged, tail-wagging creature). Our training in research methods asks us to reverse the directional flow of our early learning. Concepts and theories present us with abstract explanations of the world around us. If we hope to test these theories, we must be able to locate clear empirical representations or counterparts for the ideas/concepts presented in theoretical explanations. This step requires us to reverse our usual practice of moving from the concrete to the abstract. Research requires us to translate concepts into variables; it requires us to move from the abstract to the empirical. Seeing the world in the language of variables requires some practice – after all we are "wired" to be conceptual. Making this "down-to-earth" adjustment, however allows us to get on with the business of research.

> ### TAKE AWAYS
> - Research must confront and accommodate the conceptual nature of humans
> - The theory/research connection is an important one:
>   - Theory consists of concepts that must be translated into corresponding variables for the research process
> - Operationalization decisions:
>   - Natural or contrived measures
>   - Product or behavioral measures

- Item or composite measures
- Conceptual definitions are key to good measurement
- Conceptual definitions …
  - Clarify the meaning of abstract concepts
  - Are the starting point for the measurement process
- Operational definitions provide step-by-step detailed instructions for the measurement process
- Levels of measurement …
  - Are part of the translation process
  - Specify the "fit" between numbers and the values of variables
- Nominal level measures use numbers as labels for the values of variables: Gender: 1. Male 2. Female
- Ordinal level measures use numbers to label and "order" values of variables: Social Class: 1. Lower 2. Middle 3. Upper
- Interval level measures use numbers to label, order and indicate exact distances between values of variables: Temperature: 32°
- Ratio level measures use numbers as the actual values of variables: Number of children in ideal family: 2

Sharpening the Edge: More Reading and Searching

- As you read through this book, you will notice how often the concept of happiness is used in examples. If you are interested in finding out how happy you are at your work, you might want to visit the following web site:

  https://www.happinessatworksurvey.com/

  If you agree to take their survey, please give special attention to how they have operationalized the concept of happiness. Also note the various levels of measurement utilized throughout the survey.
- A quick way to see the connection between concepts and variables is by visiting the GSS web site. This web site lists the various concepts addressed by survey questions. Visitors can select concepts and "click" on them to activate a link to the exact questions (the operational definitions) used on the GSS as measures of the concept. Use the following steps to the see the concept/variable connection for yourself:
  1. Access the GSS homepage: http:www.icpsr.umich.edu/gss/home.htm
  2. Click on the Site Map
  3. Click on the Subject Index
  4. Find a concept of interest to you
  5. Click on it to see its corresponding GSS questions
- Good discussions of both theory and the conceptualization process are offered by Earl Babbie in his book:

  Observing Ourselves: Essays in Social Research (1998)

  In particular, see the chapters entitled "Paradigms" and "Making Distinctions."

- You can find some sociological dictionaries that can prove helpful in the conceptualization process online:

  The Open Education Sociology Dictionary: http://sociologydictionary.org/
  Sociology Guide.com: http://www.sociologyguide.com/basic-concepts/
  The Babylon 10 dictionary: http://dictionary.babylon.com/alienation/

Exercises

1 Review the four dimensions of alienation offered by Erikson (in the section "Operationalization"). Go to the GSS homepage and find the questions used to measure alienation. Assess the adequacy of the GSS questions as operationalizations for each of the four dimensions of alienation.

2 For each of the following concepts: (a) offer a clear conceptual definition and (b) suggest two questions or observations you think would be good ways of empirically documenting the concepts.

   - patriots
   - binge drinking
   - innovation
   - infantilization
   - hooking up.

3 Select one of the following concepts and devise three different operational definitions (OD) for the concept but make each OD represent a different level of measurement (i.e. nominal, ordinal, interval, or ratio).

   - Concepts:
   - couch potato
   - aggressive driver
   - a helicopter parent.

4 Use the following links to access Cheek and Buss's 13 item shyness measure (http://academics.wellesley.edu/Psychology/Cheek/research.html) and the UCLA loneliness index: http://fetzer.org/sites/default/files/images/stories/pdf/selfmeasures/Self_Measures_for_Loneliness_and_Interpersonal_Problems_UCLA_LONELINESS.pdf. Examine the items that make up each index and indicate: (a) the level of measurement achieved in each item, (b) the level of measurement achieved for the overall score generated by adding the items together.

5 Select a concept of interest to you and try your hand at devising multiple measures of that concept by using the matrix found in Table 5.1. For instance, imagine devising contrived vs. natural, and product vs. behavioral measures of happiness. A contrived product measure would be a happiness index. A natural behavioral measure might be listening for workers who whistle or sing while they work. See how creative you can be with your selected concept.

6 Do a literature search for articles about optimism. Try to find two or three different operational definitions that have been used by researchers to measure optimism. Which operational definition do you think is most "on target"?

Notes

1 http://academics.wellesley.edu/Psychology/Cheek/research.html.

2 These figures come from the AFl-CIO Average CEO Pay By State: http://www.aflcio.org/Corporate-Watch/Pay-watch-2014/CEO-Pay-by-State "Executive Paywatch": http://www.aflcio.org/cgi-bin/aflcio.pl.

3 Can you identify the level of measurement achieved in each of the above questions?

References

Babbie, Earl. 1998. *Observing Ourselves: Essays in Social Research*. Prospect Heights, IL: Waveland Press.

Black, Donald. 1976. *The Behavior of Law*. New York: Academic Press.

Durkheim, Emile. 1951. *Suicide*. New York: Free Press.

Erikson, Kai. 1986. "Work and Alienation." *American Sociological Review* 51 (February): 1–8.

Harrell, W. Andrew. 1991. "Factors Influencing Pedestrian Cautiousness in Crossing Streets." *Journal of Social Psychology* 131(3): 367–372.

Hirschi, Travis. 1969. *Causes of Delinquency*. University of California Press.

Theodorson, George and Achilles Theodorson. 1969. *A Modern Dictionary of Sociology*. New York: Barnes & Noble Books.

Chapter 6

All That Glitters Is Not Gold: Assessing the Validity and Reliability of Measures

Introducing Social Research Methods: Essentials for Getting the Edge, First Edition. Janet M. Ruane.
© 2016 John Wiley & Sons, Ltd. Published 2016 by John Wiley & Sons, Ltd.

FIRST TAKES

Be sure to take note of the following:

Good research requires quality measures – how can we be sure we have them? We must put measures through their paces

- Validity tests
  - Face
  - Content
  - Criterion
    - Predictive
    - Concurrent
- Reliability tests
  - Test-retest
  - Multiple forms
  - Split-half technique
- Measurement error – it is inevitable; idea is to control it
  - Noise
    - Many sources
  - Bias
    - Many sources

Anyone who has studied a foreign language knows all too well that some translations do not faithfully restate the original text. There is a Flickr group devoted to documenting phrases/sayings that get "lost in translation" (see https://www.flickr.com/groups/badtranslations/). As indicated in Chapter 5, whenever we translate mental abstractions into their empirical counterparts we must worry about similar problems regarding the accuracy of our translations. Does the number of toys given to a child accurately measure parental love? Does the size of an engagement ring measure a fiancé's affection? (I can see some heads nodding on this one!) Was the grade you received in your last math class an accurate measure of your knowledge of the course material? Is our "fear of crime" accurately measured by a question that asks if we are afraid to walk alone at night? In this chapter we review the various tools available to the scientist for establishing whether or not our measures are truly trustworthy or accurate. In the first part of the chapter, we look at various ways the researcher can assess a measure's validity (i.e. the extent to which it is measuring what it claims to measure). In the second part of the chapter we also address another important consideration when assessing measures: reliability. With this issue, we try to assess the extent to which a measure is able to deliver consistent or "stable" results. In conducting both reviews, we move from rather simple to more discerning tests.

Box 6.1   Comme on dit? How do you say?

Consider what happened when the following playground sign was translated from English into Spanish:

English:
   "Parental or guardian supervision is required for the use of this playground equipment. Play at your own risk."

Spanish translation:
   "Ustedes debe tener un permiso terra jugar un este campo. Violadores seran susceptibiles a accion policial."

In translating the Spanish back into English, this is what we get:
   "You should have a permit to play in this field. Violators will be susceptible to police action."

http://www.nydailynews.com/news/national/playground-signs-send-messages-english-spanish-article-1.1234911.

Measurement Validity

As indicated repeatedly in this book, the skeptical nature of scientific research demands that we put our measures of variables to the test. We must be concerned with assessing if they really do measure what they claim to measure and a number of options are available for assessing the validity or accuracy of a measure. The following sections consider tests for face validity, content validity, criterion validity and construct validity. Remember, these "tests" are presented in an order from less to more discerning or rigorous assessments.

Face Validity

The least we can ask of any concrete indicator of a mental abstraction is that it satisfies the condition of **face validity**. Assessing a measure for its face validity merely requires that we ask if the measure "looks good" on surface (face) inspection. If the "empirical translation" does not look right (or sound right) then it lacks face validity. For instance, some researchers maintain that the GSS measure of fear of crime (Is there any area right around here – that is, within a mile – where you would be afraid to walk alone at night?) lacks face validity. Critics complain that a question that asks about being afraid of walking alone at night lacks any clear or apparent connection to the concept "fear of crime." Or consider measuring the concept of "technological savvy" by asking if one knows how to use a phone. On the face of it, this measure is not very

> **Face validity** – claiming a measure is accurate because it "looks" right or appears to be getting the job done; a subjective assessment of validity.

convincing. It would be very hard to find someone in this day and age who is not familiar with how phones work so merely knowing how to use one may not be a great way to measure technological savvy. Similarly, measuring "college level math ability" with a series of simple multiplication problems does not measure up on face validity. Or think about how to measure happiness – doing so by observing if people stomp their feet raises some face validity concerns. Even claiming to be able to measure happiness by the presence or absence of a smile lacks face validity for many. Just think about the day-to-day work of flight attendants or waitresses – smiles do not always convey happiness. (See Hochschild's research on emotion work for further consideration of this issue.)

As each of the preceding examples shows, face validity is a very *subjective* test of validity. It is possible (even likely) that two different individuals might elicit two very different assessments of the face validity of a measure. What looks good to one might strike another as totally inadequate. Because of this equivocation, face validity is not considered a very demanding or convincing test of validity. While all measures should at minimum possess face validity, many researchers are not willing to settle for this most basic form of measurement validity. Pushing beyond face validity is staying true to the skeptical nature of scientific research.

Box 6.2   Newsworthy research: facing off the vote

Every major election finds polling organizations trying to get a fix on who the public will elect. In conducting their polls, the focus is typically on "likely voters." But just who is the likely voter? Not surprisingly, different polls employ different measures of the likely voter. The Gallup organization uses a series of seven questions to determine if someone is a likely voter. The Pew Research Center on the other hand determined "likely voters" via some combination of seven to nine questions.

Gallup wound up miscalling the 2012 presidential election – it had Romney winning by a very slim margin. Some feel that its "likely voter" measure was part of the reason for its error. Their measure of likely voter filtered out too many young and minority voters, two groups that were more likely to vote for Obama.

Sources: Sheppard (2012); Keeter (2012).

Content Validity

Content validity assesses how good a fit is obtained between conceptual and operational definitions – i.e. do the conceptual and operational definitions coincide or overlap?[1] Recall from Chapter 5 that conceptual (aka nominal) definitions offer theoretical clarifications of concepts. Operational definitions specify the steps or procedures involved in empirically documenting a concept. In determining

Content validity – asserting a measure is accurate because it addresses all dimensions or component of the concept's nominal definition.

content validity one is really assessing if the full *content* of the nominal definition is realized or addressed in the operational definition. This, of course, is just another way of asking the essential question of measurement validity: is the measure really measuring what it claims to measure? A few examples should help make the point.

Imagine that a researcher is interested in studying problem drinking. She uses the following nominal definition of problem drinking that she found while doing a literature search: drinking that is used to escape personal problems or that results in some kind of trouble (Thompson 1989). She measures problem drinking with the following question: Do you ever drink to escape life pressures? If this were the only question asked, the measure would be judged as lacking content validity. The full content of the nominal definition is not represented in the one question used to measure problem drinking – that is, our imaginary researcher failed to ask any questions about drinking that *results in some kind of trouble*. In order to achieve content validity, the researcher would need to ask at least one more question – one that inquired about the negative consequences of drinking.

Or consider another example. Poverty is an important issue in any society and certainly warrants accurate measurement. If we follow our own advice offered in Chapter 5, we should first clarify the meaning of poverty. Poverty is a complex concept – it indicates a deficit on two fronts: income (earnings) and assets (savings, home equity, stocks, etc.) The lack of income means that people and families have a hard time "getting by." The lack of assets, on the other hand, means that people and families have a hard time "getting ahead." So with this conceptual clarification, we can now ask how poverty is measured. Do the measures used address *both* components or dimensions of poverty? In the United States, poverty is measured with regard to income, assets are not addressed.[2] Critics of this income only approach maintain that it lacks content validity for the overall reality of poverty. An "income only" measure hides a much deeper and disheartening reality of "asset poverty." The asset poor receive virtually no help from the government. Yet those dedicated to helping the poor maintain that it is the lack of assets that keep so many impoverished individuals from any chance or hope of upward mobility.

Content validity is an important consideration whenever a researcher is working with complex, multidimensional concepts. If concepts are defined as having more than one dimension (as with the problem drinking and poverty examples), then multiple items must be used to document the concept. Consider a standard physical exam. Health is a complex concept and requires many different forms of assessment. Consequently, during a yearly physical, physicians will run many different tests (measures) to document the patients' overall health. Or think about the concept of intelligence, again a very complex concept in that it encompasses many dimensions (e.g the ability to learn, the ability to adapt, the ability to problem-solve). With such a multidimensional conceptual definition, a valid measure of intelligence would need to assess all specified components. If you visit the webpage, IQTest.com (http://iqtest.com/) you will see that this organization claims that it offers the most valid IQ measure available. Its measure of IQ assesses 13 different components of intelligence. As is true for face validity, content validity is a subjective validity test. Essentially, judgments are made (often by experts in a field) as to whether or not the selected empirical indicators really do represent the full content of concept's nominal definition.

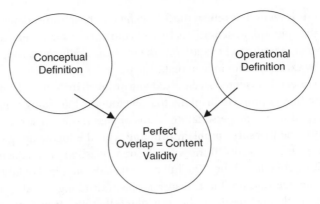

Figure 6.1   "Visualizing" Content Validity

Criterion Validity

Criterion validity – using empirical evidence to establish that a measure is measuring what it claims to measure.

Given that empirical evidence plays a central role in scientific inquiry, you may already be suspecting that some tests of validity demand more than subjective assessments. And indeed this is the case. **Criterion validity** (aka empirical validity) uses some kind of objective, empirical evidence in order to explicitly demonstrate the validity of measures. There are two common strategies for establishing criterion validity: demonstrating predictive validity and demonstrating concurrent validity.

Predictive Validity

Predictive validity – a form of criterion validity where a measure's ability to accurately predict something logically related to the measure is used as evidence of the measure's validity (i.e. to assess the predictive validity of a happiness measure, one might show how *high* happiness scores predict *low* depression scores).

With **predictive validity**, the researcher provides empirical evidence of a measure's validity by showing that the measure is able to accurately predict some outcome that should be logically related to the variable being measured. (Note that the outcome *must* be something different from the variable being measured. To predict that a measure will measure itself is nothing more than circular reasoning). The accuracy of the prediction is taken as objective evidence that the measure must be tapping what it claims to measure. If results support the prediction made, the measure is taken to be valid. If results do not support the prediction, the measure is seen as failing this test of validity. For example, imagine that someone has developed a 10-item measure (an index) of leadership ability. You examine the index items and while the items look good to you (i.e. they have face validity), you really cannot be sure if they measure leadership ability. You want some hard, empirical "proof." So what kind of "outcome" would be good evidence? Predictive validity for the measure could be demonstrated by the researcher predicting that individuals who score high on the leadership ability index will go on to actually occupy leadership roles or positions in an organization. (Future leadership *performance* would be an outcome that is logically related to leadership *ability*.) So, if the index were administered to 100 new hires in an organization, predictive validity could be claimed if after 12 months on the job, those with the highest leadership *ability scores* from 12 months earlier were actually occupying or advancing in leadership positions.

Now imagine a 20-item measure that alleges to document productive study skills in students. Having good study skills should lead to a predictable outcome: getting good grades. You could claim predictive validity for this measure if you could show that those students with the highest scores on the study skills measure were also the students with the highest grades at the end of a course. (High grades would be an outcome that is logically related to having productive study skills.) Or think again about polls that try to measure "likely voter" via a series of statements. Predictive validity could be demonstrated if researchers were able to show that those who scored high on the likely voter questions actually wound up voting in the election.

Let me review one more example from the research literature. Researchers were interested in assessing the validity of a six-item index for measuring adolescent risk-taking propensity (Alexander, Kim, Ensminger *et al.* 1990). To establish the validity of their index, the researchers predicted that there would be an association between high scores on the risk-taking index for eighth graders and their subsequent initiation of some risky behaviors as ninth graders. This is exactly what the researchers found – eighth-grade scores were associated with certain activities among ninth graders: namely the initiation of sexual activity among virgins and substance use among nonusers. Consequently, the researchers were able to claim predictive validity for their risk-taking measure.

Concurrent Validity

Concurrent validity puts a slightly different time spin on demonstrating validity. While predictive validity tests provide concrete evidence of measurement validity by making forecasts (predictions) about future outcomes, concurrent validity tests offer more timely "here and now" proof. I can demonstrate the concurrent validity of a measure by showing that the results I obtain with the measure are essentially the same as the results I obtain with another previously validated measure of the same concept. To run this test, I must administer two measures at the same time (concurrently): the one I am trying to validate along with a second measure that is already accepted to be valid. As objective proof of the new measure's validity I want to be able to show how the new measure generates scores or results that are very similar to the scores or results produced by the second already valid measure. In the end, this test is all about obtaining a high correlation between the scores of the new and the established measures. With concurrent validity, the objective evidence of my measure's validity is its ability to produce results that correlate highly with the results obtained via another established valid measure of the same concept. Again, some examples should help clarify this test.

> **Concurrent validity** – a form of criterion validity that uses an established valid measure of a variable to demonstrate the accuracy of another measure of the same variable.

Imagine that you are a medical researcher and you are working on a new procedure to measure whether or not someone has a rare genetic disorder. As it turns out, a valid test for the disorder already exists. The "old" test, however, is expensive and invasive and patients do not like to go through the procedure. (This is actually a fairly common situation in medical testing today.) Your goal is to develop a new test that is inexpensive and non-invasive. How could you prove the validity of your new test? You could administer both the old and the new procedures to the same patients in clinical trials. You can claim concurrent validity for your new procedure (measure) if it yields results that are essentially identical to the results obtained via the old procedure. The similar results would produce the high correlation "evidence" that you are looking for as proof of validity.

Or imagine that you are a smart entrepreneur looking for a way to cash in on the huge educational testing market. You know that students dread having to sit through the very long standardized tests used for admission to undergraduate and graduate study: SATs and GREs in the United States or A level exams in the United Kingdom. You decide to develop a new, shorter, more student-friendly version of these measures of academic potential. How will you prove your new short test is as good as the old long tests? If you can show that the scores obtained on the short test are highly correlated with those obtained on the old test, you will be able to claim concurrent validity for your new test (and smile all the way to the bank).

It is a common observation that humans are always looking for ways to "build a better mousetrap." Researchers are no exception to this maxim. There are many examples of researchers "tweaking" established measures in order to produce more efficient versions that are nonetheless as good as, if not better, than the originals. Consider for instance the many iterations of the most widely used measure of loneliness: the UCLA loneliness measure. It is presently in its third major modification – and with each modification findings regarding concurrent validity are issued (http://public.psych.iastate.edu/ccutrona/uclalone.htm). Or take a look at the modifications that have been made to the frequently utilized measure of shyness: Cheek and Buss's measure. Originally, the measure was a 9-item index and now there are both 20- and 13-item versions (both expanded versions correlate highly with the original 9-item index).[3]

Box 6.3   Newsworthy research: new test for pancreatic cancer is a valid success

For a truly inspirational review of how a 15-year-old developed a new "test" for detecting pancreatic cancer in its earliest (and most treatable) stage see the TEDx lecture by Jake Andraka. His new sensor technique is inexpensive and non-invasive and replaces a 60-year-old technique that misses about 30 percent of cancers and costs over $800. As you listen to the TED lecture, think about how Jake was able to demonstrate the validity of his new measure:

http://articles.mercola.com/sites/articles/archive/2013/03/04/andraka-new-pancreatic-cancer-test.aspx#!

Construct Validity

Construct validity – demonstrating the accuracy of a measure by showing it produces results consistent with theoretically based hypotheses or predictions.

There is one other validity assessment to consider – construct validity. Establishing the construct validity of a measure may well be the most demanding and involved validity test. To establish **construct validity** we use a combination of theory and hypothesis testing to demonstrate that our measures are valid ones. More precisely, we use theory to generate a series of **hypotheses** (i.e. statements that predict relationships between the measure we are trying to validate and a series of other variables). If we find support for the

> **Hypothesis** – a statement or prediction about an expected relationship between two variables.

hypotheses, we can claim construct validity for the measure we are evaluating. For instance, imagine that we are trying to assess the validity of a measure of legal social control. To test your measure you could work with Donald Black's theory of law (1976). According to Black's theory, the amount of law in society increases with culture, stratification, social integration, and social organization (as well as several other variables). If we find that our law measure behaves as hypothesized (i.e. we find an association between it and the other measures of culture, stratification, integration. etc.) we have demonstrated the construct validity of our legal social control measure.

Or imagine that you are trying to assess the validity of a new measure of social capital. Social capital refers to individuals' participation in community networks and activities. Social capital can vary greatly from individual to individual. Some of us have a lot of social capital, others have very little. A review of the literature on social capital indicates that it affects many other areas of life. For instance, social capital is hypothesized to be associated with lower stress levels, with higher feelings of self-fulfillment, with higher rates of trust, with greater accumulation of wealth, and with higher levels of education as well as with time spent on and experiences with social networking sites (Ahn 2012; Bourdieu 1986; Kraut, Kiesler, Boneva *et al.* 2001). To establish the construct validity of our measure of social capital, we would need to produce data that supported our specific social capital hypotheses: data that showed an inverse relationship between social capital and stress levels, a positive relationship between social capital and feelings of self-fulfillment, and so on.

Hopefully it is now clear that demonstrating criterion and construct validity requires much more work from the researcher than face or content validity. Indeed, demonstrating either criterion or construct validity would be small research projects in themselves. Consequently, if researchers have gone to the trouble of establishing these forms of validity they are likely to discuss their findings in their research reports. These discussions typically are presented in the methods sections of research articles (see Box 6.4 for an example).

Box 6.4 Excerpt providing evidence of validity (bold) and reliability (italics)

In the scale revision/construction sample of 326 college students the *alpha coefficient of internal consistency reliability for the 20-item shyness scales was .94 (M = 51.8; SD = 13.6)* and it **correlated .96 with the original Cheek & Buss 9-item shyness scale**. Melchior and Cheek (1990) reported that in a sample of 31 college women the 20-item scale had a *45-day test-retest reliability of 0.91*, **and correlated .69 with aggregated ratings of shyness received from family members and close friends**.

Source: The Revised Cheek and Buss Shyness Scale: *http://academics.wellesley.edu/Psychology/Cheek/research.html.*

Reliability Checks

In addition to asking if a measure is valid, we should also ask if it is reliable. In a court of law, reliable witnesses are those who can be counted on to stand by their testimony – that is, to tell the same story time after time (even under a heated cross-examination). So it is with reliable measures. A measure is considered **reliable** if it yields the same results each time it is used provided, of course, that there has been no real change in the variable being measured. In other words, reliable measures do not fluctuate – they yield *consistent* results.

> **Reliable measure** – one that produces or yields consistent or stable results.

Think about the standard device we use to measure our weight: a bathroom scale. If we were to step on and off a scale five times in a row, a reliable scale would give us the same reading each and every time. This exercise would demonstrate the reliability or the consistency of the scale. Now think about a notoriously unreliable measurement device: the standard air pressure gauge for our car tires. If you have had any experience with a simple, mechanical air-pressure gauge (the kind that resembles a writing pen in shape), you know first-hand that consistency is not often a characteristic of this tool! You attach the gauge to a tire valve and get a reading of 32 lb. You are not sure you had a snug fit so you repeat the procedure. The second time around the gauge reads 29 lb. Which reading is right? You try it a third time and find the same tire now has 33 lb. of air in it! What's going on? You are caught in the unreliable zone.

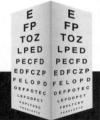

Box 6.5   Sharpening your research vision: the IKEA reliability idea

If you are a fan of IKEA you have probably seen some of their "testing" devices designed to show consumers that IKEA products stand the test of time. Walk through IKEA and you might see a kitchen drawer that has been opened and closed countless times. Or you might see a bed or couch that has withstood incessant "bouncing" tests (designed to simulate the conditions presented by kids or adults). In the final analysis, IKEA is all about showing consumers that their products are reliable – we can count on them performing as expected time after time. In research, reliable measures get the job done time after time.

Testing for Reliability

As with testing for validity, the researcher has several options to choose from when trying to assess the reliability of a measure. One test assesses consistency over time. Another assesses consistency across two forms or versions of a measure. And a third assesses the internal consistency of items in a composite measure.

Test-Retest

Both the earlier scale and tire pressure gauge examples illustrate the simplest technique we have for determining the reliability of a measure: the test-retest strategy. As the name implies, with test-retest we simply engage in the same measurement procedure two times and check to see if we get the same results both times. As empirical evidence of reliability, we look for a high correlation coefficient (ideally .80 or higher) between the two measurement outcomes or results. This all sounds simple enough and for the most part it is simple. There is one point, however, deserving of further consideration. How long should we wait between the "test" and "retest"?

> **Test-retest reliability check** – assessing the consistency of a measure by using it twice on the unit of analysis and looking for highly correlated results (provided there has been no real change in the subjects between the test and retest).

With the scale and tire gauge examples, the retesting could (and should) be done immediately. Take one measure, and then take it again. There is no complication with any immediate follow-up. The measurement devices (scales and tire gauges) cannot *remember* anything about each test and therefore cannot intentionally foil the researcher. (In fact, delaying the retest in these cases would be risky since both body weight and tire pressure could very well change over the course of time.) But now think about what might happen when we engage in some measurement involving human respondents (as opposed to scales or tire gauges). What if I were to give you a 10-item anxiety index and then immediately repeat the index so I can assess its reliability. What might happen? Chances are good that my repeating the measure will strike you as funny (or even anxiety-provoking). You may work very hard at trying to *remember* exactly how you responded the first time around and complete the second measure on the basis of memory. Think about the result: I will wind up with responses that *look* consistent between the test and retest but the consistency is "artificial," a byproduct of your good memory. So, can I avoid this problem just by waiting longer? Well, it depends on how long I decide to wait before doing the retest. Say I decide to wait a month – long enough so you could no longer remember your first set of responses. But what if I now find that your responses from the first test are very different from your responses to the second test. Does this mean my measure is unreliable? Not necessarily. By waiting the *extended* time period, I must now consider the possibility that your anxiety level has *really changed*. The low correlation between time one and time two results could reflect an unreliable index *or* it could reflect a real change in your anxiety level over time.

Clearly the time delay is an important consideration in the test-retest procedure. The researcher must find a happy medium or a Goldilocks moment where the time delay is neither too short nor too long between measurements. Take a look back at Box 6.4. You will see results from a 45-day test-retest assessment of the Cheek and Buss shyness measure. (What do you think … is 45 days between test and retest a reasonable time period for assessing a shyness measure?)

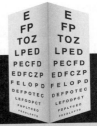

> **Box 6.6   Sharpening your research vision: "seeing" change – is it an unreliable measure or have things really changed?**
>
> The ability to assess the reliability of a measure via the test-retest technique is complicated by the fact that some variables are quite mercurial. Consider the variable political affiliation. Pollsters know all too well that this variable can change quickly (with major historical events) or change over the course of time (from week to week, from primaries to general elections or from one election cycle to another). In the months after 9/11 there was a substantial increase in the percentage of Americans calling themselves Republicans. In the 2008 presidential election, Pew Polls found that fully 15% of respondents changed their political affiliation between October 2008 and November 2008. Different results from time one to time two did not indicate a lack of reliability – it indicated how quickly people's attitudes can change.
>
> *Source:* Pew Research Center (2012)

Multiple-forms reliability check – assessing the consistency of a measure by using two forms of the measure and seeing if both forms yield highly correlated results.

Multiple-Forms Test

A researcher who has only one-time access to respondents (a likely condition in most cross-sectional, one moment in time survey research) should consider using a multiple-forms method for checking reliability. With this technique, two separate alternate versions of a measure are developed. The reliability of these measures can then be established by comparing the results obtained from each form. For good reliability, the results obtained via the two forms should be highly correlated.

The multiple-forms technique (aka alternate or parallel forms) is a fairly common strategy in survey research. For instance, experience has taught survey researchers that measures of age can be very unreliable. Indeed, demographers have long noted an amusing (but frustrating) tendency for people reporting age data: they find an age they like and then stick with it for several years! Consequently, survey researchers will often try to document the reliability of age measures via a multiple forms method. At one point in the survey, respondents may be asked to report their *age in years*. At another point in the survey they may be asked to list their *year of birth*. Phrasing the question in two different ways provides a multiple-forms scenario. Reliability is demonstrated if the results obtained from both questions are consistent.

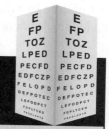

> ## Box 6.7 Sharpening your research vision: job applications – how reliable is the prospective employee?
>
> Perhaps you have had this experience when filling out a job application. Somewhere early on in the form, you are asked if you have ever been in trouble with the law. Later on you encounter a similar question but worded in a slightly different way. Did the employer lose track of the questions asked? No, what you encountered was a "reliability" check. Think of the two slightly different questions as illustrating the "multiple forms" reliability technique. If the two versions of the questions fail to produce consistent information, the chances are that the job applicant won't be getting a call back from the prospective employer.

The multiple-forms technique is rather easy to execute when we are assessing single-item measures (where one question or observation is used to measure the variable of interest). As in the age example above, we devise a question and then devise another question that essentially asks for the same information. The alternate forms technique is much more challenging when trying to establish the reliability of a multiple-item index. The challenge here is to develop two different yet functionally equivalent *composite measures*. (Composite measures use two or more items to document a variable. See Chapter 5.) If I first develop a 10-item anxiety measure, the multiple forms technique requires that I develop a *second* 10-item anxiety measure that *appears* to be "different" but is really the same as the original. This task can be quite tricky (i.e. in changing the wording of the items in the two indexes, we may actually change what it is we are measuring). Given this complication, reliability checks of multiple-item measures (indexes) often go a different route.[4]

Split-Half Test

A popular alternate strategy for assessing the reliability of a composite measure is the split-half technique. In essence, this is to see if all of the items that make up a composite measure are equivalent and consistently measuring the same concept. Reconsider again the previous 10-item anxiety index. The

> **Split-half reliability check** – assessing the consistency or stability of a composite measure by splitting the measure into two halves and checking to see if the results yielded by each half are highly correlated with each other.

split-half reliability check would entail us splitting the ten items into two sets of five items each (i.e. consider all even numbered items as a set and all odd numbered items as a separate set). Scores would be generated for each mini-group of five items. If the two sets of scores were highly correlated with each other, we would take this as evidence of the index's reliability. The coefficient that is frequently used to report the reliability of items in an index is Cronbach's alpha. The values of Cronbach's alpha range from 0 to 1. Typically an alpha value of .70 or higher is taken as a good indication of reliability.[5]

Consider a concrete example of a reliability check offered by Johnson (1991) in her work on job strain among police officers. In measuring the variable "external burnout," Johnson asked respondents their level of agreement/disagreement with the following statements:

- I treat some civilians as if they were impersonal objects.
- Working with people all day is really a strain for me.
- I have become more callous toward people since I took this job.
- I worry that this job is hardening me emotionally.
- I don't really care what happens to some citizens.
- Working directly with people puts too much stress on me.

The split-half technique tells us how equivalent or consistent these items are with each other. Johnson reports a Cronbach's alpha of .87 for these six items. Such a high value is a good sign that the measure of job "burn out" is a reliable one. Or take a look back to Box 6.4. You will see that a Cronbach's alpha .94 is reported for the Cheek and Buss 20-item shyness index.

Box 6.8   Sharpening your research vision: the relationship between validity and reliability

In terms of developing or testing the quality of measures, it is advisable to think first about reliability. If a measure is unreliable, it cannot be valid. Or to say this another way: a measure cannot be valid without it being reliable. But assessment cannot stop with reliability. A measure can be reliable without it being valid. So press on and check for validity as well.

By now you may be thinking that devising valid and reliable measures requires a lot of time and effort. You are right! But then good things come to those who wait and work. Good things also come to those who "look." When it comes to measurement, it is not always necessary to start from scratch or to reinvent the wheel. Collections of measures are available in libraries and online, which contain a variety of "ready-made" indicators for a wide range of concepts. Furthermore, these "off the shelf" measures have typically already been put through their paces and been assessed for their validity and/or reliability. A good literature review is also key to locating existing measures. If the measures have been subjected to validity and reliability testing this will surely be noted in any methods discussion (as it was, for instance, in Johnson's discussion of her job burn-out measure). Before "reinventing the wheel" in your own research efforts you should check and see if adequate "tested" measures already exist. If they do, you are free to incorporate them into your own work as long as you abide by the conditions or terms of use.

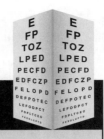

Box 6.9   Sharpening your research vision: the best things in life …

"Best" lists – the web really loves them: the best places to live, the best vacation spots, the best companies to work for, the 13 best beer countries (yes there is such a list), the best burgers … you name it and you can probably find a "best" list for it. From now on, when you see one of these lists, you will be in a position to assess if the best is really the best. Bring your research eye to those lists and assess their standards of measurement. See if you agree that the steps and procedures used to construct the lists are really measuring the best. See if you are persuaded that the procedures are capable of yielding accurate and consistent results. Anything less than this is simply not the best. (Why not give it a try right now? Check out Glassdoor.com's latest Top 50 list of the best places to work: http://www.glassdoor.com/Best-Places-to-Work-LST_KQ0,19.htm. If you agree with their measurement procedure, you will have some useful information on where to send your next resume!)

Noise and Bias

While the first part of this chapter is meant to convince you of the importance of striving to produce quality (valid and reliable) measures, it is nonetheless the case that measurement should never be thought of as a perfect process. Instead, measurement is better thought of as a process that yields *estimates* of true values. You may step on a scale and see a reading of 142 lb. Is this *exactly* what you weigh? Probably not. If you have your shoes on or if the scale is old (and has weak springs) or if you are leaning back on your heels, your true weight is probably not accurately reflected in the 142 lb. reading. It is the case that most attempts at measurement contain some degree of **measurement error**.

> **Measurement error** – error attributed to flaws in the measurement process itself; flaws that keep a measure from hitting its intended target spot on.

The following equation helps to make this point:

$$X = T + S + R$$

Where …

X = obtained results from an imperfect measurement process

T = the true value of what is being measured (i.e. the results that would be obtained under conditions of perfect measurement)

S = systematic error (aka bias)

R = random error (aka noise)

Noise – error in the measurement process that is non-patterned or non-directional.

In this measurement equation, the "S" and "R" terms constitute measurement error. One prevalent form of measurement error is known as **noise**. Noise refers to non-patterned error in the measurement process. Non-patterned error simply means that there is no set direction to the error involved in the measurement process. Sometimes the error occurs because the measurement process overshoots the true value; sometimes error occurs because the measurement process undershoots the true value. If you happen to be a fan of TV cooking shows, you may have noticed that cooks are often guilty of noisy measurement. For instance, when I measure out 3 cups of flour, I do it in a very noisy way. One cup may be slightly overfilled, one underfilled and one might be perfectly level. I have a somewhat lax attitude about measurement in baking because I am aware of a "forgiving" characteristic of noise: In the end, noise cancels itself out. In my baking example, I probably wind up with 3 cups of flour because the overfills and underfills cancel each other out. (Of course if you ask my family and friends you might learn that my "noisy" baking measurement is more of a problem than I realize!)

Not all measurement error is so forgiving. Sometimes error can be patterned. By patterned error we mean that the mistakes in the measurement process are consistently in the same direction – that is, the error may be *consistently* overestimating or consistently underestimating a true value. Patterned error with a consistent direction is known as **bias**. Early in my baking career, I consistently misread the teaspoon abbreviation for a tablespoon. Consequently, the error I introduced into my baking was always in the same direction: I always added too much (a tablespoon instead of a teaspoon) salt or baking powder! Given the patterned nature of bias, there is no chance of bias canceling itself out in the long run (as is true with noise). For this reason, bias is usually the more troublesome measurement error. (And for this reason, my baked goods were never in demand!)

Bias – error in the measurement process that is patterned or has a consistent direction.

Of these two major sources of measurement error, which one is more tolerable? The key to the answer is found in the idea of *systematic* error. Noise is non-systematic error while bias is systematic error. We can live with a little noise in the measurement process in large part because we assume it will work itself out as we continue the measurement process. Overestimates will be offset by underestimates. Nonetheless, noise in a measure decreases the measure's reliability. The consequences of bias can be more severe. Given its systematic nature, bias does not cancel itself out in the long run. Indeed *undetected* bias has the capacity to render a measure invalid. Critics of IQ tests, for instance, have long argued that these tests are biased against minorities: the questions that make up the tests are not equally meaningful to all and thereby systematically under-document the innate intelligence of some groups. Similarly, survey researchers must always consider how the selection of words can bias measures. Asking respondents about their attitudes toward *welfare* will produce lower levels of support than asking about their attitudes toward *assistance to the poor*. Asking people about their attitudes toward suicide will produce lower levels of support than asking about physician assisted death (Ramanathan 2013). While we must expect some degree of measurement error (either noise or bias) we must nonetheless try to keep both types of errors to a minimum.

Box 6.10   Sharpening your research vision:
biased consumer ratings?

As you might suspect, when I am considering a purchase, I do some preliminary research. I rarely try a new restaurant without first reading what other diners have to say about the place and the food. When I book a hotel, I always check out recent guest reviews. On Amazon, I want to read what past customers have to say about a product before I make a purchase. Is all of this checking a big waste of time? Well I hope after reading about noise and bias in the measurement process, you might have an informed opinion. We have all heard about restaurants that "stack" their reviews with false positive feedback submitted by bogus diners. And some of you have probably been "instructed" by car salespersons on the kind of feedback to offer when submitting evaluative surveys. One car salesperson actually told me that I had to give him the highest ratings or he would be at risk of losing his job. While writing this book I had yet another measurement error wake-up call. I received an email from the manufacturer of a recently purchased kitchen item. The email urged me to provide product feedback and then gave me a link to use that would *automatically* rate the product at the highest possible levels! Now I understand why when I was shopping for the product, it boasted a remarkably high "5 star" rating.

Sources of Noise and Bias

Noise in the measurement process can stem from a number of sources. Our research subjects themselves might introduce noise. Tired respondents or inattentive respondents or young respondents can all be responsible for some degree of error in the measurement process. Many colleges and universities have unofficial "party nights" where students celebrate the end of another week. Professors know first-hand that scheduling tests on the mornings after these nights is risky: the tests will be plagued by a lot of noise. Noise can also be introduced by poorly constructed measures. Excessively complicated measures, poorly designed measures or measures with vague directions can contribute to noisy measurement. Noise can also be due to human diversity. Imagine 20 undergraduates working the phone banks for an instant feedback survey of a local community campaign. It is certainly possible that each student will put his or her own spin on the survey questions and thereby add some noise to the measurement process. Given the great array of sources of noise, researchers are well advised to anticipate the most likely sources of noise in their study and do what is feasible to keep the noise level down to a minimum.

A major source of bias in the measurement process can be the expectations of the researcher. You are probably familiar with the old adage that we humans "see" what we want to see or "hear" what we want to hear. Researchers are not exempt from this tendency and may be inclined to interpret ambiguous responses in ways that confirm their expectations. Or the researcher might inadvertently communicate expectations (via head nods or voice inflections) to research subjects who might then supply the desired answer. To counteract this source of bias, some research will be conducted under "blind" conditions where those executing the research are intentionally kept in the dark about the research hypotheses or expectations.

Bias can also be built into our measurement instrument. Chapter 8 shows that questions can be phrased in such a way as to "lead" respondents to one response over another. The earliest version of the UCLA loneliness measure was suspected of introducing just such a bias into the measurement process. This is what set off the subsequent attempts to modify the measure. The influence of "expectations" can always work their way into the measurement process via the research subject. When research topics are threatening or sensitive, there is a tendency for research subjects to answer questions not honestly but rather in accordance with what they *think* the researcher wants to hear. This phenomenon is known as the "normative response bias" and can systematically distort findings in a socially desirable way. In the United States when registered voters are asked if they intend to vote in upcoming elections, most will say yes: voting is after all the responsible thing to do. In fact, voter turn-out rates indicate that these respondents are over-reporting their actual voting behaviors. Or consider Nate Silver the American statistician who has gained considerable fame in predicting the results of presidential elections. Silver was asked why other polling organizations made more sizeable mistakes in their recent election forecasts. Silver put the blame at the feet of biased data collection strategies. He thinks that polling groups that relied primarily on phone surveys, and in particular of landline phones, were systematically missing important segments of voters – voters who were more likely to vote for Democratic candidates (Silver 2012).

Since the presence of undetected bias has the potential to render our measures invalid, some researchers make a compromise with regard to bias and noise. They will intentionally introduce noise into the measurement process in an effort to keep bias at bay. Why this compromise? It has to do with the appealing feature of noise mentioned earlier: noise will cancel itself out in repeated measurement. So, in the interest of eliminating bias in an interview situation, the researcher might intentionally use multiple interviewers who are randomly assigned to interviewees. This will make for a noisy measurement process but it will preclude any systematic distortion being introduced by any one interviewer.

Measuring Up and Out

As the above discussion indicates, measurement is a tricky business. On the one hand we strive to design measures that are valid and reliable. We work to construct as perfect a measure as possible. On the other hand, we must also acknowledge that we conduct our research in an imperfect world. We are well advised, then, to acknowledge that the measurement process really represents (at best) an effort to *estimate* the "true" value of some variable. This mindset encourages us to anticipate noise and bias in the measurement process and do what we can to keep both at an acceptable level. Assuming that some measurement error is inevitable is also fully consistent with the skeptical attitude that is a defining feature of the scientific way of knowing. In doubting that measurement is perfect, we are better prepared to anticipate and catch errors. Such skepticism ultimately serves us well in our pursuit of error free knowing.

TAKE AWAYS

- Measurement is an essential but demanding part of research
  - We must always check/assess if measurement has been done right!
- Validity tests – assess if researcher is measuring what she or he claims to be measuring
  - Face – assess a measure in terms of whether or not it "looks right"
  - Content – assess a measure by comparing a variable's conceptual and operational definitions
  - Criterion – assess a measure by mobilizing empirical evidence to "show" skeptics the measure is getting the job done
    - Predictive – Evidence? Measure can make accurate predictions
    - Concurrent – Evidence? Measure is highly correlated with other valid measures of the same variable
  - Construct – assess a measure by seeing if it produces results consistent with theory
- Reliability tests – assessing if results produced via measurement are consistent or stable given repeated measurement
  - Test-retest – use measure two times and compare results
  - Multiple forms – develop two forms/versions of the same measure and see if results obtained by each are highly correlated
  - Split-half technique – use with unidimensional indexes: divide index into two parts (halves) and see if scores obtained from each half are highly correlated
- Measurement error is inevitable. The researcher's job is really about trying to minimize it
  - Noise – random or directionless error with many (and some uncontrollable) sources. Noise makes for unreliable measures
  - Bias – systematic error in that the mistake occurs in a consistent direction. Undiscovered bias will invalidate a measure

Sharpening the Edge: More Reading and Searching

- While I have confined this review of validity and reliability to just one chapter, E.G. Carmines and R.A. Zeller have devoted an entire book to measurement assessment: *Reliability and Validity Assessment* (Beverly Hills, CA: SAGE 1979)

- Here is a list of measurement reference books you might find useful in your research efforts:

  > Bruner, Gordon C., Hensel, Paul J., and Karen E. James. 2005. *Marketing Scales Handbook: A Compilation of Multi-Item Measures for Consumer Behaviors and Advertising. Mason*, OH: Thomson South-Western.
  > Carlson, Janet, Geisinger, Kurt and Jessica L. Jonson. 2014. *The Nineteenth Mental Measurements Yearbook*. Lincoln, NE: Buros Institute of Mental Measurements. Take a look at the following web site (and check to see if your local college or university provides free access): http://www.unl.edu/buros.
  > Miller, Delbert and Neil Salkind. 2002. *Handbook of Research Design and Social Measurement*, 6th edn. Thousand Oaks, CA: Sage.

Exercises

1 Access the GSS and review the topics index. Select one of interest to you that uses a multiple item index to measure the concept. Answer the following questions:
   - Does the measure have face validity?
   - What would you need to do in order to judge the measure's content validity?
   - Explain what you would do to demonstrate the measure's predictive validity.

2 Use the same index you selected for exercise 1 and offer a detail explanation of how you would demonstrate the reliability of the measure by either the test-retest or the split-half technique.

3 Reconsider Johnson's measure of external burnout. She defines this concept as "feelings of being emotionally hardened by the job and lacking compassion for citizens." Given this definition, how would you rate the content validity of her measure? Next try your hand at developing a "different" but equivalent set of burn-out items. Explain how you would go about establishing the reliability of the two forms.

4 Use the following link to find the items Pew uses to measure the variable likely voter: http://people-press.org/files/2011/01/UnderstandingLikelyVoters.pdf. Now do some digging and find the items Gallup uses the measure the same variable: http://www.gallup.com/poll/111268/How-Gallups-likely-voter-models-work.aspx.

   Compare the two sets of items. Can you discern why the two polling organizations might reach different conclusions about election outcomes given how each operationalize "likely voter"? Would you say the two measures are essentially the same? Could they be used to illustrate the "multiple forms" technique for establishing reliability?

5 Access the following list that offers Fortune's assessment of the best companies to work for: http://fortune.com/best-companies/. Find out the measurement procedures used to construct the list. Compare the standards with those used by Glassdoor.com (see Box 6.9). Which of the two does a better job on the validity and reliability fronts?

Notes

1 Within educational research, content validity refers to whether or not a selection of items accurately reflects the larger universe of items on a given topic. For instance, a one-question exam would lack content validity on a qualifying exam for a law license.

2 See http://www.census.gov/hhes/www/poverty/about/overview/measure.html for details on how the US Census calculates poverty rates.

3 See http://academics.wellesley.edu/Psychology/Cheek/research.html.

4 Access the following link to find two versions of a locus of health control measure: http://www.nursing.vanderbilt.edu/faculty/kwallston/mhlcscales.htm. Take a look at both forms and see if you agree that they are really equivalent forms.

5 Technically, Cronbach's alpha reports an average of all possible split-half combinations of all the items in an index.

References

Ahn, June. 2012. "Teenagers' Experiences With Social Network Sites: Relationships to Bridging and Bonding Social Capital." *The Information Society* 28: 99–109.

Alexander, C., Kim, Y., Ensminger, M., Johnson, K., Smith, B., and L. Dolan. 1990. "A Measure of Risk Taking for Young Adolescents: Reliability and Validity Assessment." *Journal of Youth and Adolescence* 19(6): 559–569.

Bourdieu, Pierre. 1986. "The Forms of Capital." In J.G. Richardson (ed.), *Handbook of Theory and Research in the Sociology of Education*. New York: Greenwood Press.

Hochschild, Arlie. 1983. *The Managed Heart: Commercialization of Human Feeling*. Berkeley, CA: University of California Press.

Keeter, Scott. 2012. "Determining Who Is a 'Likely Voter.'" Pew Research Center. http://www.pewresearch.org/2012/08/29/ask-the-expert-determining-who-is-a-likely-voter/.

Kraut, Robert, Kiesler, S., Boneva, B., Cummings, J.N., Helgeson, V. and A.M. Crawford. 2002. "Internet Paradox Revisited." *Journal of Social Issues* 58(1): 49–74.

Pew Research Center. 2012. "Party Affiliation and Election Polls." http://www.people-press.org/2012/08/03/party-affiliation-and-election-polls/.

Ramanathan, K. 2013. "POLL: Most Americans Support Physician-Assisted Suicide When It's Not Described As 'Suicide'". http://thinkprogress.org/health/2013/06/03/2093531/physician-assisted-suicide-described-suicide/.

Sheppard, Steven. 2012. "Gallup Blew Its Presidential Polls, but Why?" *National Journal*. http://www.nationaljournal.com/politics/gallup-blew-its-presidential-polls-but-why-20121118.

Silver, Nate. 2012. "Which Polls Fared Best (and Worst) in the 2012 Presidential Race?" *The New York Times* (November 10). http://fivethirtyeight.blogs.nytimes.com/2012/11/10/which-polls-fared-best-and-worst-in-the-2012–presidential-race/.

Thompson, Kevin. 1989. "Gender and Adolescent Drinking Problems: The Effects of Occupational Structure." *Social Problems* 36(1): 30–47.

Chapter 7

One Thing Leads to Another … or Does it? Tackling Causal Analysis

Introducing Social Research Methods: Essentials for Getting the Edge, First Edition. Janet M. Ruane.
© 2016 John Wiley & Sons, Ltd. Published 2016 by John Wiley & Sons, Ltd.

FIRST TAKES

Be sure to take note of the following:

Causal analysis – a perennial concern for researchers (and the rest of us)
- ○ Pursues explanations of events or outcomes
- ○ Distinguishes independent and dependent variables
- Two models for causal analysis
  - ○ Nomothetic – seeks general causal explanations
  - ○ Idiographic – seeks case-specific causal explanations
- Three required conditions for establishing causal connections
  - ○ Timing – independent variable must precede the dependent variable
  - ○ Association – independent and dependent variables must be associated
  - ○ Non-spuriousness – observed relationship must survive any/all tests for spuriousness
- Experiment – *the* causal design
  - ○ Superiority of experiment – is found in its "planned" control
  - ○ Control = best strategy for handling threats to internal validity
- Assessing the use of non-experimental designs for causal analysis
  - ○ The survey
  - ○ Field research

Advertisers have known it for a long time: babies make good ad copy. That babies work in advertising makes perfect sense. Who can resist a cute, inquisitive baby or toddler? Newborns delight us with their engaging curiosity about the world around them. "Why?" is a question that can keep 2-year-olds going, and going, and going. Children remind us that curiosity about how things work may be an inescapable human trait. Indeed, social and evolutionary psychologists maintain that our interest in causal analysis is "hard-wired" (Shermer 1997).[1] Michael Shermer, in embracing an evolutionary theory of our cognitive development, argues that we have evolved into "pattern-seeking, causal-finding creatures" (1997: xxiv). Interestingly enough, he also argues that it is our causal-seeking nature that leaves us so vulnerable to misinformation. We are hard-wired, he says, to *seek* patterns. We are not, however, hard-wired to detect truth or avoid errors. For that, we need to learn and apply scientific methods of knowing.

Independent variable – the cause of another variable; the variable that produces change in the dependent variable; aka predictor variable.

Dependent variable – the outcome we are trying to explain; the variable that is presumed to be the result of another.

Chapter 1 identified belief in a causal model of the universe as one of the defining features of science. Part of the scientific mindset is the assumption that every event has an antecedent event. Things don't just happen – they are caused. To reflect this commitment to causal analysis, science employs a distinctive vocabulary of **independent** and **dependent** variables to reflect the cause and effect model. A dependent variable is the entity, or phenomenon, or the *outcome* we want to explain. For instance, we might be interested in explaining why people engage in crime, family violence, join jihadist groups or why some students get higher grade point averages than others. The independent variable is the "causal agent" – that is, the factor we think is responsible for bringing about the dependent variable. You might also think of the independent variable as a "predictor" variable. Causal analysis is essentially an attempt to identify the independent variables that predict or account for select dependent variables.

Causal Models – Nomothetic and Idiographic

When pursuing causal analysis, there are two paths we might follow: the **nomothetic** path and the **idiographic** path. The nomothetic path adopts a generalist or a "macro" approach to causal analysis – it is interested in finding general causal patterns that exist over and above any one individual, case or event. With this orientation, we are interested in trying to find the *common influences* that explain a general class of actions or events (e.g. war, crime, divorce, autism, school violence, terrorism). This search for common, transcendent causal factors is fundamentally a search for an efficient model of causal analysis. Let me explain what is meant by "efficient". The nomothetic model tries to identify a few key factors that explain the most variance in our dependent variable. Variance simply refers to variation but it is the lifeblood of all analysis. If all things were the same, there would be nothing to explain. It is variation or differences that intrigue us (variance is discussed further in Chapter 12). It might help to think of the nomothetic approach as one that focuses on the "big picture" of some class of events – the picture that results when you step back and take a wide view – one that encompasses many instances of the outcome being studied – for example, divorce. Given that the nomothetic approach is seeking common factors that hold true across a class of actions, it offers a *probabilistic* explanation of outcomes. That is, nomothetic causal research allows us to identify those variables that increase the likelihood of certain outcomes. In other words, the nomothetic model may not be able to accurately predict if *you* will wind up divorced, but it will be able to identify the variables that are common across the greatest number of divorces or the variables that are the most likely causes of divorce in general. The following kinds of statements are indicative of nomothetic causal research:

> **Nomothetic model of causality** – an approach to causal analysis that seeks the common factors responsible for a general class of events; "big picture" causal analysis.
>
> **Idiographic model of causality** – an approach to causal analysis that seeks to identify the specific factors that produce a specific event.

Students reporting use of one or more packs of cigarettes per day were three times *more likely* to use alcohol, seven times *more likely* to use smokeless tobacco and 10–30 times *more likely* to use illicit drugs than were students who never smoked. (Torabi, Bailey and Majd-Jabbari 1993, my emphasis)

... people with alcohol abuse problems or those who have received treatment for the problem were no *more likely* to be chronically homeless than were other homeless people. People with a history of hospitalization for mental health problems were *more likely* to be chronically homeless than were people without a record of institutionalization. (James 1992, my emphasis)

While the nomothetic approach is interested in "general" causal explanations, the idiographic approach is dedicated to specifics. An idiographic approach has a micro focus and is much more limited in scope than the nomothetic approach. In contrast to the "big picture" approach of the nomothetic model, we might think of the idiographic approach as taking the "small picture" approach but the small picture is "blown up" or enlarged so we can see all the details. The idiographic model is interested in thoroughly explaining the sequence of events that lead to *one particular outcome*. With the idiographic approach, we might be interested in explaining our best friend's divorce (as opposed to divorce in general). Or we might be interested in explaining a fist fight that broke out today in the cafeteria (as opposed to school violence in general). We might be interested in explaining a neighbor's suicide (instead of suicide in general). Or we might want to understand how Anders Breivik went on a 2011 shooting rampage that left 77 people dead including many youths attending a summer camp in Norway (Borchgrevink 2013; Richards 2014) or what led Adam Lanza in 2012 to kill 27 people in an elementary school in Newtown, Connecticut. Since the idiographic approach is case specific, it strives to provide an extremely thorough or *exhaustive* causal explanation of some event. In this sense, then, it is said to offer a *deterministic* explanation of events: it details how one event led to another, which led to another, which ultimately led to the outcome (the dependent variable) we are analyzing. The following kinds of statements are indicative of idiographic research efforts:

> The research problem was to understand why NASA managers had launched the Challenger in January 1986, despite a recommendation by contractor engineers that the mission be delayed because of unprecedented cold temperature predicted for launch time ... The analysis showed a decision making pattern that was fundamentally like the demise of intimate relationships. The demise of the Challenger was preceded by a long incubation period filled with warning signs that something was seriously wrong with the technology. (Vaughan 2002)

> In accounting for an individual's use of marihuana ... we must deal with a sequence of step, of changes in the individual's behavior and perspectives, in order to understand the phenomenon. Each step requires explanation, and what may operate as a cause at one step on the sequence may be of negligible importance at another step ... In a sense, each explanation constitutes a necessary cause of the behavior. That is, no one could become a confirmed marihuana user without going through each step ... The explanation of each step is thus part of the explanation of the resulting behavior. (Becker 1963)

While you may not have realized it before, the idiographic approach is the one that motivates much of our day-to-day causal curiosity. We are hooked on getting the "skinny" on specific people and events. Entertainment programs and magazines thrive on satisfying the public's curiosity about what caused the latest "it" couple's break-up or about the sequence of events that led to Bruce Jenner's decision to transition. It is our desire for nitty-gritty details that keep reality crime show programs on the airwaves. Shortly after the 9/11, a NOVA special provided a detailed (minute-by-minute) analysis of the structural collapse of the World Trade Towers. (A short slide show presenting the logic and details of the collapse can be found at http://www.pbs.org/wgbh/nova/tech/world-trade-center-collapse.html). The idiographic model is also the dominant model of social workers, clinical psychologists, and historians – that is, professional researchers who are committed to unraveling causal forces in the lives of specific clients or specific historical figures and events.

There is no doubt that the idiographic approach to causal analysis can be quite interesting because of its personal, case-specific focus. If, however, our goal is to advance our understanding of *social* phenomenon, we would be well advised to become familiar with (and appreciative of) the nomothetic model. Not surprisingly, the nomothetic model is the dominant model of sociology, a discipline committed to the study of broad social patterns. The following sections focus primarily on issues that are most relevant for the nomothetic model. We return to the idiographic model at the end of the chapter.

	Nomothetic	Idiographic
Questions:	General	Specific
e.g.	What causes suicide?	What caused Robin Williams to take his own life?
Levels:	Macro	Micro
Explanations:	Probabilistic	Deterministic
Data:	Quantitative	Qualitative
Causal Standards:	3 traditional criteria	Convincing narrative that details causal mechanism

Figure 7.1   Two Approaches to Studying Causality

Nomothetic Approach: Causal Requirements

To contend that one variable *causes* another variable, three conditions or causal requirements must be satisfied: (1) the independent variable must be shown to precede the dependent variable in time; (2) the independent variable and the dependent variable must co-vary – that is they must be shown to be associated (correlated) with each other; (3) the relationship between the independent and dependent variable must survive any and all attempts to prove it spurious. These three conditions are mandatory requirements: *all three conditions must be met.* Anything less and we simply cannot claim a causal relationship. A more detailed explanation of each requirement follows.

Temporal Ordering

The time test of causality is really an exercise in logic. (Recall from the opening chapters the critical role that logic and reasoning play in the scientific way of knowing.) For any factor or event to "cause" another, it *must* precede the other in time. Reason dictates this condition. We cannot claim that a piece of bad news caused us to blow up at our kids if we got the bad news *after* we lost our temper. We cannot claim that lung cancer causes one to take up smoking if smoking precedes the development of lung cancer. We cannot posit that a patient's mid-life heart disease is the cause of his or her poor childhood nutrition. Logic dictates that the timing has got to be the other way around. The time requirement (and logic) precludes or negates all of the preceding causal claims.

> **Fixed variable** – a trait or characteristic that is imposed or assigned to an individual, often at birth (gender, age, etc.); fixed variables cannot be altered by the researcher.

At first glance the time test for establishing a causal relationship would seem to be a simple one to satisfy. In many instances, it is very easy to establish which variable precedes another in time. Sociologists, for instance, are frequently interested in studying the effects of certain **fixed variables**. Fixed variables cannot be manipulated by the researcher. That is, the specific value of a fixed variable is *not* one that the researcher is free to change or alter for the sake of study. Fixed variables are most easily understood as our ascribed statuses (i.e. statuses imposed on or assigned to us). Sex, age, ethnicity, race, birth order are all examples of fixed variables that might be of interest to a social scientist wanting to explain such things as income, political affiliation, charitable donations, depression, voting behaviors, and so on. Many fixed variables are assigned to us at birth or early in life. Given this we can easily argue that they precede other variables in time. As we move away from such fixed variables, however, figuring out the time order of independent and dependent variables becomes more challenging. Not all variables enjoy clear or obvious temporal orderings vis-à-vis each other. This, of course, is the classic chicken and egg question.

Consider the temporal ordering of depression and drinking. Which of these two variables precedes the other in time? Does one's drinking or one's excessive drinking cause depression? Or does depression cause one to seek some solace in the bottle? How about the relationship between parent–child communication levels and delinquency? Does non-communication precede delinquency? Or does trouble with the law or some authority figures give adolescents a good reason to forgo conversations with their parents? When the temporal ordering of variables is not apparent, the researcher must be prepared to build a case or justification for the ordering they endorse. Very often, this case is most persuasively made via the relevant theory associated with an area of research. The case for the time order can also be made by citing the research literature. What do other researchers maintain is the temporal ordering? What evidence exists in the literature to support this ordering? As we argued in Chapter 4, a good literature review is really an essential step in planning a good study.

Associations Between Variables

The association requirement merely asserts that if two variables are causally connected, *they must co-vary*. Are women more likely than men to report feeling stressed? (Yes, according the 2014 American Psychology Association's "Stress in America" survey). Do more hours spent on the Internet mean fewer hours spent with family? (Yes, if you live in Cyprus, Russia, or Sweden; no, if you live in Poland, Taiwan, or the United States. See Center for the Digital Future 2013) Again logic dictates the association requirement. If two variables do not move together in some patterned way, it would be foolish to try and argue that one is the cause of the other. If we cannot document an association, we should not even think about claiming a causal relationship. On the other hand, a loud and clear warning must be sounded here: merely finding an association between two variables does not automatically indicate that a causal connection exists. This point deserves a bit more attention.

Perhaps the most common lay mistake in causal analysis is to assume that if two variables are connected, they are causally related. But the simple fact is that correlations do not "make" or verify causal relationships. Not all associations or correlations bespeak causal connections. Think about the interesting associations noted by Levitt and Dubner in their work *Freakonomics* (2005). The authors ask readers to think twice before assuming (as many do) that the correlation between campaign spending and winning elections is a causal one. Or they discuss the high correlation that exists between the size of a city's police force and the number of murders. Here the authors note it would be ludicrous to think the police are responsible for the murders (Levitt and Dubner 2005). Before we can be optimistic or claim that we have found a causal connection between two variables, even those that are sequentially related, we must satisfy the third requirement for causality: we must establish that the observed relationship is *not* a spurious one.

Non-spuriousness Association

To fully appreciate why correlation is not synonymous with a causal connection, we must understand what is known as a **spurious relationship**. A spurious relationship exists when there is an *apparent* but not a genuine causal connection between two variables (e.g. variables A and B). With a

> **Spurious relationship** – one that results because two variables (A and B) are each connected to a third lurking variable (C).

spurious relationship, the appearance of a causal connection between variables A and B is due to the fact that both A and B are causally linked to a third variable C. (You might find it helpful to think of the C variable as a "lurker" variable – i.e. it is in the background, out of sight, but nonetheless still relevant.) If we are unaware of the presence and influence of the C variable, we can mistakenly conclude that A is the driving force behind B. In truth, however, C is really running the show: C causes A *and* C causes B and gives the illusion that A is causing B (see Figure 7.2a).

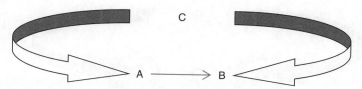

Figure 7.2a   Strengthening Your Research Vision: The Case of the Spurious Relationship Spurious relationship exists because both A and B are *each* connected to the same "lurking" background variable C.

For many years now, studies have been documenting an association between breast-fed children and higher IQ scores. At first glance, one might be tempted to assume a causal relationship: that breast-feeding makes babies smarter. (Supporters of this contention claim that the DHA found in mother's milk is what positively affects IQ.) The third requirement for establishing a causal connection, however, *forces* us to ask if a third variable might be responsible for the connection between breast-feeding and IQ scores. In suspecting a spurious relationship, we might consider that a "behind the scenes" C variable is at work. Skeptics of the observed correlation between breast-feeding and IQ scores argue that the association is due to an antecedent *social* condition. Perhaps a certain mothering style influences both the decision to breast-feed and the intellectual development of children (Lucas, Morley, Cole *et al.* 1992; Horwood and Ferguson 1998). Or think again about Levitt and Dubner's noting the positive correlation between campaign spending and winning elections. Rather than spending "buying" elections, these authors argue that it is the appeal of the candidate to voters that influences both spending and winning elections (Levitt and Dubner 2005).

In testing for spurious relationships, the researcher must be prepared to consider *any and all* rival explanations (i.e. C variables) that might account for the apparent causal connection between A and B. In essence, testing for spuriousness means that the researcher tries to control or remove the influence of the C variable on the original A–B relationship. If when controlling the C variable, the original relationship between A and B disappears, we have evidence of a spurious relationship (see Figure 7.2b). On the other hand, if when controlling the C variable, the original relationship between A and B maintains itself, we say that it has survived *this* test for spuriousness. But the researcher cannot stop here. It is essential to *repeat* this testing until we have controlled the influence of *all likely rival explanations* – that is, all likely C variables. Reviewing a specific example should help.

Imagine that we have found a positive relationship between hair length and GPA. If we took this as a causal connection, all college students would be well advised to grow their hair as long as possible! But before assuming a causal relationship exists, we must consider rival explanations of the apparent causal connection. Is there a C variable that might influence hair length and also influence GPA? Gender seems a good place to start. If we control on gender (analyze all male data separately from all female data), we would see that gender influences both A and B variables: females tend to have longer hair and higher GPAs.

In the study of domestic violence, there is a clearly documented association between alcohol use and violent behavior towards spouses. Many researchers, however, are hesitant

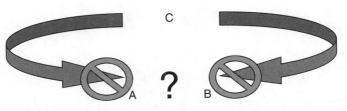

Figure 7.2b   Strengthening Your Research Vision: Testing for a Spurious Relationship Controlling the "C" Variable

Table 7.1   Some famous spurious relationships
Positive relationships have been found between each of the following sets of variables (resist drawing any causal conclusions).

Observed Associations	*Lurking C variables?*
Ice cream sales and deaths by drowning	think seasons
Number of homicides and number of churches	think population
The stork population and the birth rate	think …
Minister's salaries and the price of vodka	think …
The number of fire trucks that show up at a fire and the amount of damage done	think …
Hospitalization rates and death rates	think …

to argue a causal connection. Instead, some theorize that there is a C variable that leads to alcohol use and that also leads to violent behavior. Perhaps issues of self-esteem or power influence both the use of alcohol and the use of physical force. Finally, consider again the before-mentioned relationship between breast-feeding and IQ scores. To date, this relationship has survived all tests for spuriousness – the relationship does not disappear when such factors as prenatal care, or social status, or mother's intelligence are used as control variables (see Belfort, Rifas-Shiman, Kleinman *et al.* 2013). So is it a causal relationship? Up to this point, it is looking as if it might be the case but only more testing for other likely C variables will tell us for sure.

If you are on board with this discussion, you should now realize that testing for spuriousness is a very challenging task. How does the researcher know what to introduce as possible C variables? Once again we turn to a thorough review of the research literature for the answer. Knowing the variables that others have posited as causal agents or as likely candidates for C variables helps a researcher anticipate and prepare for adequate testing in their own work. If a researcher does not do this kind of prep work, they will likely drown in a sea of C variables. (Sorry I could not resist.)

Causal Analysis and Research Design

If our research goal is causal analysis, there is one research design or strategy that is superior to all others and should be part of our planning: the **experiment**. The term "experiment" is one that is frequently misused. Many people use the term "experiment" as a synonym for a study. This is incorrect usage. While experiments are studies not all

Experiment – a controlled study in which the independent variable is intentionally manipulated so as to observe its impact on the dependent variable.

studies are experiments. Clarifying the meaning of an experiment, then, is our first order of business. The experiment is a contrived and very controlled plan of action in which subjects are randomly assigned to two groups and where the independent variable is intentionally manipulated in one of the groups in order to assess its impact on the dependent variable. The *control* that characterizes the experiment allows the researcher to explicitly address the three previously stated requirements of causality. The experimenter controls the introduction and the manipulation of the independent variable thereby assuring that it precedes the dependent variable in time. The control achieved with randomly assigned experimental and control groups enables the researcher to clearly document any association or correlation between the independent and dependent variables. The control of the randomly assigned groups also enables the researcher to neutralize the influence of lurking C variables and thereby effectively eliminate rival explanations of changes in the dependent variable. In short, there is no better strategy for examining causal relationships than the experimental design.[2] These essentials controls are discussed here in greater detail.

Control group – a group that is identical to the experimental group except for one thing: the independent variable is intentionally withheld from the control group.

Experimental group – the group that receives or is exposed to the independent variable.

Random assignment – using chance and only chance to assign participants to the experimental and control groups.

Consider the classic experimental design and how it would allow us to investigate the causal connection between using the nicotine patch and subsequent changes in smoking behaviors. The classic experiment starts with the researcher setting up two groups: the **control group** and the **experimental group.** Ideally, these two groups will be created via **random assignment**. Random assignment means that chance and chance alone will determine the placement of study volunteers into the control or experimental groups. Random assignment helps assure that the two groups will start out as equivalent groups since pure chance determines who is placed in each group.[3] (Probability theory holds that random assignment gives us the best chance of getting equal groups.) Once we have our randomly assigned groups, we can then impose the experimental condition (i.e. the intentional manipulation of the independent variable). That is, the experimental group will receive or be exposed to the independent variable; the control group will not receive or be exposed to the independent variable. So in our present example, the experimental group will receive the nicotine patch, the control group will not. After the introduction of the independent variable in the experimental group, we will then measure the smoking activity of *both* the control and experimental groups. If we find that smoking is reduced in the experimental group, we are in a position to attribute the decrease to the nicotine patch.

How can we be so sure of our conclusion? It is all in the "controlling" design. The experimental design enables us to isolate the connection (if any) between the independent and dependent variables. We control the temporal ordering of the variables (*first* the patch, *then days later* a measure of smoking behaviors). We can clearly see any association between the patch and smoking by comparing the outcomes (number of cigarettes smoked) in the two groups. And since we start with two equivalent groups, we can dismiss any rival explanations of any observed changes in smoking outcomes. For example, we can refute the argument that the experimental group reduced their smoking because they were more motivated since the control group presumably exhibits the same level of motivation. (Random assignment allows us to make this assumption).

Experimental Design and Internal Validity

Another way to understand the superiority of the experimental design for examining causal connections is through the concept of **internal validity**. A research strategy has internal validity if it is able to eliminate alternate or rival explanations of an outcome – that is, the dependent variable. These rival explanations are known as **threats to internal validity**. The experimental design is very strong on internal validity because it is able to eliminate many standing rival explanations of outcomes. Let us consider a few common threats: history, maturation, and selection bias.

> **Internal validity**–the state or extent of accuracy with regard to a study's assessment of a causal relationship between variables.
>
> **Threats to internal validity** – rival explanations that hinder or compromise the researcher's ability to know or detect genuine causal relationships.

History

This threat occurs when some event external to a study occurs at the same time as the study. When "history" happens we can no longer be sure that any observed change in the dependent variable is due to the independent variable; history may be responsible for the change. For instance, imagine that during our nicotine patch study (which is scheduled to last a few weeks) a famous celebrity dies of lung cancer. Some might want to argue that this "historical" event (rather than the nicotine patch) is responsible for any observed changes in the study participant's smoking behaviors. History, then, can leave us in a state of uncertainty with regard to causal conclusions.

Maturation

This threat occurs when participants in a study undergo developmental changes or growth, changes that could influence the dependent variable under investigation. With this validity threat, the researcher can no longer be sure whether changes in the dependent variable are due to the independent variable or to maturation of subjects. Imagine again that our nicotine patch study is aimed at late adolescent smokers and is running for an academic year. At the end of the study period, some skeptics might want to argue that any changes observed in participants' smoking behaviors *might* be due to the patch but they might also be due to the fact that the adolescent smokers "outgrew" this phase of risky, rebellious activity. Again, when maturation occurs over the course of a study, our ability to reach causal conclusions can be compromised.

Selection Bias

This threat occurs when participants in a study are not randomly assigned to study groups. Changes in the dependent variable *might* be due to the independent variable but they might also be attributed to the peculiar characteristics of the people in our study groups. Return again to our nicotine patch study. Imagine that the researchers allowed volunteers for the study to self-select into the group receiving the nicotine patch. Any observed changes in smoking behaviors might be due to the patch but they might also be due to the fact that the extremely motivated (i.e. those desperate to quit) volunteered to be in the experimental group, that is, the group getting the patch. The selection threat then can compromise our ability to reach accurate causal conclusions.

Now consider how the basic experimental design with randomly assigned experimental and control groups can handle and very effectively dismiss these common validity threats. The presence of an experimental and a control group nicely counters the threats of history and maturation. If history happens, it happens to *both* groups and therefore drops out of consideration as a rival explanation. In other words, the history threat becomes a wash since it occurs to both the experimental and control groups. The same thing can be said for maturation since any growth or development will happen to *both* the experimental and control groups. If maturation is common to both groups, it can be eliminated as a rival explanation for changes in the dependent variable. The threat of selection bias is eliminated in the experimental design since both the experimental and control groups are randomly assigned. Random assignment assures that the same kind of people are found in both groups and that the experimental groups won't wind up with more motivated (desperate to quit) participants than the control group. In short, the experimental design is one very powerful design for controlling these and other threats to a study's internal validity.[4] (See Box 7.1 for a list of some other common internal validity threats.)

Box 7.1   Sharpening your research vision: other common internal validity threats

Testing threat – can occur whenever pre-testing is part of a study's design. With pre-testing you must ask if test "practice" or "priming" via the pre-test is responsible for the apparent connection between the independent and dependent variable.

Instrumentation threat – again occurs when there is pre-testing and post-testing. This time, you must ask if the pre-tests and post-tests differed in any way (i.e. were different instruments used in pre- vs. post-testing?). If measures do change from pre- to post-testing, you must consider that this is responsible for the apparent connection between the independent and dependent variable.

Mortality threat – this threat occurs when participants drop out of a study. You must then ask if it is the loss of these participants that really accounts for the apparent connection between the independent and dependent variable.

Regression threat – this threat occurs when participants for a study are selected based on extreme scores or conditions (i.e. very low math scores or very high stress scores). If this is the case, you must consider that extreme scores often "settle" down or bounce back to more normal scores and if this occurs it can be what accounts for the apparent connection between the independent and dependent variable.

Limits of the Experimental Design

The experiment is a powerful, efficient, and internally valid strategy for examining causal connections. Given this, it may surprise you to learn that the experiment is not the inevitable design choice in causal research in sociology or in other social sciences. This is so for several reasons: the nature of the independent variable, ethical considerations regarding the intentional manipulation of the independent variable, practical limitations on random assignment of experimental and control groups, and the limitation of experiments with regard to external validity. We now consider each of these points in more detail.

First, we should consider the kinds of variables needed for experimental research. The experiment requires an independent variable that can be imposed or manipulated[5] by the researcher. Remember, being able to *intentionally* introduce the independent variable to the experimental group while *intentionally* withholding it from the control group is key to "seeing" if the independent variable has a causal impact on outcome. Whereas a wealth of variables can be manipulated or controlled by the researcher (e.g. amount of caffeine consumed, caloric intake, amount of feedback given subjects, speed of objects, temperature), many variables of interest to social researchers simply cannot be imposed or controlled by the researcher (e.g. gender, race, ethnicity, age). In general, any variable that refers to a trait or a property of a person[6] is not one that is amenable to experimental research. We simply cannot study the effects of gender, or race, or age, or any "fixed" variable under experimental conditions since we cannot intentionally manipulate these variable as required in the experimental design. Subjects come to the experiment with their values on these variables already "set." Yet such variables are frequently the main variables of interest to social researchers.

Box 7.2   Newsworthy research: searching for the Ebola cure

In 2014, the world received a rather loud wake-up call with regard to Ebola. While some 9000 lives were lost to Ebola in 2014, it was the disease's appearance among US health care workers that prompted the sit-up and take notice in the United States. Missionary physician Kent Brantley contracted the disease while he was working in a hospital in Liberia. His health was declining rapidly or, as Brantley put it in an interview, he was "actively dying." And so when he heard that there was a new drug ZMAPP developed in Canada's National Microbiology Lab by Dr. Gary Kobinger, Brantley wanted to take the drug. The catch? The drug had only been tested on monkeys – never on humans. Dr. Brantley described his transition from doctor to patient to lab rat but admitted that he had no choice. Brantley recovered from Ebola but the scientist behind ZMAPP says it is premature to claim a real victory. Instead, according to researcher Kobinger, before ZMAPP can be considered "a real scientific fact," it will need to be subjected to randomized trial experiments on humans. These clinical trials for the ZMAPP drug are now underway.

Source: "60 Minutes, ZMAPP, A New Kind of Terrorist, Bradley Cooper", February 15, 2015. *http://www.cbs.com/shows/60_minutes/video/XnCtjhBtydCY2HwEi2o0izvu_mRmg9Qg/zmapp-a-new-kind-of-terrorist-bradley-cooper/.*

Second, the faithful execution of an experiment may create ethical and/or political dilemmas for researchers. Imagine you are a fan of head start programs and you want to do an experiment to see if such programs have long-term benefits for kids. Would it be ethical to intentionally withhold such programs from the control group if doing so might put them at a long-term disadvantage? (See the Cambridge-Somerville Youth Study discussed in Chapter 3 for a real world example of experiments causing life-long adverse consequences.) Or think about the risks of experimental research in medicine. Clearly, in medical research where experimental conditions could have negative consequences, the researcher should have great pause about proceeding. Recall the case of Dr. Olivieri from Chapter 3 on ethics. Once she discovered that the experimental drug was having an adverse effect she felt it her ethical duty to warn the parents of her research participants. And if the researcher does not pause, IRBs are often there to pull the plug. The flap over Facebook's experimenting with user emotions raised ethical concerns. (Facebook intentionally manipulated what people were seeing on their Facebook pages in order to see the emotional impact on users.) When you stop and think about it, there is a slew of important causal investigations that nonetheless present clear ethical dilemmas for the experimental design: such as the short or long-term impact of alcohol consumption or of drug use on our well-being, the impact of physical discipline on children, or the impact of various diets on our nutritional health. All of these investigations raise important causal questions, but ethical considerations must preclude pursuing such studies via the classic experimental design.

Box 7.3   Newsworthy research: using twins to study the effects of exercise

In this age of growing waistlines, interest in the benefits of exercise is growing as well. A study conducted in Finland used twins to examine the effects of exercise on health. Ten pairs of identical twins were involved in the study. Twin studies have long been used as a way to study the relative effects of nature versus nurture. But this study is of interest to us here for the ethical issues it may have encountered. The health benefits of exercise have long been established. Indeed, sports physicians note that muscles begin to atrophy within days of the cessation of exercise. So how did this Finnish study stay on the correct side of ethics since depriving someone of exercise could easily be seen as harmful? As it turns out, the study did not employ the experimental design (i.e. exercise levels were not manipulated by the researchers). Instead, the researcher located pairs of twins who were engaging in different levels of exercise: high versus low. (As it turned out, one twin in each pair had stopped exercising at his usual level while the other twin maintained his high exercise level. Ergo the quasi "experimental and control groups" were naturally established by the twins themselves.) The two groups of twins were simply compared with regard to a series of health factors (i.e. amount of body fat, insulin sensitivity, endurance levels, and amount of brain gray matter). And in case you are wondering, the twins who had maintained the higher exercise levels did indeed have better health scores on the measured outcomes.

Source: Rottensteiner, Leskinen, Niskanen *et al.* (2015).

The required random assignment of research subjects to experimental and control groups can be a deal breaker for some researchers. Depending on the research topic, random assignment may strike some as an arbitrary, unfair or unrealistic condition of the experiment. This is especially the case when exposure to the independent variable offers the possibility of some positive outcome – ostensibly those assigned to the control group are denied the opportunity of any positive outcomes that might be linked to the independent variable. In many instances, random assignment is simply beyond the purview of the researcher as, in some arenas, "assignment" decisions are the exclusive prerogative of legal notables (e.g. judges) or of other authority figures (e.g. parents).

Lastly, the experiment is by its very nature extremely weak on **external validity** – the extent to which study findings can be accurately generalized beyond the study (see discussions in Chapters 2 and 4). Earlier in this chapter, we sang the praises of the controlling nature of experiments. It is the abundance of control that makes the experiment so very effective at detecting causal connections. But all of that control comes at a price. Experimental control is a *contrived* (and therefore unnatural) condition. Consequently, the experiment may yield results that do not hold true under natural, non-experimental conditions. In other words, the experiment lacks **mundane realism** – that is, resemblance to everyday conditions. In returning to our nicotine patch example, we may find that the patch is effective under experimental conditions but not very effective when used by everyday smokers under real-world conditions. Or consider how often experimental research in the medical field, given ethical and political factors, must be conducted on animals – mice, rabbits, dogs, pigs. The external validity concern is whether or not the results obtained from animal studies can be applied to humans. The following quote about the limits of experimental research when studying certain health problems illustrates several of the limits of experimental design:

> **External validity** – the extent to which findings from one study can be accurately generalized beyond that study.
>
> **Mundane realism** – the extent to which a study resembles the conditions of everyday life.

> Scientists are still arguing about fat, despite a century of research, because the regulation of appetite and weight in the human body happens to be almost inconceivably complex, and the experimental tools we have to study it are still remarkably inadequate … To study the entire physiological system involves feeding real food to real human subjects for months or years on end, which is prohibitively expensive, ethically questionable (if you're trying to measure the effects of foods that might cause heart disease) and virtually impossible to do in any kind of rigorously controlled scientific manner. But if researchers seek to study something less costly and more controllable, they end up studying experimental situations so oversimplified that their results may have nothing to do with reality. (Taubes 2002)

Perhaps you are now asking the following question: If experiments are "problematic" for much of our social research why devote a chapter to this design? The simple fact is that the experiment is still the design that serves as the "gold standard" for assessing any piece of research pursuing causal analysis. Those who for reasons of ethics (it would be unacceptable to randomly assign participants to experimental and control groups) or of feasibility (it is impossible to manipulate fixed variables or unrealistic to randomly assign groups) cannot employ the experiment must still grapple with how to assure a non-experimental design is up to the task of causal analysis. The closer a non-experimental design comes to emulating the experimental design (e.g. see Box 7.3), the more faith we can have in any causal conclusions generated by the non-experimental study. With this in mind, we are now going to take a brief detour and review the single most popular research strategy for the social sciences and see how it fares in light of experimental standards.

Causal Analysis via Non-experimental Survey Research

In Chapter 4, on research design, we discussed how strategies fall into two major camps: those that employ experimental design and those that use non-experimental design. And as noted in the current chapter as well as previous chapters, non-experimental designs are *not* the best for pursuing causal analysis. Nonetheless, due to some very important limitations to using experiments, many researchers must settle on non-experimental approach. In this section I discuss the single most popular and efficient strategy for social research – the **survey** – and see how it tries to address the causal requirements.

Survey – data collection tool that gathers information by asking questions.

The survey is a research tool that gathers critical research information via questions. (Guidelines for conducting good surveys are discussed in detail in Chapters 8 and 9.) Surveys are incredibly versatile research instruments: there are relatively few areas of social life that cannot be effectively studied by having subjects respond to questions and/or statements about selected topics. Still, the survey is strikingly different than the experiment. Surveys do not employ experimental and control groups. They do not intentionally manipulate independent variables. Surveys are not as controlled as experiments. In fact, once questionnaires (the most common form of surveys) are delivered to potential respondents, they are entirely out of the researcher's control altogether! Indeed, pollsters are grappling anew with the problem of the growing tendency of potential survey respondents electing *not* to complete surveys. This pattern of non-response has been on the increase for the last two decades. The decidedly different design of surveys sees survey researchers delivering their surveys to either: (1) one group (sample) at one moment in time (a cross-sectional survey design), or (2) delivering the survey over time to either: (a) the same group time after time, or to (b) multiple sequential groups drawn from the same population (longitudinal designs.) (These non-experimental options are discussed fully in Chapter 4).

In forgoing the true experimental design and its intentional manipulation of independent variables, survey researchers must pursue some kind of correlational analysis in their pursuit of causal research. With correlation analysis, the researcher searches for associations or connections between various variables of interest included on the survey. For instance, on a survey I might ask about the respondent's age and his or her charitable donations in order to see if there is an association between these variables. Or I might ask about a respondent's income level and his or her political affiliation to see if these two variables are related. Indeed, with the use of a statistical package like SPSS or Stata or SAS, coupled with the information collected by surveys, the researcher can readily see if there are correlations between any of the variables measured by the various survey questions. With careful planning and forethought given to measurement, especially to levels of measurement, the survey researcher can be in a very good position for documenting any connections between variables.

So while the cross-sectional survey design significantly departs from the experimental design, it is clearly well equipped to meet at least one of the required conditions for demonstrating causality: the association requirement. With the right cross-tabs, t-tests or correlation runs, the survey researcher can easily demonstrate whether or not two variables move together (co-vary) as well as demonstrate the strength of the association. But what about the other two causal requirements: temporal ordering and establishing non-spuriousness? How does the survey fare on satisfying these conditions?

Surveys have a harder time satisfying the time order requirement of causality. This is especially the case with surveys using a cross-sectional time frame (and this is the majority of surveys). With a cross-sectional study, the researcher obtains all relevant information from respondents at a single point in time, no future follow-up contacts are made. (Cross-sectional designs are discussed in greater detail in Chapter 4). The cross-sectional time frame of surveys presents a challenge to the temporal order requirement of causality. Since all survey data is collected at one moment in time, the survey researcher does not have the option of imposing the independent variable and then later measuring subsequent changes in the dependent variable. Consequently, the typical survey researcher must pursue other ways of addressing the time order requirement of causality and establishing that the independent variable really does precede the dependent variable in time.

Perhaps the most utilized resolution of this time dilemma in cross-sectional research is the use of **retrospective questions**, in which the researcher asks a series of questions about the respondent's past. With retrospective questioning the time order of variables is made clear: events that occurred at an earlier point in time (e.g. high school experiences) clearly precede subsequent events (e.g. occupational achievements). Retrospective questions about your childhood experiences with physical discipline can be used to investigate a causal connection with your later disciplinary practices as a parent. Retrospective questions about adolescent drug use can be used in a causal investigation of mid-life health issues. Retrospective questions about peoples' experiences of the last 12 months can be used to investigate a causal link with their present attitudes toward national security. To be sure, the retrospective "fix" is not without problems. People have a remarkable capacity for forgetting or even altering past events. (Just think about Brian Williams's or Bill O'Reilly's faulty memories.) But with carefully constructed questions and with reasonable time frames, retrospective questions can make significant inroads into resolving the time dilemma of surveys.

> **Retrospective questions** – questions about a respondent's past history.

Another strategy for unraveling the time order of variables is the use of fixed variables (see section on "Temporal Ordering" in this chapter). Since fixed variables frequently reflect statuses or conditions "fixed" at birth, they logically precede all other subsequent outcomes or variables. My age (fixed by my birth year) precedes my income, my political affiliation, my attitude toward stem cell research, my views on climate change, and so on, and therefore is logically cast in the role of independent variable in a causal investigation. (Another way of making this point is to ask if any of the previously mentioned variables – income, political affiliation, attitude toward stem cell research – could *cause* my age? Whenever you find yourself answering no to such a question, you have probably identified a fixed variable.)

Perhaps the most problematic causal criterion for survey research is the test for spuriousness. Ideally, surveys are administered to representative samples of research populations (see Chapter 11 on Sampling). Since surveys do not entail the creation of randomly assigned experimental and control groups, it is difficult for surveys to conclusively address the issue of rival explanations of dependent variables. The survey researcher must engage in some heads-up thinking in order to effectively test for spurious relationships. In essence, the researcher must *anticipate* likely C variables (rival explanations) and include measures of them on surveys. (And while I may sound like a broken record – the ability to anticipate likely C variables is enhanced by a good thorough review of the research literature.) When likely C variables have been identified, measures of them can then be included on surveys. When it comes time for testing for spurious relationships, the C variables can be introduced as control variables in the analysis of our survey data – we can control their influence on the observed relationship between variables A and B. (If the observed relationship between A and B maintains itself, we can eliminate the C variable as a rival explanation of the dependent variable.) Consequently, the researcher's ability to eliminate rival explanations will ultimately depend on how thoughtful and diligent the researcher is about including survey questions about pertinent C variables.

To be sure, the experiment has a simple eloquence in its design with regard to combating rival explanations: the assumed equivalence of the experimental and control groups is a very powerful way to eliminate most internal validity threats. So without the use of experiment and control groups, the survey researcher must devise an effective "work-around." The work-around, however, can be accomplished via very thoughtful survey development and careful statistical analysis. Two variable tables that demonstrate an association can morph into three variable tables controlling for C variables. Simple correlational analysis must be ramped up to regression or path analysis. Statistics must step in to compensate for the lack of experimental and control groups. And, of course, if questions about relevant C variables are omitted from the survey, the chance to test for spuriousness will be lost. So while it is not the ideal design for causal investigations, the survey can, with enough careful planning, and statistical know-how, step up to the task of pursuing causal questions.

Causality and Field Research

Field research – data collection strategy that sees the researcher directly observing research subjects in their natural setting.

Before leaving this discussion of causal analysis, we should consider another popular research strategy – **field research** – and see how it sizes up on the causal analysis front. With field research, the social investigator directly observes people/events in their natural settings. (Field research is discussed in detail in Chapter 10.) One common goal of field research is to document the natural flow or unfolding of events. Many of the earliest field observation studies were attempts to understand how one "becomes" a … stripper, nudist, bisexual, a gang member, a biker woman, a prostitute or an "ex" deviant to name but a few topics. While we have spent the bulk of this chapter discussing the dominant causal model in sociology and other social sciences – the nomothetic model – it is now time to return to the idiographic model.

Field research is most readily and naturally aligned with the idiographic style of causal analysis. The field research commitment to directly observing events and people *over time* facilitates the detailed examination of causal sequencing that is the heart of the idiographic approach. And while the idiographic model is only interested in an exhaustive causal analysis of *one* specific event, it must still refer to basic causal standards reviewed above: time order, association, and non-spuriousness. This means that if a proposed account stipulating a causal sequence of events does not meet the time requirement, then that account must be rejected and a new one sought. For instance, if the death of a hostage can be shown to have preceded air strikes by coalition forces, then the **narrative** that the air strikes caused the death must be rejected. Additionally, however, the idiographic model must also pay attention to two more standards of causality: specifying a causal mechanism and contextualizing the event under analysis. In other words, an idiographic narrative must offer a persuasive account of how one thing led to another.

> **Narrative** – an account that details the unfolding or sequencing of an event.

As previously indicated, in providing a causal explanation of an event, the idiographic model offers a **narrative** – an account of the connections between sequential events. In this narrative, particular attention is paid to specifying the causal mechanism of some specific outcome. Narratives should contain details or "thick descriptions" that help the reader visualize and understand the unfolding or progression of events. A strong, detailed narrative should serve to strengthen the causal argument being presented. Attention is also paid to the *context* of the causal connection. Contextual analysis seeks to identify those factors that might prove relevant for fully understanding the causal sequence – how one thing led to another. If the narrative fails to offer a convincing analysis on these fronts, the causal conclusions will be compromised. Consider, for instance, the narrative offered by Rubinstein (1973) and see how it helps to illuminate the causal sequencing of events that led to a patrolman hitting an elderly black man:

A young white officer noticed a man standing near a street corner turn away as the patrol car approached. He stopped his car and rolled down the window to look at the elderly Negro man. Instead of getting out of the car, he yelled across the deserted street to him. "Take you hand out of your coat." The man had turned back toward the car when it stopped, and he had his right hand jammed inside. He did not react to the command. They were frozen for several seconds; then the patrolman repeated his demand. When the man remained silent, the officer drew his pistol, continuing to remain seated in his car. He placed his gun in plain view and again ordered the man to show his hand. The man was very agitated but he remained silent. Slowly he began to extract his hand, but he gave the appearance of concealing some intention which threatened the patrolman, who cocked his gun and pointed it directly at the man. Suddenly the old man drew out his hand and threw a pistol to the ground. He stood trembling. The patrolman uncocked his gun with a shaking hand and approached. He was on the verge of tears, and in a moment of confusion, fear, and anxiety, he struck the man with the butt of his pistol. "Why didn't you take your hand out when I told you? I almost shot you, you dumb bastard." (Rubinstein 1973, pp. 304–305)

If you call to mind any recent criminal trial, you will discover a fundamental weakness of the idiographic narrative. It is totally possible for different individuals to observe the same events and yet construct different narratives. Consider the strikingly different narratives that are likely to emerge in a typical criminal murder trial. As part of the trial, the two opposing attorneys will each present a case that they contend best describes the events that led to the murderous outcome. The defense will construct a causal narrative that exonerates the accused while the prosecutor will construct one that alleges a very different story of the defendant's guilt. Constructing a narrative does not guarantee that the causal argument is a correct one. For a timely example, consider the conflicting narratives that have been constructed regarding the summer 2014 shooting of Michael Brown in Ferguson, Missouri. Or consider the conflicting narratives floated after the 2012 attack on the American Mission in Benghazi, Libya. Some early accounts of the violence claimed it was a spontaneous mob attack while other accounts asserted the violence was a planned terrorist attack. Some accounts maintained a deliberate cover-up of an intelligence failure while a final report by the US House of Representatives concluded there was no such failure or wrongdoing (CNN Library 2014; Edwards-Levy 2014). Once again we would be well advised to invoke the skeptic mindset of science and assess the narrative's temporal argument as well as the details and the context it offers by way of elaborating causal mechanisms.

Conclusions

Trying to establish causal connections is a fundamental human and research activity. Uncovering, for example, the causes of family violence, drug addiction, eating disorders, mental illness, autism, recidivism, or terrorism, on either an individual or social level could mean life-changing consequences for countless individuals who are directly and/or indirectly affected by these problems. Similarly, *misstating* the causes of these problems could also spell life-altering *negative* consequences for countless individuals. Errors in causal analysis can be quite costly; our standards for establishing causal connections must be high.

In striving to produce high quality causal research, we are well advised to utilize the experiment – the quintessential design for detecting causality. This research design offers us the best chance of correctly identifying the causal connections between independent and dependent variables. The experiment sets the standard for assessing all causal analysis. Still, there are times when the experiment is not a practical or feasible design choice. Limitations imposed by the nature of variables being investigated, by ethical or political implications, or by the issue of external validity can force the researcher to employ non-experimental research strategies. Ultimately, however, researchers using non-experimental design will nonetheless be judged by the standards set by the experiment.

TAKE AWAYS

- Causal analysis is engaged with the "cause and effect" model
  - It is concerned with providing explanations or with answering the why and how questions
- In pursuing causal analysis, we have the choice of two approaches:
  - Nomothetic model – seeks general causal explanations
  - Idiographic model – seeks case-specific causal explanations
- There are three essential criteria for establishing causal connections
  - Timing – independent variable must precede the dependent variable
  - Association – independent and dependent variables must be associated
  - Non-spuriousness – observed relationship between the independent and dependent variable must survive any/all tests for spuriousness
- The experiment is the gold standard design choice for studying causality
  - Can readily address causal criteria
  - Most effective at handling threats to internal validity:
    - History, maturation, selection bias, mortality, and so on
- With careful planning, non-experimental designs can pursue causal analysis
  - Cross-sectional survey research with careful planning and analysis can address questions of causality via:
    - Use of retrospective questions
    - Use of fixed variables
    - Inclusion of C variables
  - Field research is a sound strategy for pursuing idiographic causal analysis

Sharpening the Edge: More reading and searching

- You will find a very down-to-earth discussion of causal relationships and validity threats in: Jeffrey Katzer, Kenneth Cook, and Wayne Crouch's *Evaluating Information*,. 4th ed. Boston: McGraw-Hill, 1998. In particular, you should consult Chapters 11 and 12.
- A thorough discussion of causality and an extensive review of internal validity threats can also be found at Bill Trochim's webpage. Once at the page, follow the links for "Establishing Cause & Effect," "Single Group Threats," Multiple-Group Threats," and "Social Interaction Threats":
  http://trochim.human.cornell.edu/kb/

Exercises

1 Consider a recent major film that tells a causal story (e.g. *The Imitation Game*, *The Theory of Everything*, *Still Alice*). Which model of causality is most clearly illustrated in the work?

2 Recently efforts have been made to bring lawsuits against fast food chains on behalf of clients who say that fast foods have caused them serious health problems. Which criteria of causality will be the most challenging one(s) for plaintiff lawyers to satisfy?

3 You have been asked to develop a questionnaire that will investigate the causal connection between drinking and family violence: is alcohol use/abuse a major cause of the use of violence against loved ones? Itemize the kinds of questions you would want to ask. Which of the questions will allow you to address the issue of a spurious relationship between alcohol use and violence?

Notes

1 For a good discussion of cognitive scientists' views on this matter as well as a discussion of sociologists' objections to this position, see Cerulo (2002).

2 To be sure, causality is studied by various methods. Science historian Naomi Oreskes in an interesting TED lecture ("Why We Should Trust Science") discusses how "modeling" techniques were once popular strategies for testing causal ideas. Today, computer simulation is used to "model" causal explanations. It is such simulation that is behind the scientific claims of global warming. In the present discussion of causal analysis, we are focusing on techniques that are standard in the social sciences.

3 Some researchers use "matching" techniques for establishing the experimental and control groups (– i.e. assign an equal number of men and women to both groups, or assign an equal number of college graduates to both groups). But this process demands prior knowledge about what variables require matching. Purists insist that a true experiment must use random assignment.

4 Other common threats are testing, instrumentation, mortality and regression, contamination and compensation. See "Expanding the Essentials" for links to learn more about these threats.

5 Some researchers call these kinds of variables "active variables."

6 Some researchers make the distinction by calling these kinds of variable "attribute" variables.

References

American Psychology Association. 2015. "Stress in America." http://www.apa.org/news/press/releases/2015/02/money-stress.aspx.

Becker, Howard. 1963. *Outsiders*. New York: The Free Press.

Belfort, Mandy B., Rifas-Shiman, Sheryl L., Kleinman, Ken P., Guthrie, Lauren B., Bellinger, David C., Taveras, Elsie M., Gillman, Matthew W., and Emily Oken. 2013. "Infant Feeding and Childhood Cognition at Ages 3 and 7 Years: Effects of Breastfeeding Duration and Exclusivity." *JAMA Pediatric* 167(9): 836–844.

Borchgrevink, Aage. 2013. *A Norwegian Tragedy*. Polity.

Center for the Digital Future. 2013. *World Internet Project*. International Report. http://www.digitalcenter.org/wp-content/uploads/2013/12/2013worldinternetreport.pdf.

Cerulo, Karen. 2002. *Culture in Mind: Toward a Sociology of Culture and Cognition*. New York: Routledge.

CNN Library. 2014. "Benghazi Mission Attack Fast Facts." December 2. http://www.cnn.com/2013/09/10/world/benghazi-consulate-attack-fast-facts/index.html.

Edwards-Levy, Ariel. 2014. "Most People Have No Idea What a House Benghazi Investigation Just Found." *Huff Post*. Politics. http://www.huffingtonpost.com/2014/12/05/benghazi-poll_n_6277742.html.

Horwood, John and David Ferguson. 1998. "Breastfeeding and Later Cognitive and Academic Outcomes." *Pediatrics* 101(1): 379–385.

James, F. 1992. "New Methods for Measuring Homelessness and the Population at Risk: Exploratory Research in Colorado." *Social Work Research and Abstracts* 28(2): 9–14.

Levitt, Steven and Stephen Dubner. 2005. *Freakonomics*. New York. Harper Collins.

Lucas, A., Morley, R., Cole, T.J., Lester, G., and C. Leeson-Payne. 1992. "Breast Milk and Subsequent Intelligence Quotient in Children Born Preterm." *The Lancet* 339: 261–264.

Rottensteiner, M., Leskinen, T., Niskanen, E., Aaltonen, S., Mutikainen, S., Wikgren, J., Heikkilä, K., Kovanen, V., Kainulainen, H., Kaprio, J., Tarkka, I.M., and U.M. Kujala, UM. 2015. "Physical Activity, Fitness, Glucose Homeostasis, and Brain Morphology in Twins." *Medicine & Science in Sports & Exercise* 47(3): 509–518. doi: 10.1249/MSS.0000000000000437.

Richards, Barry. 2014. "What Drove Anders Breivik." *Contexts* 13(4): 42–27.

Rubinstein, J. 1973. *City Police*. New York: Farrar, Straus & Giroux.

Shermer, M. 1997. *Why People Believe Weird Things*. New York: W.H. Freeman.

Taubes, Gary. 2002. "What if it's all Been a Big Fat Lie?" *The New York Times Magazine*, July 7. http://www.nytimes.com/2002/07/07/magazine/what-if-it-s-all-been-a-big-fat-lie.html.

Torabi, M., Bailey, W., and M. Majd-Jabbari. 1993. "Cigarette Smoking as a Predictor of Alcohol and Other Drug Use by Children and Adolescents: Evidence of the 'Gateway Drug' Effect." *Journal of School Health* 63(7): 302–307.

Vaughan, D. 2002. "Signals and Interpretive Work: the Role of Culture in a Theory of Practical Action." In Karen Cerulo (ed.), *Culture in Mind: Toward a Sociology of Culture and Cognition*. New York: Routledge.

Chapter 8

The Questionnaire: Would You Mind Taking the Time to Answer a Few Questions?

Introducing Social Research Methods: Essentials for Getting the Edge, First Edition. Janet M. Ruane.
© 2016 John Wiley & Sons, Ltd. Published 2016 by John Wiley & Sons, Ltd.

FIRST TAKES

Be sure to take note of the following:

Survey research

- The dominant data collection tool in the social sciences
- Finding out by asking questions – familiar but not necessarily easy

Two forms: interviews and questionnaires

- Questionnaire: a popular and extremely versatile tool
    - Not as simple as it looks
    - Securing good response rates is critical
- Need good quality control
    - Wording
        - Follow the "rules"
    - Sequencing
        - Order matters
    - Formatting
        - Appearance matters
- Mailed and online questionnaires
    - Require some special considerations

Your next trip to the supermarket can provide a good gauge of our dependence on one basic tool for knowing. While waiting in the checkout line, take a look around at the tabloids and you will find yourself adrift in a sea of questions. Who are the latest celebrities to abandon Twitter? Will Prince Charles ever serve as King of England? How long will Oscar Pistorius actually spend in prison for the killing of his girlfriend? Is the Jenner family happy about the arrival of Caitlyn? Is Justin Bieber about to be deported? Will George and Amal's marriage really last? Is it true that Vladimir Putin suffers from a form of autism? Similarly, a sampling of morning, afternoon, and evening talk shows or Web pages remind us that "inquiring minds" want to know the answers to many, many questions. Posing and answering questions seems to be at the heart of our popular mass media culture.

Finding out by asking questions is not the exclusive domain of news tabloids and talk shows. It is also the heart of survey research – the primary data collection tool of the social sciences. Simply put, the **survey** is a research instrument that allows us to gather critical information by posing questions to respondents. In general, we follow one of two paths in survey research. We ask our questions via an **interview** or we ask our questions via a **questionnaire**. An interview is the more *personal* form of survey research – questions are posed in a face-to-face or telephone exchange between the interviewer and the respondent. (The interview technique is the focus of Chapter 9.) A questionnaire is a

Survey – a data collection tool that gathers information by asking questions.

Interview – a form of survey research where questions are posed person to person.

Questionnaire – a form of survey research where questions are posed via a self-administered instrument.

self-contained, self-administered instrument for asking questions. While the questionnaire lacks the personal touch of the interview, it can nonetheless be an extremely efficient data collection tool. Indeed, the self-sufficiency of questionnaires makes them the most popular survey option. A good questionnaire can "stand on its own" and enable a researcher to collect data without requiring any personal contact with the respondent. This trait means that questionnaires can transcend most barriers of time and space. By utilizing the mail system (snail mail or email), a researcher can execute a national or an international survey without *anyone* ever "leaving home."

And as news tabloids and talk shows reveal, there is hardly any limit to what it is we can find out by asking questions. Indeed, the survey is a popular tool for data collection precisely because it is so versatile. Any one of the several goals of research (exploration, description, explanation, or evaluation) can readily be pursued via survey research. Similarly, there is no limit to the kinds of information we might obtain via questions. We can ask questions to find out objective facts and conditions (What is your age? Where were you born?) We can ask questions about behaviors. (Do you smoke? Do you participate in any team sports? Did you vote in the last election?) We can ask questions to learn people's attitudes, beliefs or opinions. (Do you think there will ever be peace in the Middle East? Do you favor a mandatory waiting period for the purchase of handguns? Is the president doing a good job with the economy? Should the retirement age be increased?) We can ask about people's future hopes and expectations. (What's the highest educational degree you plan on obtaining? How many children do you see in your future? Do you expect to see a solution to global warming in your lifetime?) We can ask questions about knowledge. (In your state, is it possible to legally charge husbands with raping their wives? Which nation has the highest infant mortality rates or the highest education levels?) Indeed, as long as we pay careful attention to how we phrase our questions, there is virtually no limit to what we might find out via surveys (see Box 8.1).

Box 8.1   Research in the news: survey overload in schools?

Most parents when they send their children to school expect them to be getting an education. But schooling these days often is accompanied by relentless data collection. Specifically, there is growing concern that students are subjected to questionnaires that extend beyond any educational mission. It is not unusual for students to receive questionnaires that ask about their health, sleeping habits, sexual activity, drug use, and disciplinary histories. Why such a wide range of issues? Well some of the data collection is serving third parties that use the student information for non-educational interests: marketing and target advertising. Many parents regard the rampant questioning of students as an invasion of privacy and they want something done about it. In 2015, President Obama proposed the Student Digital Privacy Act. This bill seeks to ensure that data collected in schools or other educational settings/contexts is used only for educational purposes.

Sources: Barnes (2014); Greenfield (2015); White House Press Release (2015).

For many, survey research is a natural and familiar way of gathering information, as second nature to us as talking and writing. This familiarity causes some to think that survey research is easy. Many adopt an "anyone can do it" attitude. (Think of all of the businesses that utilize surveys to learn more about their customers.) As we will see in this chapter, however, such an attitude is extremely naive. Much thought must be given to the exact wording of our questions, the structure of our questions, and the way we sequence and format our questions. This holistic approach is mandated by the fact that survey research has a terribly vulnerable Achilles heel. The fact is that we can ask great questions and still fail at survey research! How so? Above all else, successful survey research requires that we secure respondents' *cooperation*. We must convince potential respondents that our questionnaire is worth their time and effort and we must convince them that the questions are worthy of honest accurate answers.

Neither of these tasks is easy but both are hurdles that the researcher *must* try to overcome. Despite their popularity, questionnaires tend to suffer low **response rates** (i.e. the percentage of potential respondents who actually return a completed questionnaire). While a response rate of 70% or more is needed for sound, responsible analysis and reporting, it is not unusual for questionnaires to face response rates of less than 40 or 50%. Indeed, many polling organizations today are grappling with the problem of low cooperation rates (which have been steadily declining since the mid-1990s) and are brainstorming about ways to overcome this problem.[1]

> **Response rate** – the percentage of contacted respondents who complete surveys.
>
> **Social desirability bias** – a measurement error caused by people responding to questions in a way that makes them look good; over-reporting "good" behaviors or under-reporting discrediting behaviors.

The issue of respondent honesty is more difficult to assess and control. Perhaps it is just human nature, but many of us like to present ourselves in the most favorable light. This tendency to answer questions in a "socially appropriate way" is referred to as a **social desirability bias**. Surely this explains respondents' tendency to over report "good things": for example the amount they give to charity, the happiness they derive from their marriages or how often people claim they attend religious services. We also tend to underreport our negatives: such as how much alcohol we drink, the amount of time we spend in front of the TV, how often we tell lies. Americans apparently "fudge" quite a bit when it comes to self-reporting eating habits:

> Forty pounds of white bread, 32 gallons of soft drinks, 41 pounds of potatoes and a couple of gallons of vegetable oil in which to fry them. No, it's not a roster of provisions for the troops on the Fourth of July. It's a sample of what the average American eats in a year.

> Bear in mind, that's only what consumers admit to eating. If there is one thing researchers have learned while surveying the nation's gastronomic habits, it is that, whether from modesty or sheer denial, Americans are prodigious liars about how much they really eat. (Winter 2002)

In short, survey research in general and questionnaire development in particular are anything but "no brainers." This kind of research requires a lot of attention to many different details.

The Way We Word

In survey research, the exact questions we ask constitute our **operational definitions** (see Chapter 5 for a full discussion of operational definitions). That is, the concepts we are interested in studying (e.g. fear of crime) are measured via the questions or statement we pose to respondents (e.g. to measure fear of crime, the GSS asks, "Is there any area right around here

> **Operational definition** – set of instructions (i.e. questions and response options) for measuring a variable.

where you would be afraid to walk alone at night?" Yes/No). Given that survey questions are our measures, the assessment of measurement validity and reliability demands that we give careful attention to the exact wording of our questions. We must choose our words wisely. An early experiment on question wording by Donald Rugg found that American's support for freedom of speech was drastically altered by different wordings of the following questions:

- Do you think the United States should *forbid* public speeches against democracy?
- Do you think the United States should *allow* public speeches against democracy?

The "forbid" question generated a much lower agreement rate (54%) than the "allow" question (75%) (Schuman 2002). Similarly, several decades later, Smith (1987) found that respondents to the GSS responded more negatively to the term "welfare" than the term "poor." A recent survey found that public opinion about government surveillance was impacted by the wording of the questions: when the surveillance was described as being court approved or as a way to fight terrorism, approval rates were 12% and 9% higher than when these words were not used (Pew Research Center 2013). When asking questions about the public's attitudes toward abortion, might it make a difference if the words "end pregnancy" were substituted for the word "abortion"? Sociologist Howard Schuman (2002) suspected the switch would lead to an increase in support for legalized abortions but was surprised to find no difference between the two wordings. The "public speech" and the welfare and surveillance examples clearly show us that wording *can* matter. And while the "abortion" example runs counter to the researcher's expectations, his findings nonetheless yield some valuable insight into the measurement process. *All* the examples reveal the importance of considering and evaluating the impact of the words we use in our measures.

The Rules

Survey data is only as good (i.e. as valid and reliable) as the questions posed and all too often these questions leave much to be desired. Quality survey data require us to follow certain rules for asking questions. The rules that follow might strike you as common sense. Faithful adherence to them, however, is not so common.

The Questions We Pose Should be Clear in Meaning and Free Of Ambiguity

This rule sounds simple enough. A moment's reflection, however, will reveal how our everyday speech is laden with ambiguity. Consider the following questions.

- Do you exercise on a regular basis?
- What is your annual income?

At first glance these questions may strike you as perfectly adequate for "finding out" some key information about the respondent. Both questions, however, are plagued by ambiguity. How, for instance, should the respondent interpret the phrase "regular basis" in the exercise question? Does regular mean that someone exercises daily or simply that they exercise several times a week? If respondents faithfully jog every Saturday morning, should they answer this question in the affirmative? In general, frequency terms like "regularly," "often," and "seldom" are inherently vague and contribute imprecision to the measurement process. We should think twice about freely using them in our questions. A better strategy is to use more precise language in the question and quantitative response options that help standardize people's experiences:

How many days do you exercise per week?

1. I do not exercise
2. 1–2 days a week
3. 3–4 days a week
4. 5–6 days a week
5. 7 days a week

Similar observations can be made about the income question. Does income refer to *earned* income or to all money payments one receives in a year? Is the question asking about net or gross income? Is the question asking about personal income or family income? The critical point is this: ambiguous questions produce ambiguous data. The more ambiguity we leave in our questions, the more ambiguity we will encounter in our findings. The survey researcher is obligated to remove as much guesswork from questionnaire items as possible.

Survey Questions Should Use Common Everyday Language; Avoid the Use of Specialized Language such as Jargon, Abbreviations or Acronyms

This rule is especially noteworthy for those of us trained in the social sciences as well as for those doing research on behalf of special interest groups. The various disciplines of the social sciences are replete with their own special language, a language that helps identify us as members of our respective fields. Sociologists, for instance, speak of families of orientation vs. families of procreation. They speak of our anomic society and the collective conscience and of social capital. These terms, while meaningful to sociologists, are clear examples of the rather mystifying jargon of a discipline. It would be a serious mistake for a sociologist to use these terms when posing questions to respondents (e.g. What was the size of your family of orientation?) Similarly, it would be a mistake to use terms that assume respondents' knowledge of abbreviations or acronyms associated with special interest groups. Questions about the respondent's support for the NRA may find them focusing on the right to bear arms but it is also possible that some respondents will simply not know the letters stand for the National Rifle Association and give you their thoughts about protecting redheads (National Redheads Association). Asking questions about GM food or MMR vaccine or about PGS will not work for those unfamiliar with the issues of genetically modified food or the measles vaccine debate or the recent hubbub over Great Britain's plan to move forward on three-parent babies (and the need for pre-implantation genetic screening.)

Survey Questions Should Use Neutral Language; Emotional or Leading Language Should Be Avoided

All of us know the power of words. Words can cut, sting, placate, or motivate. The power of words does not disappear in survey research. Emotional language can produce biased responses by "pushing our buttons" and encouraging respondents to react to the language *used* in a question rather than to the issues raised by a question. Consider the following question found in a Greenpeace survey about marine mammals:

> On December 31, 1992, a United Nations ban on the use of high seas driftnets, the modern monstrosities of plastic filament that trap and kill any living creature that enters their paths: dolphins, seals, marine birds, even whales, went into effect. Presently there is no way to ensure that the ban is working or that driftnets are no longer being used. Would you support an international system to monitor and enforce the UN driftnet ban?

As you read this question, if you found yourself having an emotional reaction to the idea of monstrous nets trapping and killing defenseless marine life, you experienced first-hand the influential power of language.

Typically emotional language is used to lead respondents to the desired response. Leading questions suggest to the respondent that one response is better than or preferred over another.[2] Clearly, the above question on the use of driftnets is not neutral. The question is trying to lead the respondent to a stand that supports the banning of driftnets. To avoid leading questions, the survey researcher must phrase questions in such a way as to make respondents feel that all answers are equally legitimate. Consider how the following questions violate this principle:

- What do you find offensive about flag burning?
- Why is hitting children wrong?

Both of these questions lead the respondent by suggesting a desired response: flag burning is offensive and hitting children is wrong. As presently phrased, the questions are telling the respondent that alternate views of flag burning (i.e. an act of free speech) or of hitting children (i.e. an acceptable disciplinary tactic) are not appropriate *regardless of how the respondent may actually feel.* Or take a look at a question posed by Fox News in a survey regarding government surveillance: "Does it feel like the federal government has gotten out of control and is threatening the basic civil liberties of Americans, or doesn't it feel this way to you?" Given the phrasing, it might not surprise you to learn that 68% of respondents agreed that the government is out of control (Dimock 2013).

Box 8.2   Sharpening your research vision: words that work … or at least "work" the audience

In 2007, political consultant Frank Luntz made quite a splash with his book *Words That Work: It's Not What You Say, It's What People Hear.* Luntz had already made a name for himself by helping the Republican Party launch the *Contract with America* and win back the House of Representatives for the first time in four decades. He was in demand as the guy who could help politicians, business leaders and just about anyone who was in need of words that would work for them. Luntz advises clients to recognize the power of words and to select words strategically. So what is part of the Luntz legacy? He advised Republican politicians to replace the elitist sounding "estate tax" with the more personal (indeed) "death tax." (Who would ever be *for* a death tax?) He urged the phrase "drilling for oil" be restated as "exploring for energy." And he still advocates that future Republican discussions about social security must be cast in the language of "retirement security." As you read current public opinion polls, be sure to pay attention to the actual language used in the questions. You may well find some of Luntz's words and ideas at work.

Survey Questions Should be Simple and Easy for Respondents to Answer

Again, this rule may strike you as so obvious that it need not be stated. Still, it is a rule that is frequently violated. For instance, surveys often pose "double-barreled" questions that are not easy to answer. Double-barreled questions are those that ask the respondent two (or more) questions under the guise of one question. Consider the following item that appeared on recent survey on community policing:

- How do you rate police response time to emergency and non-emergency calls?

Respondents were provided with just one set of response alternatives (answers ranging from adequate to inadequate) despite the fact that they were really being asked to assess two different kinds of police activity: emergency and non-emergency calls. Respondents who had different experiences for emergency and non-emergency encounters with the police would find this question impossible to answer as currently phrased.

Questions can also prove difficult to answer when they ask respondents to perform unreasonable calculations. A medical researcher may want to know about respondents' health risks. Asking how many cigarettes the respondent smokes in a year (or even in a month) is not a good way to get this information. Years and months are not the usual time-frames smokers use to quantify their smoking habits. (Smokers usually characterize their habit in terms of daily consumption: e.g. a pack a day.) Similarly, a researcher may be interested in obtaining information about household spending. Asking respondents about their annual expenditures for food, however, would not be a user-friendly question. In fact, the calculations required to answer this question would encourage a high non-response rate – that is, rather than doing the calculations, respondents would be tempted to skip the question altogether. The researcher would be better advised in this situation to ask a question about respondent's average food bill for a typical time period (e.g. a weekly grocery order). Once this basic information is obtained, the researcher can then do the calculations needed to estimate yearly food expenses.

Questions that fail to follow rules of good grammar can also prove difficult for respondents. Particularly troublesome are questions that employ a double negative. Double negatives *don't make no good sense in our writing or in surveys.* (See what I mean?) If the respondent is forced to re-read a question in an attempt to figure out what it is really asking, then the question is not an acceptable one. Consider the following double-negative question that was used in a Roper survey of American's beliefs about the Holocaust:

- Does it seem possible or does it seem impossible to you that the Nazi extermination of the Jews never happened?

With this wording of the question, 22% of respondents indicated that they thought it possible the Holocaust never happened! Jewish leaders were shocked by these findings. Researchers reconsidered the actual phrasing of the question and determined that the use of a double negative (impossible and never) in the original question was the culprit behind the surprising findings. The question was asked again without the confusing double negative phrasing.

- Do you doubt that the Holocaust actually happened or not?

This time the percentage of respondents who thought the Holocaust probably didn't happen fell to less than 3%.

The Structure of Questions: Closed and Open-Ended Questions

In addition to carefully considering the exact wording or phrasing of our questions, survey researchers must also decide the amount of freedom they want to give respondents when answering the questions posed. This freedom issue is addressed by the use of closed or open-ended questions.

With **closed-ended questions**, the researcher provides a set of pre-determined response alternatives for the respondent to use when answering the question. With **open-ended questions**, respondents are free to devise their own unique answers to the questions posed. You have probably encountered these two versions of questions in a typical classroom exam. The multiple-choice questions on an exam illustrate closed-ended questions. The essay portion of an exam illustrates the open-ended style of questions.

> **Closed-ended questions** – questions that supply pre-determined response options.
>
> **Open-ended questions** – questions that require respondents to supply their own answers.

There are a number of considerations that should influence the use of closed or open-ended questions. Providing a pre-determined set of responses is advisable when it is possible to anticipate the full range of potential responses and when these responses are relatively few in number. Questions about respondent's marital status, political affiliation, or favorite fast food chain would all be good candidates for closed-ended questions. Open-ended questions are advisable when posing a complex question that defies any ready or apparent answer. The open-ended approach is also recommended when we are interested in obtaining the respondent's unique views on an issue or topic. Questions about respondents' career plans or hopes for the future or about their views on charging adolescent law offenders as adults would be good candidates for open-ended questions.

In deciding on closed or open-ended questions, the researcher should also consider the advantages and disadvantages of each style of questioning. As you probably know from experience, closed-ended questions are easier to answer. (How often have intentionally skipped circling an answer on a multiple-choice exam because it was just too much trouble?) Since closed-ended questions are easy to "answer" they tend to cut down on non-responses. They also carry a clear benefit for the researcher: They reduce the time and effort needed to code responses for data entry and analysis. "Coding" decisions are achieved via the pre-determined response alternatives. These advantages, however, also alert us to some disadvantages of closed-ended questions. Because closed-ended questions are "easy" to answer, they may encourage respondents to circle or check a response even when the responses do not really "ring true" for the respondent. (Again, think about your experiences with multiple-choice exams. Any time you "guess" at an answer you are pretending to know something you really do not know.)

Box 8.3   Sharpening your research vision: would you like that question open or closed?

Schuman conducted an interesting experiment that shows respondents will often take the path of least resistance when answering survey questions. He asked respondents their thoughts about the most important problem facing the country today. For the first group studied, he left the question open-ended – people had to come up with their own entries. He asked a second comparable group of respondents the same question but this time he also presented a set of options for the respondents to choose from. The listed options were culled from the *least prevalent* responses obtained from the group completing the open-ended question – that is, fewer than 3% of the open-ended respondents identified the listed problems as important. Schuman also gave the second group the opportunity to specify a totally different problem if they were not satisfied with the listed options. Despite the closed-ended list being decidedly low-priority problems, the respondents to the closed-ended question chose one of the "rare" listed options as the most important problem facing the country. Schuman notes then that the form of a question, open or closed, becomes an important frame of reference for respondents.

Source: Schuman (2002).

Closed-ended questions can also misrepresent or obscure true differences or similarities in respondents' answers. Consider, for instance, the following question about a person's generosity:

How generous a person are you?

1. Extremely generous
2. Somewhat generous
3. Not so generous
4. Not at all generous.

One person may donate $100.00 a year to their favorite charity and select option 1 (extremely generous) to describe him/herself. Another person may donate $1000.00 a year to their favorite charity and also select option 1. There is a tenfold difference in these respondents' money-giving behaviors yet both respondents would receive the same variable value (1) in terms of their closed-ended responses. Conversely, we can also imagine a scenario where persons donating $100.00 might characterize themselves as extremely generous while others donating the same amount might characterize themselves as "somewhat generous." Here we have the "same" behaviors appearing as different responses in our closed-ended question. You can imagine how these misrepresentations can confound the researcher's data analysis. Extreme variation is "hidden" in the first scenario while identical behaviors yield "false" variation in the second scenario. Since the study of variation is the driving force of research analysis, the problem of obscuring variance in the measurement process is a significant concern. (See Chapter 12 for further discussion.)

The clearest advantage of open-ended questions is that they do not put words in respondents' mouths. This feature means that open-ended questions may do a better job than closed-ended questions at measuring what *respondents* actually think or do (and not just measure what the *researcher believes* respondents think or do; see Box 8.3). Open-ended questions also allow researchers to find out something unanticipated. The freedom offered with open-ended questions means that respondents may report something the researcher would never have thought of including in a closed-ended set of responses. Once again, however these advantages foreshadow some of the disadvantages of open-ended questions. Giving respondents total freedom to supply their own answers means that the researcher will have to work harder at coding responses. Indeed, it is possible that responses will be widely different from one person to the next.

Open-ended questions are also "harder" for respondents to complete. They require respondents to work harder in the sense that they have to "write" something in order to provide an answer. Consequently, open-ended questions suffer a lower response rate than do closed-ended questions. (Again, think about a typical exam. Essay questions are usually more work for students since they actually have to write out answers and not just select a listed option, so it is not so unusual to find students leaving essay questions blank. Writing out a response to a question you really do not know how to answer may be more trouble than it's worth.) And since open-ended questions required respondents to compose an answer, there is also a minimal level of education or language fluency needed by respondents.

Closed vs. Open-Ended Questions and Levels of Measurement

Our selection of closed or open-ended questions carries implications for the level of measurement we achieve in our survey items. As we change the response alternatives we offer in our closed-ended questions, we can change the level of measurement achieved. Consider the following questions:

- Do you rent DVDs?
    1. yes
    2. no
- Do you rent DVDs?
    1. never
    2. rarely
    3. occasionally
    4. often
- In the last two weeks, how many times did you rent DVDs? (Please specify an exact number_____)

The first item reaches the nominal level of measurement. The numbers attached to the various response alternatives merely label two qualitatively different answers: yes and no. The second item with its different set of fixed choices reaches the ordinal level of measurement. The numbers attached to the various response alternatives express a rank ordering – as the numbers increase from 1 to 4 so too does the frequency with which one rents videos. A switch from the closed-ended forms to an open-ended question about renting videos enables the researcher to achieve the ratio level of measurement. The "number" attached to the third item above is an actual count of the number of times the respondent rented videos in the last two weeks.[3]

Exhaustivity – an essential trait for closed-ended questions that requires all relevant response options being presented to respondents.

Mutual exclusivity – an essential trait for closed-ended questions requiring that provided response options do not overlap each other.

Closed-ended Options: How Many?

One other issue deserves careful consideration when constructing closed-ended questions. The most basic question is how many response categories should be listed? For nominal level measures, the number of categories should be **exhaustive** and they should be **mutually exclusive**. To offer an exhaustive set of response options, the researcher should include as many options as needed to cover all feasible answers. In short, the provided response options should be *empirically determined* – listing all the options that actually exist. Mutually exclusive response options are ones that do not overlap. Here the goal is to give respondents only one place to "land" or go when choosing an answer.

For some variables, these conditions of exhaustivity and mutual exclusivity are easily met. In asking a closed-ended question about respondent's sex, the researcher only need supply two response options: male and female.[4] These choices are both exhaustive and mutually exclusive. Asking about area of residence is a good candidate for a closed-ended question – urban, suburban, rural. But now think about asking a closed-ended question about respondent's college major, the challenge of providing an exhaustive list of options is much greater. Some colleges offer hundreds of majors! Here the researcher must figure out an acceptable solution. She or he might list broad categories of majors (e.g. social science major, natural science major, business major) in order to keep the list of options to a manageable size. If the researcher goes down this route, it is always wise to include an "other" option for the student whose major does not fall into any of the conventional categories. (The "other" category allows the researcher to satisfy the condition of exhaustivity.) But rather than trying to provide a full list of options, the researcher might decide the question is better posed as an open-ended one that invites the respondent to write in the name of their major. The researcher would then face the task of reviewing all the responses and imposing an after the fact coding scheme.

Sometimes our attempts to achieve exhaustivity lead us to make mistakes regarding mutual exclusivity. Consider for example asking a question about student status and providing the following "empirically based" options:

What is your student status?

1. undergraduate
2. graduate
3. full-time student
4. part-time student
5. day student
6. night student

The researcher has tried to cover all bases in the listed options but in doing so there is clear overlap between the options. The student respondent might legitimately want to select both options 3 and 5 (a full-time and a day student). The remedy is to maintain a strict focus in questions. If you want information about "level" (undergraduate vs. graduate), "load" (full vs. part-time), and "timing" (day vs. night), ask three separate questions.

Like nominal level measures, ordinal response options must also be mutually exclusive and exhaustive. This rule, however, does not tell the whole story. In creating a ranked list of response alternatives, the researcher has considerable latitude. For instance, he or she must decide the number of ranked alternatives to offer. In measuring the level of agreement with certain views the researcher might provide three alternatives (agree; neutral; disagree), four alternatives (strongly agree; agree; disagree; strongly disagree), five alternatives (strongly agree; agree; neutral; disagree; strongly disagree), or perhaps six alternatives (strongly agree; mostly agree; agree somewhat; disagree somewhat; mostly disagree; strongly disagree). The choice of response alternatives should be guided by our research needs – how fine-tuned or precise do we want the information to be? The number of response alternatives also influences how much "hedging" respondents are allowed. An even-numbered set of ordinal response categories forces respondents to come down on one side of an issue:

1. strongly agree ⎫
2. agree ⎬ one side
3. disagree ⎫
4. strongly disagree ⎬ the other side

An odd numbered set of ordinal response categories allows respondents to take a "middle" position and avoid committing themselves to either side of an issue:

1. strongly agree
2. agree
3. neutral (a middle, fence-sitting location)
4. disagree
5. strongly disagree

Again, the researcher should be aware of these implications and make an informed decision as to whether an odd- or even-numbered set of choices is preferable. For instance, there are many political issues where knowing the percentage of the undecided or unsure would be a very valuable piece of information for political operatives. Offering a "fence sitting" middle option, then, would be a smart choice in supplied responses.

One additional warning is worth noting. Mutually exclusivity is often violated by ordinal level questions that offer numerical ranges as options. Consider the question of how many times one has eaten at a fast food restaurant in the last month. This question might provide the following response options:

1. 1–5 times
2. 5–10 times
3. 10–15 times
4. more than 15 times

Respondents who have had fast food 10 times have two selections available to them – option 2 and option 3. This violates mutual exclusivity. When offering numerical ranges as response options, care must be taken not to fall victim to this all too common overlapping mistake.

Putting It Together

As indicated in the opening pages of this chapter, one of the major obstacles that must be overcome when using questionnaires to gather information is the problem of cooperation. Recall, the point made earlier that questionnaires must function as "stand alone" tools – they must contain everything needed to get respondents to answer the questions posed. This means that the questionnaire is required to do all that it can to persuade potential respondents to cooperate and supply the requested information. Certain questionnaire design and formatting issues are critical to securing this cooperation.

First Things First – Persuasive Cover Letters or Introductions

While tempting, it is a mistake to think that a good survey starts with a good question. Good surveys really start with a good sales pitch. Before a respondent ever looks at specific questions, she or he must first be convinced that the survey in hand is a worthy one. The very best questions will never do a good job at collecting information if the entire questionnaire winds up in the respondent's wastebasket. To preclude this cruel (and all too common) fate, a questionnaire must first *sell itself* to the potential respondent. This is best accomplished with a persuasive introductory statement or cover letter (for mailed questionnaires). The introduction should serve to assure the respondent of the survey's importance and legitimacy. It should convince the respondent that the time they spend filling out the questionnaire will be time well spent. To accomplish this, the researcher is well advised to specifically address the saliency of the research topic. Tell the respondents why your project matters and why their cooperation is so critical. Introductions and cover letters should also directly address the issues of confidentiality or anonymity (see Chapter 3). The researcher should tell respondents how their privacy will be protected. When cover letters are used they should be personalized: they should address the respondent by name or by a semi-personal category (i.e. Dear Audubon Member but not "Dear Occupant") and should bear the personal signature of the researcher. Cover letters should also contain phone numbers or email addresses that the respondent may use to obtain additional information about the study. When possible, it is best for cover letters to be printed on letterhead that will lend credibility to the research project.

Primacy Effects

After presenting respondents with a persuasive introduction to your project, it is best to open the survey with interesting or pleasant questions that are easy to answer. Remember, you must still be concerned with securing the respondent's cooperation – even a powerful introduction or cover letter will find it hard to overcome a tedious or boring or threatening set of opening questions. For this reason, many experts advise that questionnaires should *not* begin with background or demographic questions. Such questions often strike respondents as either invasive or dull. Similarly, do not start with provocative, open-ended questions! While you may think this a good way to grab the respondents' attention, it is just as likely that they will find this approach presumptuous or offensive. Any questions that might threaten the respondent should really be delayed until *after* you have won the trust of your respondent. Instead, consider starting off with some interesting opinion or attitude questions – such questions will help reinforce the point that the researcher is really interested in hearing what is on the respondent's mind. Consider, for instance, how the Pew organization starts its annual Global Attitudes surveys. They intentionally present a non-controversial, ice-breaking question: "How would you describe your day today? Has it been a typical day, a particularly good day, or a particularly bad day?" (Poushter 2014). If you can use a safe, non-threatening question to get respondents thinking and *talking about themselves* you have a good chance of keeping them onboard with the rest of your questionnaire.

Sequencing

The order or sequence of our survey items can greatly influence the respondent's decision to supply the requested information. Getting off on the wrong foot may mean the researcher will never see their survey returned to them. Sequencing can also influence the quality of the information we obtain. Which questions should be placed at the start, at the middle and at the end of the survey? Is it appropriate to group certain questions together? Will the order or flow of the questions influence people's answers? Consider once again the question about government surveillance presented in a Fox News survey: "Does it feel like the federal government has gotten out of control and is threatening the basic civil liberties of Americans, or doesn't it feel this way to you?" This question was then followed by this question:

> As you may have heard, the U.S. Justice Department secretly seized extensive telephone records of calls on both work and personal phones for reporters and editors working for the Associated Press in the spring of 2012. At the time, the news organization, using government leaks, had broken a story about an international terrorist plot. The government obtained the phone records without giving the news organization prior notice, as is customary. Do you think the government was probably justified in taking these actions or does this sound like the government went too far?

Sixty percent of respondents indicated that the government went too far. The sequencing of the two questions as well as the language and extensive "set-up" for the second question no doubt helped to keep most respondents in the "too far" camp (Dimock 2013).

Logical Flow

It is usually a good idea to try to achieve some logical order to the questions you pose in a questionnaire. You might consider grouping questions by a time-order (e.g. you might first ask questions about the respondent's adolescent years and then ask questions about their young adulthood). Or you might group questions by topics (i.e. put all questions about family together and all questions about work together, etc.). As you move from one group of questions to another, you should try to assist the respondents in making any necessary mental shifts demanded by the new group of questions. Transitional statements can help respondents achieve the right mindset for the new set of questions: "Now I want to shift the focus to your high school years …"

When deciding on the order of questions, the researcher must be cognizant of the fact that earlier questions can influence respondents' answers to later questions. (See above discussion of the sequencing of questions on a Fox News survey.) If we first ask respondents if they consider themselves overweight and then ask them about their eating habits, we can expect that their answers to the first question will influence what they say to the second question. Knowing what to do about the effect of question order, however, can be tricky business. Researchers might follow a number of strategies. They might simply decide to be sensitive to the possibility that question order may influence responses. The "order" effect could then be part of their data analysis. The researcher might pre-test the questionnaire and explore with the "trial" respondents whether or not the order of the questions influenced their responses. A more formal strategy might be to develop two forms of the final questionnaire with different question ordering adopted in each form. This solution would enable the researcher to empirically assess if question order actually influenced responses.

To Ask or Not to Ask

A sure-fire way to discourage respondents' cooperation is to force them to read questions that are not relevant to them or their experiences. Respondents who have no children should not have to contend with a slew of questions about their parenting practices. Respondents who are unemployed will not appreciate reading a series of questions about their current job. Respondents who are not married will not appreciate a series of questions about the division of domestic chores with their non-existent spouses! We can most effectively spare respondents from questions that are not relevant to them by using filter and contingency questions. A **filter question** is one that determines if it is appropriate or necessary for the respondent to read a subsequent set of questions. **Contingency questions** are a subset of questions that are only answered by those who have been given the "green light" by a preceding "filter" question. For example, if respondents answer "yes" to the filter question asking whether or not they have any children, they might then be instructed to go on to a set of questions regarding their interactions with their children. Those who do not have children would be instructed to skip these questions and to move on to the next relevant section of the questionnaire. When setting up filter and contingency questions, it is best to set the contingency questions "apart" from the rest of the questions and use arrows or lines to direct appropriate respondents to these sections of the questionnaire.

> **Filter question** – a question that determines if respondents should answer or skip follow-up question(s).
>
> **Contingency question** – a question that is limited to those respondents who have been "cleared" by a preceding filter question.

1. Do your currently smoke cigarettes?
    1. Yes (if yes, please answer questions 2 and 3)
    2. No (if no, please skip to question 5)

> 2. In the past year, have any family members or close friends tried to get you to stop smoking?
>   1. yes
>   2. no
> 3. In the last year, have you tried to stop smoking cigarettes?
>   1. yes
>   2. no

The Long and the Short of It

Not surprisingly, researchers usually prefer long questionnaires (and interviews) to short ones. Long questionnaires are more cost efficient – once we have respondents at hand, we are tempted to get as much information from them as possible. The risk of giving into the "economy" size questionnaire, however, is great. Generally as the length of questionnaires increases, the response rate decreases (Smith 1994). Lengthy questionnaires can discourage respondents from starting or completing the survey. While there are no hard and fast rules about questionnaire length, it is generally advised that questionnaires should be designed so that they take no more than 30 minutes to complete (Monette, Sullivan, and DeJong 1998). That said, some survey researchers contend that length is not nearly as important as difficulty for discouraging respondents. A 40-minute survey might feel like a 20-minute survey if the questions are simple and you can keep your respondents engaged in the task at hand (Henning 2013).

Formatting

The way a questionnaire appears on paper (or on a computer screen) is certainly relevant to securing respondents' cooperation. Questionnaires that look unprofessional, sloppy or cramped will not inspire respondents to put pencil to paper (or finger to keyboard, mouse, or tablet). The formatting or presentation of our survey questions is also an important consideration in developing valid and reliable measures. If we do not pay sufficient attention to how our questions appear on paper we may wind up with some unfortunate surprises (see Box 8.4). If you find this hard to believe, just recall the fiasco that developed on Election Day 2000 in Florida! In retrospect, was it really such a good idea to use a "butterfly ballot" – that is, one that staggered the candidates' names on two separate pages and positioned the selection column down the center? (See Figure 8.1.) Clearly, there were many Florida voters who maintained that the markings on their ballots did not accurately record (measure) their true voting intentions. If you take a careful look at the ballot you will see that Democratic candidate Al Gore appeared in the second box on the left side of the ballot but punching the second hole on the ballot actually recorded a vote for the Reform Party candidate Pat Buchanan!

| **Box 8.4** | Sharpening your research vision: little things matter |

Tom Smith of the National Opinion Research Center has found that "little things" can matter quite a bit when it comes to formatting surveys. All of the following "simple" mistakes can decrease data quality and undermine replication efforts:
- misalignment of response boxes
- overly compact (dense) question formatting
- faulty placement of filer and contingency questions
- leaving too little space for answers to open-ended questions.

Source: Smith (1993).

While the Democratic candidates appeared in the second box on the left side of the ballot, punching the second hole on the ballot recorded a vote for the Reform Party candidates.

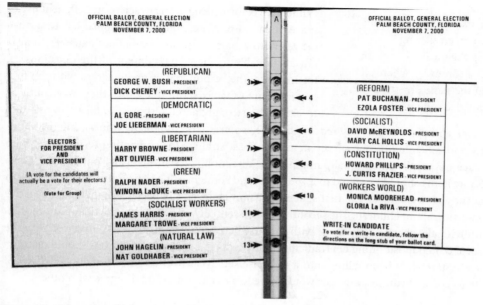

Figure 8.1   The Butterfly Ballot of 2000. *Source:* Anthony at en.wikipedia (Own work) [Public domain], via Wikimedia Commons

Formatting decisions are particularly relevant for closed-ended questions. What is the best layout for the response alternatives? Should they be listed vertically or horizontally? In general, vertical listing of response options is thought to lead to fewer errors. Should we have respondents indicate their answers by filling in circles ⬤ or checking boxes [√]? Should we use letter or number prefixes for identifying the various response alternatives? (Numerical prefixes enable us to "pre-code" response alternatives and thereby facilitate data entry.) These decisions are not irrelevant. The survey researcher must give serious thought to which option will produce the least amount of measurement error. (Some pre-testing can help with these decisions, see "Pre-testing" below).

Frequently, we will pose a series of questions that all employ the same response alternatives. We might present a series of statements and ask respondents the degree to which they agree or disagree with each statement. This style of questioning invites the use of matrix formatting where statements are vertically stacked on the left of the page or screen and the response alternatives are vertically stacked on the right side of the page or screen.

For each of the following statements, please indicate whether you strongly agree (SA), agree (A), disagree (D), strongly disagree (SD) or are undecided (U):

	SA	A	D	SD	U
Children should be seen and not heard	[ ]	[ ]	[ ]	[ ]	[ ]
Children are our most precious commodity	[ ]	[ ]	[ ]	[ ]	[ ]

Response set – occurs when respondents fall into a pattern when answering questions, rendering the measure invalid; most likely to occur in an index where all items are worded in the same direction (i.e. all negative or all positive statements).

While matrix formatting is an attractive and efficient use of space, it can also invite trouble: a response set. **Response set** refers to a pattern in the respondent's answers that is not attributable to the actual content of the questions. If, for instance, the respondent strongly agrees with the first few items in a matrix set of questions, they may continue to check the strongly agree response to all the remaining items *without ever actually reading them!* Response sets can greatly undermine the validity and reliability of our survey items. The best strategy for combating response set is to discourage it by intentionally mixing the "direction" or sentiment of your matrix items. Some items should be stated in a "positive" and some in a "negative" direction. Look again at the above example. The first statement about children can be seen as making a negative assertion about children. The second item is essentially a positive statement about children. Individuals who strongly agree with the first item would be expected to disagree with the second. Juxtapositioning contradictory statements in a matrix of questions should discourage respondents from falling into a response set. To answer an intentionally mixed set of items consistently, respondents would have to agree to some and disagree with others.

Pre-Testing

After developing a good solid questionnaire, the researcher should always plan on conducting a pre-test. There is no better way to see what others think about the questionnaire than to ask them. To pre-test, we should administer the questionnaire to a small group of people who closely resemble our research population. (Those involved in a pre-test are no longer eligible for inclusion in your final sample.) A particularly effective technique is the "think aloud" (Patten 2001) or what some call the cognitive interview. Here we ask respondents to talk about their reactions to each of the items on the survey – how did they understand the questions and the response options? This is a most effective strategy for seeing if both the researcher and the respondent are "on the same wavelength" and for detecting bad questionnaire items. To strike a more technical note, the "think aloud" provides critical feedback for assessing a question's validity and reliability. Pre-testing also allows the researcher to assess the impact of word selection, question sequencing and various formatting and layout issues. While cognitive interviews are frequently conducted in person, some researchers find they can also be conducted over the phone (Noel 2013).

Return to Sender: The Special Challenge of the Mailed Questionnaire

Throughout this chapter we have made repeated reference to the importance of obtaining respondents' cooperation and securing a high response rate in survey research. All that we have said so far is directed at building a good survey instrument as a way of encouraging high response: pay attention to question content and form, pay attention to formatting and question sequencing. Below are a few more tips that are particularly relevant when using the mail system for the delivery and the return of our surveys.

Cover Letter

As indicated earlier, the best strategy for increasing the response rate to a mailed questionnaire is a strong, persuasive cover letter. Convincing respondents that your research project is a worthy one will go a long way toward encouraging them to complete it and return it to you.

Make Returning Easy and Attractive

You need to stay one step ahead of all the reasons why a respondent may not return your questionnaire. You should not give respondents any reasons for *not* cooperating. Provide a self-addressed stamped envelope. Resist making the questionnaire any longer than it really needs to be. It is always easier to convince someone to fill out a short rather than a long questionnaire. Timing of mailed surveys is also relevant to good response rates. You should avoid sending questionnaires out at "busy times" of the year. Don't expect people to pay attention to your questionnaire request at holidays, at tax time, or at the start of school years. You should also think twice about sending out questionnaires during the height of the vacation season. Questionnaires may languish in mailboxes for two or three weeks while the respondent is off on their annual camping trip.

You might also consider some kind of payment or incentive for your respondents. Before you dismiss this idea as beyond your budget, remember that it is the gesture not the amount that seems to count. The payment you offer might be a token or a symbolic one. You might include a few pennies for your respondents' thoughts. You might offer coupons or bookmarks or even a list of useful URLs relevant to the survey's topic. Some suggest treating respondents to "first class" postage for use on a mailing of their choice! If the survey is about a special interest, consider offering a token gift reflecting the interest (e.g. nature clubs might include a pack of seeds or a thematic bumper sticker). The idea is simply to let the respondents know that you are not taking their time and input for granted.

Systematic Follow-up

In the interest of securing good response rates, you should also plan on conducting systematic follow-ups with your respondents. If they have not returned their questionnaires by the appointed time, you should be prepared to contact them (either by mail or phone) and address once again the importance of both the study and their input. You should also be prepared to send out a second and even a third copy of the questionnaire. Such systematic follow-ups have been credited with significantly increasing final response rates.

Delivering Questions Electronically

The computer age has opened yet another major avenue for delivering questionnaires to respondents: questionnaires can be delivered via email or launched via web pages or via apps on smartphones. Proponents of electronic surveys contend that such surveys are the wave of the future. There are several pluses to Internet surveys. They can greatly increase the convenience for respondents who can answer on their own timetable. They are also credited with reducing social desirability bias – respondents to online surveys feel less compelled to answer questions in a self-enhancing way. And given the increasing number of homes with computers and Internet connections (it is estimated that nearly 90% of US adults use the Internet [DeSilver 2014]), it is quite likely that the electronic questionnaire may well become the telephone interview of tomorrow. Many of you are probably already familiar with SurveyMonkey. It is the world's most widely utilized online survey software and is responsible for nearly 3 million online surveys each day (DeSilver 2014). In 2014 Pew Research Center launched the American Trends Panel. This ongoing research effort involves a representative sample of 3000+ individuals who have agreed to take monthly online surveys[5] that will provide Pew with more detailed information about the respondents than Pew is able to get with their more traditional phone interviews.

The Trends Panel group will also allow Pew to collect data from the same individuals over time and thus open the door to analysis of individual change (Goo 2014; see Chapter 4 for more on the longitudinal panel design). Just after the 2014 mid-term elections, *The New York Times* and *CBS News* announced their plan to utilize the services of a UK research firm – YouGov – to test drive a new non-probability sample consisting of 100,000 participants who have agreed to take exclusively online questionnaires. The large sample size reflects a calculated decision to "grow" the sample as a way of capturing the diversity of the target population. (See Chapter 11 for more detailed discussion of probability vs. non-probability samples.)

But serious drawbacks also exist with online surveys and researchers are advised to proceed with caution. Perhaps the biggest problem entails achieving a good representative sample via an online survey. Probability sampling is the key to representative samples. But probability sampling requires the use of a **sampling frame** – that is, an exhaustive list of all of the elements in the research population. Since such a list is not readily available for all email or Internet users, probability samples are something of a stumbling block for those wanting to do representative sampling in conjunction with online questionnaires. Consequently, researchers who conduct online surveys must weigh the costs of missing key portions of the general population who are less likely to have access to the Internet, such as the elderly, the poor, those living in rural areas, and those with less education. Conversely, given the incredible "linking" capacity of the Web, online surveys are often accessed by *inappropriate* respondents who are not part of the intended sample. Given these serious drawbacks, major polling and survey organizations are putting their heads together to figure out how to incorporate other technological avenues such as cell phone apps and text messaging to advance the cause of survey research.

> **Sampling frame** – an exhaustive listing of all the elements in a research population.

Box 8.5   Newsworthy research: professional questionnaire respondents

Looking for a job? Perhaps you should consider becoming a Turker. Turkers are a new group of professional online questionnaire respondents who work for Amazon's Mechanical Turk. The group stands 500,000 strong and members are ready to launch into response mode at a moment's notice. Since the pay for completing any one survey is quite low, some Turkers increase their earnings by completing as many surveys as possible. One interviewed Turker reported completing approximately 20,000 surveys during a five-year period for various academic researchers. Others report completing 40,000 or more online surveys. In fact, more and more social psychology surveys are coming to rely on Turkers for obtaining their data.

This online survey work may help some pay their bills or earn some extra spending money, but what does it mean to have "professional" survey takers? It is a question that is troubling many academic researchers who fear that "super Turkers" (the small fraction of workers who complete an extremely large number of surveys) may be responsible for skewing survey results. Super Turkers "know the drill" of online questionnaires and tend to respond to human nature questions in a non-natural, experienced way. On the other hand, some researchers report that Turkers make for better respondents than undergraduates or the general public. They don't just "phone it in" – many take professional pride in their work. In fact, there is an online community (Turker Nation) set up to check for inappropriate behavior by Turkers. To be sure, this is not the last we will hear about Turkers. They provide great fodder for methodological thinking (and maybe a job for struggling students).

Source: Marder (2015).

And while electronic surveys dramatically increase the ultimate reach of surveys, they do not offer any magical fixes for the inherent problems of questionnaires. Electronic surveys must still grapple with the myriad challenges presented throughout this chapter: question wording, question sequencing, formatting, survey and item non-response, and so on. Concerns over issues of anonymity and/or confidentiality will likely loom large given the public's wariness about the Internet's profound potential for privacy abuse (see Chapter 3 and Cole 2001). In short, online questionnaires have secured a place in survey research and as issues of restricted access and privacy are resolved, that place will likely be a most secure one in the world of market, political, and social research.

Ask and You Shall Receive

In considering the various research options for systematically gathering information, the questionnaire has earned the right to be a perennial favorite. It is the real workhorse of research tools – a frequent choice of researchers because of its versatility, its time and cost efficiency, and for its overall ability to get the job done. Still, questionnaires are not foolproof. Indeed any fool can develop a questionnaire and by now you have probably been subjected to quite a few foolish questionnaires! Hopefully this chapter has convinced you that much care and work must go into questionnaire construction if we are to reach the goal of asking the right questions in the right way in order to obtain valid and reliable information.

TAKE AWAYS

- Survey research is the mainstay of social and marketing research
  - The questionnaire is a "stand alone" instrument for obtaining information (If it cannot stand on its own, more work needs to be done!)
  - The interview is the more personal/social form of survey research
- Quality control issues are key to effectively combatting low response rates that typically plague questionnaires. For a quality questionnaire, attention must be given to:
  - The actual wordings of questions:
    - Follow the "rules"
    - Make informed decisions about closed or open-ended questions
    - For closed-ended questions make smart decisions about options
  - The placement and sequencing of questions
  - The formatting of the entire questionnaire
- Mailed and online questionnaires present special challenges
- Be ready to see more options with technological advances

Sharpening the Edge: More Readings and Searching

- The Pew Research Center for the People & the Press covers an array of topics relevant to survey research. Visit their site at:

  http://www.people-press.org/methodology/our-survey-methodology-in-detail/
- Take a look at the following pages to learn more about what polling organizations are considering as strategies to battle low-response rates:

  http://www.pewresearch.org/fact-tank/2014/07/28/qa-what-the-new-york-times-polling-decision-means/
- For a short but informative chapter on "conceptual fundamentals" in questionnaire construction, see:

  Michael Patton's "Thoughtful Questionnaires" in *Practical Evaluation* (Newbury Park: Sage, 1982)
- For a more thorough review of survey issues, see:

  Seymour Sudman, Norman Bradburn and Norbert Schwarz's *Thinking About Answers: The Application of Cognitive Process to Survey Methodology* (San Francisco: Jossey-Bass, 1996)
- There are a number of good Internet sites devoted to the survey method. The reader will certainly find something useful at any of the following locations:

  The American Statistical Association offers an online booklet devoted to explaining survey research to the general public: https://www.whatisasurvey.info/

  The homepage for the General Social Survey offers links to GSS Methodological Reports on various survey issues. Once on the homepage look under the section for GSS Publications and click on the link for Reports and then the link for GSS Methodological Reports: http://www3.norc.org/GSS+Website

Bill Trochim's web page is (as usual) filled with very useful information on the topic of surveys: http://trochim.human.cornell.edu/kb/survey.htm
- For those who want to learn some more about Luntz's words that work, the following link will take you to a list of best the 21 words he thinks will work best in the 21st century: https://designfortheeveryman.wordpress.com/2012/01/31/21-words-for-the-21st-century-from-author-frank-luntz/
- Those wanting to hear some words from Luntz himself might enjoy the following lecture: http://www.milkeninstitute.org/events/conferences/global-conference/2012/panel-detail/3559

Exercises

1 Devise three different questions (and answer choices when appropriate) to measure respondents' (a) commuting routine, or (b) family food budgets. Have one question capture the information at the nominal level, one at the ordinal level, and one at the ratio level of measurement

2 Critique the following questions. Revise as needed:
- Why should evil rulers like Saddam Hussein be removed from office?
- Do you think IT should be a required component for every college major?
- Are you a regular contributor to non-profits?
- How much money do you spend each year on highway tolls?

3 Find either an online or a recent direct mail survey and critique its content and format.

4 Revisit Johnson's index of job "burn-out" presented in Chapter 6 'Split-Half Test'. What changes might you now recommend for this index?

5 Imagine that you want to find out if respondents have a good idea of how many calories they typically consume in a day. Devise a series of questions that you think would be a good set of measures.

6 What "grade" would you give to the following questions that actually appeared on some recent surveys:
Q: Do you support or oppose laws that allow people to register to vote and cast a ballot at the polls on Election Day?
  ☐ Support – These laws help increase participation in our elections.
  ☐ Oppose – These laws increase the likelihood of voting irregularities.
Q: In your view, what is the single biggest problem with elected officials in Washington, DC today?
  ☐ They are out of touch with regular Americans.
  ☐ They are under the influence of special interests.
  ☐ They only care about their political careers.
  ☐ They are too partisan and unwilling to compromise.
  ☐ All of the above.
On a surgery center survey:
Q: In general, how do you rate our facility? Excellent / Good / Average / Needs to improve.

Notes

1   See http://www.pewresearch.org/fact-tank/2014/11/24/facing-challenges-pollsters-broaden-experiments-with-new-methodologies-2/ for some of the ideas the Pew polling organization is investigating.

2   You should understand that "leading" respondents is exactly what many organizations want to do. Their surveys are not conducted to learn the "truth" but rather to obtain favorable results for their cause or mission. The educated respondent needs to be on guard.

3   The general rule of thumb is to utilize ratio level measures whenever it is feasible. The ratio level is considered the "highest" level of measurement because of its versatility. With ratio level data, the researcher can always "collapse" data into lower ordinal or nominal level data. The ratio level also offers the most versatility in terms of statistical analysis. For some kinds of information, however, respondents are often reluctant to answer open-ended ratio level questions (e.g. questions asking for exact yearly income or exact ages). In such instances, lower level closed-ended questions can be the better choice.

4   With the increasing interest in gender identity, there is a growing recognition of the need to supply a third "other" option.

5   Approximately 90% of participants will take online surveys. Those without Internet access will complete mail or phone surveys (Goo 2014).

References

Barnes, Khaliah. 2014. "Student Data Collection Is Out of Control." *The New York Times*, December 19. http://www.nytimes.com/roomfordebate/2014/09/24/protecting-student-privacy-in-online-learning/student-data-collection-is-out-of-control.

DeSilver, Drew. 2014. "Facing Challenges, Pollsters Broaden Experiments with New Methodologies." Pew Research Center. FactTank, November 24. http://www.pewresearch.org/fact-tank/2014/11/24/facing-challenges-pollsters-broaden-experiments-with-new-methodologies-2/.

Dimock, Michael. 2013. "Polling When Public Attention is Limited: Different Questions, Different Results." Pew Research Center. FactTank, May 22. http://www.pewresearch.org/fact-tank/2013/05/22/polling-when-public-attention-is-limited-different-questions-different-results/.

Goo, Sara. 2014. "How Pew Research Conducted the Polarization Survey and Launched a New Research Panel." Pew Research Center. FactTank, June 12. http://www.pewresearch.org/fact-tank/2014/06/12/how-pew-research-conducted-the-polarization-survey-and-launched-a-new-research-panel/.

Greenfield, Beth. 2015. "Data Collection at Schools: Is Big Brother Watching Your Kids?" Yahoo! Parenting, February 23. https://www.yahoo.com/parenting/data-collection-at-schools-is-big-brother-111889795072.html.

Henning, Jeffrey. 2013. "Is the Ideal Survey Length 20 Minutes?" ResearchAccess, December 24. http://researchaccess.com/2013/12/survey-length/.

Luntz, Frank. 2007. *Words that Work: It's Not What You Say, It's What People Hear*. New York: Hyperion.

Monette, D., Sullivan, T., and C. DeJong. 1998. *Applied Social Research: Tool for the Human Services*. Fort Worth, TX: Hold, Rinehart & Winston.

Noel, Harmoni. 2013. "Conducting Cognitive Interviews over the Phone: Benefits and Challenges." AAPOR. American Association for Public Opinion Research.

Pew Research Center. 2013. "Government Surveillance: A Question Wording Experiment." July 26. http://www.people-press.org/2013/07/26/government-surveillance-a-question-wording-experiment/.

Poushter, Jacob. 2014. "Who's Having a 'Good' or 'Bad' Day Around the World?" Pew Research Center, December 30. http://www.pewresearch.org/fact-tank/2014/12/30/having-a-typical-day-in-2014-youre-not-alone/.

Schuman, Howard. 2002 "Sense and Nonsense about Surveys." *Contexts* (Summer): 40–47.

White House. 2015". FACT SHEET: Safeguarding American Consumers & Families." January 12. http://www.whitehouse.gov/the-press-office/2015/01/12/fact-sheet-safeguarding-american-consumers-families.

Chapter 9

Having the Talk: Person to Person Information Exchange

Introducing Social Research Methods: Essentials for Getting the Edge, First Edition. Janet M. Ruane.
© 2016 John Wiley & Sons, Ltd. Published 2016 by John Wiley & Sons, Ltd.

FIRST TAKES

Be sure to take note of the following:
- The interview is the *personal* form of survey research
  - It is also very social
    - Interviewing takes two
    - Needs social skills
    - Needs rapport
- In-person interviewing
- Structured vs. unstructured interviews
  - Qualitative (intensive) interviews
- Phone interviewing
  - Some special considerations
- Focus groups – using group discussions to learn more

Every Sunday morning, *Meet the Press* and *Face the Nation* vie for the most compelling one of these. David Frost, largely due to his ability to charm, was thought to be one of the best at them (and he will always be remembered for his sessions with Richard Nixon). Charlie Rose has earned a faithful audience for the sessions he conducts around his large wooden table. The French have great respect for their own Anne Sinclair and her exchanges with people in high places. After the Charlie Hebdo attacks in Paris, the Islamic State group published an exchange with "France's most wanted widow." No self-respecting police show could get through an episode without going at one "in the box". And most of us need to go through one to land a job. What is the common ingredient that crosses so easily between the worlds of news, entertainment, and our everyday work lives? The interview. Of all the data collection techniques available in our search for information, the interview strikes many as the single best device for promoting understanding and "getting at the truth."

In popular culture, the interview is the hallmark of a person's claim to fame. You know you have made it when Barbara Walters wants to interview you for her "most fascinating people of the year" special. An interview with Oprah tells us you have either arrived or that you are about to have a big career boost. Indeed, the interview may be the best sign of someone's "fifteen minutes of fame." Many a magazine can move more copies by promising a revealing "sit down" with the latest celebrity. And even people who might have good reasons to avoid talking nonetheless often agree to an interview in order to clear the air or get their story out.

The interview also has a prominent place in our everyday lives. The interview is a staple of many academic experiences: admission to programs or graduate schools and selection for scholarships or fellowships. Entry to the work realm often turns on the all-important "first" and hopefully subsequent interviews. (Tips on good interviewing strategies are standard entries in job-hunting advice web sites and manuals.) And if we turn a sociological eye to our dating rituals, we will quickly realize that the interview process is clearly part of the "getting to know you" phase of dating. Indeed, a new time sensitive industry has emerged around this interview part of dating: speed dating. In these intentionally short (5–8 minutes!) "dates" participants quickly exchange vital information about themselves. This time and cost-efficient meeting puts the interview function of the first date "front and center" (see Box 9.1).

Box 9.1   Speed dating: faster and easier than ever

The firm 8minuteDating.com offers subscribers eight great 8-minute dates on one fun night in either the United States or Canada. SpeedDate.com has upped the ante. It has taken the original concept of an extremely short date and added an appealing techno-logical twist: SpeedDate.com offers *online* 3-minute dates. This international service presents members with dating opportunities in countries from A to Z: Afghanistan to Zimbabwe! SpeedDate.com claims to be the world's largest speed dating site with over 11 million members worldwide. Dating without ever leaving home – what's not to like?

The popularity of the interview is not limited to the worlds of news and entertainment or work and dating – it is present in the world of research as well. Perhaps the positive reaction to interviews is due to the fact that interviews enjoy a much higher response rate than their impersonal sibling, the questionnaire. A well-executed interview study can achieve response rates of 80–85%. Perhaps some researchers feel that interviews make more sense than questionnaires. Questionnaires can too often be dismissed as either superficial or tedious endeavors. Critics of closed-ended questionnaires complain that they put words in respondents' mouths – they do not permit the researcher to collect in-depth, meaningful or rich information. Critics of open-ended questionnaires complain that respondents are not likely to invest the time required to write out answers to these probing yet "impersonal" surveys. Perhaps too it is our social nature that makes interviews an attractive research option. No doubt, the appeal of the interview for many is its focus on the individual and its reliance on just plain talk. Many of us are flattered at the prospects that someone else is really interested in *talking* with us, in making us the focus of attention. With the interview, the researcher takes the time to contact the research subject, to build rapport, and to listen to, interact with and "get to know" the research subject. (Perhaps some of you are familiar with the Jimmie Kimmel skit "Lie Witness News" where his team conducts on the street interviews with ordinary people who are asked about totally fake news items. It is a pretty convincing display of just how enamored people can be with an interview.)

Box 9.2   Having our say: StoryCorps

The interview is an attractive and intriguing exchange for many people. Many of us (perhaps most) would like a chance to tell our stories. Since 2003, StoryCorps, a non-profit organization, has offered one of the largest oral histories projects in the world. StoryCorps gives ordinary individuals a chance to be interviewed about their lives. Each participant is given 40 minutes to tell their story. To date more than 50,000 interviews have been conducted and are archived in the American Folk Life Center in the Library of Congress. You can listen to the stories or receive weekly updates at the following site: https://app.etapestry.com/hosted/StoryCorpsInc/OnlineForm.html.

Conversational Exchange

In large part, the **interview** refers to the personal exchange of information between an interviewer and an interviewee. Good interviews strive to make the exchange a comfortable, conversational one (though it would be naive to think of an interview as *just* a conversation, as you will see as you read on). As in everyday conversations, participants should experience the interview as a pleasant social encounter. To a large extent, achieving this standard depends on the researcher's ability to establish "social harmony" or good **rapport** with the interviewee. The interviewer must be able to put respondents at ease, express interest in, and be able to listen actively to, respondents and assure them that they will be supported throughout the entire process. Indeed, establishing good rapport is key to getting the cooperation that is central to the survey method in general. If respondents do not agree to talk, the data collection process is foiled. The rapport issue demands that the interviewer's social skills must be sharp. It also alerts us to the fact that not all social researchers will be good at the interview process – some lack the social skills demanded by the interview process. In her book about *bacha posh* in Afghanistan (young girls being raised as boys until they reach puberty), the author speaks of the extended time required for her to be able to gain the trust of locals to talk about this practice (Nordberg 2014).

> **Interview** – a personal exchange of information between an interviewer and an interviewee.
>
> **Rapport** – a condition of ease or trust in the interview situation.

While the interview strives to achieve a conversational exchange of information, it would be a mistake to equate interviews with everyday conversations. As you well know, ordinary conversations can be a series of meandering "talking points" that are meant to entertain more than to inform. Depending on our level of interest, we can let points slide in our everyday talks with others. Listening "with half an ear" is a rather common technique in everyday conversations. The interview cannot be this casual. The interview is a *purposeful* conversation wherein the interviewer has a set research agenda – that is, key points or questions that must be addressed and a level of understanding that must be pursued. To facilitate accomplishing these research goals, interviewers typically employ either an interview guide or an interview schedule. **Interview guides** are relatively unstructured tools that list the general topics, issues or ideas to be covered in an interview. Guides produce unstructured, qualitative and often intensive interviews. They give respondents considerable latitude in determining the actual content of the interview. In essence, they allow the interview to be respondent-driven – that is, the respondent is given sizeable leeway to take the interview where the respondent wants to take it.

> **Interview guides** – unstructured talking points to be covered in an interview.
>
> **Interview schedules** – structured list of questions (and often set response options) to be used during an interview.

Interview schedules, on the other hand, are much more structured than guides. Schedules will list the exact questions and, if the questions are closed-ended, the exact answers to be presented to all respondents. Consider for instance the schedule used in the World Values Survey which looks at the impact of cultural values and beliefs on social and political life. The survey has been conducted since 1981 and takes great care in developing the interview schedule that will be used in nearly

100 different countries that contain nearly 90% of the world's population. The survey uses a common set of questions that are developed first in English and then translated into the national languages of the participating countries. (The questions are then translated back into English to make sure that nothing is "lost" in translation.) Such structured schedules produce more standardized interviews and when using a forced-choice, closed-ended question format, a more quantitative interview. (With closed-ended interview questions, answers can be reduced to the pre-coded numbers attached to the response options.) For a highly structured interview situation, results will be quantified and reported via numbers and statistics. (See data from the GSS [http://www3.norc.org/GSS+Website/] or from the Eurobarometer Survey [http://ec.europa.eu/public_opinion/index_en.htm] or from the World Values Survey [http://www.worldvaluessurvey.org/WVSContents.jsp] for examples.)

Unstructured Interviews

One's choice of interview style – unstructured or structured – depends on the research goal. Unstructured interviewing is a good idea when pursuing an exploratory piece of research, when trying to paint a thorough descriptive picture of some phenomenon or some process, or when trying to understand a respondent's unique experiences or perspective. The unstructured (aka qualitative) interview is the tool for hearing the respondent's story in their own words and for tapping into the meanings of their lives. Given this last point, unstructured interviewing has a firm place in field research or ethnographic research (see Chapter 10 for further discussion.)

Unstructured interviewing can also be an effective strategy for countering memory failure or respondent resistance. Giving the respondent more control over the pace and direction of the interview can empower respondents. Qualitative interviewing allows respondents to get to topics on their own terms, pace, and comfort levels. Following their own pace may also help respondents "stumble" on to memories that would not be so easily retrievable under more direct questioning. In their study of women's ways of knowing, Belenky, Clinchy, Goldberger, and Tarule (1986) clearly saw the value of unstructured interviewing:

> Each interview began with the question, "Looking back, what stands out for you over the past few years?" and proceeded gradually at the woman's own pace to questions concerning self-image, relationships of importance, education and learning, real-life decision-making and moral dilemmas, accounts of personal changes and growth, perceived catalysts for change and impediments to growth, and visions of the future. We tried to pose questions that were broad but understandable on many levels. (Belenky, Clinchy, Goldberger, and Tarule 1986, p. 11)

Or consider the advice offered by StoryCorps to help participants who have agreed to "interview" a family member or friend for this oral history project. The advice is consistent with conducting an unstructured interview:

> Trust your instincts. When you hear something that moves you, ask more questions. Sometimes your storyteller will need "permission" to explore a certain topic; you can simply say "Tell

me more." Feel free to ask questions in whatever order feels right, and don't let them constrain the conversation. Real moments are the best moments. (http://storycorps.org/what-to-expect/)

The unstructured qualitative interview might initially strike some as the simplest interview option: you just sit back and let the respondent talk. But this attitude belies the work that must go into a qualitative interview. Some may say that talk is cheap but the serious interviewer must regard talk as a more precious commodity. Robert Weiss (2004) says that good interviewing provides "windows into people lives." Arguably, getting people's stories in their own words is the most valid measurement option one can achieve. Still, none of this happens "automatically." Quality interviewing requires a special skill set, one that requires special training that not all of us possess or will ever develop.

One special challenge of the unstructured interview is keeping respondents on point. The latitude extended to respondents might result in some straying off course. The interviewer must make an informed decision about when the wondering is productive and when the respondent must be reeled back in. Another issue that needs special attention is the issue of respondent honesty. To be sure, some people will embellish their stories – consider the recent flaps involving NBC news anchor Brian Williams or Fox's Bill O'Reilly and their "faulty" war coverage memories (Connor 2015; Roig-Franzia, Higham and Farhi 2015). While the immediate goal is to get respondents talking, the diligent interviewer must also be on the ready for detecting false claims. Since humans can be very good at misleading others, this is a rather daunting task. Still, the skilled interviewer will use details and the contexts of accounts and personal observations as indicators of the validity of the information (Weiss 2004).

Structured Interviews

When the researcher wants to provide a descriptive overview of a research population with regard to, for instance, their behaviors, attitudes, or values, or when the researcher wants to standardize the interview process, structured interviewing is the more appropriate strategy. Structured interviewing is also appropriate for quantifying information about the research population. Unless we ask the same questions of all, we will not be in a position to say what percentage favor or oppose a certain social policy or what percentage engage in certain behaviors. You may already be familiar with the General Social Survey (GSS). It is a prime example of a highly structured interview conducted on a regular basis in the United States. Consider the following GSS questions along with the instructions for the interviewer (presented in capital letters) used to assess respondents' attitudes toward abortion:

Please tell me whether or not you think it should be possible for a pregnant woman to obtain a legal abortion if … READ EACH STATEMENT, AND CIRCLE ONE CODE FOR EACH[1]
A. If there is a strong chance of serious defect in the baby?
B. If she is married and does not want any more children?
C. If the woman's own health is seriously endangered by the pregnancy?
D. If the family has a very low income and cannot afford any more children?

    E.   If she became pregnant as a result of rape?

    F.   If she is not married and does not want to marry the man?

    G.   The woman wants it for any reason?

Each interviewee is asked to respond to each statement with the *same set* of response options: yes, no, don't know or no answer. By sticking with this regimen, a quantitative profile of respondents can easily be generated.[2]

Developing an Unstructured Guide

Since the unstructured interview guide consists of general topics or issues to be covered, you might think it is an easy tool to develop. But the truth is that developing a good guide really requires much careful thought and work. Lofland and Lofland (1995) offer a series of suggestions for preparing a guide. The first step is for the researcher to enter what they call the *puzzlement phase*. In this phase, the researcher works at articulating all the things about the research topic that are puzzling. Suppose you want to do a study on personal webpages. In thinking about the topic, the researcher might "puzzle" over the following: What is the function of a webpage? When does someone decide they "need" their own page? Are personal webpages "reality" or "fantasy" documents? Should access to pages be open or restricted? During this phase, which may go on for days or weeks, the researcher jots down all of his or her thoughts about the topic. (Lofland and Lofland recommend using a separate note card for each question or issue). To get a full array of ideas/questions, the researcher should ask others what they find puzzling about the topic and/or consult articles/books on the topic.

Once the puzzlement phase is finished and the researcher has accumulated a stack of cards, the cards can be sorted into several internally consistent piles. A review of the piles should help the researcher assemble a general outline as well as a sequencing of questions for the guide. It is also a good idea to supplement the guide with well-placed probes.

> **Probes** – follow-up questions used in the interview process in order to get respondents to provide additional information.

Probes are questions used to follow up on points mentioned, but not fully explicated, by the respondent. Careful probing can often be the key to an "Aha" insightful moment in an interview. Listing probes on the guide serves to remind the interviewer to pursue important lines of inquiry.

In his discussion of qualitative interviewing, Weiss presents a different strategy than Lofland and Lofland noting that it is usual for questions to be developed *during* the interview. Still, he notes there are standard ways to "structure" the non-structured exchange: (1) keep respondents focused on concrete observations; (2) Ask respondents about recent events; and (3) keep checking for and asking for detail (2004). Getting these tasks accomplished means that the interviewer must be ready to probe and encourage the respondent to expand or dig deeper. But to do so successfully, Weiss also notes the importance of having established a productive partnership between the interviewer and interviewee.

An interviewer's social skills are certainly called into play when conducting a qualitative interview. Since this style of interviewing is very dependent on the respondent's willingness to talk in detail, the researcher must create a warm and supportive "talk" environment. To accomplish this, two strategies are most important: the interviewer must know how to be an "active" listener and the interviewer must know how to handle respondent silences.

Verbal mirror – an interview technique where the interviewer periodically offers a summary paraphrasing of respondent's answers.

Active Listening

The idea of an active listener might strike some readers as an oxymoron – listening would seem to suggest a silent passive role for the interviewer. In fact, good listening calls on the researcher to actively attend to what the respondent is saying. In effect, the researcher must "hang on" the respondent's every word. Active listening entails the interviewer periodically supplying a **verbal mirror** of what the respondent is saying In providing a verbal mirror, the researcher paraphrases in a clear, concise, and non-evaluative way exactly what the respondent has communicated. Imagine a college student who has just described her first year at college as a disaster – a series of failed courses. The interviewer might say "So what I'm hearing you say is that freshman year was not so good for you in terms of academics." The verbal mirror shows the respondent that the researcher is indeed listening to everything. It also gives the respondent a chance to correct any misunderstandings by the interviewer. In her work on oral histories, Borland (2004) notes that what the interviewer "hears" is often in conflict with what the interviewee "says" due to historical, cultural, political, and philosophical differences between the two parties. She believes that researchers must be sensitive to these interpretive conflicts and not assume one perspective necessarily "trumps" the other. Most importantly, though, the verbal mirror provides the respondent with an opening to say more – to continue the dialogue and delve deeper into the topic.

Another essential ingredient of active listening is the previously mentioned probe. A probe is a follow-up technique that encourages the respondent to further elaborate or clarify a point of discussion. To encourage a respondent to say more, the interviewer might simply employ a quizzical look until the respondent starts talking again. The interviewer might also probe with a well-placed "Uh-huh" or "Go on" or an encouraging nod of the head. At times, however, the probe needs to be stated more explicitly. Imagine a college student saying she wants to get her own apartment because home life is so stressful. The interviewer might ask the respondent to discuss in more detail what makes home so stressful and how apartment living would relieve these stresses. Knowing when and how to probe effectively are two critical interview skills. The following two excerpts illustrate these points. The first excerpt from John Kitsuse's research on the imputation of the status homosexual shows how probes can clarify respondent's answers. The second excerpt from Angrosino's research with the mentally challenged shows how probes can help keep respondents focused.

Kitsuse's work:

I: What happened during your conversation?

S: He asked me if I went to college and I said I did. Then he asked me what I was studying. When I told him psychology he appeared very interested.

I: What do you mean "interested"?

S: Well, you know queers really go for this psychology stuff.

I: Then what happened?

S: Ah, let's see. I'm not exactly sure, but somehow we got into an argument about psychology and to prove my point I told him to pick an area of study. Well, he appeared to be very pensive and after a great thought he said, "Okay, let's take homosexuality."

I.   What did you make of that?

S: Well, by now I figured the guy was queer so I got the hell outta there. (Kitsuse 2002, p. 98)

Angrosino's work:

Researcher: Tell me about what you did at your uncle's café.

Yes, Uncle John. He's a great guy. I really love him.

R: What did you do there?

He cooks all his own food. Even bakes. Bread, cakes.

R: Did you help him?

He opens every day for breakfast and then he stays open until really late. He never likes to turn people away.

R: Did you help him in the kitchen?

Oh, yeah. I like to help. He's just like my Pop. They always want to help people. That's why he brought the café when he retired. He wanted to help people. People always need good food, he says. (Angrosino 2001, p. 253)

Silences

Speech, we are told, is silver but silence is golden. While active listening is important, this technique should never cause the interviewer to interrupt important respondent silences. Rather early in our training as social beings, we learn the value of friendly banter that can keep awkward silences at a minimum. Think about your own awkwardness when you encounter a deafening silence at the other end of a phone conversation – if you are like most people you will rush in to fill the void. Or watch how many teachers react to non-response from students – many will rush in and resume talking to end the deafening silence! The researcher, however, must put this convention aside during a qualitative interview. Moments of silence in an interview should be appreciated as instances of thoughtful punctuation. Frequently, there is something to be learned from the silence. It should be treated as a data point on par with words. The researcher should note silences in their files and even record the length of silences.

Some interviewers use a silence as a kind of probe – a silent probe. If the interviewer can learn to let the silence stand, the respondent may very well "break the silence" by providing more information. If the researcher rushes in and prematurely disrupts the silence, important data may be lost forever – the respondent may feel embarrassed or erroneously assume that what they were about to say was unimportant. As a result, important information may be lost forever. A good interviewer will learn to respect silences. In doing so, the researcher is apt to discover how silences can be springboards into important topics of discussion.

The Interview Schedule

When the researcher is interested in standardizing the interview process (i.e. making the experience the same for all respondents), the interview guide of the qualitative interview is replaced by an interview schedule. The points addressed in Chapter 8 on questionnaire construction can be applied to the development of the interview schedule: questions should have a singular focus and use neutral language – they should not lead the respondent. Response choices should be mutually exclusive and balanced (see Chapter 8 for more rules).

Perhaps the biggest challenge to conducting a structured interview is the fact that such interviews can have a rather artificial feel to them. This is especially a dilemma in the most structured of interviews – that is, an interview where *both* questions and response options are standardized. A highly structured schedule can be thought of as a script that is used by the interviewer to ensure that all respondents experience the same interview process. The schedule will typically contain the introductory comments to be made by the interviewer, a list of the exact questions (and response options) to be presented (in order and verbatim) in the interview, a list of the authorized probes and follow-ups for any open-ended questions, and a space for writing in the answers to open-ended questions. In these scenarios, the respondent may come to believe that the researcher is less interested in hearing what is on the respondent's mind than in checking off boxes on the schedule. Since scripting can make the standardized interview feel stilted and unnatural, there is an added social burden on the interviewer: she or he must work to keep the whole process engaging and informative. Part of this work is "rehearsing" with the interview schedule so that it can be delivered in an engaging way. No interviewer should ever appear as if they are reading the questions "cold." Indeed, the interviewer might do well to think about the structured interview as a performance that must have the appearance of spontaneity. Once again, then, we see the importance of the interviewer's social skills. The initial rapport established between the interviewer and the respondent will certainly help in keeping the exchange natural. Active listening (even to closed-ended responses) is also an essential strategy. And approaching the exchange as a professional yet engaging performance is useful as well.

Covering Sensitive Topics

While the personal touch of the interview is perhaps its greatest strength, it can be a distinct disadvantage under some circumstances. Covering sensitive or threatening topics can be quite challenging in personal interviews.

> **Normative responses** – answering questions in a socially desirable way.

Respondents may resist talking about matters they consider too private, or personal, or discrediting: sexual behaviors, family finances, parental disciplinary practices, drug use, and so on. Respondents might also be tempted to provide **normative responses** (i.e. answering questions in a socially desirable way). The first line of defense against these problems is good rapport. Having trust in the interviewer can help the respondent navigate their way through difficult topics. Discussion of sensitive topics can also be facilitated by carefully matching interviewers and interviewees: for example have men interview men, women interview women, age-mates interview age-mates, or minorities interview minorities. Matching has been shown to be particularly effective in combating normative responses. Finally, another effective strategy for covering sensitive topics is to change the *format* of the information exchange. When it comes time to cover threatening topics, the researcher can hand the respondent a self-administered form (or an electronic device) that contains all sensitive questions. The respondent can then answer the questions privately and return the form in a sealed envelope or hand back the laptop or cell phone to the researcher. This technique has been employed successfully in the GSS for questions on personal sexual behaviors (Smith 1992). Surely new technology and smarter smartphones will only make such practices easier to incorporate into the interview process.

Phone Home

An extremely popular variation on the one-on-one personal interview is the next best thing to "being there" survey – the telephone interview. This technology dependent technique sees the interviewer questioning respondents by phone and recording their answers (often with the assistance of computers). Reliance on telephone interviewing has increased dramatically in the last few decades, especially in the areas of market, political and public opinion research. Pew Research Center, for instance, uses phone interviewing as its primary mode of data collection (Smith 1990; Opdenakker 2006; Pew 2015a). And if you have had any experience on the job market, you probably have been through some telephone interviewing yourself – it is often a preliminary step to securing a personal interview.

There is much to recommend telephone interviews. Telephone interviewing is much more economical than personal interviews, costing anywhere from one-third to one-tenth the cost of an in-person interview. They are also a relatively fast research option. As shown by public opinion polling, telephone interviewing can give us almost instant feedback on the public's reactions to national or world events. Telephone interviewing has also been offered as a solution for reaching respondents with busy schedules, in widely dispersed or geographically remote and/or dangerous locations, as well as for reaching secluded or disabled respondents (Mann and Stewart 2000; Noel 2013). Phone interviewing can be set up so that computers generate phone numbers via random digit dialing (aka RDD). In this way, respondents are able to provide answers under conditions of total anonymity. Computers can also assist in the verbatim recording of respondents' answers. Lastly, phone interviews can be less intrusive or threatening than in-person interviews. For respondents, letting someone "into" their home via the phone is easier and certainly less risky than opening the front door to a stranger. Similarly telephone interviewing holds a safety appeal for the *interviewer* as well. Conducting phone interviews in high crime areas or in strife or war torn areas of the world is a safer option than going door to door for in-person interviews.

Phone interviewing also has a great "reach" potential: In the United States only 2% of homes are without either a landline or cell phone (Pew Research Center 2015ab). A World Bank study estimates that 75% of the world population has access to cell phones and, depending on the country, the access can be much higher: 90% in Russia and 94% in Iraq. Furthermore the World Bank sees the mobile cell phone movement at the very *start* of its growth curve (World Bank 2012).

On the other hand, telephone interviewing has some clear weaknesses. While phones may make it easier for us to "reach out and touch" someone, contact is not as easy as it seems at first. Relying on telephone directories, for instance, will give us a rather biased sampling frame (a list of members in our research population.) Think about it a minute – what numbers will never make it into our samples?[3] Owing to the limitations of telephone directories, many researchers will employ some form of computer generated random digit dialing (RDD) to select numbers for telephone interviews. RDD overcomes the problem of unlisted numbers in directories, but it also produces many unacceptable numbers (e.g. out-of-service and business numbers). For every 5 or 6 numbers dialed, the researcher may well find that only one connects with a residential target.

Reaching a working number does not guarantee connecting with the right party. To get a full appreciation of the many obstacles that can thwart phone interviewing, it is worth a visit to the Q & A page housed by the Survey Research Center at Berkeley (http://srcweb .berkeley.edu/res/tsamp.html). Here you will find close to 50 different problems one might encounter when trying to conduct a phone interview. Phone answering machines, busy lifestyles and endless ringing and busy signals all but assure that interviewers must be prepared to make many call-backs (up to 20) before they reach the targeted party. And of course, *reaching* the right party does not in itself guarantee an interview. Especially in these days of aggressive telemarketing and call-screening phone features, people may be less inclined to cooperate with *any* unsolicited phone calls. Not surprisingly then, phone interviews have a lower response rate than in-person interviews.

Cell phones also complicate the telephone interview. Over the last ten years there has been a dramatic increase in the number of people who have dropped landlines and gone totally wireless for phone service. At the time of writing, in the United States one in four Americans use only cell phones and nearly another fifth receive most of their calls via cell phones (Pew Research Center 2015ac). Since "cell phone only" users tend to be a different demographic (younger users and minority users) special efforts must be made to assure cell-only adults make it into samples. While landlines are assumed to be shared devices in households, cell phones are considered personal devices. Major polling organizations are still debating whether or not this distinction makes a significant difference in sampling.

For those who answer landline phones, attempts are made to randomly select a member of the household for survey participation – this random selection process is *not* used when contact is made via cell phones. Cell phone interviews are also more costly than landline interviews – anywhere from one and a half to two times more expensive. Cell phones typically allow for easy call screening, which adds a selectivity issue to sampling. Cell phone calls can easily be compromised by environmental factors (public settings, in-transit [car, bus, train] settings.) And they typically have lower response rates than landline interviews. Finally, poor call quality can also present special problems for the cell phone interview (Pew 2015d).

Because of the limitations imposed by the less personal phone exchange, telephone interviews must be rather short and uncomplicated – getting answers to in-depth, open-ended questions is particularly challenging. Additionally, research has shown us that follow-ups and probes are harder to execute in the telephone interview. It is also harder (though it can be done with pre-planning) to incorporate visuals in the phone interview (Noel 2013). Maintaining control over the interview process can be challenging. During phone exchanges, other people or activities in the home or call environment can easily distract respondents. And at any point in a phone interview, the respondent might decide the interview has lasted long enough and simply terminate it by hanging up. Finally, telephone interviews present a certain "coverage problem." As we have seen, cell-only phone users are a large and growing proportion of phone users. The percentage of cell-only users is higher for young adults and for blacks and Hispanics – groups that are already frequently missing from survey research. And while 98% of American homes have phones, phonelessness is more likely to occur in certain regions (e.g. US South) and among certain age groups and certain racial and ethnic groups (younger age groups, Hispanics and Native Americans in the United States). Lastly, there is the growing problem of refusals. Over the last two decades, the non-cooperation rates have been steadily increasing (Pew 2015e). Depending on the focus of the interview, these coverage differences could bias the results of phone surveys.

The More the Merrier – Focus Groups

I hope by now that you appreciate that there is a significant difference between questionnaires and interviews. The interview is a data collection technique that is dependent on *social interaction* – the give and take between the interviewer and interviewee. There is one special type of interview situation – the focus group – that fully recognizes the value of social interaction per se as an important source of data, insight, and understanding. **Focus groups** are guided *group discussions* of selected topics. With this technique, the researcher will assemble approximately 6–12 people for the specific purpose of discussing a common concern, issue, event, program, or policy. Advocates of focus groups maintain that the social interaction between group members will

> **Focus group** – a guided group discussion/ exchange "focused" on a select topic.

produce a dynamic and insightful exchange of information that simply would not be possible in any one-on-one interview situation. The give and take of the focus group exchange gives the researcher a chance to learn more about what people think of the topic at hand as well as to learn more about *why* they think as they do. The insight generated by focus groups makes them rather valuable tools for a variety of research purposes: market research, political analysis, and evaluation research.

In recent years, major broadcasting organizations have assembled focus groups to provide immediate insight into citizen reactions to presidential debates. Some polling organizations use focus groups as a way to test their survey instruments by having group members discuss the specific survey questions. Any many of you are probably aware of how major movie or television studios will frequently rely on focus groups to decide the ending of a movie or the fate of a TV pilot. Training in focus group research can open some fairly lucrative job possibilities.

While focus groups are decidedly different from the traditional one-on-one interview, both techniques are similar in their dependence on talk. Focus groups only work if respondents agree to talk. Indeed, it is the give and take, the point–counterpoint between group members that is critical to providing insight into the process of constructing viewpoints on various issues, attitudes, or positions. As is true for traditional interviews, certain social skills are required of the focus group moderator. Since the special contribution of focus groups is attributed to the dynamics of the group, the moderator has a special burden to facilitate group interaction. A particularly tricky dilemma faced by the moderator is to "run" the focus group without imposing his or her own viewpoint on the group. The moderator must guide discussion without overly directing it. In general, lower levels of moderator involvement are usually adopted in more exploratory focus groups. Higher levels are called for when seeking answers to specific questions or when testing specific research hypotheses.

Expressive role – sees focus group moderator attending to the emotional needs and dynamics of the group.

Instrumental role – sees focus group moderator attending to the social interaction dynamics of group (e.g. keeping members focused, preventing cross-talking).

In guiding focus group discussions, the moderator must be ready to play two roles: an expressive and an instrumental role. In the **expressive role**, the moderator will attend to the socio-emotional expressions of the group and closely attend to the content of the discussion – treating all participants as equals and keeping the tone of the discussion friendly and engaging. In the **instrumental role**, the moderator must make sure that the ground rules for the group are known and honored by all. The moderator, for instance, will inform the group that everyone's opinions are valuable, that no one should dominate the discussion, and that cross-talking or verbal put-downs will not be allowed. In fulfilling one's instrumental duties, the moderator will also take care to strategically place focus groups members around the discussion table: dominants should be seated immediately next to the moderator while shy individuals should be seated where it is easiest to maintain a direct line of eye contact with the moderator. (Decisions about dominant or shy group members are made during a period of planned small talk that should precede the start of the focus group session.) As part of the instrumental role, the moderator will also be sure that the research agenda is followed and that the group stays on schedule.

In his work *Talking Politics*, Gamson (1992) employed focus groups to better understand how working-class people come to form their opinions on political issues. His comments on running the groups are quite informative about focus groups in particular, and about interviewing in general:

> To encourage conversation rather than a facilitator-centered group interview, the facilitator was instructed to break off eye contact with the speaker as early as politeness allowed and to look to others … when someone finished a comment. We relied mainly on two facilitators, both women, matching their race with that of the participants … If a discussion got off track, the facilitator moved it back on by going to the next question on the list. But we encouraged a conservative approach to what was considered off the track since, in negotiating meaning on any given issue, participants typically brought in other related issues. Once most people had responded to a question and no one else sought the floor, the facilitator moved to the next question on the list. These follow-up questions also served as a reminder of the issue in the event that a discussion had rambled. (Gamson 1992, pp. 17–18)

Karen Cerulo used focus groups as well in *Deciphering Violence: The Cognitive Structure of Right and Wrong* (1998). Her book examines media portrayals of violence and the varying effects such stories have on the reading and viewing public. Cerulo contends that focus groups are especially well suited to studies addressing culture and cognition.

> Focus Groups provide a unique research vehicle. The technique is designed to capture "minds at work" as participants evaluate particular stimulus materials … focus group interactions encourage subjects to air, reflect, and reason their views aloud. Each session becomes a self-reflexive exercise that is unlikely to emerge from other data-gathering techniques. Further, focus groups are structured such that a study's participants interact *with each other* as opposed to interacting one-on-one with an investigator. In this way, researchers avoid the very real risk of channeling subject responses. The method places the greatest emphasis on the subjects' point of view. (Cerulo 1998, pp. 112–113)

Training Issues

By now it should be clear to the reader that interviewing (one-on-one and group) requires special social skills and training. Researchers are well advised to select their interviewers carefully. Good interviewers must be motivated individuals who are willing to hit the pavement (or work the phones) in order to secure interviews. They must be persistent as repeated call-backs are frequently needed to land interviews. They must be flexible people who are willing to work around respondents' schedules. (This often translates to scheduling interviews for evenings or weekends.) Interviewers must come across as non-judgmental individuals who can inspire the trust of respondents. This can be a particularly challenging skill to master. Establishing good rapport is key to getting respondents to "open up" in an interview but this opening up can also mean that interviewers will hear truths or views they do not necessarily share with the respondent. Such moments need to be carefully handled by the interviewer if the conversation is to continue. Consider the following exchange between a researcher talking to the owner of a local bar in a neighborhood that was part of the researcher's childhood:

> I then asked him how the neighborhood had changed since the 1950s. He looked at me for a moment and out poured a string of epithets and expletives about how blacks had destroyed what had once been a beautiful, cohesive community. The intensity and maliciousness of his comments caught me off-guard but did not surprise me. I have been privy to such language before. What was startling was his assumption that my partner and I would be responsive to such an ugly racist creed. (Gallagher 2004, p. 206)

Good interviewers must be able to think on their feet and quickly determine the correct "tone" or style to adopt for any given interview. They must hone their sales skills in order to sell both the project and themselves to potential respondents. On this last point, interviewers must understand the importance of first impressions – good first impressions can be the difference between respondent cooperation and refusal. Even seemingly simple things like clothing decisions may mean the difference between a successful or unsuccessful interview. In general, partisan clothing is not a good idea – wearing a Yankees cap may set up a barrier with a Red Sox fan. Wearing your Denmark jersey may not go over well with a fan of Sweden football.

Good social skills are essential but successful interviewing also requires specific training. Though it may appear simple for hosts of late-night talk shows, a good interview does not just happen. (And truth be told, not all people with talk shows are good interviewers.) Part of the reason why interviewing is the most expensive data collection technique is the fact that training good interviewers is time-consuming and costly. Talk, at least as a data collection tool, is really not cheap at all. The interviewer should have a good understanding of the research project – its purpose and how the guide/schedule serve that purpose. It is also a good idea to provide interviewers with a crash course in methods. They need to understand the basics of sampling and the importance of a random selection process. They need to understand the importance of the operationalization process and measurement validity. This insight should help stave off any temptations to change or modify the interview guide.

Trainees also need to appreciate how interviewers themselves can introduce bias into the measurement process via their reactions to and recordings of respondents' answers. In qualitative interviewing projects, interviewers must learn how to become active listeners. Trainees must learn when and how to use effective probes. They must learn how to reign in respondents who are wandering off the subject or pursuing irrelevant tangents. For more standardized projects, interviewers must be trained in how to faithfully execute interview schedules while maintaining enthusiasm. For both interview conditions, interviewers must also master the social skills that will help them establish and then maintain the necessary rapport with respondents. Interviewers must also pay attention to how they bring an interview to a close. They need to strike the right balance between abrupt endings and long goodbyes. Interviewers should also learn the value of "debriefing" themselves. Once they have left the actual location of the interview, they should write down any interesting thoughts or observations regarding the interview. Such notes can prove quite helpful in the analysis phase.

Training should always involve some practice sessions. Running through several mock interviews is an essential preparation step. These practice interviews will help interviewers get comfortable with the questions, spot potential trouble spots and prepare acceptable clarifications. It is also a good idea for interviewers to commit to memory the opening portions of interview guides or schedules. With enough practice, the interviewer should be able to conduct a smooth-flowing, natural-sounding interview.

Tools of the Trade

Despite the clear importance of the human touch and social skills in conducting successful interviews, the interviewer is well advised to acknowledge the critical "supporting" role of technology in the process. No matter how diligent interviewers believe they can be in recording respondents' answers, they should always consider making audio recordings (and for focus groups, video recordings) of interview sessions. This step merely acknowledges the importance of faithfully capturing the data without introducing any errors. Relying exclusively on note-taking during the interview runs the risk of distorting information because of selective or faulty memories and/or poor recording skills. Furthermore, the attention and care the interviewer gives to recording duties may come at the expense of attentive listening. Interviewers who are worried about "getting it all down" may not be so ready to pursue strategic probes and follow-ups. Given these considerations, the best line of advice is to plan on recording interview sessions. That said, the final decision to record or not to record must rest with the respondent. If the respondent is not comfortable with recording, it should not be done. Recording under protest is unlikely to yield a productive interview exchange.

Regardless of whether or not interviews are recorded, the interviewer should *always* take extensive notes during the session. (In focus groups, the task of recording notes is often given to one or two people not conducting the interview.) The best advice is to act as if no recorder is running. With this approach the researcher will always have a written record of the interview session. If an audio record exists as well, it can be used to amend or supplement the notes taken during the interview. Written verbatim transcripts are particularly important in unstructured interviews since the respondent's exact answers constitute the data that the researcher will analyze. In short, written transcripts are our data sets. There is no justification for skipping this step of data preparation. Indeed, experienced interviewers know all too well that the presence of a transcript greatly facilitates the job of analysis. Transcripts can be read and re-read and compared and scrutinized in the service of thorough analysis. By way of analyzing qualitative interview transcripts, Weiss advises that they be approached as word puzzles that see the researcher search for "meaning units" – entries that address the same idea or issue. Those units are then sorted and integrated in order to construct the resulting narrative (Weiss 2004). Consider how Nordberg solved the "puzzle" in her analysis of interview data with Afghans addressing the differences between men and women in Afghan culture:

> When I asked Afghans to describe to me the difference between men and women, over the years interesting responses came back. While Afghan men often begin to describe women as more sensitive, caring, and less physically capable than men, Afghan women, whether rich or poor, educated or illiterate, often describe the difference between men and women in just one word: *freedom*.

> As in: Men have it, women do not. (Nordberg 2014bb)

The Final Word

As the preceding review indicates, talk is an important research tool. It is also a versatile one. With the selection of in-person interviews, phone interviews, and group interviews the researcher has the ability to custom-fit the element of talk to the research job at hand. Whether the research task is exploratory or explanatory, quantitative or qualitative, simple or complex, the interview may well be the right way to talk yourself into a good study.

TAKE AWAYS

- The interview is the personal form of survey research
  - It is also the more social form–it takes two for a good interview
    - A partnership based on good rapport between researcher and subject is essential
- Person-to-person interviews can offer more than just talk
  - Researcher can "read" much from body language and social setting
- Unstructured (Qualitative) interviews can provide a rich data source
  - They are best for tapping into meaning behind behaviors/attitudes
- Structured interviews are more similar to the questionnaire
  - They need to abide by all the rules governing quality questionnaires
- Phone interviews are seen as a quicker, cheaper alternative to personal interviews but …
  - Phone interviews present their own challenges (harder to establish rapport, harder to control, harder to probe, etc.)
  - Phone interviews are also facing declining response rates
- Focus groups take advantage of social interaction as a source of information
  - They can be a rich and informative source of data for a select topic

Sharpening the Edge: More Reading and Searching

- The Library of Congress has an American Memory collection of interviews with former slaves. Some of these interviews can be accessed online:
  http://memory.loc.gov/ammem/collections/voices/
- The StoryCorps program offers people a chance to record their stories for posterity. More than 50,000 interviews are archived. (Some of the interviews are available via NPR's listen page.) A collection of questions that participants might use in the interviews can be found at:
  http://storycorps.org/historias/historias-questions/
- The Roper Center offers a page that gives a good tutorial on polling:
  http://www.ropercenter.uconn.edu/education/polling_fundamentals.html
- The Survey Research Center at the University of California at Berkeley offers a Q & A series that covers many of the challenges encountered in telephone sampling:
  http://srcweb.berkeley.edu/res/tsamp.html

- Useful information on focus groups (i.e. planning, running, analyzing results, etc.) can be found in:

    David Morgan's *Focus Groups as Qualitative Research* (Newbury Park, CA: Sage, 1996) and in Morgan's 2004 article "Focus Groups," in Sharlene Nagy Hesse-Biber and Patricia Leavy's (eds.) *Approaches to Qualitative Research* (New York: Oxford University Press)

- As is so often the case, Bill Trochim's webpage offers a very informative overview of the interview process that covers everything from preparing to execution:

    http://www.socialresearchmethods.net/kb/intrview.php

- No one who is seriously considering an interview project should proceed without reading:

    John and Lyn Lofland's *Analyzing Social Settings*, 3rd edn. (Belmont, CA: Wadsworth, 1995)

Exercises

1 Using the steps outlined in the chapter, devise an unstructured guide for use in a study of: (a) long-distance commuting marriages, or (b) participation in x-treme sports, or (c) families engaged in home-schooling.

2 Record two to three nights each of two competing late night "talk" shows. Critique the interview styles and skills of each show's host. In particular, pay attention to styles of interviews (structured or unstructured). Do you think talk show hosts are making good choices on this front?

3 Visit a few online sites that offer advice for job-hunting interview skills. Would the tips work well in a research setting?

4 To get an idea of how much the interviewer can bring to an unstructured interview, try the following. Develop one interview guide on a topic of your choice. Give the guide to two interviewers who will both use the guide to interview the same person. (Explain to the interviewee that the interviewers are practicing their interview techniques.) See what similarities or differences emerge via the two interviews.

Notes

1 Instructions for interviewer.

2 For a percentage breakdown of answers through the years, you can visit the GSS homepage (http://www3.norc.org/GSS+Website/) and look under the subject heading "Abortion."

3 If we use telephone directories to generate samples, residences without phones and those with unlisted numbers will never make it into the sample. A very famous example of the dangers of working with such restricted lists is the 1936 Literary Digest poll concerning the Roosevelt vs. Landon presidential election. The Literary Digest used telephone directories and automobile ownership lists to generate a sample of voters. The poll predicted that Landon would win the election in a landslide. In fact, Roosevelt had a landslide victory. How did the Digest get it so wrong? An upper-class bias was produced in their sampling technique – only the wealthiest Americans in 1936 owned phones and automobiles. Poor Americans were not included in the Digest poll and poor Americans were solidly behind Roosevelt and his New Deal.

References

Angrosino, Michael. 2001. "How the Mentally Challenged See Themselves" in Alex Thio and Thomas Calhoun (eds.), *Readings in Deviant Behavior*, 2nd edn. Boston: Allyn & Bacon.

Belenky, Mary, Blythe Clinchy, Nancy Goldberger, and Jill Tarule. 1986. *Women's Ways of Knowing: The Development of Self, Voice and Mind*. New York: Basic Books.

Borland, Katherine. 2004. "'That's Not What I Said': Interpretive Conflict in Oral Narrative Research." In Sharlene Nagy Hesse-Biber and Patricia Leavy's (eds.), *Approaches to Qualitative Research*. New York: Oxford University Press.

Cerulo, Karen. 1998. *Deciphering Violence: The Cognitive Structure of Right and Wrong*. New York: Routledge.

Connor, Jackson. 2015. "Bill O'Reilly's Alleged Lies Now Fill A Book." *The Huffington Post*. April 7. http://www.huffingtonpost.com/2015/04/07/media-matters-oreilly-killing-truth-e-book_n_7019488.html.

Gallagher, Charles. 2004. "White Like Me? Methods, Meaning and Manipulation in the Field of White Studies. In Sharlene Nagy Hesse-Biber and Patricia Leavy's (eds.), *Approaches to Qualitative Research*. New York: Oxford University Press.

Gamson, Joshua. 1992. *Talking Politics*. New York: Cambridge University Press.

Kitsuse, John. 2002. "Societal Reaction to Deviant Behavior." In RonaldWeitzer (ed.), *Deviance and Social Control: A Reader*. New York: McGraw-Hill.

Lofland, John and Lyn Lofland. 1995. *Analyzing Social Settings: A Guide to Qualitative Observation and Analysis*, 3rd edn. Belmont, CA: Wadsworth.

Mann, Chris and Fiona Stewart. 2000. *Internet Communication and Qualitative Research*. London: SAGE.

Nordberg, Jenny. 2014a. *The Underground Girls of Kabul: In Search of a Hidden Resistance in Afghanistan*. New York: Crown.

Nordberg, Jenny. 2014b. "The Afghan Girls Who Live as Boys." *The Atlantic.com*, September 8. http://www.theatlantic.com/features/archive/2014/09/the-underground-girls-of-kabul/379762/.

Opdenakker, Raymond. 2006. "Advantages and Disadvantages of Four Interview Techniques in Qualitative Research." *Forum Qualitative Sozialforschung / Forum: Qualitative Social Research*, 7(4), Art. 11. http://www.qualitative-research.net/index.php/fqs/article/view/175.

Pew Research Center. 2015a. "Mixed-Mode Surveys." http://www.people-press.org/methodology/collecting-survey-data/mixed-mode-surveys/.

_____. 2015b. "Random Digit Dialing – Our Standard Method." http://www.people-press.org/methodology/sampling/random-digit-dialing-our-standard-method/.

_____. 2015c. "Cell Phones." http://www.people-press.org/methodology/sampling/cell-phones/.

_____. 2015d. "Cell Phone Surveys." http://www.people-press.org/methodology/collecting-survey-data/cell-phone-surveys/.

_____. 2015e. "The Problem of Declining Response Rates." http://www.people-press.org/methodology/collecting-survey-data/the-problem-of-declining-response-rates/.

Roig-Franzia, Higham, Manuel Scott and Paul Farhi. 2015. "Within NBC, An IntenseDdebate over Whether to Fire Brian Williams." *Washington Post*. February 11. http://www.washingtonpost.com/lifestyle/style/within-nbc-an-intense-debate-over-whether-to-fire-brian-williams/2015/02/11/8e87ac02-b22f-11e4-886b-c22184f27c35_story.html.

Smith, Tom. 1992. "A Methodological Analysis of the Sexual Behavior Questions on the GSS." *Journal of Official Statistics* 8: 309–26.

Weiss, Robert. 2008. "In Their Own Words: Making the Most of Qualitative Interview." Goodwin, Jeff and James Jasper (eds.), *The Contexts Reader*. New York: Norton.

World Bank. 2012. Press Release "Mobile Phone Access Reaches Three Quarters of Planet's Population." Press release, July 17. http://www.worldbank.org/en/news/press-release/2012/07/17/mobile-phone-access-reaches-three-quarters-planets-population.

Chapter 10

Field Research: Welcome to *My* World

Introducing Social Research Methods: Essentials for Getting the Edge, First Edition. Janet M. Ruane.
© 2016 John Wiley & Sons, Ltd. Published 2016 by John Wiley & Sons, Ltd.

FIRST TAKES

Be sure to take note of the following:

Fieldwork – the naturalistic data collection tool

- It is about location
  - How should the researcher enter the field?
- It is about immersion
  - Walking a mile in someone's shoes
  - Talking with field participants
- Take note(s) of it all
  - Field notes – the qualitative data file
  - Tactics for managing field notes
  - Recording techniques
  - Creating files
- Fieldwork presents some special challenges for:
  - Ethics
  - Sampling

Think for a moment. What is the best way to *really* know what it means to be a member of the Royal Family or a White House staffer, a member of the Papal Swiss Guard, in the cast of a Broadway production, or perhaps a short-order cook? If you are thinking you would like to spend some time with these people on their own turf and follow them through their daily routines, you are thinking like a field researcher. Those dedicated to field research see much wisdom in pursuing the advice of "walking a mile in someone's shoes" in order to know something about their life and their experiences. In essence, this "put yourself in my place" way of knowing is at the heart of field research (ethnographic research, a term borrowed from anthropology, is a common synonym). In pursuing this data collection strategy, we take our study to the natural "field" or setting of our research topic and we literally watch (and listen to) what happens. In trying to find out how folks can make it (or not) by working at low wage jobs in America, Barbara Ehrenreich (2001) moved across the United States taking jobs as a waitress, a hotel maid, a house cleaner, a nursing home aide and as a salesperson at Wal-Mart. While she was pleasantly surprised to learn that she could "do" the work, she also learned first-hand about some stubborn and often belittling realities that keep low-wage workers in these jobs.

Of all the data collection techniques available to the social researcher, field studies may have the most intuitive appeal. After all, field research is essentially about watching and talking to people. It entails spending time observing the normal or natural flow of social life in some specific social/cultural setting. To some degree, all of us have engaged in such observations at one time or another. People-watching is a good way to pass the time and/or amuse ourselves during long layovers at airports or long waits in hospital emergency departments. Few of us, however, have taken our people-watching as seriously as the field researcher. **Field research** involves an extremely systematic and rigorous study of everyday life with researchers committed to long-term observation. To maximize their understanding of some social phenomenon, they will actively seek out interactions with specific people or in specific places. Their observations will be conducted in the interest of answering specific research questions. And for many practitioners, field research outscores the other data collection options in terms of measurement validity – seeing is believing, as it were. Field researchers are also committed to a full documentation of their observations by recording complete notes about their field observations.

> **Field research** – an extremely systematic and rigorous study of everyday life that sees the researcher observing and interacting with subjects in their natural settings (aka ethnographic research).

Location, Location, Location … and More

To fully appreciate field research, we must view it with an eye to two separate research endeavors. First, field research entails conducting our research in a *certain place or setting* (i.e. the natural setting of the phenomenon being studied). Our field studies might take us to an urban police precinct, an international refugee camp or a religious pilgrimage. Field research also entails a *certain way of knowing* (i.e. knowing that comes from immersing ourselves in the social world of our research setting). It is this feature of field research that sees the researcher trying to understand the meaning of events from the perspective of those being studied. While both of these features are defining ones for field studies, they are also challenging ones.

In entering the natural setting of some social phenomenon, the researcher must confront access problems. Not all settings (or more pointedly not all the people in them) will welcome the researcher with open arms. Successful entry requires the researcher to do some background homework about the setting and its local culture. The researcher might actually need the assistance of a gate-keeper to gain access. **Gatekeepers** are individuals who can give the researcher legitimate access to the field. Consider for instance Early and Aker's (1993) research on suicide in the black community. Suicide is always a difficult phenomenon to study both quantitatively (where statistics can be less than totally trustworthy owing to political and/or religious influences), and qualitatively (where access problems can be insurmountable.) It is interesting to note, then, that Early and Aker elected to talk to black pastors as important sources of information for understanding this phenomenon in black communities. In entering the field, the researcher must also take great care not to disrupt its "naturalness." Indeed, if the setting significantly changes by virtue of the researcher's presence, the purpose of our research is seriously undermined. This problem of disrupting the routine creates **reactivity effects** in field research and it demands some careful attention in the planning stages of our research.

> **Gatekeepers** – people who can help or limit researchers' access to the field.
>
> **Reactivity effects** – the change in individual's or the group's behaviors that is due to a researcher's presence.

Box 10.1   Sharpening your research vision: embedded journalists: an exercise in field research?

It is now a rather common view that American support for the Vietnam War was lost over US kitchen tables. Historians and journalists alike acknowledge that pictures of the war shown on the nightly news (while people were having their family meals) did much to make the public weary of the war and to fuel anti-war sentiment. In the years since Vietnam, the military has re-thought the role of journalists in covering subsequent military conflicts in light of the media's power to shape public opinion. By the time of the 2001 Afghanistan war, the Pentagon was embedding journalists with the troops. With this arrangement, reporters would travel with soldiers provided they followed the rules – that is, reporters could not travel on their own and there could be no "off the record" interviews. At first glance, embedding reporters might seem like an exercise in field research – one that would offer the public authentic and rich data about the war. But those who are critical of this approach point out some of the potential downsides to embedded reporting, downsides that we will recognize as part of field research in general. Recall the importance of "gatekeepers" in field research. Ideally, gatekeepers provide access to key players in the field. But with embedded journalists, the military gatekeepers limited access of reporters.

A second concern in field research is "**going native**". This is when researchers lose their objectivity and become one with their research subjects. Indeed, it seems that many of the embedded reporters

> **Going native** – occurs when a field researcher loses his or her objectivity and over-identifies with research subjects.

"went native" and in abandoning their objectivity they wound up making a case for the Pentagon's war. Many reporters befriended soldiers and understood that the soldiers were their protectors. Given the heavy reliance on air power and long-range artillery, reporters got a bird's eye view of "launchings" but seldom saw the destruction on the other end of the launch. In the meantime, journalists from other nations were covering a war that looked very different from what their embedded American counterparts were seeing. Seeing may be "believing," but you have to be sure you are seeing it all.

Levels of Involvement

In immersing oneself in the field, researchers must decide the level of involvement they will assume. It is helpful to think about participation as varying along a continuum from low to high. The various levels of involvement – complete observer → observer as participant → participant as observer → complete participant – have both advantages and disadvantages.

Complete Observer

In entering the field as complete observers, researchers minimize their immersion in the social phenomenon being investigated. This strategy is really one of *non-participatory* observation. The researcher tries to remain as detached as possible from the situation being observed. Complete observation may be accomplished via some kind of hidden observation (e.g. watching children play through a two-way mirror or observing taped behavior) or via simple detachment (observing hospital emergency room behaviors by sitting in the waiting area). In all likelihood, field subjects will be totally unaware of the ongoing research efforts. Consequently, researchers who hope to keep reactivity effects to a minimum frequently adopt the complete observer role. The detachment of the complete observer is also seen as a good strategy for maintaining objectivity and limiting the chances of the researcher "going native" (losing objectivity by over-identifying with the research subjects).

The shortcoming of the complete observer strategy, however, is somewhat apparent. Critics argue that the distance and detachment implied in this role limits the amount of insight or understanding that can be achieved by the researcher. Remember that achieving an understanding of the meaning of the subjects' world is one of the goals of field research. Some would also argue that any kind of hidden or disguised observation raises ethical dilemmas since research subjects are denied the chance to give their informed consent to the research project. Sometimes the choice of complete observation is a forced one given the clear boundary between researcher and subjects. Consider for instance, Barbara Myerhoff's (1989) observation study of a senior citizen's group in California or Barrie Thorne's (2001) study of children's playgroups. In both instances, natural age differences precluded the researchers from adopting a decidedly participatory stance.

Observer as Participant

With this level of involvement, the researcher acknowledges her or his research agenda and participates to a limited degree in the field. By way of example you might envision a researcher studying a weight watchers' group who tells the members about the research project and who attends weekly meetings but does not commit to the dieting process. This strategy is more ethically defensible than the complete observer who is doing covert observation, but it too has a drawback. In going public about one's research agenda and in limiting one's involvement, field interaction may be strained and once again insight might be limited or superficial. There is also a greater chance that this level of involvement will encounter stronger reactivity effects. Subjects might also resent and frankly not trust a researcher who is not really "all in." Sean Kidd in his study of "street youth" (2004) relates how it took weeks of positive encounters and a personal testimonial from one street youth before the researcher was seen as trustworthy. Still, there are many field projects where the researcher's involvement is necessarily limited. For a good example of such restricted involvement see Anderson and Calhoun's work on male street prostitutes (2001). The authors readily acknowledge that "learning from doing" was not a legitimate option for them.

Participant as Observer

The participant as observer becomes fully involved with the group or setting under study and is totally open about their research agenda. In entering the field this way, the researcher is trying to maximize participation while maintaining the ethical high ground. Initially, there may be some concern that the known research agenda will encourage the reactivity effect. Sincere involvement, however, can do much to build trust and effectively offset these effects. Many researchers who have adopted this level of involvement maintain that with time and effort, they come to enjoy full acceptance in the field. A good illustration of this level of involvement is found in Mitchell Duneier's work (2001) on New York City street vendors. Duneier devoted considerable time to "clearing" his research interest and project with other key vendors before he ventured into street sales himself. Indeed, he observed street vendors for two years and completed a book manuscript about the everyday life of vendors before deciding to start his project anew. He felt his work needed "more" than observation alone was providing and eventually he ventured into working street sales himself.

Complete Participant

In adopting the complete participant role, the researcher *appears* to be a genuine participant in the group or setting being observed. In effect, researchers acting as complete participants are involved in *covert* research – they only let research subjects see them as participants, not as researchers. There is a level of intentional deception with the complete participant role. This level of involvement is often justified as necessary for gaining access to controversial or illicit research settings. Consider Laud Humphrey's (1970) study of tearooms – public rest rooms used for homosexual encounters. Humphrey posed as a "watch queen" at rest rooms in public parks in order to observe fleeting homosexual acts between strangers. (Watch queens are lookouts who warn participants of approaching police.) Humphrey defended his covert tactics on the grounds that a "declared" researcher would never have been permitted to observe this activity.

Following the same line of reasoning, this level of involvement is also pursued in the interest of lessening reactivity effects. While it is true that a covert researcher should not destroy the natural dynamics of the field under investigation, it is nonetheless true that the complete participant will inevitably affect the social setting. As apparently genuine group members, complete participants will influence group interactions. Perhaps more than any other level of involvement, the complete participant also runs the risk of "going native" and abandoning their scientific stance. The full immersion necessary to achieve complete participation could very well encourage a loss of objectivity on the part of the researcher. Lastly, since complete participation is a covert activity, critics fault it on ethical grounds. Subjects observed without prior knowledge of the research project have absolutely no chance of providing their informed consent. For this reason, some researchers forcibly assert that there is never a defensible reason for this level of involvement (see Erikson 1967).

Low involvement   High involvement

Complete observer	Observer as participant	Participant as observer	Complete participant
Look without taking part in action	Limited participation	Full participation and research agenda is known	Full participation but research agenda is secret

Figure 10.1   Levels of Field Involvement

There is one other access issue to be considered. Some researchers think it important to conduct field research as "insiders" while others prefer adopting the outsider role. Although there is some overlap between these distinctions and the selected levels of involvement discussed above, the insider/outsider categories raise some different issues as to what the researcher "brings" to the study by virtue of his or her own statuses. The argument for taking the insider approach is that the researcher, by having the specialized knowledge of the group being studied, will be able to conduct more insightful analysis. The insider might also have an easier time being accepted by others, and recognized as being "one of them." So in various studies of athletes, some researchers feel that their own athletic training or conditioning is important for establishing their legitimacy in the field.

One of the early "classics" of field research was Nels Anderson's 1923 study of hobos – a study facilitated by the fact that Anderson himself had spent time riding the rails before he pursued graduate study at the University of Chicago. There are some who make the argument that the insider status is a requirement for effective study of gender-based or race-based groups or cultures. A slightly different twist on conducting research as an insider sees the researcher recruiting and training members of a group or community (clearly "insiders") to work as participant observers. (See for instance Angotti and Sennott 2014 study of a South African community and its public conversations about HIV/AIDS.)

The argument for entering the field as an "outsider" is that the researcher benefits from having a more naive position with regard to the field setting and participants. The outsider is free of "blinders" – and will "look and listen" without having any preconceived ideas (or biases) of what is important or significant, or any preconceived notions of how things "work." Many ethnographers believe that the best observation strategy is to approach a setting or a scene as a "stranger." Assuming the outsider role makes it easier to do this. Seeing the scene or group as something "strange" also makes it easier for the researcher to ask what Ruth Horowitz calls the "dumb questions." The status as outsider permits the researcher to reveal their "ignorance" about the settings or about observed behaviors – for example, "I know this may sound dumb to you but …" On the other hand, outsiders may well face a bigger challenge earning the trust of those in the field. The need to strike the right balance finds some ethnographers exploring the use of "internships" in certain settings. By assuming an internship position, the researcher is free to "ask" and learn and also able over time to establish more situated knowledge associated with an insider's viewpoint.

Field Research Tasks

The most basic task of field research is to provide descriptions of the social realm or setting being studied. This description process is not as easy or straightforward as it may sound. Indeed, the biggest challenge is often that of deciding just what the researcher should pay attention to or describe. Description is necessarily a selective and a partial process. In large measure, the process of looking and recording will be guided by the researcher's theoretical and conceptual assumptions (again showing us the importance of the theory/research link). It will also be influenced by the researcher's own history, biography, and training.

Thick descriptions – highly detailed accounts of what the researcher has observed or experienced in the field.

The descriptions provided should be **thick descriptions** (Geertz 1973). Thick descriptions are highly detailed accounts of what the researcher has experienced in the field. In providing thick descriptions the researcher is trying to explicate the connection between behaviors or events and their contexts. A concentrated effort is made to identify the *subjective* meanings people attribute to events. The researcher tries to describe social life from an "inside perspective" so as to enhance what Weber called "*verstehen*" (understanding). The researcher tries to adopt what Matza calls an "appreciative" stance (1969). In so doing, he or she strives to understand and communicate not only *what* happens but also *how field subjects themselves interpret and understand what happens*. The goal is to discover how respondents' lives are "lived." The following quote from Goffman about his year of fieldwork at St. Elizabeth's Hospital (a federal mental institution) in Washington, DC speaks to this point:

> My immediate object in doing field work at St. Elizabeth's was to try to learn about the social world of the hospital inmate, as this world is subjectively experienced by him … I passed the day with patients … It was then and still is my belief that any group of persons – prisoners, primitives, pilots, or patients – develop a life of their own that becomes meaningful, reasonable, and normal once you get close to it, and that a good way to learn about any of these worlds is to submit oneself in the company of the members to the daily round of petty contingencies to which they are subject. (Goffman 1961, pp. ix–x)

The thick description of fieldwork feeds a narrative that aligns with the idiographic model of causality (see Chapter 7). The contextual details offered in observations and interviews enable or support the analysis of the causal sequencing of specific events. Still, description is just the *initial* task of field research. The goal of providing thick descriptions of field events and behaviors is to transcend particular events and identify general patterns or regularities of social life. Consequently, field research typically has an inductive quality to it that is different from survey research. In survey research, theoretical ideas are often stated and then "tested" via survey questions. In field research, the researcher starts first by closely examining the social world. These observations are then used to inductively arrive at theoretical propositions that are informed by the field observations. In following this inductive path, field research is most often associated with developing or building "grounded theory."

As the name implies, this theory is "grounded" or based in the setting being studied (Glaser and Strauss 1967). (See Chapter 4 for more on distinction between inductive and deductive research.)

Another distinctive feature of field research is its ongoing, dynamic approach to data analysis. In survey research, data collection and analysis are separate stages of work: that is, first we administer our questionnaires and collect our data and then we enter that data into our computers for analysis. Analysis starts only *after* the data collection phase is complete. In field research, this separation between data collection and analysis simply does not exist. Rather, in field research, analysis is ongoing and occurs at all points of the field study. As theoretical "leads" appear, the field researcher is well advised to follow up on them. Theoretical hunches from yesterday may direct our data collection decisions of tomorrow. Analysis is a continuing process that occurs as data are collected, recorded and reflected upon.

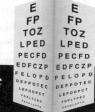

Box 10.2   Sharpening your research vision: distinctive characteristics of field research

Field Research

- essentially a qualitative endeavor
- aligned with the idiographic causal model
- inductive style of research supporting the development of grounded theory
- data collection and analysis – not distinct or separate stages of research process.

Informal Interviews

Field research is not restricted to just what the researcher sees. Much understanding is gained by listening to the noises, sounds, talk, and conversations of the field. An important tool for gaining this level of understanding is the **informal interview**. These interviews are usually less structured than those discussed in Chapter 9. This is largely due to the dynamic nature of field studies. The researcher may make an on-the-spot decision to ask questions as the need or opportunity arises. In the early phases of field research, the informal interview may simply be a series of broad overview or general information questions. As the research progresses, questions will become more focused and specific (Bailey 2007). As the study progresses, informal interviews are also likely to be supplemented by intensive, in-depth (aka qualitative) interviews with key members of the field. These in-depth interviews are key to obtaining "authentic data" from the field participants, to getting their views or takes

Informal field interviews – less structured and often unscheduled interviews that emerge from an exchange during field observations.

on reality. An important ingredient of the in-depth interview is *active listening*. The phrase may strike some as odd; many think of listening as a "sit back" and passive strategy (i.e. as in "you talk and I'll listen"). But active listening requires the researcher to be very attentive to what is being said by the interviewee. Paying attention and probing at critical moments or actively seeking to make the implicit explicit – all of these things are part of the researcher's duties in an in-depth interview exchange. Being a good active listener promotes the in-depth understanding and the rich data we hope to achieve in qualitative field studies. Anderson and Jack (1991) detail a strategy for listening that entails attending to: (1) self-evaluative statements made by participants, (2) reflective statements made by participants, and (3) the logic and internal consistency of participants' statements.

Carol Bailey (2007) notes that a key difference between formal and informal interviews is that the latter are really reciprocal exchanges. There is a give and take between the researcher and field members – both engage in the sharing of ideas, information, emotions, and so on. This reciprocal sharing is particularly important in field studies because it helps establish and maintain rapport. It also helps to eliminate the typical hierarchical nature of relationships between researchers and respondents. Informal interviews are also interested in capturing the context of talk and conversation. In this way, they help to advance the cause of thick description.

Notes

While field research is a rather dynamic undertaking, there is one essential *constant* in such studies: field notes. In survey research, our data winds up in the form of a data file (i.e.

> **Field notes** – a written record (as well as any audio or photographic evidence) of the researcher's field observations and experiences.

a block of numbers that represent respondents' answers to survey questions). In contrast, the data file of field research consists of recorded **field notes** (i.e. the words or images used to record the researcher's ideas, field observations, and interviews). Our research findings or conclusions will be based on a careful analysis of what it is we have logged in our field notes. Anyone who is not interested in faithfully recording field notes should *not* be doing field research. No field notes, no data, no go. It's as simple as that.

In the best of all possible worlds, field notes consist of a faithful recording of what we observe while in the field.[1] In effect, they depend on our ability to "pay attention" – that is, on our ability to watch, listen, smell, feel, and sense what is going on around us. How much of what we observe should be recorded? This is a difficult question to answer. Ultimately, we must trust the field researcher to decide what "counts" as important evidence or data. Still, if there is a side to "err" on it is arguably better to collect as much data as possible. Given its dynamic or emergent nature, it may be weeks or even months before the field researcher discovers the significance of her observations. Consequently, the more details recorded in one's field notes, the better one's documentation of insights or conclusions. Ultimately, field notes should be rich enough to help or enable someone reading them to "be in" or have a "near experience" of the place or event described.

In light of the importance of logging field notes, you might now be thinking that researchers must enter the field with recording equipment in hand. And, in a sense, this is true. Field researchers would never want to be in the field without their powers of observation "activated" or without a trusty notebook and pen. Yet, the actual recording of field information can be a tricky undertaking. Recall the point made earlier: field researchers are loath to do anything that might disrupt the naturalness of the setting being observed. Consequently, making the recording process an obvious or explicit one is not a good idea. It is not unusual – in fact it is rather typical – for the actual recording of full field notes to be delayed until *after* the researcher has left the field. Two of the premier authorities on field research, John and Lyn Lofland (1995), recommend that field researchers master two techniques that will make note-taking as unobtrusive yet as accurate as possible: mental notes and jotted notes.

With the practice of **mental notes**, the field observer tries to mentally capture or "freeze" a moment or event. The researcher makes a concerted effort to snap or draw as detailed a mental picture as possible, one that will survive in the mind's eye until the actual later recording of field notes. **Jotted notes** refer to the practice of recording short but evocative words or phrases that will serve as cues to fuller ruminations once the researcher has left the field. To minimize any disruption of the natural flow, jotted notes are best

> **Mental notes** – a detailed "mental recording" on an event/exchange in the field.
>
> **Jotted notes** – brief, perfunctory short-hand notes taken while in the field that will serve to enhance recall once the researcher has left the field.

recorded as inconspicuously as possible. The Loflands also recommend a practice they call "fuller jottings." This simply refers to the researcher taking advantage of any opportunity (a train ride home or waiting for a show to start) where mental and jotted notes can be supplemented. A researcher observing the interactions in a neighborhood bar might make jotted notes while appearing to doodle on napkins or beer coasters or while appearing to work on a crossword puzzle. Fuller jottings might be made while waiting for their take-out food on their way home. The idea behind mental notes and jotted notes and fuller jottings is to develop skills that will support the practice of recording fuller notes once the researcher has left the field.

While the exact content of field notes will inevitably vary from one study to the next, there are essentially five elements that should be included in all notes (Lofland and Lofland 1995):

- a basic record of each observation period
- afterthoughts and previously forgotten observations
- ideas for analysis
- the researcher's personal impressions and/or emotional reactions
- notes or ideas for future observations.

Basic Record

The basic record offers a running, chronological account of all research activities. The basic record should include information on dates, times, and durations of each observation session. It should include a detailed description of both the setting and the people in those settings, as well as the observed behaviors and interaction. In writing these descriptions, it is best to be as concrete and objective as possible. The Loflands advise us to keep the focus on "raw behavior." Opinions or judgments should be kept separate from factual descriptions. But it is also important to remember that the researcher should not just function as a human tape recorder. Instead, field observations are about making the connections between actions/behaviors and context. Providing thick descriptions of what one has observed in the field is predicated on the assumption that the *context* of behaviors is an important resource for understanding those behaviors.

In making notes on field locations or settings, particular attention should be given to the exact physical layout of the setting (providing a diagram or photos is a good idea), as well as the details with regard to such things as colors, furnishings and lighting of the setting. Good field notes should actually allow the reader to "visualize" the people, places, things, and events encountered in the field. If you have any doubts as to the significance of this kind of information, imagine what understanding would be lost if you were not able to consider or "see" how the physical environment of a nursing home or a hospital influences the interactions that take place there. Descriptions of settings should also detail the smells and the sounds as well as the lighting and colors of settings. (Again, think of the hospital and the significance of this kind of data – think hallway noises or the sounds of medical equipment or of patients in distress. Or to get an immediate feel for the significance of lighting, think about its importance in a theatre production.)

In addition to describing the physical environment, the basic record should also include a physical and social description of the main players in the field. How many people are there? How do they occupy the space? What do they look like? How do they sound? What information do they communicate to others via their clothing, hairstyles, accessories, or other "props"? How do they behave? What are the lines of interaction between players? (Diagrams are often useful to depict such dynamics.) Who are the social isolates and the social butterflies? What kind of verbal and non-verbal communication is taking place? Is there a special language of the setting?

Particular care should be taken when recording talk and conversation. Lofland and Lofland (1995) recommend developing a system where it is quite clear whether the notes are recording paraphrases vs. exact quotes of others or if the notes are recording the researcher's own thoughts and reflections. (So a researcher might indicate direct quotes by bolding them while paraphrases might be shown in italics. Personal thoughts might be recorded in a larger font.) All of these kinds of details belong in field notes – it constitutes the researcher's data. Consider the following "raw notes" taken by Allard in her study of inner-city high school students. See how they help you get a "feel" for and an image of the setting:

Health Resource Center: first official visit.

Tuesday afternoon observation (been here before with a student, but this is first time I've been here in for an extended period of time. Started at about 11:50 when the third period ended and first lunch sitting starts and left just after the end of the last period after the last lunch sitting at 1:50pm-ish.

More about the room: it's not really an inviting place and I can't say I love being there. There is no natural light and the overhead florescent light is flickering and driving me crazy (maybe that's a new thing or maybe I didn't notice before). The walls are made of cinder blocks, pretty much like the rest of the school and are painted the same "puke yellow" color as many of the other rooms (thanks 9th grader student for telling me that color description – it's actually pretty accurate and it's just as depressing as you'd think it was). One wall has metal brackets all over it with a lot of leaflets on all manner of things, but mainly sex education information (I've seen some of these leaflets left up on the third floor, suggesting at least that students have taken such literature at some point).

The floor has worn carpet tiles on it (same as the main school office and other administrative offices I've seen) There is one desk with one office chair and one classroom plastic chair in front of it. There is a huge wicker bowl full of condoms next to an equally huge plastic bowl of candy on a low bookshelf.

ADDITION: I later learn that there is an initiative called "candy program" (explains the big bowl of candy!) which allows students to come in and get free candy, thus giving cover for those who are embarrassed to get condoms (they are side by side – idea is you grab a handful of candy and a handful of condoms at the same time), plus it just lures more students – candy seems to work as an amazing bribe here, and anyone who comes in then are exposed to literature, condoms and if she's there – the counselor.

There is a steady stream of kids coming in and out of center all during that period. The students don't stay long, just grabbing what they need and chit chatting to their friends – from what I could hear a lot of the time it wasn't anything about the material or purpose of the visit. I counted about 12 student visitors over this period (one female (I recognize as being in the 11th grade – don't know her name) came back twice by herself, but most students came with someone else. Most of the visitors were girls …

Student visits went up at the end of each lunch shift: I guess that the center's high visibility since it's right next to dining hall helps. Plus nearly all students go to the lunch room at some point in the day – a teacher told me nearly all students qualify for free lunches so most go as it's often their only warm meal of the day (must check that stat with the admin and others later).

Unlike the other time I was here with a student (there was a school counselor staffing then), today there is just a short (we're talking not much more than 5 foot here) young looking white female. I have never seen her in the school before. She has long brown hair in a ponytail; she is wearing jeans and a sorority sweatshirt and college age, but looks much younger. We get chatting almost immediately (she wants to do know what I am doing there and I explain my project and she seems cool with it). She told me she volunteers as part of a community service requirement of her college …

The volunteer was at times visibly uncomfortable with the few students who actually spoke to her (like me, most students ignored our presence completely). One set of students picked up on her nervousness – a young male (I've not seen him before so I am figuring he is in another track than the one I am involved in) asked the volunteer "are you a virgin?" and the three girls he was with (also students I was not familiar with, but looked younger than him) all laughed loudly. The volunteer looked pretty mortified and blushed, didn't say a word and turned and busied herself with something else. The group then left the office with a handful of candy and nothing else. I thought the volunteer would say something to me, but she didn't. I didn't want to bring it up and embarrass her more, though typing this up now I wish I had. I wonder if she'll come back.

Source: Allard, Faye. Excerpt from her original field notes for her 2008 study, "Mind the Gap: Examining the Gender Differences in African American Educational Achievement."

> ## Box 10.3   Field notes and visualization
>
> The following excerpt is from Donald Ball's article "An Abortion Clinic Ethnography." It provides a detailed description of an abortion clinic's physical layout.
>
> Spatially, the waiting room is L-shaped and extremely large; approximately 75 feet long and 50 feet wide at the base leg. Its size is accentuated by the fact that most of the room is sunken about three feet below other floor levels. Fully and deeply carpeted, well furnished with several couches, arm chairs, large lamps, and tables … Both the size of the room and the placement of the furniture function to provide private islands … space is structured so as to create withdrawal niches for each set of patrons.
>
> *Source:* Ball (1967).

Afterthoughts

As hard as we might try, it is unlikely that we will faithfully record everything from an observation session during the initial post-field recording session. Sometimes we will find ourselves remembering events or episodes or learning new information at a later time (see example of new information in the Allard extract). These lapses or additions should not go unrecorded. (Indeed, they might be valuable sources of insight as to what is happening in the field or happening within the researcher.) Instead, they should become part of the record as soon as we recall them. As the events are recalled, care should be taken to fill in details from the original timeline.

Ideas for Analysis

While writing up field notes, the field researcher will surely have some flashes of insight into possible patterns emerging in the data. These ideas should be recorded as they occur and reviewed as observations continue. These insights might prove to be rich fodder for more rigorous analysis. When an idea occurs, take note of it. Ideas that are forgotten will never have a chance of having a pay-off.

Personal Impressions and Emotional Reactions

Recording one's personal feelings may seem at odds with the objective mission of scientific research. Yet, making such notes a part of the record is what allows the researcher to consider precisely how our subjective states may taint or color our "objective" reading of situations. The tone that characterizes a given event may be more a function of the researcher's mood than a genuine aspect of the field experience being described.

Notes for Future Observations

This last standard feature of field notes might best be thought of as a running "to do" list. As the researcher concludes the latest set of notes, she or he should explicitly list those things that still need to be done in future sessions: such as interviews with key players, observations of special events, first-hand encounters of field ceremonies or rituals. Items that remain from previous lists should be carried over onto subsequent lists. As one's field-work progresses, this "to do" list should grow smaller and smaller. Indeed, the size of the list may be taken as a rough indicator of the timeline for a field project. When there is relatively little left to do, the researcher should be preparing to leave the field and to devoting more attention to final analysis and write-ups.

The commitment to field notes must be strong. Again, if you do not plan to log them faith-fully, then you should go another data collection route. The time delay between observation and recording sessions should be kept to a minimum (we should never let more than a day go by between observing and recording!) The Loflands have suggested that for any one hour of observation, one should be prepared to record up to 13 pages of notes (Lofland and Lof-land 1984)! While others may find this 13 to 1 ratio extreme, it is still widely accepted that one should spend more time writing up field notes than actually spent in the field. Because the task of recording notes can be so daunting, some advise that field researchers should do their observations in relatively short time blocks (e.g. around three hour sessions). If you couple this with the estimated time commitment for writing up field notes, you will quickly realize that field research is a full-time commitment. If all of this sounds like more work than you care to do, then stand forewarned that field research may not be the data collection strategy for you. To be sure, field research requires endurance. It is not unusual for studies to last for years. By the time Palmer (1989) completed his "immersion" into the culture of paramedics, he had spent several years collecting his data, including logging over 500 hours with emergency medical personnel and making nearly 100 emergency runs with paramed-ics. Mitch Duneier (1999) devoted five years to his study of New York City street sellers of used books and magazines. Alice Goffman spent six years living in an inner-city Philadel-phia neighborhood where she documented the social world of people "on the run" from the law (2014). Randy Blazak's study of skinheads entailed seven years of data collection (2011).

Files

As stated earlier, the content of field notes constitutes the raw material for data analysis. But given the fact that field notes are likely to yield pages and pages for analysis, how should the field researcher proceed? One essential technique is the creation of files. There are essen-tially four different types of files that enable the researcher to transform field notes into meaningful and useful categories. With the advent of word processing programs, creating these files is a rather straightforward "cut and paste" operation.

Chronological Files

Chronological files organize the full record of all the notes and thick descriptions in a series of folders ordered along a logical calendar timeline. For instance, the researcher might create a series of folders organized by each week of observation. These files should help the researcher "see" the big picture of the research project. They should also help the research "see" any change over time. Finally, chronological files, since they contain a full listing of all thick descriptions, should help the researcher see all events in context.

Analytical Files

These files are created in order to help the researcher make sense of the data. Consequently, you might think of these files as the "idea" files. As indicated in the section on field notes, ideas for analysis should be recorded for each observation period. These ideas or hunches or themes that might be productive leads for analysis should subsequently each receive their own folders. The folders would then be filled with all *pertinent* entries from the field notes. Unlike the chronological file, the analytic files will be "cut and paste" files. That is, these files will not be a source of the full record of observations. Rather they will only contain notes that illustrate the idea or theme of a particular folder. A literature review will often suggest general themes or ideas that might be relevant for organizing notes. While the specific field experience will certainly suggest some topics for analytical files, within sociology, folders are often established for main concepts of our discipline: norms, roles, values, conflict, interactions, groups, and so on.

Mundane Files

Mundane files organize all the information from your field notes into the most obvious categories. Bailey (2007) suggests that these files consist of the "people, places, events, and things" of the researcher's field observations. For instance, the field researcher should consider establishing a separate folder for each major player in the field. Major events or field episodes should have their own folder. If observations varied by morning, afternoon, and evening hours, each time period should have its own mundane folder. If observations occurred across several settings, each location should have its own mundane file. Like analytical files, mundane files will consist of "cut and paste" entries – that is, pertinent entries will be culled from the entire field record and filed in the relevant folder. The idea behind mundane files is to create a system that will allow the researcher to access all information about major categories (people, places, events, themes, etc.) as quickly as possible. (Imagine the newspaper editor telling a reporter to bring her everything they have on _____. The existence of mundane files is what makes this sort of thing possible.)

Methodological Files

This last set of files would contain any, and all, notes about one's research procedures. Notes on how the researcher selected the field site, decided on observation periods, selected key informants, made sampling decisions, and so on, should all be found in these files. These files will prove most relevant during the write-up phase of research when one needs to justify or explain or elaborate on various methodological strategies and decisions.

The creation of files, like the recording of notes, deserves the most serious attention of the field researcher. The good news is that in creating files, the researcher is actively involved in the analysis of field data. In identifying the various folders and thinking about the appropriate placement of entries, the researcher is doing the work of analysis. *Understanding* what one has seen in the field *requires* the researcher to engage the data in this way. In a very real sense, the more the researcher puts into field notes and files, the more he or she will get out of them: nothing ventured, nothing gained.

Just as there are statistical packages to help with the analysis of quantitative data files, there is computer software available to help with the analysis of qualitative data. Some of the more popular programs are NVivo and HyperRESEARCH and Atlas.ti. While some maintain that analyzing qualitative data is more an art than a science (and thus fear that analysis will be mis-served by computer programs), there is much to recommend using analysis software. The sheer volume of data that can accrue in field research can make the analysis task a daunting one. Computer programs can help the researcher avoid feeling overwhelmed by their qualitative data.

The Ethics of Fieldwork

Perhaps it is because field research is seen as a natural form of data collection that it demands more attention on the ethics front. Recall from Chapter 3 that researchers must attend to issues such as not doing harm to research subjects, obtaining informed consent from those subjects and respecting their privacy. It is the last two of these listed concerns that present a special challenge to the field researcher. If the naturalness of field research is its greatest strength, there is an argument to be made that obtaining informed consent undercuts this strength. Consider that the principle of informed consent had its origins in medical research. It was intended to assure that patients and/or their care-takers were aware of what their treatment entailed – both the benefits and the risks. And the timing of obtaining informed consent was clear: it is sought before the start of any treatment. Imposing this model on the field setting, however, strikes some as unnatural or intrusive or even unnecessary. After all, the field researcher is not proposing a "course of treatment." Rather she or he is merely wanting to "look and listen" to what is naturally occurring.

Often in fieldwork, there is no clear or formal start to a project. Researchers might first see if they can find a place in the field from which to conduct their research. Consequently, there may be many false starts. Furthermore, informed consent requires that potential subjects be given enough information about the study to enable them to decide for themselves if they want to participate. As we noted in Chapter 3, the issue of knowing how much information to share about a given study is problematic. Clearly it should not be "too little" and it should not be "too much", but where is the "just right" line? The more vocal critics of the current operational standards in fieldwork claim that researchers often err on the side of providing "too little" information. Critics maintain that given researchers' need to gain access to the field and establish productive relationships in the field, they too often are less than honest or forthcoming about their projects (Thorne 2004). Often field subjects have a mistaken understanding of the field researcher's role or they construct their own frames for understanding the researcher's role. Yet if that misunderstanding "helps" the gathering of data, some (many?) researcher will allow it to stand.

Field research with its emergent twists and turns adds yet another layer of uncertainty to the informed consent dilemma. It is quite possible that a field project ends up being a very different project than the one started. If such change occurs, does the original informed consent still hold? One might also ask how long informed consent "lasts." Since some projects can go on for extended time periods, and fields can change over time with new players entering and old ones exiting, should the field researcher be continually "renew-ing" informed consent? Another twist is added by the social dimensions of field research. Researchers try very hard to establish good rapport and trusting relationships with their subjects. What should the field researcher do when the research subjects become "friends"? Some researchers may welcome this change in status because it might provide better access to more insightful data but others feel that befriending subjects could be a slippery slope, one that has a usurious quality to it.

These complexities surrounding field research also hold implications for the other main-stay of ethics: the right to privacy. Some researchers maintain that public field settings, by their very location, are free of any assumptions of or rights to privacy. But as we reviewed in Chapter 3, the location of a study does not totally settle the private/public line. Indeed, the case can be made that participants in public settings actually expect *more* privacy. (Think about the last time you rode in an elevator or on a crowded subway. My guess is that you avoided looking directly at other riders if they were strangers to you. Similarly, if someone stares at you in public, you are likely to take offense and perhaps even let that someone know you are upset.) Just because someone is going about their natural, everyday activities does not mean they want a "formal" audience – that is, a researcher who is intent on look-ing and listening. Indeed Lofland (1973) notes that one of the ways we protect privacy in public settings is by controlling or minimizing eye contact. Very often in more private field settings, the privacy issue is also side-stepped. A rather common practice in field research in private locations or organizations is to obtain informed consent from "gatekeepers" or authority figures that control access to the setting. Such arrangements not only render moot the individual's right to give their own informed consent, but also undercut the entire pri-vacy issue. In his research on prostitution in South Korea, Heiner (2008) contacted manag-ers (pimps) in order to obtain permission to interview the pimps' "girls."

Sampling Issues in Field Research

The idea of sampling in field studies presents an interesting challenge for the researcher. In survey research, samples are often selected with an eye toward their representativeness vis-à-vis a larger population. The field researcher does not typically have this grand concern about obtaining a representative sample. Indeed, the researcher's selection of a location often is gov-erned by very practical concerns about access. Researchers might try out several locations and see which one works best in terms of gaining access and securing a productive place for themselves in the location. Still some attention needs to be given to sampling strategies. There are four non-probability strategies worthy of careful consideration: quota sampling, snowball sampling, theoretical sampling, and deviant case sampling. (A thorough discussion of sam-pling and various probability and non-probability techniques can be found in Chapter 11.)

Quota Sampling

If groups or social processes being studied have clearly defined categories of participants or cases, then some kind of quota sample can be used. For example, in their study of commuting practices for workers in Cambridge, UK, Guell and Ogilvie (2013) tried to maximize diversity with regard to gender, age, and area of residence. They also were interested in securing different categories of commuters in their sample: those walking to work, biking to work, driving to work, or taking public transportation.

Snowball Sampling

This sampling strategy is useful when research participants are hard to identify or may not be open to being approached by a stranger. To get this sample started, the researcher finds an initial contact and then asks if that contact can provide leads for other possible participants. In essence, this sample is built around social networks and referrals. Jackson (2003) used snowball sampling in her exploratory study of child to mother violence. She started with three initial contacts and grew her sample to twenty.

Theoretical Sampling

This sampling strategy is guided by emerging research findings. The researcher decides the next sampling move based on what the field notes indicate are important considerations. This sampling strategy continues until a "saturation" point is met where a new location or interview does not offer any new information.

Deviant Case Sampling

This strategy intentionally uses cases or participants that are "exceptions" to regular patterns as a way to learn more about those patterns. So in a study of a neighborhood bar and its group of regular customers, the researcher might spend some time observing or interviewing a patron who is not considered a "regular."

No matter which strategy (or combination) is used, the field researcher must always be considering whether or not the locations selected for observation are representative of the larger research population. Mario Small, for instance, notes that many, many qualitative studies of poor neighborhoods used the city of Chicago for their field location. Yet Small notes that Chicago is quite different from the "average" poor neighborhood in the United States (Small 2015). And the researcher should also try to assess the extent to which the actual observations made within the setting might be considered representative of all possible observations.

The Validity of Field Research

If you are reading this book from beginning to end, you may now be wondering how field research measures up on the various validity issues: measurement, internal (causal), and external. For some, there is no better way of empirically documenting the world around us than through natural observational methods. As the opening paragraph suggests, much understanding can come from going to your research subjects and spending time in their terrain. Measuring parental love by watching parent–child interactions over time and under a variety of circumstances may offer a degree of accuracy that cannot be matched by questions or indexes designed to measure parental love "on paper." Directly observing residents of long-term care facilities or patients in hospice care will yield a level of understanding of "lived experiences" that is not possible to obtain via survey research. And because of its extended time commitment and its attention to details, fieldwork is strong on some of the essential ingredients for the process-analysis of idiographic causal research.

Field researchers are present to witness the unfolding of events and outcomes. And while some might be quick to give field research low grades in terms of external validity, such judgments are really misguided. Indeed, by making careful sampling decisions (e.g. by increasing the number or the variety of observations made in one's study, or by varying the locations of observations) the field researcher may be able to make some informed generalizations. Of course, the accuracy of such generalizations can be directly tested by careful replication. By repeating one field study in other settings or with other groups, the researcher can directly address the generalizability of a given set of research findings. Currently, there is a new found appreciation for comparative work that systematically examines fields or groups or organizations in different locations.

TAKE AWAYS

- Field research is the most *natural* way to collect information about the world around us
  - ○ The researcher goes to his or her subject and meets them in their own natural settings
  - ○ It utilizes all the researcher's senses: look, listen, feel, smell, taste
- Location is key
  - ○ Researcher must find a place in the field
    - – Placement options vary along a continuum from complete observation to complete participation
  - ○ It is about immersion:
    - – Walking a mile in someone's shoes
    - – Hearing subjects' stories in their own words
- The data file is distinctive – it consists of words/images rather than numbers
  - ○ Qualitative data is used to construct a story or narrative which
    - – Supports an idiographic approach to causality
    - – Typically follows an inductive style of research
  - ○ Field research presents special challenges with regard to:
    - – Ethics – problems of informed consent and privacy loom large
    - – Sampling – non-probability techniques come to the forefront

Sharpening the Edge: More Reading and Searching

- Much will be gained by visiting the field via one of the great works. You might try William Foote Whyte's *Street Corner Society* (Chicago: University of Chicago Press, 1955). After reading this classic, you might then see how the work has held up over the years by reading the April 1992 issue of the *Journal of Contemporary Ethnography*. This issue contains essays that offer critiques of Whyte's work as well as responses to those critiques.

- For a study that may ring closer to home, you might also want to read Jay MacLeod's *Ain't No Making It: Aspirations and Attainment in a Low-Income Neighborhood*. 2nd expanded edn. (Boulder, CO: Westview Press, 1995). This work shows how a good research project can be borne in the classroom as MacLeod initiated the field study to complete a research requirement.

- Anyone planning on doing a field research project would be well served by reading Carol Bailey's work *A Guide to Field Research*, 2nd edn. (Thousand Oaks: SAGE, 2007). Many consider the following (and updated) as the essential text for anyone contemplating field research: John Lofland, David Snow, Leon Anderson, and Lyn Lofland's *Analyzing Social Settings: A Guide to Qualitative Observation and Analysis* (Cengage 2005).

- "All things qualitative" is the focus of the Qualitative Blog – a useful monthly bulletin that offers training, tools and tips for the qualitative researcher. It is published by International Institute for Qualitative Methodology (IIQM):
  https://iiqm.wordpress.com/about/

- A good online review of many of the issues/topics encompassed by qualitative research (including a discussion of how to select a computer program for field notes) can be found at Colorado State University's Writing Studio page:
  http://writing.colostate.edu/guides/guide.cfm?guideid=63

- To find more information about qualitative research, visit QualPage on the web. In particular, see the link to "Qualitative Data Analysis" for a series of options for analysis of field data:
  http://www.qualitativeresearch.uga.edu/QualPage/

- If you are thinking about a career in qualitative research you might want to visit the Qualitative Research Consultants Association web site:
  http://www.qrca.org/?page=aboutus

- For another web site containing qualitative research information/links go to:
  http://www.communicationresearch.org/qualitative.htm

Exercises

1 Practice your hand at taking field notes by providing a detailed description of location you "know" but have never really thoroughly described (e.g. classroom, dorm room, family kitchen, neighborhood bar). Be sure to pay attention to all the pertinent categories that go into good field notes (description of physical layout, descriptions of major players and their interactions, etc.). What kinds of things did you discover once you started "paying attention"?

2 Find a public setting where you can practice your hand at field observation. Plan on spending two 30-minute sessions in the setting. In one of the sessions, force yourself to take only *mental* notes (i.e. do not use any obvious recording tools). In the second session, go prepared with pen and paper and take notes while in the field. Afterwards, critique the two sessions. In particular, focus on how the presence/absence of explicit note-taking influenced the quality of your notes as well as the quality of the interactions in the field.

Notes

1 Actually the recording of field notes should begin before the researcher enter the field. As soon as the researcher has an idea and starts any preliminary work for the study, the process of recording field notes should begin.

References

Allard, Faye. 2008. Excerpt from her original field notes for her dissertation research: "Mind the Gap; Examining the Gender Differences in African American Educational Achievement". University of Pennsylvania.

Anderson, K. and D. Jack. 1991. "Learning to Listen: Interview Techniques and Analysis." In Sherna B. Gluck and Daphne Patai (eds.), *Women's Words: Feminist Practice of Oral History*. New York: Routledge.

Anderson, Leon and Thomas Calhoun. 2001."Strategies for Researching Street Deviance." In Alex Thio and Thomas Calhoun (eds.), *Readings in Deviant Behavior*, 2nd edn. Boston: Allyn & Bacon.

Anderson, Nels. 1998. *On Hobos and Homelessness*. Edited and introduction by Raffaele Rauty. Chicago: The University of Chicago Press.

Angotti, Nicole and Christie Sennott. 2014. "Implementing 'Insider' Ethnography: Lessons from the *Public Conversations about HIV/AIDS* Project in Rural South Africa." *Qualitative Research*. doi:10.1177/1468794114543402.

Bailey, Carol. 2007. *A Guide to Field Research*, 2nd edn. Thousand Oaks: SAGE.

Ball, Donald. 1967. "An Abortion Clinic Ethnography." *Social Problems* 14: 293–301.

Blazak, Randy. 2011. "White Boys to Terrorist Men: Target Selection of Nazi Skinheads" *American Behavioral Scientist* 44: 982–1000.

Duneier, Mitchell. *Sidewalk*. 1999. New York: Farrar, Straus, and Giroux.

Early, Kevin and Ronald Akers. 1993. "'It's a White Thing': An Exploration of Beliefs about Suicide in the African-American Community." *Deviant Behavior* 14: 277–296.

Ehrenreich, Barbara. 2001. *Nickel and Dimed: On (Not) Getting by in America*. New York: Owl Books.

Erikson, Kai. 1967. "A Comment on Disguised Observation in Sociology." *Social Problems* 14: 366–373.

Geertz, Clifford. 1973. *The Interpretation of Cultures*. New York: Basic Books.

Glaser, Barney and Anselm Strauss. 1967. *The Discovery of Grounded Theory*. Chicago: Aldine.

Goffman, Alice. 2014. *On the Run: Fugitive Life in an American City*. Chicago: The University of Chicago Press.

Goffman, Erving. 1961. *Asylums*. New York: Anchor Books.

Guell, Cornelia and David Ogilvie. 2015. "Picturing Commuting: Photovoice and Seeking Well-being in Everyday Travel." *Qualitative Research* 15(2): 201–218. doi:10.1177/1468794112468472.

Heiner, Robert. 2008. "Prostitution and the Status of Women in South Korea." In Robert Heiner (ed.), *Deviance Across Cultures*. New York: Oxford University Press.

Jackson, Debra. 2003. "Broadening Constructions of Family Violence: Mothers' Perspectives of Aggression from Their Children." *Child and Family Social Work* 8: 321–329.

Kidd, Sean. 2004. "'The Walls Were Closing In, and We Were Trapped': A Qualitative Analysis of Street Youth Suicide." *Youth & Society* 36: 30–55.

Lofland, Lyn. 1973. *A World of Strangers. Order and Action in Urban Public Space*. New York: Basic Books.

Lofland, John and Lyn Lofland. 1984. *Analyzing Social Settings: A guide to Qualitative Observation and Analysis*, 2nd edn. Belmont, CA: Wadsworth.

Lofland, John and Lyn Lofland. 1995. *Analyzing Social Settings: A Guide to Qualitative Observation and Analysis*, 3rd edn. Belmont, CA: Wadsworth.

Matza, David. 1969. *Becoming Deviant*. New Jersey: Prentice-Hall, Inc.

Palmer, C. Eddie. 1989. "Paramedic Performances." *Sociological Spectrum* 9: 211–225.

Small, Mario. 2015. "Qualitative Research, Randomized Control Trials, and Causal Inference." The Eastern Sociological Society Annual Meetings, New York City. February 26–March 1, 2015.

Thorne, Barrie. 2004. "You Still Takin' Notes?" Fieldwork and Problems of Informed Consent." In Sharlene Naby Hesse-Biber and Patricia Leavy (eds.), *Approaches to Qualitative Research*." New York: Oxford.

Chapter 11

Sample This! How Can So Few Tell Us About So Many?

Introducing Social Research Methods: Essentials for Getting the Edge, First Edition. Janet M. Ruane.
© 2016 John Wiley & Sons, Ltd. Published 2016 by John Wiley & Sons, Ltd.

FIRST TAKES

Be sure to take note of the following:
- The practice of sampling – a very common undertaking
- Populations vs. samples (and other key terms)
- Representative samples: obstacles, challenges, and solutions
  ◦ Probability samples
  ◦ Using sampling frames and random selection
- Non-probability samples
  ◦ What to do when the use of sampling frames is not possible
  ◦ No claim of representativeness
- Estimating error due to sampling
  ◦ Confidence levels and margins of error

Most of us have some first-hand experience with the world of sampling. In our everyday experiences, we use samples to give us a glimpse or a "taste" of some larger entity. Indeed, samples work their way into our lives on a fairly regular and far-reaching basis. For instance, many colleges now require various majors to assemble portfolios containing samples of the students' work over their college careers. Likewise, job applicants might be asked to submit samples of their professional work product as part of the application process.

In reaching into our mailboxes on any given day, the chances are good that we will pull out a trial pack of the newest super-strength painkiller. We cannot watch a feature film without first being "treated" to short snippets of coming attractions. And as news reports so clearly demonstrate, investors the world over closely monitor the movement of key samples of stocks – the *Dow Jones Industrial Average*, the *S&P 500*, the *Nasdaq*, China's *Shanghai Composite*, Germany's *Dax,* Canada's *TSX 60*—for their daily dose of insight into the entire stock market. While each of these examples is quite different, they all help establish a simple point: samples play a central role in our obtaining and processing information.

The everyday uses of **samples** take their cue from the world of formal research. Researchers are often interested in learning something about large groups or aggregates of peoples or things. These larger collectives are referred to as **research populations**. We might be interested in studying the elderly, elementary school kids, millennium babies, Jihadists, blog postings, or Facebook pages. As these examples suggest, many research populations are simply too large to be studied in their entirety. In fact, the study of entire populations is so unusual that we have a special term for it: a **census**. Studying an entire population is such an arduous undertaking that even the US government with all of its resources only attempts a census of the US population once every ten years!

Research population – the total collection of the people, places or things we are studying.

Samples – a smaller subset of a research population.

Census – a study that collects information about every element in the research population.

If we are not willing or able to study a research population in its entirety, what can we do? We can elect to study smaller *subsets* of our research population – that is, we can study samples. Researchers may want to know something about the changing aspirations of college students in the United States. To get this information, however, the researcher need not survey *all* college students. Instead, a carefully selected small group – a sample of college students – can get the job done. Similarly, researchers might be interested in the violent content of video games. In carrying out this study, it is most likely that those involved in the research will analyze the content of a select group – a sample – of the various video games on the market. Drug companies test new drugs not on all targeted patients but rather on a much smaller group – a sample – of willing volunteers.

Samples, then, offer a practical solution to the daunting task of studying entire populations. We can use samples to "stand in" for a larger population. In this sense, samples can be very efficient devices – they allow us to look at the "few" in order to know about the many. Working with samples saves time and money. When doctors need to check our blood, they don't have to "drain" our entire circulatory system – a few ounces will do it. Wine tasters do not have to consume the whole bottle to assess a wine – a mouthful is sufficient (despite the false claims of some tasters). Ideally, samples "work" when they "mimic" or accurately depict the larger whole or population from which they come.

Samples that do a good job at conveying accurate information about the whole are referred to as **representative samples**. Representative samples allow the researcher to take the information obtained from the small sample and generalize it back to the entire population. So, if the average age of individuals in your sample is 32, and your sample is a representative one, the researcher can safely conclude that the average age in the population is likely 32 (with some minor adjustments, as we will see). This ability to generalize sample findings or information to the larger population is known as **sample generalizability**. When our generalizations are accurate, we speak of the findings having strong **external validity.**

Representative sample – a subset of a research population that accurately captures the variation found across the entire population.

Sample generalizability – the ability to generalize findings derived from a sample back to the entire research population.

External validity – exists when findings from a sample can be accurately applied to the entire population or when findings from one study can be accurately applied to other groups.

Using samples to make accurate generalizations about populations is a central concern of good sampling. This point alerts us to one important caveat about samples. Only representative samples are trustworthy in providing information about entire populations. Can we assume that most samples are good, representative ones? Well, let us look once again at some of our common sampling experiences.

Reconsider for a moment those movie trailers that precede the feature film. Coming attractions clearly illustrate just how misleading some samples can be. As you well know, movie attractions typically pack the less than two-minute "sample" of the coming attraction with the funniest or most dramatic or the most action-packed moments of the new release. All too often, however, the trailer widely misrepresents what the viewer will find in the rest of the film. Technically speaking, these small samples of feature films contain **sampling error**. Sampling

Sampling error – error that results from the fact that data is collected from subsets of research populations.

error refers to the inaccuracies of samples vis-à-vis their populations. Or think about a very common tactic used by many cable news programs. When talking about a controversial issue, some show hosts will urge their viewers to get out their cell phones and call to let the host know where the viewers stand on the issue. Sometime before the program ends, the host will announce how the sample of callers responded: "You have spoken …" But *who* exactly is the *you* that has responded? The hosts like to claim that they have a wide viewership and that somehow these quick call-in samples enable them to say how America thinks about gun control or immigration or ISIS. But the truth is that if you are not a fan of the show, you will not be watching and thus will never call in. And even if you are a fan of the show, not all fans will call. So who has spoken? Only that group who happens to be listening and willing to call – hardly a representative sample of the US population. And once again sampling error lives!

Sample statistic – a value for a variable obtained from sample data.

Population parameter – the true value of a variable for the entire population.

Sampling error is attributable to the fact that samples are typically imperfect. That is, they do not always accurately reflect the whole population. Let's return for a moment to the previous age example. While the average age in the *sample* is 32, the average age in the *population* is likely to be slightly different – say 31 or 33. This difference between a **sample statistic** (a value based on or derived from sample data) and a **population parameter** (the true value of a variable for the entire population) constitutes sampling error and it is something to be expected in the sampling process. Our goal in obtaining samples, then, is to try to select samples that minimize sampling error (*totally* eliminating it is really too much to expect). Why is it that some samples do a better job than others at representing their populations and minimizing sampling error? We consider this question next.

Obstacles to Representative Samples

As noted, the quality of samples can vary widely. The sample of blood drawn in the doctor's office is safely taken to be representative of all the blood in our body. On the other hand, we would be foolish to be so trusting of the typical movie trailer for coming attractions. Why the difference? Sampling with regard to the blood running through our veins is non-problematic because the blood in our body illustrates a **homogeneous population.** Homogeneous populations are those that consist of identical elements. **Elements** are the entities that make up a population. The blood running through our *feet* is the

Homogeneous population – a population that consists of identical elements.

Elements – the entities (people, places, things) that make up a research population.

Heterogeneous population – a population that contains diverse elements.

same as the blood running through our *hands*, through our *hearts*, and so on. Sampling from homogeneous populations is easy. If all the elements or members of a research population are identical to each other, then a sample of one would be sufficient to tell us about the entire population! Consequently, physicians are usually satisfied with one sample of blood when doing a blood work-up.

The trouble for social researchers is that homogeneous populations are relatively rare in the social world. The research populations that social scientists study are typically **heterogeneous** ones – that is, they are typically characterized by great diversity. For an illustration of population heterogeneity, consider once again the typical movie and its featured trailer. Feature movies often run over 100 minutes in length. As movie fans know, these 100+ minutes can contain a lot of variation. The average movie will contain slow moments, exciting moments, funny moments, poignant moments, dull moments, tedious moments, and so on. This variety in the total collection of a movie's moments or scenes illustrates the concept of population heterogeneity. If you think about it, population heterogeneity is just what we want in a full-length film. These 100+ movie minutes would be painfully boring if we were to see essentially the same scene over and over again (Bill Murray's *Groundhog Day* notwithstanding).

Population heterogeneity simply acknowledges the fact that many populations contain a great variety or diversity of elements. Think for a moment about your local college population or about a typical workplace. Despite the fact that college students all have college in common or office workers all share a common employer, there is still a great amount of diversity in both populations. College students vary in social class, gender, race, ethnicity, age, religious background, marital status, size, interests, and so on. The same can be said about office workers. In many areas of life, we appreciate this diversity. Variety, we say, is the spice of life. For some, monotony, or the same thing over and over, is a fate worse than death.

The simple fact is that population heterogeneity is one of the realities of life and, as it turns out, it is one of the great obstacles to obtaining good representative samples. The more heterogeneous a population, the more difficult it is to obtain a sample that adequately captures *all* the variation therein. If movie trailers were to faithfully represent *all* the moments of the feature film, they would have to show the good and the bad, the exciting and the boring. This, of course, does not make for good business if you are trying to sell tickets! This point brings us to yet another obstacle to good samples: the sample selection process.

How is the Sample Selected?

As suggested by the movie trailer example, the desires, motives, or biases of those selecting samples can certainly undermine the sample's ability to accurately represent the population. Those who select the scenes to include in movie trailers are not really interested in presenting a representative sample of movie moments. Instead, they are interested in presenting the scenes that have the best chance of convincing people to buy tickets. Individuals who book guests for television talk shows are not necessarily interested in representative samples either. The shows may advertise that they will feature "mothers who date their daughters' boyfriends." In reality, however, talk shows will likely book only those mothers who will do the most for ratings: such as the outrageous, the outspoken, the flamboyant. Similarly, people who conduct mall surveys for marketing researchers can easily stray from selecting representative samples. Surveyors might purposely avoid certain people (the disheveled, the elderly, and geeks) and happily pursue others (young, attractive potential dates). While these decisions may make sense for the survey worker, they seriously undermine the selection of a representative sample. Clearly, leaving the selection process open to such influences as personal motives and agendas greatly challenges the goal of achieving a representative sample.

Box 11.1   Research making news: desperately seeking subjects

All research (except censuses) depends on the use of samples for the purpose of data collection. In survey research, researchers come to depend on individuals as their data source. So the question is "how do researchers get these individuals?" One answer may surprise you. The Internet has opened up a whole new world of recruitment possibilities. Amazon's *Mechanical Turk* is an online forum for workers (who are paid very low wages) to complete surveys or perform other HITs (Human Intelligence Tasks). Relying on crowdsourcing, Amazon is able to recruit a group of professional survey takers for researchers. The pay for any one survey is quite low (virtually a few cents) and that helps to explain why some workers wind up completing tens of thousands of surveys. Everyone has got to make a living, right? For their part, researchers who turn to Turkers (that's what these online survey workers are called) for their sample get what they need: willing subjects to complete their surveys. Indeed some researchers say they would rather use Turkers than have to rely on undergraduates (the other frequently tapped pool for academic research – see Box 1.3 in Chapter 1). But is there a latent downside to going this route? Some say yes. David Rand of Yale University's *Institution for Social and Policy Studies* and an early supporter of Mechanical Turk, is now sounding a warning about its limitations. Rand's research finds that Turkers average 20 surveys a week versus the one survey per week completed by college undergraduates. This high rate of survey completion makes Turkers a "seasoned" group of workers, and a group that Rand fears may no longer be the best subjects for use in studies that so frequently examine *natural human impulses*. The fact is that Turkers take surveys that frequently repeat questions or blocks of questions. Turkers, in turn, get experience (or practice) in answering these questions. This experience creates a condition of "non-naiveté" that sets them apart from other survey takers. Turkers' responses to survey items, then, may not be representative of the more "naive" members of a research population. What does this mean for the results of studies relying on Turkers? That's what David Rand and other critics want to know.

Size Matters (To a Degree)

Some samples do a poor job representing their populations because they are too small. While small samples can adequately represent homogeneous populations (remember, a sample of one is all that's needed to perfectly represent a totally homogeneous population), diverse populations require larger samples. The reasoning is straightforward, the more heterogeneity in the population, the more elements we need to include in the sample in order to represent all the diversity.

There is a catch-22, however, with the issue of size. Earlier we noted that sampling was an attractive option in research because it is so efficient. Samples allow us to use a few to learn about the many. Large samples, however, can undermine this efficiency. Consequently, researchers recognize a point of diminishing return with the issue of sample size. While, in general, it is true that larger samples will be more representative than smaller ones, the advantages can be outweighed by the increased cost. Doubling sample sizes will double the cost of sampling but it will not necessarily double the accuracy of sample data. Indeed, probability theory indicates that increasing the size of a carefully selected random sample from 1000 to 2000 (a 100% increase) will only increase the accuracy of the sample by 1%! (Newport, Saad, and Moore 1997). Consequently, larger is not necessarily better when it comes to samples. Instead, researchers will employ ratios that establish acceptable sample sizes for various population sizes. As a general rule, the larger the population size, the smaller the sampling ratio needed to obtain a representative sample. Gallup and other major survey groups are able to obtain accurate information about our national population[1] by using sample sizes of between 1000 and 1500 (Newport, Saad, and Moore 1997). Box 11.2 presents the standard sampling ratios for various population sizes.[2]

Box 11.2   Sharpening your research vision: conventional sampling ratios

For a very small populations (under 200), do a census

For a population of:	Use a ratio of:
500	50%
1000	30%
10,000	10%
150,000	1%
1 million	0.025%

A Representative Sample – Take A Chance

The best strategy for overcoming these obstacles to obtaining a representative sample entails the use of some kind of **probability sampling**. A probability sampling technique is one where the probability of selecting any element or member of the entire population is known. The key to probability sampling is found in the **random selection** process. A random selection uses chance, and chance alone, to determine which members or elements of the population are selected for inclusion in the sample.

Probability sample – one where the probability of selecting any element or member of the entire population is known.

Random selection process – a technique for selecting a sample where chance and only chance determines which elements get included in a sample.

A random selection process is frequently employed whenever people are concerned with the perception of fairness. Think about what occurs when it is time for selecting a winner of a raffle. All tickets are placed in a basket where they are "mixed" or tumbled and then someone will (often ceremoniously) select a winner by pulling one ticket from the basket. This ritual is done primarily to offer a vivid demonstration that the drawing was not rigged in any way. Chance and chance alone determines which one name gets pulled from the basket. Or think what goes on in elementary school classes when it is time to put on a special school event. In the interest of fairness, the selection process is often taken out of the hands of the teacher (who might play favorites in selecting students) and instead put into a hat! To carry out a random selection of students for the event, all the names of members of the class (the population) are placed in a hat. A small set of names (the sample) is then randomly drawn. In pulling a name from the hat, every element in the population (i.e. every name in the hat) has a known and equal chance of being selected for the sample. The selection of names is repeated until the desired number of students is obtained for the sample. The names selected are determined by chance (and not by teacher bias or student popularity). This is a classic illustration of a random selection process. The more our sample selection process resembles this chance drawing, the more confident we can be that our sample will be a representative sample. Indeed, a major premise of probability sampling is that a sample will be representative of its population if all members of the population have an equal chance of being selected for the sample.

The idea of chance playing a significant role in selecting a good representative sample may strike some as odd. After all, our culture often warns against our leaving important outcomes to chance. We are urged to be prepared, to leave nothing to chance. We buy insurance and draw up wills in order to guard against disasters, diseases and death – the fickle finger of fate. And such advice is sound when we want outcomes that complement our personal preferences, traits or lifestyles. As indicated above, if we want samples that reflect our preferences, we should be deliberate in selecting them (i.e. booking the most loquacious guests for a talk show). But if we want samples that truly represent their population, we need to eliminate our personal preferences (biases) and allow chance to guide the selection process. Chance is our best antidote to idiosyncratic preferences and biases.

Sampling frame – an exhaustive list of each and every element that makes up a research population.

The Sampling Frame

In order to employ probability sampling, the researcher must work with a **sampling frame**. A sampling frame refers to an exhaustive listing of all the elements that make up a research population. The sampling frame is an essential ingredient for probability sampling. Indeed, it is the sampling frame that enables the researcher to "know" the probability of elements being selected for a sample. If a researcher knows that a sampling frame contains 1000 elements, then he or she also knows that *any one* element has one chance in 1000 of being selected for the sample. Without this total listing of all the population elements, probability sampling is impossible.

Obviously, before frames can be constructed, the researcher needs to have a clear definition of the research population. Clear population definitions will help the researcher identify the specific group the sample needs to represent. Vague or ambiguous definitions of research populations will only lead to problematic sampling frames and samples. Rather than defining one's research population as supporters of public television, we would do better to clearly state all the delimiters of the population we want to represent with our sample: for example, individuals who have pledged financial support to their local public broadcast stations in a given year. Instead of broadly defining our research population as sociologists we might do better to specify the population as current members of the *American Sociological Association*. Achieving this level of specificity when defining our research populations greatly enhances our ability to assemble or find a good sampling frame.[3]

Constructing good sampling frames, then, becomes a critical task in probability sampling. Ultimately, the adequacy of our samples really depends on the adequacy of our sampling frames. Good frames ("on target", complete, accurate, non-redundant lists of elements) will make for good samples. Bad frames (lacking focus, incomplete, inaccurate or redundant lists of elements) will make for bad or misleading samples. (One of the reasons offered by the Gallup organization for its miscall of the 2012 US presidential election was Gallup's use of a "biased" sampling frame. See Box 11.5.) The time spent clarifying the definitions of our research populations and evaluating sampling frames is time well spent.

While the researcher may actually have to construct a sampling frame from the ground up, many research populations have readily available sampling frames. If you want to interview a sample of sociology majors, it is likely that the registrar's office or the sociology department could supply a list containing all the relevant names. A minister who wants to send a questionnaire to a sample of parishioners is likely to have a readily available list of the members of the congregation to use as a sampling frame. With this list in hand (and once it is checked for any glaring errors like missing names or repeated names), the researcher can then go about selecting a variety of probability samples. Box 11.3 contains a list of all the recipients of the Nobel Peace Prize since the award's inception in 1901. A researcher interested in studying this research population could use the list in Box 11.3 as a sampling frame for drawing a probability sample of recipients.

Box 11.3	List of nobel peace prize recipients, 1901–2014	
1901	Jean H. Dunant, Frédéric Passy	Switzerland, France
1902	Élie Ducommun, Charles A. Gobat	Switzerland, Switzerland
1903	Sir William R. Cremer	Great Britain
1904	Institute of International Law	
1905	Baroness Bertha von Suttner	Austria
1906	Theodore Roosevelt	United States
1907	Ernesto T. Moneta, Louis Renault	Italy, France
1908	Klas P. Arnoldson, Fredrik Bajer	Sweden, Denmark
1909	Auguste M. F. Beernaert, Paul H. B. B. d'Estournelles de Constant	Belgium, France

1910	Permanent International Peace Bureau	
1911	Tobias M. C. Asser, Alfred H. Fried	Netherlands, Austria
1912	Elihu Root	United States
1913	Henri La Fontaine	Belgium
1914		
1915		
1916		
1917	International Red Cross	
1918		
1919	Woodrow Wilson	United States
1920	Léon V. A. Bourgeois	France
1921	Karl H. Branting, Christian L. Lange	Sweden, Norway
1922	Fridtjof Nansen	Norway
1923		
1924		
1925	Sir J. Austen Chamberlain, Charles G. Dawes	Great Britain, United States
1926	Aristide Briand, Gustav Stresemann	France, Germany
1927	Ferdinand E. Buisson, Ludwig Quidde	France, Germany
1928		
1929	Frank B. Kellogg	United States
1930	Nathan Söderblom	Sweden
1931	Jane Addams, Nicholas Murray Butler	United States, United States
1932		
1933	Sir Norman Angell	Great Britain
1934	Arthur Henderson	Great Britain
1935	Carl von Ossietzky	Germany
1936	Carlos de Saavedra Lamas	Argentina
1937	Viscount Cecil of Chelwood	Great Britain
1938	Nansen International Office for Refugees	
1939		
1940		
1941		
1942		
1943		
1944	International Red Cross	
1945	Cordell Hull	United States
1946	Emily G. Balch, John R. Mott	United States, United States
1947	Friends Service Council, American Friends Service Committee	Great Britain, United States

1948		
1949	Lord John Boyd Orr of Brechin Mearns	Great Britain
1950	Ralph J. Bunche	United States
1951	Léon Jouhaux	France
1952	Albert Schweitzer	France
1953	George C. Marshall	United States
1954	Office of UN High Commission for Refugees	
1955		
1956		
1957	Lester B. Pearson	Canada
1958	Georges Pire	Belgium
1959	Philip J. Noel-Baker	Great Britain
1960	Albert J. Luthuli	South Africa
1961	Dag Hammarskjöld	Sweden
1962	Linus C. Pauling	United States
1963	International Red Cross, League of Red Cross Societies	
1964	Martin Luther King, Jr.	United States
1965	UN Children's Fund (UNICEF)	
1966		
1967		
1968	René Cassin	France
1969	International Labor Organization	
1970	Norman E. Borlaug	United States
1971	Willy Brandt	Germany
1972		
1973	Henry Kissinger, Le Duc Tho (declined)	United States, North Vietnam
1974	Eisaku Sato, Sean MacBride	Japan, Ireland
1975	Andrei Sakharov	Soviet Union
1976	Mairead Corrigan, Betty Williams	Northern Ireland, Northern Ireland
1977	Amnesty International	
1978	Anwar Sadat, Menachem Begin	Egypt, Israel
1979	Mother Teresa of Calcutta	Albania – India
1980	Adolfo Pérez Esquivel	Argentina
1981	Office of UN High Commission for Refugees	
1982	Alva Myrdal, Alfonso Garcia Robles	Sweden, Mexico
1983	Lech Walesa	Poland
1984	Bishop Desmond Tutu	South Africa

1985	International Physicians for the Prevention of Nuclear War	United States
1986	Elie Wiesel	Romania-United States
1987	Oscar Arias Sanchez	Costa Rica
1988	UN Peacekeeping Forces	
1989	Dalai Lama	Tibet
1990	Mikhail S. Gorbachev	Soviet Union
1991	Aung San Suu Kyi	Myanmar
1992	Rigoberta Menchú	Guatemala
1993	Frederik W. de Klerk, Nelson Mandela	South Africa, South Africa
1994	Yasir Arafat, Shimon Peres, Yitzhak Rabin	Palestine, Israel, Israel
1995	Joseph Rotblat Pugwash Conference	Poland-Great Britain
1996	Bishop Carlos Ximenes Belo, José Ramos-Horta	Timor, Timor
1997	Jody Williams International Campaign to Ban Landmines	United States
1998	John Hume, David Trimble	Northern Ireland, Northern Ireland
1999	Médecins Sans Frontières	Switzerland
2000	Kim Dae Jung	South Korea
2001	United Nations Kofi Annan	Ghana
2002	Jimmy Carter	United States
2003	Shirin Ebadi	Iran
2004	Wangari Muta Maathai	Kenya
2005	International Atomic Energy Agency (IAEA), Mohamed ElBaradei	Austria, Egypt
2006	Muhammad Yunus, Grameen Bank	Bangladesh, Bangladesh
2007	Intergovernmental Panel on Climate Change (IPCC), Albert Arnold Gore Jr.	Switzerland, United States
2008	Martti Ahtisaari	Finland
2009	Barack Obama	United States
2010	Liu Xiaobo	China
2011	Ellen Johnson Sirleaf, Leymah Gbowee, Tawakkol Karman	Liberia, Liberia, Yemen
2012	The European Union	
2013	Organization for the Prohibition of Chemical Weapons	
2014	Kailash Satyarthi	India
	Malala Yousafzai	Pakistan
2015	National Dialogue Quartet	Tunisia

Some Probability Samples

Researchers interested in probability sampling techniques have their choice of several options. We review some of the most standard selections below.

Simple Random Sample The most basic probability sample is the **simple random sample** – a selection process that affords every element in a population an equal chance of being selected for the sample. This sampling technique sees the researcher executing the following *simple* steps: (1) numbering all the elements in the sampling frame, and (2) randomly selecting some of the numbered elements for inclusion in the sample. For example, if we numbered all of the Nobel Peace Prize winners listed in Box 11.3, we would be set up to do a simple random sample of the winners. Random selection can be done with the assistance of a table of random numbers (a table of random numbers can usually be found in an appendix of a statistics book or you can find a table online (e.g. http://www.stattrek. com/statistics/random-number-generator.aspx). In using such a table, the researcher selects a number (by chance) from the random numbers table. (Selecting a number by chance is as simple as dropping your finger on the table and seeing what number you land on.)[4] The element in the sampling frame with that number then gets included in the sample. This step is repeated until the desired sample size is achieved.

> **Simple random sample** – one in which all elements of sampling frame have a known and equal chance of being selected for the sample.

Systematic Random Sample As you might imagine, the simple random sample is simple for small research populations, but it quickly gets tedious for larger populations. A **systematic sample** is a reasonable alternative. A systematic random sample employs a systematic "skip" pattern that can speed up the random selection of elements for the sample. The skip pattern is determined by the sampling interval – a set distance between elements in the sampling frame. This set distance is calculated by dividing the total population size by the desired sample size.

> **Systematic random sample** – one which uses a random starting point and then employs a systematic skip pattern (sampling interval) to select every kth (e.g. 5th, 10th, 12th, etc.) element for inclusion in the sample.

So let us go through the steps needed for selecting a systematic random sample. Once again the researcher will start with a sampling frame. Next, a sampling interval needs to be calculated. This is done by dividing the total population size by the desired sample size. So, if we have a population of 10,000 and we want a sample of 500, we would work with a sampling interval of 20 (10,000/500=20). Next, we will use a table of random numbers to select the *first* element for inclusion in the sample. (In using the table of random numbers we want to randomly select a number that falls within our sampling interval. In the current example, we want a randomly selected number between 1 and 20). If our random starting point were number 8, we would include elements number 8, 28, 48, 68, and so on, in our sample. (We would continue selecting every 20th element until we reached our desired sample size of 500.) Once a starting point is determined, the rest of the elements for inclusion in the sample will be systematically selected by incorporating the sampling interval into the selection process. The sampling interval, because it is a systematic skipping pattern, speeds up the selection process. Or consider drawing a systematic sample of Nobel Peace Prize winners listed in Box 11.3. Since 1901, there have been 128 Nobel laureates. Say we want a sample size of 30,[5] this would give us a sampling interval or a "skip" pattern of 4 (128/30 = 4.26). We would use the table of random numbers to select a starting point that falls within our sampling interval (a number from 1 to 4). Doing just this, I randomly selected the number 3 as my starting point. Consequently, looking back at my sampling frame (the list of winners in Box 11.3), I would select Élie Ducommun for the sample and every fourth winner thereafter (e.g. Baroness Bertha von Suttner, Klas P. Arnoldson, and so on.)

Stratified random sample – one that organizes the sampling frame into homogenous subgroups based on a critical variable to assure that a representative sampling of the values of this variable is achieved.

Stratified Sampling   Recall from our earlier discussion that representative samples are more easily obtained from homogeneous than from heterogeneous populations. **Stratified random sampling** takes advantage of this insight. With this technique, the researcher organizes the sampling frame into relatively homogeneous groups (strata) before selecting elements for the sample. This step increases the probability that the final sample will be representative in terms of the stratified groups. So, if we are particularly concerned that our sample faithfully represents the research population in terms of gender, we would stratify the sampling frame on gender (i.e. we would list/group all males together and then list/group all females together). We would then proceed to draw either a simple or a systematic sample in each group. If a researcher sees a critical need for faithfully representing some key variable (e.g. gender, race, ethnicity, political affiliation, age) then they would be well advised to stratify the sampling frame along the values of that variable.

There is one hitch to stratified sampling. It often requires the researcher to have quite a bit of information about the research population at his or her fingertips. Consider, for example, the sampling frame for Nobel Peace Prize winners. On the basis of first names, we could easily stratify the list by gender. (Although some first names may not be obvious and so even here we might need to do a bit more verifying work when creating these separate lists.) But if we wanted to stratify the list on another variable (e.g. recipient's age at time of award, or their occupation, or race), we simply could not do it with the minimal information contained in the list presented in Box 11.3. We would first have to obtain this additional information about each winner in order to create these subdivisions within the sampling frame. If the additional information required for stratification is not readily or easily available, stratification may not be a practical endeavor.

Cluster sample – one that is selected in stages, enabling the use of successive sampling frames for progressively larger clusters of the ultimate sampling unit.

Cluster Sampling   We have already noted that a sampling frame is an essential ingredient for probability sampling. And we have noted that often sampling frames might be relatively easy to obtain. What, however, happens when an exhaustive listing of all the elements in a research population is an impossible or unreasonable proposition? Say you want to sample high school students in your home state or region. Do you really have to start by compiling a list of every single high school student in your state? Fortunately, the answer is no. Cluster sampling is a probability technique that can be used when the construction of a sampling frame is *theoretically possible* but not a very feasible course of action.

Cluster sampling requires the researcher to approach the sampling process in multiple stages. The idea is to identify naturally occurring and increasingly inclusive "clusters" of one's ultimate sampling unit. Imagine you want to study graduating high school seniors in your state. Where do seniors "exist"? They exist in high schools. Where do high schools exist? In cities. Where do cities exist? In states. Finally we are at the "top" cluster (or primary unit) for our sampling problem. Now the researcher starts working backwards. Is it reasonable to construct a sampling frame of all the cities in a state? Yes. (In fact one probably already exists on the state's homepage.) From this sampling frame, one can select a simple, a systematic, or a stratified sample of cities. Is it possible to construct a sampling frame listing all the high schools for the selected cities? Yes. From this list, one can then select a sample of high schools. Is it possible to construct a sampling frame of graduating seniors for the selected schools? Yes (and once again this list probably already exists in the selected schools' registrar's office.)

As you can see, cluster sampling is not for the faint of heart. It entails much more work and effort than other probability techniques. And a "heads-up" warning must be issued for this technique: since cluster sampling entails *repeated* sampling it presents greater opportunity for sampling error. Indeed, we must assume that each sampling event contains some error and that this error will be compounded as the sampling continues. Still, it offers a practical solution to obtaining a representative sample of very large research populations. And, typically, cluster sampling is conducted by major organizations (e.g. governments, corporations) that have in-house experts to calculate the sampling error that accompanies this technique. If you visit the homepages for national and international social surveys, you will likely find links leading to information about sampling procedures, and you will also see how committed these groups are to obtaining representative samples. For instance, the European Social Survey (ESS) adheres to the following standard when sampling: "an optimal sample design for cross-cultural surveys should consist of the best *random sampling practice* used in each participating country" (emphasis added). In practice, this means that the ESS utilizes sampling frames listing residents in some countries (e.g. Norway, Sweden, Switzerland, or Denmark), sampling frames listing households in other countries (e.g. Netherlands or the UK), or it will utilize multi-stage cluster sampling in countries lacking reliable registries of residents or households. No matter what, however, some form of probability sampling is employed: "Individuals are selected by strict random probability methods at every stage" (http://www.europeansocialsurvey.org/methodology/sampling.html).

Box 11.4   Sharpening your research vision: major
probability and non-probability samples

Probability	Non-probability
Require a sampling frame	No sampling frame used
Assumed to be representative	Cannot assume representativeness
Simple random	Convenience
Systematic random	Snowball
Stratified	Purposive
Cluster	Quota

Non-Probability Techniques

As cluster sampling shows us, researchers sometimes have to be extremely creative (and patient) in constructing sampling frames. Nonetheless, we must also acknowledge that not all research scenarios allow for probability sampling. There are times when the essential ingredient for probability sampling – the sampling frame – is impossible for the researcher to construct. Imagine that you want to study the homeless in your local city. Is probability sampling possible? Can you assemble (either immediately or eventually) a sampling frame? That is, can you construct a list that contains the names of all the homeless individuals in your area? I think most of us would have to answer no. Unlike high school students whose names and addresses are certainly known to administrative offices, the homeless are essentially an anonymous research population. Even groups that befriend the homeless (e.g. soup kitchens or religious organizations), often do so under conditions that safeguard anonymity.

As another example, think about the task of sampling heavily tattooed individuals or "collectors" as they are known in the field (Vail 2001). This is a group that is decidedly "marked" as outside mainstream society. How realistic is it to construct an exhaustive list of such people? Some people with full-body tattoos go to great lengths to hide this fact from conventional others. They wear concealing clothing at work and are quite selective in revealing their tattooed selves to others (Sanders 1999). Compiling an exhaustive list of your research population, then, will be an unrealistic (and certainly incomplete) undertaking.

So, what is the sampling alternative when probability sampling is impossible? The researcher who cannot construct a sampling frame must consider a non-probability sampling technique. As is the case with probability sampling, the researcher has several non-probability sampling options to consider.

Convenience Samples

Probably the oldest sampling strategy is the convenience sample (aka accidental sample). As the name implies, this technique builds a sample on the basis of finding conven-ient or readily available individuals. Those who are selected for the sample are those who are close at hand. If you have ever been asked to fill out a questionnaire in your university student center or as you exited a voting/polling location, you have had first-hand experi-ence with a convenience sample. Clearly, there is an obvious shortcoming to this kind of sampling. Individuals who are not "conveniently" located have no chance of being selected for such samples. For instance, students who never frequent the student center, or voters who were not at the polls at the time surveying was being done, or citizens who voted by mail would never have a chance of making it into the previously described convenience samples. The omission of all but the most conveniently accessed elements in a population greatly undermines the representativeness of a convenience sample.

> **Convenience sample** – one that uses readily available (close at hand) elements.

Snowball Samples

Snowball sampling is essentially a sampling strategy built around social networks and referrals. (The technique's name invokes the image of rolling small snowballs into larger and larger snowballs – i.e. the kind that form the base of a snowman.) The researcher will start the sampling process by contacting a few individuals for inclusion in the sample. These people will then be asked for names of additional people who might be willing to be part of the research project. Snowball sampling might be a good technique to consider for the tattoo project mentioned above. After making contact and winning the trust of a few "collectors" the researcher would then ask these individuals for names of other collectors. The new names would then be contacted and asked for names of still more collectors. This process is repeated until a satisfactory sample size is achieved. Weston (2004) used this technique to gather a sample for her study of the lesbian and gay community in San Fran-cisco. She used her personal contacts to generate a list of initial potential subjects. Then she asked those folks to suggest names of other potential participants. There is again a clear shortcoming of snowball samples. Individuals who are "loners," who are not "networked" with others in the research population will likely be excluded from snowball samples.

> **Snowball sample** – one that uses referrals or social networks to build a sample.

Quota Samples

It is perhaps useful to think of the quota sample as the non-probability equivalent of the stratified sample. Here the researcher selects sample members on the basis of key traits assumed to characterize the research population. Sampling is then conducted in such a way as to fill set quotas for these traits. You may have been involved in such a sample if you have ever been approached in a mall by a marketing researcher looking to fill a quota for some predetermined charac-teristics (e.g. female, contact wearers in their 20s). Once researchers fill a quota on one set

> **Quota sample** – a sample that recruits elements in order to fill pre-determined desired categories of elements that "represent" the population (aka a non-probability stratified sample).

of characteristics, they move on to another (e.g. male contact wearers in their 20s). Again, this process is repeated until every specified quota is filled. In its sampling procedures, the World Values Survey is committed first to full probability sampling but it *might* resort to quota sampling if practical limitations necessitate. In such instances, the primary sampling and interim units are selected via probability techniques. It is only in the last stage of sampling that quota techniques might be employed within relatively small final clusters that have themselves been selected via a random process.[6]

Purposive Samples

Purposive sample – a sample that uses special knowledge to intentionally "hand pick" elements for a sample.

You might want to think of this kind of sample as "the researcher knows best" sample. What I am getting at here is that a purposive sample utilizes specialized knowledge or insight to select the elements for the sample. For instance, there was a time in American politics when the state of Maine, because of the timing of its state elections, offered good insight into the political climate in the rest of America. (The phrase was "As Maine goes, so goes the nation.") Political analysts then were well advised to take a look at Maine voters if they wanted to know how the rest of the country was leaning. So it is with a researcher's use of purposive sampling. For instance, the field researcher might use her field observations to get a good idea of the persons who should be included in qualitative intensive interviews. Or the researcher studying home foreclosures might, because of their preliminary work, already have a good idea of the best cities to include in their study sample.

There is a clear risk entailed in this kind of sampling. It is quite possible that the researcher does *not* "know best" and will hand pick an inadequate or misleading sample. It is also possible that the researcher will introduce a bias into the sampling process. Researchers may get the results they desire by selecting a sample that will confirm their expectations. (Maine stopped being the bellwether state for forecasting presidential elections in 1936. In that year, Maine was one of only two states that did not vote for Franklin Roosevelt! In fact, over the years, Maine has voted more often for losing rather than winning presidential candidates; This Day in Quotes.com 2014.)

The most important point to remember with all of these non-probability techniques is that they cannot be assumed to produce representative samples. Sampling strategies that are not based on probability theory and techniques leave the researcher in the dark with regard to either estimating sampling error or achieving any degree of confidence in how well the sample truly represents the larger population. For these benefits, the researcher *must* employ some form of probability sampling.

Estimating Sampling Error

In the end, the researcher wants a sample that does a good job at providing information about the entire research population at hand. In other words, the researcher wants to work with a representative sample. As we have seen, the best chance one has of obtaining a representative sample is via some kind of probability sampling. In effect, probability sampling increases the *probability* of obtaining a representative sample. But does it *guarantee* a representative sample? Well, look again at the term *probability sampling* and you will have the answer. Probability sampling makes representative samples a more *likely* but not a guaranteed outcome. What's the researcher to do? Doesn't this uncertainty undermine one's ability to generalize sample information back to the entire population? Yes and no. While it is true that probability sampling does not offer guarantees, it does allow the researcher to cope with the uncertainty of achieving a representative sample. Probability sampling enables the researcher to calculate confidence intervals that *estimate* the amount of sampling error that exists in the sample.

Box 11.5 Newsworthy research: what went wrong in 2012?

The polling world shook a little in November 2012 when the Gallup Organization "blew" its read of the 2012 presidential election. Gallup has been in the polling business for 75+ years and is regarded by many as the most trusted polling organization in the world. But in 2012, Gallup was essentially the lone wolf in its polling results which forecasted a win for Romney and a loss for Obama. In fact, Obama won re-election and did so by a very handsome margin (51% for Obama vs. 47% for Romney). To be sure, Gallup and the rest of the polling world wondered what happened and Gallup launched a review of its practices. In its final report about their miscalculations, a number of factors were cited as contributing to their forecast failure. Gallup, like other polling organizations, was interested in screening for those who were most likely to cast a vote in the election and seeing who these likely voters were favoring during the months, and then weeks, leading up to the election. In retrospect, Gallup concluded that the questions they used to measure "likely voters" may have introduced a bias into their polling results – a bias that favored hearing from white Republican voters. These voters were more likely to support Romney. Gallup also concluded that they *oversampled* in the Mountain and Central time zones, thus introducing another pro-Romney bias. And lastly, Gallup used a sampling frame based on landline phone service (rather than its previous random digit dialing technique from previous election polls.) This sampling frame decision resulted in Gallup working with an older and more Republican sample. Clearly research methods matter and as Gallup has learned, bad decisions in measurement and/or sampling can be costly.

Confidence Intervals

When using information obtained from a sample to infer something about the larger population, the researcher should always acknowledge the possibility of some sampling error. That is, she or he must be prepared for the possibility that samples never perfectly reflect their respective populations. There is always some lack of "fit" between the sample and

Confidence interval – a range of values attached to a sample statistic that indicate the adjustment that is likely needed to capture the true population value.

Confidence levels – the selected degree of certainty researchers work with when trying to estimate population values from sample statistics; social researchers usually work at the 95% or 99% confidence levels and therefore strive to be accurate 95% or 99% of the time.

Margin of error – the range of values needed to correct a sample statistic for a given level of confidence.

its parent population. To acknowledge this lack of fit the researcher can calculate a correction factor – a **confidence interval** – to use in conjunction with any sample data. This factor suggests how the sample data should be amended or adjusted in order to bring it more closely in line with the true population value.

In everyday life, we use such correction factors whenever we find ourselves making "give or take" statements. Someone asks you to estimate the amount of time you spend each day on the Internet. You say three hours *give or take 30 minutes*. Someone asks how much you spend on gas for your car each month. You say $400, *give or take $50*. Your amended "give or take" statement illustrates the correction term needed to improve the accuracy of your estimate. As it turns out, researchers also make use of such accuracy adjustments. These correction terms are a function of **confidence levels** and a corresponding **margin of error** – that is, we state how confident we are that the true population value actually falls somewhere within a range of values that supplement a sample statistic. So in estimating the average age in a research population (say the membership of a national bird-watching organization) the researcher might report an average age of 55 (+/−2). Fifty-five is the average age in the sample used for the study and the +/−2 is the correction factor – that is, the **margin of error** or the range of values within which the average age for the entire population of bird watchers is expected to fall.

Confidence interval – consists of a sample statistic +/− the margin of error.

Confidence intervals are always stated for corresponding confidence levels (i.e. the degree of confidence the researcher has that the stated interval really captures a true population value). Most often, social researchers elect to work at the 95% or 99% confidence levels. With these levels, the researcher is calculating confidence intervals that have either 95 chances in 100 or 99 chances in 100 of "capturing" the true population value in the specified range of values (the margin of error). If you have taken a statistics course, you have probably encountered these terms before. In order to increase one's level of confidence, one must set wider or more inclusive ranges of values within which population values might fall. Increased confidence, then, comes at the cost of decreasing precision. Many national polling organizations work with the 95% confidence level when providing estimates of overall population values. At the end of a report of US adults' favorability ratings of Benjamin Netanyahu (45% just prior to his appearance before Congress in March 2015) the Gallup Poll stipulated the following: "For results based on the total sample of national adults, the margin of sampling error is ±4 percentage points at the 95% confidence level" (Dugan 2015).

While all of this may sound unduly complicated or involved, it really is an extremely valuable benefit of probability sampling. This chapter began by noting that samples are often used to give us insight into larger populations. In the final analysis, sample accuracy is an extremely important issue. Ultimately, we want to have some confidence that our sample is trustworthy regarding the information it provides about the population. One particular political event will help make this point. In the final days of the 2000 presidential election, pollsters were claiming that the November election was literally too close to call. For example, a CBS News poll in early October found 46% (+/−3) of likely voters sampled intended to vote for Bush while the percentage intending to vote for Gore was 47% (+/−3). If you do the math (i.e. if you add or subtract the correction factor for each percentage) you will see that the pollsters were admitting that *either* candidate might actually have the edge in voter support in the population at large. You remember that the pollsters were indeed correct. The presidential election was extremely close (so close that contested ballots in one state determined the outcome of the election and only after the decision was punted to the US Supreme Court). Without the use of probability sampling, these kinds of accurate insights about populations would be impossible to make.

Just a Sampling of the Issues

Sampling is a common and useful strategy for gathering information. Oddly enough, however, it is still an idea that prompts considerable skepticism. A telling Gallup poll on American's confidence in polls illustrates this point. Gallup discovered that while most of us trust what polls tell us about public opinion, we do not believe that samples of fewer than 2000 respondents can accurately tell us about the views of all Americans (Newport, Saad and Moore 1997).

This skepticism about sampling has worked its way into an important political debate. In a 1999 ruling, the US Supreme Court held that sampling violates federal census law and consequently could not be used in the 2000 census. (The Clinton administration contended that the 1990 census had missed 4 million Americans in the total population count. Administration lawyers argued that sampling was necessary in order to provide an accurate count of the US population for the 2000 census.) The court's 5–4 decision left open the question of whether sampling is an unconstitutional census practice. Given the political implications of the sampling issue (e.g. possible reapportionment of Congressional districts and the federal monies and power attached), there is little doubt that this question will be revisited in future censuses. Although given the public's declining trust in science, it is hard to know if sampling will ever win the day in this battle.

Despite the skepticism and the political intrigue that surrounds sampling, it is a firmly established social and research practice. It is also a trustworthy practice – good probability sampling techniques can give us remarkably accurate information about entire populations. Good, representative samples, however, require a lot of care and effort. Hopefully, this chapter has offered a reasonable sampling of the issues that must be considered in order to achieve good results.

TAKE AWAYS

- Sampling – the next best thing to censuses!
  - A very practical alternative to a census
- Samples always contain some degree of error vis-à-vis the entire population.
- Probability sampling:
  - Affords the best chance of obtaining a representative sample
  - Utilizes sampling frames and a random selection process
  - Allows us to estimate the amount of sampling error
  - Some common probability samples include:
    - simple random sample
    - systematic sample
    - stratified sample
    - cluster sample
- Non-probability samples are used when sampling frames do not exist or cannot be constructed.
  - Some common non-probability samples are:
    - convenience sample
    - snowball sample
    - purposive sample
    - quota sample
- Sampling error is inevitable
  - Probability samples allow us to estimate error due to sampling
  - Non-probability samples do not allow any estimating of sampling error

Sharpening the Edge: More Reading and Searching

- An interesting webinar on the wisdom (or not) of reporting margins of errors for much polling and marketing research can be found at:
    http://www.huffingtonpost.com/annie-pettit/stop-asking-for-margin-of_b_6579466.html
- Check in with the American Association of Public Opinion Research site and see the results of recent efforts to compare the effectiveness of probability vs. non-probability sampling in polling efforts:
    http://www.aapor.org/AAPORKentico/Communications/Public-Statements/Further-ing-Our-Understanding.aspx
- While much of social research utilizes sampling, we should not look a population gift-horse in the mouth! You can find a vast array of census data at the American FactFinder web page:
    http://www.census.gov/
    click on the link to American FactFinder.
- A brief review of sampling terminology as well as of the "great" moments in the development of sampling can be found in an article by Tommy Wright of the US Census Bureau:

"Selected Moments in the Development of Probability Sampling: Theory and Practice." *Survey Research Newsletter* 13 (July 2001).

- The Gallup Poll is dependent on good sampling, as well as on American's faith in sampling. Not surprisingly, then, the Gallup site offers a very cogent, reader-friendly explanation of probability sampling. See the article "How Polls are Conducted":
  http://www.gallup.com/help/FAQs/poll1.asp
- You can follow the latest polls on US elections and public opinions at HuffPost Pollster:
  http://elections.huffingtonpost.com/pollster
- Visit Mark Blumenthal's page "Mystery Pollster" for some interesting reads on polling:
  http://www.mysterypollster.com/main/2005/09/gallups_poll_on.html
- Several Internet sites are available for helping researcher calculate the right sample size for a given study "How to Determine Sample Size":
  http://www.isixsigma.com/library/content/c000709.asp
- The Survey System's "Sample Size Calculator":
  http://www.surveysystem.com/sscalc.htm
- Qualtric's "Determining Sample Size: How to Ensure You Get the Correct Sample Size":
  http://www.qualtrics.com/blog/determining-sample-size/
- And here's a page that discusses sample size for qualitative research:
  http://www.quirks.com/articles/a2000/20001202.aspx

Exercises

1   Obtain a membership list for a group, organization, or cause with which you are familiar. Following the steps outlined in this chapter, draw a simple random sample of names from the list. Critique your sample in terms of its representativeness. What steps would you suggest taking to improve your chances of obtaining a truly representative sample?

2   Imagine you have been hired by a college's food service office to help them figure out their menu "hits and misses."(A) You come up with the idea of checking the cafeteria garbage containers in order to figure out what students liked and disliked on the menu. What research population is being targeted by this strategy? What kind of sampling strategy is this? What are the obvious downsides to this strategy? (B) After two weeks of checking out garbage, you decide to change tactics and talk to students while they sit in the cafeteria eating their food. What research population is being targeted now? What kind of sampling strategy is this? What are some of its obvious downsides?

3   Read the article by Frank Newport, Lydia Saad and David Moore, "How Polls are Conducted" (http://media.gallup.com/PDF/FAQ/HowArePolls.pdf). According to the article, what is the one requirement for being included in a Gallup National Poll? Provide a concise definition of Gallup's sampling frame for national polls. Who is not included in Gallup's sampling frame for a national poll? Does this exclusion concern you or not?

4   Consider the best sampling frame for a study of voters. Random digit dialing has been the technique of choice for many years but more recently, many polling organizations have been using voter registration lists for their sampling frame. What do you see as the advantage and disadvantage to selecting a sample via each of these strategies.

Notes

1 In the 2012 US presidential election, the Gallup organization miscalled the election. Gallup Polling consistently showed Romney running ahead of President Obama and winning the election by 1–3 percentage points. One reason cited for Gallup's failure was the poll's overrepresentation of Republican voters throughout the 2012 polling (Shepard 2012).

2 This last point about sample size is one that confuses many students of sampling. Reason would seem to dictate that larger populations would require larger samples to represent them. And indeed, if you take another look at the table, the largest population sizes do require the largest samples. It is only the sampling *ratio* that is small.

3 Such specificity helps the researcher construct a good sampling frame but it does come at a cost – it can decrease the researcher's ability to generalize. Using the ASA membership list means that the researcher is limited to generalizing about *ASA* sociologist, not *all* sociologists. If there is a big gap between these two populations, the researcher may want to rethink this strategy.

4 Numbers in tables are often presented in sets of four or five digits. (If you google images of tables of random numbers, you will see the variety of offerings.) The researcher must determine how many of the digits to consider when identifying random numbers. So, if the sampling frame contains 1000 elements, the researcher might decide to use the first four digits in a table that offers five digit sets.

5 Technically, with such a small research population, the researcher should consider conducting a census rather than engaging in sampling.

6 http://www.worldvaluessurvey.org/WVSContents.jsp.

References

Dugan, Andrew. 2015. "Netanyahu's Favorable Rating Improves in US Gallup Polling." http://www.gallup.com/poll/181778/netanyahu-favorable-rating-improves.aspx?utm_source=Politics&utm_medium=newsfeed&utm_campaign=tiles.

Newport, F., Saad, L. and D. Moore. 1997. "How Polls Are Conducted." In M. Golay, *Where American Stands*. New York: John Wiley & Sons, Inc.

Sanders, C. 1999. "Getting a Tattoo." In E. Rubington and M.Weinberg (eds.), *Deviance the Interactionist Perspective*, 7th edn. Boston: Allyn & Bacon.

Shepard, Steven. 2012. Gallup Blew Its Presidential Polls, but Why? *National Journal*, November 18. http://www.nationaljournal.com/politics/gallup-blew-its-presidential-polls-but-why-20121118.

Shepard, Steven. 2013. "Gallup Post Mortem Leads To Polling Changes." *National Journal*, June 4. http://www.nationaljournal.com/blogs/hotlineoncall/2013/06/gallup-post-mortem-leads-to-polling-changes-04.

This Day in Quotes. 2014. "As Maine Goes, So Goes: (a) the Nation (b) Vermont …" November 4. http://www.thisdayinquotes.com/2009/11/as-maine-goes-so-goes-vermont.html.

Vail, D. Angus. 2001. "Tattoos are Like Potato Chips … You Can't Have Just One." In Alex Thio and Thomas Calhoun (eds.), *Readings in Deviant Behavior*, 2nd edn. Boston: Allyn & Bacon.

Weston, Kath. 2004. "Fieldwork in Lesbian and Gay Communities." In Sharlene Naby Hesse-Biber and Patricia Leavy (eds.), *Approaches to Qualitative Research*." New York: Oxford.

Chapter 12

Show Me the Numbers: Descriptive Statistics and Inferential Statistics

Introducing Social Research Methods: Essentials for Getting the Edge, First Edition. Janet M. Ruane.
© 2016 John Wiley & Sons, Ltd. Published 2016 by John Wiley & Sons, Ltd.

FIRST TAKES

Be sure to take note of the following:
- Using numbers to paint a picture
  - Descriptive statistics
  - Numbers for summarizing/organizing data
    - Presenting numbers to reveal frequencies, averages and differences
- Using numbers to "extend" findings
  - Inferential statistics
  - Numbers for moving from samples to populations
- The normal curve
  - The basis for inferential statistics
  - Supports the estimating of sampling error
- Sampling distributions are "normal"

At this point, we are nearing the end of this brief introduction to social research methods. One major transition topic (or is it terrifying topic?) must be considered: social statistics. In the first half of this chapter, we will review the topic of descriptive statistics. In the second half of the chapter we will kick it up a notch and review the basics of inferential statistics.

How Did We Get to This Point?

So far we have devoted most of our attention to the systematic collection of information. We have given attention to planning, and design, and sampling. We have considered in some detail the issue of measurement as well as the major tools or techniques the social sciences employ in the name of executing measurement: questionnaires, interviews, and field research. In trying to make the connection to statistics, it is helpful to recall the definition of measurement offered in Chapter 5: *measurement refers to the process by which we attach numbers to the values of variables.* As we learned in Chapter 5, numbers do not always mesh well with the values of our variables. Indeed, we distinguish between various levels of measurement as a way to indicate the "fit" (or misfit) between numbers and the values of variables we are measuring.

When the numbers we use merely identify qualitative differences between the values, we have a nominal measure (e.g. the variable gender where we attach the number 1 to the value male and the number 2 to the value female.) When numbers indicate a rank ordering to the values of our variables, we have an ordinal level of measurement. (e.g. measuring one's interest in politics as 1 = low, 2 = medium, 3 = high). When the numbers attached to the values indicate equal distance between values, we have achieved the interval level of measurement. (e.g. consider measuring the daily high temperature with a Fahrenheit thermometer: the difference between 32° and 33° is the same as the difference between 82° and 83°). When the numbers we use in the measurement process are actual "counts" of some variable, we have achieved the ratio level of measurement (e.g. measuring one's community spirit by the actual number of times one has attended a community event in the past three months).

We take the time to review levels of measurement here because it helps to clearly establish the role of statistics in social research. (If you are hazy on any of this, you may want to revisit the materials in Chapter 5 as well as parts of Chapter 9.) In the simplest sense, **statistics** can be thought of as *a set of techniques used to analyze the results of measurement.* Or to say it another way, *statistics is a set of tools for organizing data.* You might even think of statistics as a "hack" (dare I say this?) or a "shorthand" for helping us understand data.

> **Statistics** – techniques used to analyze or organize data; set of tools for analyzing data.

What is data? **Data** is what we produce through the measurement process. Data refers to *information that has been "numerically transformed."* Look again at the preceding paragraph for a concrete example. Say on a survey we collect information about respondents' gender. Via the measurement process, we numerically transform this information when we record all gender data for our respondents as either a number 1 for males or a number 2 for females. Similarly, respondents' interest in politics may be reported as low, medium, or high. We take this information gathered from our respondents and create "data" out of it when we record a response of low interest as a number 1, a response of medium interest as a number 2 and a response of high interest as a number 3. When we have transformed all the information we have collected, we are left with a **data file/set.** It is this data set – this matrix of numbers – that we want to analyze. Once we have a **quantitative data file**, it's time to talk statistics.

> **Data** – information collected via the measurement process; information that has been numerically transformed.
>
> **Data file** – a matrix of data (aka data set).
>
> **Quantitative data file** – a collection or matrix of numerical values of variables measured.

For those readers who may feel intimidated by the word statistics, it is worth repeating the following: statistics is merely a set of tools for organizing data. We mislead ourselves if we think they are anything more than this. They are not the goal of research; they are not truth (ergo the popular adage about levels of deceit: lies, damned lies, and statistics). They are simply tools to be used in the service of research or more specifically in the service of *understanding.* And as is true with most tools, they really can make our work easier *if* … if we know which tools are right for the job. Attacking a Phillips head screw with a hammer or even a flat head screwdriver is misguided. So too is trying to open a corked wine bottle with a can opener. Similarly, using the wrong statistical tool for the data at hand will produce unsatisfactory results. The goal of this chapter is to introduce you to some basic ideas that should go a long way in helping you get comfortable with going to the statistics toolbox or more confident in your understanding the use of those tools by others.

Getting Organized

Descriptive statistics refer to a set of techniques that organize, summarize, and provide a general overview of our data. They are numbers that give a quick summary of some variable for the entire sample. Perhaps the most basic way of getting such an overview is with the tool known as the frequency distribution. The **frequency distribution** provides an ordered listing (e.g. from high to low) of the values of

> **Descriptive statistics** – techniques that organize, summarize, and provide a general overview of data.

Frequency distribution – an ordered listing (from high to low) of the values of a variable along with a tally of the number of times each value occurs.

a variable along with a tally of the number of times each value occurs. The frequency distribution allows us to take an unwieldy set of scores and present them in a more manageable, coherent form. It clearly presents the range of values for a variable and the number of cases for each value. Imagine how useful this simple device is for a teacher who wants to review how students perform on a major test. A frequency distribution would show her each test grade and the number of students earning it. This really can be an eye-opening exercise.

In creating frequency distributions, we usually group values of continuous variables into class intervals or ranges of values (e.g. 0–4, 5–9, 10–14 etc.). This is an important facet of getting organized. A set of 100 different values can be reduced to a more manageable number of ten 10-point intervals (0–9, 10–19, 20–29, 30–39, etc.) or to five 20-point intervals (0–19, 20–39, 40–59, etc.). In deciding on the size of the intervals, it's best to use ranges that are easy to digest and that help reinforce meaningful differences in values. Intervals of 5, 10, or 20 are commonly used.

Figures 12.1 and 12.2 illustrate the organizing power of a frequency distribution. Figure 12.1 shows a set of test scores for a group of 23 students as they appeared on an alphabetized grade sheet. Figure 12.2 shows the frequency distribution when using a five-point class interval. The numbers in the frequency column of Figure 12.2 tell us just how many scores fall within each range.

	65	79	86	75
85				
	75	59	94	79
88				
	64	74	72	94
57				
	87	82	77	72
81				
	99	55	85	

Figure 12.1   Ungrouped Scores

Scores	Frequencies
95–100	1
90–94	2
85–89	5
80–84	2
75–79	5
70–74	3
65–69	1
60–64	1
55–59	3

Figure 12.2   Frequency Distribution, Grouped Scores

Summarizing Descriptions

Another way to organize data is by offering summaries of it. Such summaries are the heart and soul of descriptive statistics. You are probably more familiar with summarizing statistics than you may realize. Think about the last time you got a test back in one of your classes. Chances are that someone in the class asked for feedback on the overall class performance. Generally, we want this kind of "big picture" information so that we can put our own test score in perspective. By way of getting the big picture, we usually are interested in knowing the *average* test score. Someone is also likely to ask about the *range* of all scores – what was the highest grade, what was the lowest? In asking for these summaries, we are acknowledging the importance of two important descriptive statistical tools: measures of central tendency and measures of variation.

Central Tendency

Measures of central tendency provide us with a kind of statistical shorthand – that is, they offer *one* number that best represents or summarizes an entire set of scores or values. If you want to know the average test score for your latest class exam, you are requesting a measure of central tendency that is known as the mean. If you want to know the most frequently occurring test score, you are requesting the mode. If you want to know the score that falls in the middle of all the scores (once they are ordered), you are requesting the median.

> **Measures of central tendency** – a single number that indicates the typical or "average" score in a data set.

A **mean** is the arithmetic average of a set of scores or values. In saying that the mean is an arithmetic average, we are indicating that some mathematical procedure is involved in its calculation. To calculate the mean, we must add all the values in a set of scores together and divide by the total number of scores. In our class test example, we would sum the scores for each and every student in the class and divide by the total number of students. The resulting number (quotient) would be the mean or average score for the entire class. Consider the following set of scores: 46, 46, 50, 52, 65. We calculate the mean by dividing the total of all the scores (259) by the number of scores (5). The mean is 51.8 (259/5 = 51.8).

> **Mean** – the arithmetic average of a set of scores.

There are three important points for you to remember about the mean. First, the mean is the only measure of central tendency that is influenced by *every* value in a set of scores. Second, given the way it is calculated, it is totally possible to get a mean value that is different from all of the other scores in a distribution; the mean does not have to be an actual value in a set of scores (case in point: calculate the average of 1 and 2; 1 + 2 = 3; 3/2 = 1.5). Third, given how we calculate the mean as an arithmetic average, the mean turns out to be the number that is the balancing point in a set of values. The distance between the mean *and all the numbers above the mean* is equal to the distance between the mean *and all of the numbers below the mean*. The importance of this last point will become apparent once we move on to the topic of variation.

We can also summarize data by reporting two other measures of central tendency: the mode or the median. The **mode** refers to the most common or the most frequently occurring value for a variable. In the following set of numbers, it is easy to visually spot the one value that occurs most often – 46.

> **Mode** – the most frequently occurring value for a variable.

$$46, 46, 50, 52, 65$$

The mode is the simplest measure of central tendency – it can easily be gleaned from looking at a variable's frequency distribution. Find the value that occurs most often and you will have found the mode. For instance, look at Table 12.1 and you'll easily see the mode for the gender composition of European Monarchies in 2015 (http://www.dulminis.nl/europe/hos.htm).

The **median** is a "midway" measure of central tendency. The median summarizes data by identifying the value that falls in the middle of a set of values or scores that are arranged from lowest to highest. With an odd number of values, the calculation of a median is simple – the median is the value that falls smack in the middle of the list.

> **Median** – the score that falls in the middle of an ordered set of scores.

$$46, 46, 50, 52, 65$$
$$\text{Odd}: \text{Median} = \text{middle value} = 50$$

When we are working with an even number of values, we calculate the median by taking an average of the two middle values (i.e. we add the two middle values together and divide them by 2: the resulting number is the median).

$$46, 46, 50, 52, 65, 68$$
$$\text{Even}: \text{Median} = \text{average of two middle scores} = 51$$

Our choice of mean, mode, or median is really one of finding the right statistical tool for the job. The mode is the *only* appropriate measure of central tendency when our data is measured at the *nominal level of measurement*. Remember that the numbers attached to the values of nominal measures are merely *labels* used to distinguish *qualitatively different values* (e.g. in measuring gender, 1 = male; 2 = female). The calculation of a mean (adding and dividing the values) for nominal level data would not make sense. We can only add and divide numbers; we cannot add and divide labels. Think about it: calculating the mean for a mixed gender group would yield some number between 1 and 2. In a group of 20 where half of the group were men and half were women, the "average" gender value would be 1.5! This does not make sense for our data since the *only* acceptable values for gender are 1 for male or 2 for female. Consequently, we need another measure of central tendency for nominal level data. The mode can get the job done since it does not require any mathematic calculations – it summarizes data by telling us the most frequently occurring value of a measured variable. So if we had a group of 30 students – 20 males and 10 females – the mode would be the value used to indicate males.

Table 12.1   Gender composition of European Monarchies, 2015

European monarchs	Frequency
Males	9
Females	2

The median is the appropriate measure of central tendency when the set of scores we are trying to summarize contain some extreme scores (aka outliers). Extreme scores are those that are markedly different from most of the scores being described. If we calculate a mean under these conditions, the mean will be pulled in the direction of the extreme scores. (Remember, the mean has the distinction of being influenced by *every* value in a set of scores.) When this happens, the mean will not do a good job at representing the entire set of scores. It will be distorted by the extreme value(s). When confronted with the presence of extreme scores, the median will do a better job of summarizing the data.

The mean is really only appropriate for use with interval and ratio level data. It is only at these levels of measurement that the numbers attached to values of the variables can be treated as "real" numbers. Only real numbers are eligible for mathematical operations like addition and division (the two operations required to calculate any mean).

Describing Variation

Variety, we are told, is the spice of life. It is also an important idea for describing and summarizing data. Again, think about your last class exam. You may learn from the instructor that the class average for the exam was 75. You get your exam back and see you have scored an 85 on the test. You are way ahead of the crowd, right? Well it depends. Before knowing how you did in relation to your classmates, you really need to know how much grade variation or diversity there was in the entire class. Did most students score around 75? Or did most people score in the high 90s with a few students really bombing the exam and thereby pulling the average score down to 75? (This example, by the way, shows how outliers can pull a mean in their direction.) We really need to get this kind of information in order to have a full big picture. We need some measure of variability. As with measures of central tendency, there are three important measures of variability in our statistical toolkit: the range, the standard deviation and the variance.

The **range** does exactly what the word suggests – it conveys the distance between the highest and the lowest values in a set of scores. The range is a quick but rather crude measure of variability. It is crude in the sense that it is calculated using only two values in an entire set of scores – the

> **Range** – a number that reports the distance between the highest and the lowest values in a set of scores.

highest and the lowest. This can be misleading. Consider the following test scores:

10, 85, 85, 85, 85, 100

The range for this set of scores is 90 – that is, the highest score (100) minus the lowest score (10). Yet to look at the entire set of scores is to see far less variability than is suggested by a range of 90. Four of the six scores are identical to each other! For a more sensitive gauge of variability, we need a measure that will use more than two scores in its calculation. Ideally, we would want a measure that takes *every* score into account when calculating a summary description of variability. The **variance** does exactly this – it uses every single score in a set of scores when calculating a summary measure of variability.

> **Variance** – a summary measure of the overall variation in a set of scores; the squared average distance of scores from the mean.

The logic of calculating the variance is fairly straightforward: to assess total variation (i.e. variance) take each score in the set and calculate its distance from the mean of the set of scores. This should give us a good overall idea of total variability in a set of scores. It all sounds good in theory – let's try it in practice. Let's try calculating the variance for the set of six scores cited above: 10, 85, 85, 85, 85, 100. Since every score needs to be considered in relation to the mean, we must first calculate the mean. Add all six scores together (you should get 450) and divide by six. When we do this, we find the mean to be 75. (Here, by the way, is yet another example of how the mean need not be an actual value in a set of scores.) Now we are ready to calculate the distance between each score and the mean. To do this we simply subtract the mean from each score:

$$10 - 75 = -65$$
$$85 - 75 = 10$$
$$85 - 75 = 10$$
$$85 - 75 = 10$$
$$85 - 75 = 10$$
$$100 - 25 = 25$$

Now add up all of these "distances" from the mean. The average distance is 0! Did we do something wrong? No. The result really makes perfect sense if we remember the mathematical significance of the mean. It is the "balancing point" in a set of values – it is the exact point in a set of scores where all the scores above the point perfectly balance all the points below. We "see" this in the above example by virtue of the fact that the total for all positive numbers (i.e. points above the mean) is exactly equal to the total for all our negative numbers (i.e. points below the mean). Add these two numbers together (+65 and –65) and we get zero.

To calculate an "average" for the amount of variation in our set of scores, then, we must do something to accommodate this "balancing" feature of the mean. We must do something to get rid of the inevitable zero in the numerator. (Remember what we learned back in first grade math: having a zero in the numerator will always give us a zero for the quotient – zero divided by zero is always zero.) The solution to the zero-balance problem is to *square* each "distance" score before adding them together. These squared deviation scores then become the basis for calculating the variance. Again, we should try it with the above scores to help make the point. Add together the squared deviations for each of the scores and you'll see you no longer get a sum of zero:

$$-65^2 + 10^2 + 10^2 + 10^2 + 10^2 + 25^2 = 5250$$

The variance is finally calculated by taking the total of the squared deviations (5250) and dividing by the total number of scores. (Actually, the total number of scores minus 1. This adjustment reflects the conservative nature of research to which we have referred so often in this book. The n – 1 adjustment deflates the denominator and thereby yields a larger estimate of variation – smaller denominators always yield larger quotients. Overestimating variation is seen as the more cautious or prudent move in social research given the heterogeneity of our research populations.)

When we divide 5250 by 5 ($n - 1$) we come up with a quotient or variance of 1,050. On one hand we know this measure *must* be better than the range since it involves every score in its calculation. Still, the number (1050) looks bizarre given that our original set of scores were numbers ranging from 10 to 100! What happened this time?

Recall that to overcome the zero-balancing feature of the mean, we squared each score's deviation from the mean. Our variance measure is expressed in these squared units. In order to get back to the *original* units of our test scores, we need to "undo" this squaring. We have one last statistical tool for accomplishing this: the **standard deviation**. We calculate the standard deviation by taking the square root of the variance. With this simple step, we return the variance to the original units of our original data. Taking the square root of 1050 leaves us with 32.4 – a number much more in line with our original set of scores.

> **Standard deviation** – the average distance between any one score and the mean; the square root of the variance.

The standard deviation is best thought of as an index of the average amount of variability in a set of scores. One could say that the standard deviation takes the best feature of the variance measure (i.e. taking every single score into account when calculating variation) and goes one better. The standard deviation is expressed in the same units as the original scores we are trying to describe. One might also say that the standard deviation "complements" the mean. The mean reports the average score that best represents a set of scores. The standard deviation conveys the average distance between any one score and the mean. The standard deviation is also like the mean in that it is sensitive to extreme scores. Indeed, this characteristic is apparent in the set of numbers we have been using. Our calculated standard deviation reflects the influence of the extreme distance between the mean we calculated (75) and the very low score of 10.

It Takes Two to Tango … and to Correlate

> **Univariate analysis** – analysis of a single variable.
>
> **Bivariate analysis** – analysis that looks at two variables at a time.

Up to this point, we have been considering how best to summarize the data we have collected on a single variable – for example, reporting the "average" gender in a group (via the mode) or reporting the average test score and average variation in test scores for a group (via the mean and the standard deviation). Focusing on a single variable is referred to as **univariate analysis**. Another important way to organize data is by reporting the overall association between two variables (referred to as **bivariate analysis**). Is there a relationship, for instance, between test scores and amount of time spent studying for the test or between age and driving ability? As one variable increases, does the second also increase? Or perhaps as one variable increases, the second decreases. To answer such questions we need to mobilize a set of statistical tools known as correlation coefficients.

A **correlation coefficient** is a number that summarizes the degree to which two variables move together. Correlations range in value from –1 to +1. When the coefficient is 1 (either –1 or +1), the two variables are perfectly "in sync" with each other – a unit change in one is accompanied by a unit change in the other. If the variables are moving in opposite directions (one increases as the other decreases), it is a negative relationship. We indicate a negative relationship by using a minus sign before the coefficient. If the variables are moving in the same direction (both are increasing or both are decreasing together), we denote that by reporting the coefficient as a positive number. When the coefficient is 0, there is no relationship between the two variables – that is, one variable does not have any connection with the other. Typically, coefficients fall somewhere between no relationship (0) and a perfect (totally covarying) relationship (+/–1). The closer the coefficient is to +/–1, the stronger the relationship between the two variables. The closer the coefficient is to 0, the weaker the relationship between the two variables.

> **Correlation coefficient** – a number that indicates the degree to which two variables covary.
>
> **Pearson coefficient** – a statistic for indicating the strength and direction of a linear relationship between two interval or ratio level variables.
>
> **Spearman rank coefficient** – a statistic for indicating the strength and direction of a correlation between two ordinal level variables.
>
> **Phi coefficient** – a statistic for indicating the strength of association between two binary (dichotomous) variables.

There are several correlation coefficients we can calculate to summarize the relationship between two variables: for example, the Pearson correlation coefficient, the Spearman rank coefficient, and the Phi coefficient. As we saw when selecting the right statistical tool for reporting averages, the level of measurement for our variables must guide our selection of the right correlation coefficient to use with our data. The **Pearson coefficient** should be used when we are looking for the association between two variables measured at the interval or ratio level: the correlation between income and size of saving accounts in dollars; the correlation between height and weight, the correlation between years in school and size of vocabulary. The **Spearman rank coefficient** is appropriate when looking for an association between two ordinal level variables: the correlation between letter grades (A, B, C, etc.) and level of interest in school (high, medium, low); the correlation between birth order (first, middle, last) and self-esteem (low, medium, high); the correlation between fabric weight (light, medium, heavy) and sun block protection (low, medium or high). The **Phi coefficient** should be used when looking for an association between two dichotomous (two values) nominal level variables: the relationship between gender and party affiliation (Republican, Democrat); the relationship between marital status (married, not married) and voting preferences (e.g. Clinton, Bush again!); the relationship between employment status (employed, unemployed) and support of welfare reform (yes, no).

Picture This

As we have tried to demonstrate in the preceding pages, we can offer a decent overview of what our data looks like via some key statistical tools: that is, measures of central tendency, measures of variation, and measures of association. Using various visual displays of data can further enhance the big picture of our data. Graphs and charts are tools for converting numbers into visual displays. Pictures, after all, are said to be worth a thousand words. As it turns out, pictures are also worth a whole lot of numbers. According to Edward Tufte, perhaps the reigning king of graphic excellence, graphs are essential devices for effective communication (Tufte 2001). Graphs and charts work well in communicating information because they take advantage of the fact that the human mind is extremely visual in nature (Bowen 1992; Tufte 1997; 2001). Indeed, Tufte reports that the human eye is capable of processing 625 data points per square inch of space (Tufte 1997).

Graphing 101

Before we start, it would help to review the basics of graphing. Most of the devices we cover in the following section all start with the same basic model: two straight lines at a right angle to each other. The horizontal line is referred to as the X axis (aka the abscissa). The vertical line is referred to as the Y axis (aka the ordinate). Quantitative variables can be plotted along either the X or Y axis. Qualitative variables, on the other hand, should *only* be plotted along the X axis. The visual field (i.e. the area between the X and Y axis) will display bars, dots, or lines by way of communicating information about data.

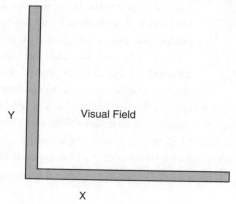

Figure 12.3 Basic Line Graph

Picturing Frequency Distributions and Central Tendency

When we want to show the frequency with which values occur in a group of data we can use bar charts, histograms, or frequency polygons. As indicated, the issue of level of

> **Bar chart** – a visual display of the frequency distribution for a nominal level (aka categorical) or a discrete variable (bars should not touch each other).

measurement should guide our graphing selection. The **bar chart** is appropriate for displaying the frequency distribution of a variable measured at the nominal level. Each category or value of the qualitative variable is represented by its own bar along the X axis. The height of each bar visually communicates the relative frequency (as indicated by the Y axis) of each value (along the X axis). Figure 12.4 shows that the mode can be quite obvious in a bar chart.

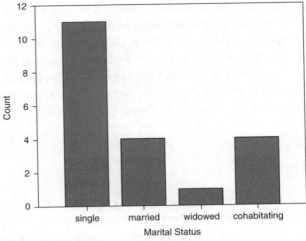

Figure 12.4   Bar Chart, Marital Status of Class of Students

Histogram – a visual display of the frequency distribution of a variable measured at the interval or ratio level (bars should touch to convey the continuous nature of variables).

Frequency polygon – a line graph connecting the midpoints of a histogram.

The histogram and the frequency polygon are both appropriate visual displays for frequency distributions of quantitative variables. In both devices, the numerical categories of our variable are displayed along the X axis while frequency information is displayed along the Y axis. The **histogram** uses a series of connected bars to present frequency information. Each bar corresponds to the class intervals of the variable plotted along the X axis. The histogram can be quite useful for spotting outliers or gaps in data. The **frequency polygon** replaces the continuous bars of the histogram with dots and a continuous line to display frequency information. The line connects the midpoints of each class interval that is plotted along the X axis. Again, either device offers quick visual feedback of averages (look for the highest bar of the histogram or the peak of the polygon.)

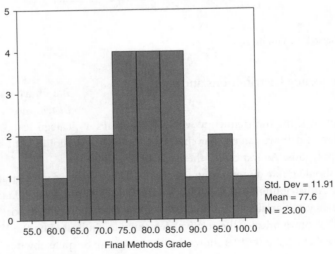

Figure 12.5   Histogram of Methods Grade from Figure 12.1

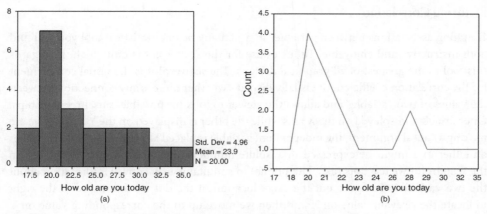

Figure 12.6   (a) Histogram of Student Ages (b) Polygon of Student Ages

Picturing Variation

Histograms and frequency polygons can also show us something about variation. This is most effectively accomplished by comparing either graph of our data to three standard models for depicting shapes of frequency distributions. Take a look at Figure 12.7. In polygon A we see a visual depiction of a set of scores that have a small amount of variation between them. We "see" this by virtue of the fact that the curve is very narrow indicating that most of the scores are clumped together around the center point of the curve (the mean). Polygon B shows us the graph of a set of scores with a moderate amount of variation – the graph resembles a bell-shaped curve. Finally, polygon C depicts a set of scores that have quite a bit of variation between them, ergo the larger the "spread" of the curve around the mean. To the extent that we can "match" our histograms or frequency polygons to one of the models in Figure 12.7, we enhance our ability to communicate the variation found in our data.

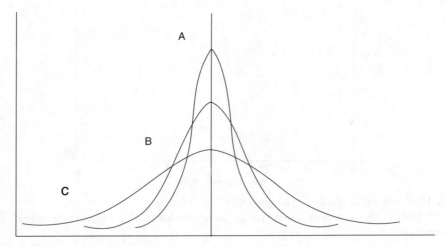

Figure 12.7   Pictures of Variation

Picturing Correlation

Graphing associations between variables may actually be one statistical tool you will find both instructive and enjoyable. Tufte's praise for the scatterplot is quite high; he regards this tool as the greatest of all graphical designs. The **scatterplot** is the visual complement for the correlation coefficient. It visually displays whether there is any connection between the values of two variables and allows the viewer to look for possible causal relationships. One variable is displayed on the X axis while the other is displayed on the Y axis. (If we are making a causal argument, the independent variable is placed along the X axis). The values on either axis might be expressed in absolute numbers, percentages, rates, or scores. In the scatterplot we use dots (aka data points) to simultaneously convey information about the two variables. To figure out the exact location of the dot we first move to the right to locate the relevant value on X and then we move up to the corresponding value on Y (the use of graph paper helps in locating the exact point of intersection). A dot is displayed for every case in our data set. Figure 12.8 shows the scatterplot for a perfect positive correlation between two variables.

Scatterplot – a device for visually displaying any shared variation between two variables

This scatterplot depicts a "perfect" positive relationship because each unit of increase on the X variable is associated with a matching unit of increase on the Y variable: as we move from one unit to the next on the X variable, we see an identical movement from one unit to the next on the Y variable. Creating a scatterplot for relationships between two variables is always a good idea – it will show you if and how the two variables are related. The graphs in Figure 12.9 show scatterplots of "less than perfect" relationships. The first one shows a negative relationship (Pearson r = −.803) between time spent exercising and number of self-reported symptoms. The second one shows a positive relationship (Pearson r = .607) between educational levels for parents.

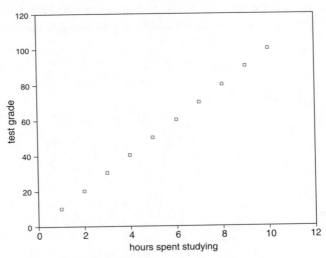

Figure 12.8   Scatterplot of a Perfect (Hypothetical)* Correlation
* hypothetical because there really is not a perfect association between time spent studying and grades earned.

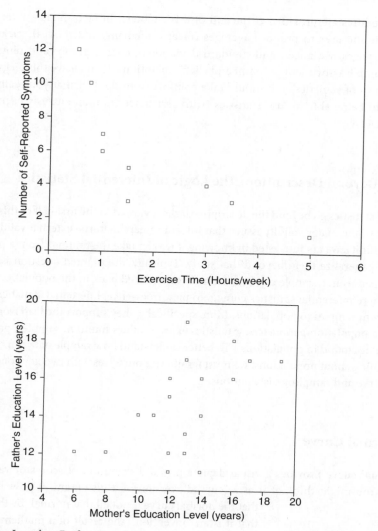

Figure 12.9   Less than Perfect Correlations

SPSS

We have covered quite a few important statistical tools in this chapter and you may be feeling like your boat is about to go down in the rough sea of statistics. The good news is that I would not put anyone in this boat without some buoyant life preservers. Every technique reviewed in this chapter is easily executed with the help of SPSS (or any other statistical package like SAS or STATA). While I have tried to give you a conceptual introduction to some very key statistical techniques, all the detailed instructions for executing these techniques can be gleaned from any number of tutorials and/or books devoted to

SPSS (some links are provided at the end of this chapter). In fact, the latest versions of SPSS enable the user to produce averages (means, medians, and modes), measures of variation (ranges, variances, and standard deviations), charts, graphs and plots with a relatively simple assortment of "point and click" operations. If you leave this chapter with a better grasp of statistics, you should take comfort from the fact that you really are on your way to being able to "do" statistics (with assistance from an analysis package like SPSS or STATA).

Moving Beyond Description: The Logic of Inferential Statistics

Inferential statistics go beyond the descriptive tasks reviewed in the first half of this chapter. Recall one of the major validity issues that inform research efforts: external validity. With external validity, we are interested in knowing if we can take the findings from a particular study and generalize them beyond that study. Typically, the pointed question is whether data obtained from a sample can be accurately generalized back to the population at large. Here is where inferential statistics come into play. In essence, inferential statistics support the leap from samples to populations. More specifically, they support the leap from sample *statistics* to population *parameters*. (Statistics express values found in samples; parameters express values found in populations.) To better understand how sample data can be used to say something about populations, we must familiarize ourselves with two key concepts: the normal curve and sampling distributions.

The Normal Curve

The **normal curve** provides a visual depiction of a distribution of scores or values on a variable. You might think of it as a "curved" version of a histogram. It is worth noting that the normal curve is not all that normal. By that I mean that it is an "invention," the result of a mathematic equation. But while the normal curve is a theoretical or hypothetical device, its value as a statistical tool is quite real. For example, the normal curve is essential to testing hypotheses about group differences or about relationships between variables. It is also an essential tool for generalizing from samples to populations.

Normal curve – a hypothetical bell-shaped distribution of values of a variable; the horizontal axis displays all possible values of the variable and the vertical axis displays the probability of the occurrence of the values.

Despite its hypothetical nature, the normal curve often does match real world scenarios. For instance it is generally held that the normal curve accurately describes the distribution of IQ scores in the general population. Measures of memory, reading ability, and job satisfaction are also normally distributed variables. The normal curve does a good job describing the values on such variables as height and weight in the population at large. Two nineteenth-century researchers (Belgian mathematician Lambert Adolphe Jacques

Quetelet and English scientist Sir Francis Galton) discovered this useful insight about the normal curve as they set about plotting the values of some common characteristics of individuals (height, weight, chest size, visual acuity, etc.). They noticed as they plotted more and more values that a common visual emerged. Across all the variables they plotted, the pattern of the frequency distribution of values resembled a bell-shaped curving line. (You will often find the normal curve referred to as a bell-shaped curve.) Researchers take advantage of this fact and apply the normal curve and its properties to the actual data they have collected. With this application, they establish a pathway for moving from samples to populations.

The normal curve has many defining and noteworthy features. In addition to its bell shape, the normal curve is unimodal – it has only one point (data value) of maximum frequency. This point of maximum frequency is at the exact center of the curve. And it is at this center point that the mean, median, and mode can all be found. The normal curve is also symmetrical – the area left of its dead-center mean is identical to the area to the right of the mean. Lastly, the area under the curve is very *predictable*. Let me explain.

While the term "normal curve" focuses our attention on the *curve* formed along the outer edges of the distribution, our interest is really in *the area under the curve*. If you look at Figure 12.10, the picture is meant to convey the idea that *all* of the values in a distribution (e.g. all weights, all heights, all IQs) fall *between* the curved line and the baseline of the figure. And using the properties of the normal curve, researchers cast this area in the language of probabilities; they treat the area under the curve as predictable. In our everyday understanding of probability, the connection between probability and prediction is apparent. We understand that events having a high probability of occurrence can also be thought of as predictable. If your grandmother has always called you on your birthday, it is probable she will call you again on your next birthday. In fact, with a sufficiently high probability, we can actually make predictions (i.e. there's a 95% or a 99% chance that your grandmother will call).

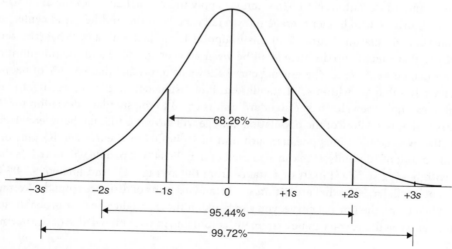

Figure 12.10   Area Under the Normal Curve – Set Proportions

Using the normal curve, researchers can make predictions about variables that are "normally distributed." For any variable that is normally distributed, statisticians tell us that we can *predict* the percentage of cases that fall between certain standard distances or areas under the curve. These standard areas are marked out in reference to the curve's dead center (i.e. in reference to the mean). The normal curve always depicts three standard distances to the right of (above) the mean and three standard distances to the left of (below) the mean. These set distances are referred to as standard deviations and are represented using what statisticians call "Z scores" or standard scores.

How does all of this translate into practice? When we claim that a variable is normally distributed (like height) we can safely make predictions about the distribution of values around the mean of the variable. Figure 12.10 shows us the predictions (probabilities) that we can assume anytime a variable is thought to be "normally distributed." Note that 34.13% of the cases will have values (e.g. heights) that fall in the area between the mean and one standard unit of distance below the mean. Since the normal curve is symmetrical (the area to the left of the mean is identical to the area to the right of the mean), we can also predict that 34.13% of the cases will have values that fall in the area between the mean and one standard unit of distance above the mean. Adding these two areas together we can say that 68.26% of the values of a normally distributed variable will fall between −1 and +1 standard units from the mean value of the variable. Continuing to follow the information presented in Figure 12.10, the normal curve also allows us to predict that 95.44% of a normally distributed variable's values will fall between −2 and +2 standard units of distance from the mean. Finally, virtually all cases/values (99.74%) will fall between −3 and +3 standard units of distance from the mean.

Let us go back now and illustrate the points of the previous paragraph with a concrete example. IQ is a variable presumed to be normally distributed in the population. In saying this we mean that the majority of IQ scores in a population will hover around the average (mean) IQ with only a very few people having extraordinarily high or extraordinarily low IQs. Let us say, for the purpose of this example, that the average IQ is 100 with a standard deviation of 10. How can we apply the normal curve in the analysis of IQ? First, anyone who has an average IQ will fall exactly in the middle (dead center) of the curve. Note that in Figure 12.10 this midpoint is marked with a 0. Why? The zero indicates that there is no distance at all between an average value and the midpoint of the normal curve. Second, the normal curve allows us to predict that 68.26% of people will have IQs that are within +/−1 standard unit of distance from the average IQ. In our current example the value of the standard unit is equal to the standard deviation for IQ (i.e. 10). That is, 68.26% of the population at large will have IQs that fall between 90 and 110 (the average IQ minus one standard unit of 10 points or the average IQ plus one standard unit of 10 points). We can also predict that 95.44% of people will have IQs that fall within +/−2 standard units of distance from the average IQ. And finally 99.74% of the people will have IQs that are within +/−3 standard units of distance from the average IQ. When using the normal curve, you can bank on these "predictions" or probabilities. In fact, as we will see, you can be extremely "confident" in your knowledge of the normal curve.

Think of the power of this tool! Once you assume or establish that a group of values or scores are normally distributed, you are entitled to make predictions about the percentage of cases that will be found within set distances from the mean of the group. This knowledge is key to helping us with the dilemma of inferential statistics – that is, gathering data from samples and using it to make inferences about populations. In the next section, we will examine why this is so.

Repeat After Me

Imagine a typical research endeavor. You are the head of a company with a social conscience. You are considering various healthcare and childcare programs for your company. You want to know what your employees think. Your nephew, who is working as a summer intern, tells you he can help with this task. He draws a simple random sample of employees and gives them a brief questionnaire to learn about some key characteristics (age, years of education, number of children). He also asks them about their views on healthcare and childcare programs. You ask if he can generalize what he has learned from the sample to your entire population of employees. Your nephew has a crisis of uncertainty. Thus he decides to take another sample of workers and redo the survey with them. Much to his dismay, he finds that the two samples don't match! The samples yield different statistics with regard to average age, the average income, the average number of children, average number of visits to doctors in the past year, and so on. A little panicked, your nephew draws yet another sample and again finds there are differences between the samples. He continues to draw samples until … you fire him. Must things have ended this way? (At least this is what your sister wants to know!!)

In the above scenario, the nephew faced the classic sampling quandary. How is it possible to use data from a *sample* to generalize to a *population*? Just because we find the average age to be 38 in our one sample, is it reasonable to say that 38 is the average age for the *entire population* from which the sample was drawn? Junior's experiences would seem to suggest not. What's the researcher to do? Remember the normal curve!

In his panic, the nephew started a process of repeated sampling and continued to draw sample after sample after sample from the same population. He did this in hope of getting closer to the true population values on key variables. In one sense, he had a good idea. If he drew enough samples from the same population and then took an average of the obtained sample data (e.g. an average of the average ages found in each sample), he would have come close to discovering the true population value. Unfortunately, researchers do not have the luxury of working this way. We do not take "repeated" samples; we select and work with only *one* sample. But if we take care in how we select our one sample, we can assume that it does indeed give us data that is generalizable. How is this possible? Well you should already have some idea about an answer: a probability sampling technique will give us the best crack at obtaining a representative sample. And, in turn, a representative sample does the best job at depicting an entire population. Combining good sampling with the insights provided by the normal curve will cinch our ability to make inferences from our sample to the population.

The Sampling Distribution

Let me introduce you to another extremely important hypothetical device: a sampling distribution. A **sampling distribution** is a hypothetical distribution of a sample statistic – a distribution that *would* be produced through repeated sampling. For instance, a sampling distribution of means would result from graphing the means of every possible sample (an infinite number) that one *could* draw from a particular population. If the nephew in our previous example had graphed the frequency distribution of the average ages or average incomes in each and every sample he drew, he would have produced a sampling distribution of these means.

Sampling distribution – a hypothetical distribution of a sample statistic that would be produced via repeated sampling.

The sampling distribution is a hypothetical distribution; in reality we never actually engage in repeated sampling. Still, this hypothetical distribution yields some important theoretical observations. First, in a sampling distribution of means, the average of all the sample means (the mean of means) is equal to the true population mean. This is an important point since we are so often trying to estimate population means from sample means. Second, if we are working with sufficiently large number of samples, we can assume the sampling distribution *is normally distributed*. Thus any and all properties of the normal curve can be applied to the sampling distribution. This insight will prove critical to any researcher who works with one sample but wants to use it to say something about an entire population.

Consider, for instance, using the mean age in a sample to infer the mean age in a population. Based on what we know about the normal curve, we can say that there is a 68.26% probability that our one particular sample mean falls within +/−1 standard unit from the mean of the sampling distribution (aka the true population value). There is a 95.44% probability that our *one* sample would fall between −2 and +2 standard units of distance from the mean. Finally there is a 99.74% probability that our one particular sample would fall between −3 and +3 standard units of distance from the mean.

Putting it Together

If we merge two types of knowledge – empirical and theoretical – we will be in a good position to infer population values from sample statistics. By taking knowledge gained from our sample and merging it with knowledge of the properties of the normal curve – we can calculate the gap or the amount of error that results from collecting data from a sample rather than the entire population.

Let us consider one more time the sampling dilemma cited earlier – how can we go beyond our sample statistics and infer population values? For instance, how can we use data about a sample mean to estimate the corresponding population mean? The answer to this question is found in our calculating a **confidence interval**. A confidence interval refers to the range of values (i.e. a "correction factor") we attach to sample statistics in order to capture true population values. The formula for the confidence interval is as follows:

> **Confidence interval** – the range of values we attach to a sample statistic that indicate the adjustment needed in order to capture the true population value.

$$CI = \bar{X} +/- (SE \times Z)$$

As this formula indicates, a number of things go into increasing our confidence in sample statistics. The X bar in the formula indicates that our best starting place for estimating a population value is the corresponding sample value. The +/− signs indicate that some quantity will either be added to or subtracted from the sample mean in order to bring it closer in line with a true population value. Why is it either? Well, think about the symmetrical nature of the normal curve. If our one sample and its mean value falls to the left side of the normal curve, it will *underestimate* the true population value and we will have to add something to $\bar{X}$ for a better estimate of the true population value. If our one sample and its mean value falls to the right side of the normal curve, the $\bar{X}$ will *overestimate* true population values and we will need to subtract an amount from $\bar{X}$ in order to bring it in line with the true population value. Finally, look at the part of the formula enclosed in parentheses. Together the product of SE and Z will provide us with what is known as the **margin of error** of the confidence interval (see section 'SE–The Standard Error' below). This margin of error will be the exact amount that will either be added to or subtracted from the sample mean in order to bring it closer in line with a true population value.

Before moving on, let me assure you that you have probably already been exposed to the margin of error via major news agencies or polling organizations. During election years when major news agencies report the percentage of voters supporting the major candidates, they always report the margin of error for their results. In order to zero in on true population values (and come closest to accurately calling the election), the networks will typically report their estimates of voter preferences to within a +/−3 margin of error. This means that if the networks report that 45% (+/−3) of Americans sampled support candidate A, they are acknowledging that the support in the general population may actually be as high as 48% (45% + 3%) or as low as 42% (45% − 3%). In other words, the networks are hedging their bets and will consider their estimates of voter preference to be right if the final vote falls within this six percentage point spread. Similarly, if you have ever read any Gallup poll results, you may have noticed that they report their findings to be accurate within a margin of error of plus three or minus three percentage points. (http://www.gallup.com/poll/faq/faq000101.asp).

Now that we have the logic of the confidence interval down, it is time to see how to "solve" the formula. The good news is that we really do have all the necessary numbers to plug into the formula at our fingertips. The $\bar{X}$ will be obtained from our sample. We can easily determine the value of SE by using two additional pieces of sample information: the standard deviation and the sample size. We can also easily determine the appropriate Z value for the formula by using our knowledge of the normal curve.

SE – The Standard Error

You can think of the **standard error** as the error we can expect by using a sample to learn about a population. You have already spent some time considering this idea in the chapter on sampling. Sampling is a good thing – it allows us to do research in a timely and cost-efficient way. However, it is not without its limitations. Samples will seldom if ever perfectly capture the population they purport to represent. We must assume they will always contain some error. The SE is a calculation that allows us to quantify that error.

> **Standard error** – a measure of sampling error – the error due to samples being imperfect subsets of the entire population.

We calculate the SE using two basic pieces of data from our sample: the standard deviation and the sample size. Recall that a large standard deviation indicates more variation between values in our sample (e.g. more variation in variables such as income, years of education, number of children, hours devoted to community service). If we have done a good job selecting a sample, the sample should reflect (albeit imperfectly) the variation in the population. The more variation in a sample, the more variation we can expect in the population.

The other key piece of sample data we use in calculating the sampling error is the sample size. Recall from Chapter 11 that larger samples are more representative than smaller samples. This stands to reason: larger samples get us that much closer to entire populations. Ergo, our calculation of the standard error should be tempered by sample size. Consequently, we calculate the standard error by dividing the standard deviation by the square root of $n-1$. (Again we use $n-1$ for the same reason as given earlier in the chapter – it yields a more conservative estimate of the standard error.)

Z Values

> **Z scores** – values that correspond to the standardized area under the normal curve.

Once we use our sample data to calculate the value of SE, we can move on to figuring out the value of Z. The normal curve helps us with this piece of the puzzle. **Z values** (aka **Z scores**) correspond to the area under the normal curve. That is, when we talk about the normal curve and its standard units of distance from the mean, we are talking about Z scores. We have already considered three Z scores in some detail: a Z score of $+/-1$ encompasses 68.26% of the area around the mean; a Z score of $+/-2$ encompasses 95.44% of the area under the curve; a Z score of $+/-3$ encompasses 99.74% of the area under the curve. While we previously presented these areas in terms of probabilities and predictions, we can also talk of these areas in terms of *confidence levels*.

Think once again about the sampling distribution – that is, the distribution that would occur via repeated sampling. Instead of saying that 68.26% of all samples in a sampling distribution fall within $+/-1$ standard unit from the mean, we could express this idea as a statement of confidence. We can be 68.26% confident that any one sample falls between $+/-1$ standard unit of distance from the mean (or between the Z scores of $+1$ and -1). We can be 95.44% confident that any one sample falls within +/−2 standard units of distance from the mean and so on. In short, the Z value for our formula will be determined by the level of confidence we want to achieve when making statements about populations based on sample data. For a 95% confidence level (a level adopted by many social researchers), we use a Z score of 1.96. (This Z value should make sense to you once you recall that a confidence level of 95.44% corresponds to a Z score of 2. Being slightly less confident – just 95% – gives us a Z score just a little less than 2: 1.96). If we want a higher level of confidence, say 99%, we use a Z score of 2.56. Increasing our confidence level will always produce a larger (wider) margin of error – but in doing so, we increase the likelihood that the true population value will fall somewhere within our +/− range. (The Z score values for any level of confidence can be gleaned from a Z score table. Such tables are usually part of appendixes of statistics books.)

A Concrete Example

Imagine that based on information from a representative sample of 100 students at your college, you calculate the average age to be 24 and the standard deviation on the age variable to be 5. Is it safe to generalize that this is the average for the entire student population at large? To answer this question with some confidence, we need to calculate the confidence interval. We start with the formula and plug in the relevant numbers:

$$CI = \overline{X} +/- (SE \times Z)$$

From our sample date, we know that $\overline{X}$ is equal to 24. Using our sample data we can figure out the value for SE.

$$SE = s/\sqrt{n-1}$$

To solve for the SE we will divide the standard deviation of 5 by 9.9 (the square root of 99),

$$5/9.9 = .5$$

Next we want to multiply the SE by the Z score for our desired level of confidence. If we want to be 95% confident in our estimation of the average age in the population, we need to plug the Z score of 1.96 into the formula:

$$CI = 24 +/- (.5 \times 1.96)$$
$$CI = 24 +/- .98$$

We can be 95% confident that the average age in the population is 24 years, give or take about one year (.98 ≈ 1).

Now try one more example at a higher level of confidence. A recent survey of a sample of 100 of our sociology majors indicated that their average GPA was 3.1 with a standard deviation of .5. What number should I report if I want to be 99% confident in reporting the average GPA for all my methods students? Once again, solving the confidence interval formula will give us the answer:

$$CI = \overline{X} +/- (SE \times Z)$$

From the sample data, we know that $\overline{X}$ is equal to 3.1. Using our sample data we can once again figure out the value of SE:

$$SE = s/\sqrt{n-1}$$

To solve for the SE we will divide the standard deviation of .5 by 9.9 (the square root of 99).

$$.5/9.9 = .05$$

Next we multiply the SE by the Z score for the 99% level of confidence. To be 99% confident we must plug a Z value of 2.56 into the formula:

$$CI = 3.1 +/- (.05 \times 2.56)$$
$$CI = 3.1 +/- .13$$

We can be 99% confident that the average GPA for all my methods students is a 3.1 +/−.13 – i.e. the population value falls somewhere between 2.97 and 3.23.

Bringing it Home

In the second half of this chapter, we have reviewed how a few important hypothetical statistical tools – the normal curve and sampling distributions – can help us with one important task for inferential statistics: concluding something about a population based on information from a sample. In particular, we have seen how to calculate a confidence interval for sample means – an interval that has a known likelihood of including a true population value. This is not all that can be said on the topic of inferential statistics, but it is a good – some would say essential – starting point. Understanding the logic of the normal curve and seeing how it factors in achieving certain levels of confidence in the conclusions we draw from sample data is vital to making a successful transition to inferential statistics.

TAKE-AWAYS

- Descriptive statistics
  - Numbers for summarizing/organizing data
    - Frequency distributions

- Measures of central tendency (statistics that tell us what things look like "on average"): mean, median, mode
- Measures of dispersion (statistics that help us "see" the spread or variation in data): range, variance, standard deviation
- Measures of association (statistics that help us "see" if two variables are connected): Pearson, Spearman and Phi coefficients
- Graphic displays: bar charts, histograms, polygons, scatterplots
- Inferential statistics
  - Numbers for moving from samples to populations
    - Sample statistics for estimating population parameters
- The normal curve
  - A graphic display of a frequency distribution of a variable that resembles a bell-shaped curve
  - The basis for inferential stats
  - Supports the estimating of sampling error
- Sampling distributions are "normally" distributed
  - Key idea to using sample statistics to estimate population parameters

Sharpening the Edge: More Reading and Searching

- For those starting to tread the statistical waters take heart! There is a lot of help available online. There are several online statistical glossaries:

  Hoffman's "The Internet Glossary of Statistical Terms": http://www.animatedsoftware.com/statglos/statglos.htm

  Statsoft Glossary: http://www.statsoft.com/textbook/glosfra.html

  David Lane's Hyperstat Glossary: http://www.davidmlane.com/hyperstat/glossary.html

  SurfStat glossary: https://surfstat.anu.edu.au/surfstat-home/glossary/glossary.html

- For more extended explanations, there are also several online statistics texts:

  You might find the Electronic Stats textbook very helpful (see especially its link to Elementary Concepts): http://www.statsoft.com/Textbook

  Another online statistics text, HyperStat Online, can be found at: http://davidmlane.com/hyperstat/

  And yet another helpful online statistics text is Gerald Dallal's *The Little Handbook of Statistical Practice.* http://www.jerrydallal.com/LHSP/use.htm

  A good online stats tutorial is offered by the Khan Academy: https://www.khanacademy.org/math/probability

- For online information on graphical displays see:

  Albert Goodman's "Graphical Data Presentation": http:www.deakin.edu.au/~agoodman/sci101/chap12.html

- There are also a few books that might prove useful for students without strong math backgrounds:
  Neil Salkind's *Statistics for People Who (Think They) Hate Statistics*. 5th edn. (Thousand Oaks: SAGE, 2014)
  Lloyd Jaisingh's *Statistics for the Utterly Confused*, 2nd edn. (New York: McGraw-Hill, 2006)
- For the ultimate word on graphic displays of information see Tufte's work, *The Visual Display of Quantitative Information*, 2nd edn. (Graphics Press 2001).
- There are several online SPSS tutorials available:
  "SPSS Tutorials: The Ultimate Guide for Mastering SPSS": http://www.spss-tutorials.com/spss-main-goals/
  "SPSS Step by Step Tutorial": http://www.datastep.com/SPSSTutorial_1.pdf

Inferential Statistics

- For a basic review of the ideas behind inferential statistics see Richard Lowry's "Concepts and Applications of Inferential Statistics" and its accompanying website:
  http://vassarstats.net/textbook/; http://vassarstats.net/
- The following interactive tutorial should also help you determine the accuracy of samples (it includes a review of the normal distribution):
  http://wise.cgu.edu/sdmmod/index.asp
- For a short but informative discussion and insightful demonstration of a sampling distribution see David Wallace's web page:
  http://faculty.uncfsu.edu/dwallace/ssample.html
- Some help in finding the right statistical tool for a particular data set can be found at Bill Trochim's "Selecting Statistics:"
  http://www.socialresearchmethods.net/selstat/ssstart.htm
- Part of the reason so many people find statistics frustrating is because the numbers can be so easily "manipulated" or misused by those who cite them. For a very good review of how to empower yourself as a consumer of statistics see Joel Best's *Damned Lies and Statistics:*
  Untangling Numbers Form the Media, Politicians, and Activists, updated edn. (Berkeley: University of California Press, 2012)
- David Salsburg's *The Lady Tasting Tea: How Statistics Revolutionized Science in the Twentieth Century* (New York: W.H. Freeman and Company, 2001) is also a book worthy of your time. Salsburg organizes his work around individuals who made significant contributions to the development of modern statistics. He puts a face on Pearson's *r* and Gosset's (Student's) *t*. He presents this history in a very readable and engaging style (and without relying on any mathematical formulas).
- For a still relevant classic about how statistics can be misused, take a look at Darrell Huff and Irving Geis's *How to Lie with Statistics* (New York: Norton, 1954, 1982, 1993).

Exercises

Descriptive Statistics

1 Consider the following set of scores in a history test. Which measure of central tendency should the teacher use when reporting the average score for the class? Why?

Scores: 81, 80, 81, 100, 75, 79, 78

2 For the same set of test scores above, would it be a good idea for the teacher to report the range of the test scores as a way of showing the variability of the scores? Why?

3 Try your hand at SPSS. Enter the above data as values for the variable Test1.

3.1 Click on the SPSS icon on your computer screen (or click on the start column and scroll up the column until you find the SPSS option).

3.2 A window with various options will appear on the screen.

- If you are unfamiliar with SPSS, you should select the circle next to **Run the Tutorial** and click OK.
- Once you have some idea of how SPSS works, you can select the circle next to **Type in Data** and click OK.

3.3 If you are working in SPSS 10.0 or higher, you should access the "Variable View" screen by clicking on this tab in the lower left corner of the screen.

In the variable view screen, each variable is represented by a row containing default information about each variable.

- Start by assigning a new variable name to replace the default name.
- Click on the first cell in the "Name" column.
- Delete the default name (if there is one).
- Type in Test1 as the name for our one variable and hit the enter key.
- At this point, we can leave the rest of the default settings as they are.

3.4 Click the tab for data view.

- The Test1 column should be highlighted.
- Type in the first test score in the first cell and hit enter.
- Repeat this step until all 7 scores are entered.

3.5 Click Analyze (in tool bar running across top of screen).
- Click Descriptive statistics.
- Click Descriptives.
- Click Right arrow key to move Test1 into right box.
- Click OK.

3.6 Find the Mean and the Standard deviation in the output. How do they help you understand the answers to problems 1 and 2?

3.7 While still in SPSS, click on Graphics
- Select histogram.
- Use the right arrow key to move Test 1 into the right box.
- Click OK.

What does the picture tell you about your data set?

Inferential Statistics

1 Earlier in the chapter (see section "The Normal Curve"), we identified several variables that are thought to be normally distributed. Try to identify 2–3 variables that you think are *not* normally distributed. Draw a hypothetical curve that best reflects the "abnormal" distribution of the variables you've selected.

2 Imagine you are working with a set of "memory" scores that are normally distributed. The mean for the set of scores is 80 and the standard deviation is 8. What is the probability that a score falls between 72 and 88? How does the area under the normal curve help you "see" the answer?

3. A recent survey of a randomly drawn sample (n = 200) of your town neighbors discovered that residents make an average of 14 calls a year to the town hall to complain about garbage/recycling services (with a standard deviation of 5). What is the average number of complaint calls you should report for the whole town if you want to be 99% confident about your findings?

References

Tufte, Edward. 1997. *Visual Explanations: Images and Quantities, Evidence and Narrative.* Cheshire, CN: Graphics Press.

Tufte, Edward. 2001. *The Visual Display of Quantitative Information*, 2nd edn. Cheshire, CN: Graphics Press.

Chapter 13

Pulling it Together: A Final Synthesis

In this last chapter, I want to offer a strategy for how you might best pull together all of the previous chapters into a coherent whole. It is in effect my offering of the final "take away" for the entire book. I could at this point offer a rehash of the major points covered in each chapter but I would rather try something that might prove more useful (and also have a greater chance of being read.) I think the best way of seeing the big picture of this book is by your imagining yourself facing the task of writing up the results of a study. How might you approach this task? In the very few pages that follow, I hope to help you realize that this exercise is a useful one for seeing how all of the "parts" of the research process presented in this text really do fit together. A useful first step might be to look again at Box 4.1 in Chapter 4 that offers an overview of the research process.

Box 13.1   The "steps" of the research process

Idea phase – Formulate a good research question
  Review the literature
  State/share your theory
  Ask your questions or state your problem or hypotheses

Design phase
  Given your research question/issue, develop an overall design or blueprint for:
    Collecting the data
    Units of analysis
    Sampling
    Measurement
    Planned analysis

Data collection phase
  Pretesting
  Pilot studies
  Final data collection

Analysis phase
  Select the right statistics/techniques for answering the research question

Writing/communication phase
  Share the details as well as the results of your executed study in a well- crafted written report/article

---

Another quick tip for imagining how one might write up the results of a research project is to find a research article that "speaks to you" and use it as a model to guide your own work. There is a standard "form" to all good research articles. As you conduct a literature review, you will notice how articles share a common structure: an opening or introductory section, a methods section, an analysis and findings section (aka results) and a conclusions section.

But here is the most compelling reason for why I want you to imagine yourself facing the task of writing up the results of a research project. If we were to do a quick summary of how to approach this task, we would in effect, review the various components of good research methods presented in this book. To write about a research project, we would need to:

- provide some background on and justify the project
- share specifics of the design or provide a blueprint for the project
- share the specifics of our sampling strategy and data collection strategy/tools/decisions
- share our data analysis plans and results
- share our thoughts on the significance of our findings
- offer some concluding comments and ideas about future research.

As it turns out, each of these tasks is facilitated by the various chapters of this book. Let me present a brief summary or roadmap.

Providing Background For and Justifying the Research Project

This step requires the writer to bring the research issue/topic "front and center" as well as to put the topic in some kind of context. Is the topic a timely or urgent one? Is the topic about a totally new or growing or perennial problem? Does it involve an issue that invites competing views or explanations? Just what is the compelling reason for pursuing the project at hand? By way of justifying the research project at hand, the role or place of theory in the project and how we used theory to "frame" the project should be discussed. Were we trying to test a specific theoretically deduced hypothesis? Were we interested in building theory from our project? Were we trying to resolve a theoretical debate? The idea is to use the introduction to share the thought process that generated the current study. Are there different views on the conceptualization of the major theoretical issues, concepts or constructs? What informed the decision regarding the best conceptual definitions of key concepts? How did our theoretical orientation inform the selection of overall design or the formulation of specific research questions or specific research tools? Were mixed methods used and if so why?

These details are critical since they lay the foundation for so many of the additional planning and execution decisions that will follow. Only by knowing the "starting point" can others evaluate the ensuing decisions for the research project. Justifying our project would also require us to show our knowledge of the relevant research literature. This step is critical to convincing skeptics that we really have the right to conduct our project. The writer is also tasked with figuring out how to organize our literature review so as to best use it as a "bridge" to our own project. About one-third of this book offers information that is highly relevant to laying the foundation that should be shared in the introductory section of a research article. The role and placement of theory in the research process is discussed in Chapters 1 and 2 and in more detail in Chapter 4. The conceptualization process is reviewed in Chapter 5. The literature review process in discussed in detail in Chapter 4.

Sharing the Specifics of our Project Planning

Once we have clarified our theoretical foundation and discussed and assessed the relevant literature, we need to move on to the nitty-gritty of research and share the details of project planning. This step would have us explaining the specific design we settled on (i.e. experimental or non-experimental), the time element we settled on (i.e. cross-sectional or longitudinal), the sampling strategy (i.e. probability or nonprobability) and the specific data collection tools we used to gather our empirical evidence (i.e. experiments, questionnaires, personal interviews, focus groups, field research, etc.) If mixed methods were used, an explanation of the rationale for this decision is in order. If there were ethical concerns that influenced these decisions, now is the time to discuss them.

This section of the paper will often feature two separate subsections: one devoted to the all-important issue of sampling and one devoted to the equally important issue of measurement. For the sampling discussion, the writer should share the specific sampling strategy used in the study (i.e. indicate whether a probability or non-probability sample was used and then identify the specific strategy employed). Some discussion or recognition of whether or not the sample can be regarded as representative is in order. Any limitations of the strategy should be acknowledged as well as the any steps taken to correct them. In addition to information about the sampling *strategy*, information about the *actual obtained* sample should also be featured. There should be a basic description of the resulting sample. The writer should specify the final sample size actually obtained (and the calculated response rate if surveys were used or the mortality rate if a panel study was conducted). Some basic demographics that will help the reader "see" the sample (i.e. percent male/female, average age, racial breakdowns, etc.) should also be shared.

The subsection on measurement should provide all the details of our specific measurement decisions. Explicitly state the major concepts and explain the selection of their empirical counterparts – that is, the corresponding variables. Share the exact operational definitions of major variables. Provide specifics regarding the levels of measurement. Report the acceptable range of values for composite measures. Offer any details available about the validity and reliability of the measures. What steps were taken to control for error (i.e. bias and noise) in the measurement process? Remember that one of the defining traits of science is its insistence that research findings must be replicated to be considered truly trustworthy. Providing the details expected in the methods section of a research article is essential support for replication efforts of other researchers. At the end of any "methods" section of a research article, the reader should have a clear understanding of exactly what was done to whom (or what) in the name of collecting the empirical evidence needed to address the research question. Again, each of these points receives considerable attention in several chapters of this book. Chapter 1 reviews the logic of scientific methods. Chapters 5 and

6 are devoted to the measurement process. Chapters 7–10 review specific data collection tools. Chapter 11 is all about sampling.

Sharing the Specifics and Results of Analysis

The next major task in a research report is to talk about analysis – what techniques were used and what were the obtained results. The writer needs to convince the readers that proper procedures were employed in the analysis and that they were used correctly. This step would have us attending to such issues as levels of measurement and how they in many ways "dictate" our analysis decisions. The results section of a research article must also pay careful attention to the effective display of the findings. Wise choices need to be made about appropriate graphics, tables, and figures. To be sure, becoming proficient in statistical analysis warrants a separate course of study as well as books dedicated to the task of analysis, but Chapter 12 provides a short primer on some of the basics of descriptive and inferential statistics.

Offer a Discussion of the Significance of our Findings

Often this section starts with a brief review of the major findings presented in the previous section. We would also need to explicitly address the results vis-à-vis our original research questions. Do the findings support or contradict our expectations? Do the findings make sense in light of the literature reviewed for the study? How or where does the study "fit" into the existing literature? What assumptions are being made in order to trust the findings? Are there other viable interpretations of the findings? Here the writer might also want to address whether or not statistically significant findings are also meaningful – that is, do the results merit further attention? Does the research help to clarify any of the theoretical points raised in the opening section of the paper? Has the research resolved any theoretical controversies or revealed new ideas to be explored? Does the research advance the general understanding of the research issues or topic? Since the writing tasks of a discussion section have us looking once again at the issues raised in the introduction of the article, the chapters of the book guiding this earlier work are once again relevant for writing a discussion.

Offer Some Concluding Remarks/Observations

Here is the writer's chance to do some constructive reflection on his or her project. Conduct a self-assessment of the strengths and weakness of all of the decisions made throughout the entire process. What shortcomings or limitations of the research are now apparent that were not so obvious earlier? Were there sources of error or possible error that need to be acknowledged? Were there critical measures that were not included in the study? What are the next needed or reasonable steps for future research? How might future research be improved? Are there important policy implications?

Seeing the Big Picture

As ironic as it might seem at first, thinking about writing a research report really is a pretty good strategy for *preparing* yourself for conducting a quality research project. Pondering in advance what an audience of well-intentioned skeptics will expect to see in your work will give you a heads-up about the care you need to take and the standards you need to consider in planning and executing a project. Thinking about what is entailed in writing about research will also put you in a better position for reading and assessing the written work of other researchers. Hopefully, this book has given you a much better understanding of what it takes to produce a quality piece of research. It should also help you know the kinds of standards you should apply when assessing what others report about their research efforts. In either case, a sound, working knowledge of scientific research methods should serve you well. Adding the ways of scientific knowing to your own stock of knowledge will not only empower you but it also will give you a clear edge in understanding the world around us. In the end, that is a pretty good pay-off.

Glossary

Anonymity   collecting data in such a way as to preclude being able to identify or link specific persons with the information they have given the researcher.

Antecedent variable   one that comes earlier in a causal sequence or chain, preceding both the independent and dependent variables.

Authoritative knowledge   knowledge based upon credentialed expertise (i.e. specialists or respected sources of information).

Bar chart   a visual display of the frequency distribution for a nominal level (aka categorical) or a discrete variable (bars should not touch each other).

Bias   error in the measurement process that is patterned or has a consistent direction.

Bivariate analysis   analysis that looks at two variables at a time.

Census   a study that collects information about every element in the research population.

Certificate of confidentiality   a form obtained through the National Institutes of Health (NIH) to safeguard against forced disclosure of confidential research information.

Closed-ended questions   questions that supply predetermined response options.

Cluster sample   one that is selected in stages, enabling the use of successive sampling frames for progressively larger clusters of the ultimate sampling unit.

Cohort   a group defined by a common event (i.e. experiencing a common life circumstance within a specified period of time).

Common sense knowledge   knowledge based on personal experiences.

Composite measure   a multiple item measure; several indicators are used together to measure a complex concept (see Rosenberg's self-esteem measure in Box 5.6 for an example).

Concepts   mental abstractions/images that serve to categorize ideas, places, things, or events.

Concurrent validity   a form of criterion validity that uses an established valid measure of a variable to demonstrate the accuracy of another measure of the same variable.

Confidence interval   the range of values we attach to a sample statistic that indicate the adjustment needed in order to capture the true population value; consists of a sample statistic +/− the margin of error.

Confidence levels   the selected degree of certainty researches work with when trying to estimate population values from sample statistics; social researchers

Introducing Social Research Methods: Essentials for Getting the Edge, First Edition. Janet M. Ruane.
© 2016 John Wiley & Sons, Ltd. Published 2016 by John Wiley & Sons, Ltd.

usually work at the 95% or 99% confidence levels and therefore strive to be accurate 95% or 99% of the time.

Confidentiality   protecting the privacy of research subjects by promising not to disclose the person's identity or link their information to them personally.

Conflict paradigm   a theoretical framework that presents the social world as conflict-laden where special interest factions compete for dominance or control.

Construct   a concept or mental abstraction that is not directly observable.

Construct validity   demonstrating the accuracy of a measure by showing it produces results consistent with theoretically based hypotheses or predictions.

Content validity   asserting a measure is accurate because it addresses all dimensions or component of the concept's nominal/theoretical definition.

Contingency question   a question that is limited to those respondents who have been "cleared" by a preceding filter question.

Contrived measures   measures intentionally designed or developed by the researcher in order to generate empirical evidence of a variable.

Control group   the group in an experiment that does not receive the independent variable; group that is identical to the experimental group except for one thing: the independent variable is intentionally withheld from the control group

Convenience sample   one that uses readily available (close at hand) elements.

Correlation   a patterned connection or relationship between two variables.

Criterion validity   using empirical evidence to establish that a measure is measuring what it claims to measure.

Cross-sectional research   research where data is collected at one single moment in time.

Data   the information collected via research efforts; the result or outcome of the measurement process.

Data file   a matrix of data (aka data set).

Deductive research   research that starts in the realm of theory and deduces questions or hypotheses to be tested with empirical data.

Dependent variable   the outcome we are trying to explain; the variable that is presumed to be the result or consequence of another.

Descriptive research   research that offers a detailed picture or account of some social phenomenon, setting, experience, group, and so on.

Descriptive statistics   techniques that organize, summarize, and provide a general overview of data.

Ecological fallacy   an error that occurs when data is collected about groups or aggregates but conclusions are drawn about individuals; an analysis mistake that occurs when findings that occur at the group level of analysis are assumed to apply as well at the individual level of analysis.

Elements   the entities (people, places, things) that make up a research population.

Empirical evidence   tangible, sensory evidence.

Empirical generalizations   generalizations based on observed patterns in the data.

Empiricism   knowledge based on sensory evidence: seeing, hearing, touching, tasting, smelling.

Evaluation research   research that assesses the impact of some program or policy or intervention.

Event-based design   a plan that sees data collected at multiple points in time from a specific segment of a population that shares a common event; aka cohort analysis.

Exhaustivity   an essential trait for closed-ended questions that requires all relevant response options being presented to respondents.

Experiment   a contrived highly controlled data collection strategy where the researcher intentionally manipulates the independent variable in order to assess its impact on the dependent variable.

Experimental group   the group in an experiment that is intentionally exposed to or receives the independent variable.

Explanatory research   research that undertakes or pursues investigating causal relationships between variables.

Exploratory research   research undertaken for the purpose of shedding light on a little understood or researched setting, group or phenomenon.

Expressive role   sees focus group moderator attending to the emotional needs and dynamics of the group.

External validity   the extent to which research findings can be accurately generalized from a sample to a population or from one group to another; accuracy with regard to findings being correct when applied beyond any one study/sample.

Face validity   claiming a measure is accurate because it "looks" right or appears to be getting the job done; a subjective assessment of validity.

Field notes   a written record (as well as any audio or photographic evidence) of the researcher's field observations and experiences.

Field research an extremely systematic and rigorous study of everyday life that sees the researcher observing and interacting with subjects in their natural settings (aka ethnographic research).

Filter question a question that determines if respondents should answer or skip follow-up question(s).

Fixed sample panel design a plan that sees data collected at two or more points in time from the exact same sample – i.e. exact same group of people.

Fixed variable a trait or characteristic that is imposed or assigned to an individual, often at birth (gender, age, etc.); fixed variables cannot be altered by the researcher.

Focus group a guided group discussion/exchange "focused" on a select topic.

Frequency distribution an ordered listing (from high to low) of the values of a variable along with a tally of the number of times each value occurs.

Frequency polygon a line graph connecting the mid-points of a histogram.

Gatekeepers people who can help or limit researchers' access to the field.

Going native occurs when a field researcher loses his or her objectivity and over-identifies with research subjects.

Heterogeneous population a population that contains diverse elements.

Histogram a visual display of the frequency distribution of a variable measured at the interval or ratio level (bars should touch to convey the continuous nature of variables).

Homogeneous population a population that consists of identical elements.

Hypothesis a statement or prediction about an expected relationship between two variables.

Idiographic model of causality an approach to causal analysis that seeks to identify the specific factors that produce a specific event.

Independent variable the variable presumed to cause another variable; the variable that produces change in the dependent variable; aka predictor variable.

Inductive research research that starts in the realm of empirical data and uses the patterns found in the data to induce/generate broader empirical generalizations.

Informal field interviews less structured and often unscheduled interviews that emerge from an exchange during field observations.

Informed consent an ethical mandate that stipulates that potential research participants must be fully informed about all aspects of a research project that might influence their decision to participate.

Instrumental role sees focus group moderator attending to the social interaction dynamics of group (e.g. keeping members focused, preventing cross-talking).

Internal validity accuracy with regard to claims of causal connections between variables/the extent to which a research design is capable of detecting a true causal relationship

Interval level measure one that uses numbers to identify, order and indicate equal distance between the values of a variable.

Intervening variable one whose placement is between the independent and dependent variables; it serves to explicate or mediate the causal connection.

Interview a form of survey research where questions are posed person to person; a personal exchange of information between an interviewer and an interviewee.

Interview guides unstructured talking points to be covered in an interview.

Interview schedules structured list of questions (and often set response options) to be used during an interview.

Intuitive knowledge knowledge derived from extraordinary or paranormal sensations or sources.

Item measure a single indicator used to document a concept (i.e. one question is typically used to measure gender or age or marital status).

Jotted notes brief, perfunctory short-hand notes taken while in the field that will serve to enhance recall once the researcher has left the field.

Longitudinal research research that collects data at two or more points in time.

Macro theory very broad explanations of large scale social processes or institutions.

Margin of error the range of values needed to correct a sample statistic for a given level of confidence.

Mean the arithmetic average of a set of scores.

Measurement the process by which numbers are attached to the values of variables (alternate: the process by which abstract concepts are translated into empirical indicators).

Measurement error error attributed to flaws in the measurement process itself; flaws that keep a measure from hitting its intended target spot on.

Measurement process the process by which abstract concepts are translated into empirical variables.

Measurement validity the accuracy or extent to which measures empirically document what they claim to document.

Measures of central tendency a single number that indicates the typical or "average" score in a data set

Median the score that falls in the middle of an ordered set of scores.

Mental notes a detailed "mental recording" on an event/ exchange in the field.

Meso theory explanatory framework that focuses on mid-size groups or levels of interaction that occur between the macro and micro levels.

Micro theory explanations of social processes that focus on behaviors of small group or person-to-person interactions.

Mode the most frequently occurring value for a variable.

Multiple-forms reliability check assessing the consistency of a measure by using two forms of the measure and seeing if both forms yield highly correlated results.

Mundane realism the extent to which a study resembles the conditions of everyday life.

Mutual exclusivity an essential trait for closed-ended questions requiring that provided response options do not overlap each other.

Narrative an account that details the unfolding or sequencing of an event.

Natural measures measures that utilize naturally occurring evidence by way of empirically documenting a variable.

Negative correlation a connection between two variables which sees the values of each variable moving together but in the opposite direction of each other.

Noise error in the measurement process that is non-patterned or non-directional.

Nominal level measure one that uses numbers to identify or label the values of a variable; aka categorical measure.

Nomothetic model of causality an approach to causal analysis that seeks the common factors responsible for a general class of events; "big picture" causal analysis.

Normal curve a hypothetical bell-shaped distribution of values of a variable; the horizontal axis displays all possible values of the variable and the vertical axis displays the probability of the occurrence of the values.

normative responses answering questions in a socially desirable way.

Open-ended questions questions that require respondents to supply their own answers.

Operational definition an empirically based definition of a variable that indicates all of the steps required to actually measure the variable; set of instructions (i.e. questions and response options) for measuring a variable.

Operationalization process process of finding reasonable and accurate empirical indicators for concepts.

Order paradigm a theoretical framework that presents the world as a well-integrated whole with interdependent and functional parts.

Ordinal level measure one that uses numbers to rank order the values of a variable.

Panel mortality the loss of research participants over time from a fixed sample.

Paradigm a grand theoretical framework, schemata or orientation for viewing social phenomenon.

Pearson coefficient a statistic for indicating the strength and direction of a linear relationship between two interval or ratio level variables.

Phi coefficient a statistic for indicating the strength of association between two binary (dichotomous) variables.

Population parameter the true value of a variable for the entire population.

Positive correlation a connection between two variables which sees the values of each variable moving together in the same direction.

Predictive validity a form of criterion validity where a measure's ability to accurately predict something logically related to the measure is used as evidence of the measure's validity (i.e. to assess the predictive validity of a happiness measure, one might show how *high* happiness scores predict *low* depression scores).

Probability sample one where the probability of selecting any element or member of the entire population is known.

Probes follow-up questions used in the interview process in order to get respondents to provide additional information.

Purposive sample a sample that uses special knowledge to intentionally "hand pick" elements for a sample.

Qualitative data research information that is expressed via words/images

Qualitative research an approach to documenting reality that relies on words and images as the primary data source.

Quantitative data   research information that is expressed via numbers; the result of a measurement process that expresses values of variables via real numbers

Quantitative data file   a collection or matrix of numerical values of variables measured.

Quantitative research   an approach to documenting reality that relies heavily on numbers both for the measurement of variables and for data analysis.

Questionnaire   a form of survey research where questions are posed via a self-administered instrument.

Quota sample   a sample that recruits elements in order to fill pre-determined desired categories of elements that "represent" the population (aka a non-probability stratified sample).

Random assignment   using chance and only chance to assign participants to the experimental and control groups in an experiment.

Random selection process   a technique for selecting a sample where chance and only chance determines which population elements get included in a sample.

Range   a number that reports the distance between the highest and the lowest values in a set of scores.

Rapport   a condition of ease or trust in the interview situation.

Ratio level measure   one that uses numbers to express values of variables as real numbers or counts; aka quantitative measures.

Rational knowledge   knowledge derived from the power of reasoning to deduce logical conclusions about reality.

Reactivity effects   occur when research participants become aware of the measurement process and consequently change/alter their behaviors as a result; the change in individual's or the group's behaviors that is due to a researcher's presence.

Reliable measure   one that produces or yields consistent or stable results.

Repeated cross-sectional design   a longitudinal research plan that sees data collected at two or more points in time from different samples of the same research population (aka trend design).

Replication   repeating a study to see if original results/findings are obtained again with different subjects or under different settings.

Representative sample   a subset of a research population that accurately captures the variation found across the entire population.

Research population   the total collection of the people, places or things we are studying.

Response rate   the percentage of contacted respondents who complete surveys.

Response set   occurs when respondents fall into a pattern when answering questions, rendering the measure invalid; most likely to occur in an index where all items are worded in the same direction (i.e. all negative or all positive statements).

Retrospective questions   questions about a respondent's past history.

Right to privacy   the right to control when and under what conditions others will have access to information about us.

Sample generalizability   the ability to generalize findings derived from a sample back to the entire research population.

Sample statistic   a value for a variable obtained from sample data.

Samples   a smaller subset of a research population.

Sampling distribution   a hypothetical distribution of a sample statistic that would be produced via repeated sampling.

Sampling error   error that results from the fact that data is collected from subsets of research populations.

Sampling frame   an exhaustive list of each and every element that makes up a research population.

Scatterplot   a device for visually displaying any shared variation between two variables

Scientific knowledge   knowledge derived from the merger of theory and research; knowledge based on the integration of rational reasoning and empirical evidence.

Simple random sample   one in which all elements of sampling frame have a known and equal chance of being selected for the sample.

Snowball sample   one that uses referrals or social networks to build a sample.

Social desirability bias   a measurement error caused by people responding to questions in a way that makes them look good; over-reporting "good" behaviors or under-reporting discrediting behaviors.

Spearman rank coefficient   a statistic for indicating the strength and direction of a correlation between two ordinal level variables.

Split-half reliability check   assessing the consistency or stability of a composite measure by splitting the measure into two halves and checking to see if the results yielded by each half are highly correlated with each other.

Spurious relationship   one that results because two variables (A and B) are each connected to a third lurking variable (C).

Standard deviation   the average distance between any one score and the mean; the square root of the variance.

Standard error   a measure of sampling error; the error due to samples being imperfect subsets of the entire population.

Statistics   set of tools for analyzing data techniques used to analyze or organize data.

Stratified random sample   one that organizes the sampling frame into homogenous subgroups based on a critical variable to assure that a representative sampling of the values of this variable is achieved.

Survey   a data collection tool that gathers information by asking questions.

Symbolic-interactionist paradigm   a theoretical framework that views social reality as constructed via the social interactions of individuals and groups.

Systematic random sample   one which uses a random starting point and them employs a systematic skip pattern (sampling interval) to select every kth (e.g. 5th, 10th, 12th, etc.) element for inclusion in the sample.

Test-retest reliability check   assessing the consistency of a measure by employing it two times on the subjects and looking for highly correlated results (provided there has been no real change in the subjects between the test and retest).

Theoretical (aka nominal or conceptual) definitions   definitions that clarify the exact meaning of concepts being measured by offering synonyms for the concepts; aka dictionary definitions.

Theory   a set of propositions or statements about how the world or some entity operates.

Thick descriptions   highly detailed accounts of what the researcher has observed or experienced in the field.

Threats to internal validity   rival explanations that hinder or compromise the researcher's ability to know or detect genuine causal relationships.

Traditional knowledge   knowledge based on the passing of time.

Triangulation   refers to using multiple or mixed data collection strategies in the study of a topic.

Unit of analysis   the what or who being analyzed; the level of life about which data are collected.

Univariate analysis   analysis of a single variable.

Valid measures   measures that actually measure what they claim to measure; measures that document what they claim to document.

Value   a specific category or attribute of a variable (for the variable car transmission, the values are stick shift or automatic).

Variable   an empirical representation/indicator of abstract concepts; any trait or characteristic that can vary or have more than one value/category.

Variance   a summary measure of the overall variation in a set of scores; the squared average distance of scores from the mean.

Verbal mirror   an interview technique where the interviewer periodically offers a summary paraphrasing of respondent's answers.

Z scores   values that correspond to the standardized area under the normal curve.

Index

Page numbers in *italics* refer to boxes, figures, tables or tips.

Introducing Social Research Methods: Essentials for Getting the Edge, First Edition. Janet M. Ruane.
© 2016 John Wiley & Sons, Ltd. Published 2016 by John Wiley & Sons, Ltd.